RUSSIAN LITERATURE

Ideals and Realities

PETER KROPOTKIN

RUSSIAN LITERATURE

Ideals and Realities

INTRODUCTION BY GEORGE WOODCOCK

BLACK ROSE BOOKS

Montreal/New York

BLACK ROSE BOOKS No. T152
Paperback ISBN: 0-921689-84-5
Hardcover ISBN: 0-921689-85-3

Canadian Cataloguing in Publication Data

Kropotkin, Petr Alekseevich, kníâz', 1842-1921
   Russian literature, ideals and realities

ISBN 0-921689-85-3 (bound)   ISBN 0-921689-84-5 (pbk.)

   1. Russian literature—History and criticism.
I. Title

PG3012.K72 1991   891.7   C91-090151-1

Library of Congress Catalog No. 90-83627
Cover design: Pierre-Paul Pariseau

Editorial Offices
BLACK ROSE BOOKS
3981 St-Laurent Boulevard,
Suite 444
Montréal, Québec
H2W 1Y5 Canada

Mailing Address
BLACK ROSE BOOKS
P.O. Box 1258
Succ. Place du Parc
Montréal, Québec
H2W 2R3 Canada

U.S. Orders
BLACK ROSE BOOKS
340 Nagel Drive
Cheektowaga, New York
14225

Printed and bound in Québec, Canada
on acid-free paper

PREFACE

A WESTERN reader, when he makes acquaintance with Russian literature, is usually impressed by its general sadness and the absence from it of the joy of life, the happiness of existence. This impression is quite correct: a striking note of sadness resounds in our literature; and even with those of our poets and novelists, like Púshkin, Gógol, or Tchéhoff, whose first productions were full of the joys of youth, gladness soon disappeared, and sadness took its place.

This feature of Russian literature was noticed more than once, and as the same character prevails in the Russian and South Slavonian folk-songs, the favourite explanation is, that melancholy and sadness are specific features of 'the mystical Slavonian soul.' Some would even see in them a characteristic of 'Eastern races.'

Leaving aside physiological guesses about 'races' and the 'mystical soul' explanation which explains nothing, but merely restates the fact in different words, the very history of the Russian nation, the raids of the Mongols, the Tartars, the Turks, with their usual sequel of murder and slavery, the hard struggle with an inclement nature, the wide expanse of the Steppes, the endless forests, and later on serfdom, —all these could not but leave deep traces of sadness in the Russian character.

However, the folk-songs of all nations bear the same traces of sadness, due to similar causes. But in Western Europe the written literature soon freed itself from the resignation of the early folk-lore. So that, properly put, the question is,—Why has the nineteenth century Russian literature retained that sad, melancholy character?

Some sort of reply to this question was already given in this book when I mentioned in brief biographical notes the hard lot of so many of our leading writers. The striking percentage of Russian poets and novelists who were imprisoned, exiled, or sent to hard labour, had already been noticed by an English reviewer of the first edition of this book, even though I had made no special point of this aspect of the literary profession in Russia.

The persecutions which our literature and, in fact, whole generations of 'intellectuals' have lived through in the nineteenth century would fully explain the absence of a real joy of life in our literature.

However, there is also another, even more characteristic, feature in our literature to which I would like to draw the attention of the Western reader. It is the presence of a certain deeply rooted inner force, which one feels in Russian works of art, literary criticism and science,—a force which has never been quelled and, in spite of all obstacles, has always kept before the Russian reader the higher ideals, the higher aspirations of mankind, reminding him that real happiness can only be found when one has joined in the endeavour for attaining the higher forms of human development.

In the first chapter of this book I have mentioned the hard lot which befell the freemason Nóvikoff,

the Christian mystic Lábzin, and the political writer
Radíscheff; but I might have shown also how a whole
generation of 'intellectuals' was persecuted at the
same time, with the intention of weeding out the
ideas of the British eighteenth-century philosophers,
the French encyclopædists, and the French Revolution, and how the teachings of the German mystics
and metaphysicians—Schelling, Fichte, and Hegel—
penetrated instead.   Since that time the persecutions
never discontinued, taking an especially acute character
every twenty years or so, when whole generations of
writers and thinkers saw their intellectual leaders
arrested, exiled, or sent to hard labour, while the
remaining ones lived under the menace of a similar
fate.   The generation of Púshkin, Odóevskiy, and
Ryléeff—the so-called Decembrists of 1825, of whose
sad fate I speak in Chapter II. of this book—was
followed in 1849 by the 'circles' of Petrashévskiy,
where the teachings of the French Socialists—Fourier,
Cabet, and Pierre Leroux—were discussed.   The result
being that again a whole generation, including Dostoyévskiy, the critics Byelínskiy and Máykoff, the
satirist Schédrin, the poet Pleschéyeff, and quite a
number of men of mark who played later on a prominent part in the work of liberation of the serfs, was
accused of a dangerous conspiracy, arrested, condemned
to be shot, sent to hard labour, or exiled.

Then came, after a short interval of relative freedom,
the persecutions of 1863, and with them began the era
of uninterrupted persecutions of literature, art, science,
and the Universities, which lasted till the year 1905.
These were years when nearly every one of the younger
writers had to make acquaintance with imprisonment

or exile, and these were periods when in almost every intellectual family there was some one of its members or friends in prison or in exile.

No wonder that all joy of life disappeared from the literature of those years. How could a novelist depict the happiness of existence in this beautiful world, when nowhere he could see that happiness? Tchéhoff's sad irony and Górkiy's angry rebellion were a necessary outcome of real life.

But even amidst the gloomy conditions of those years Russian literature remained true to its mission. It retained its inner force, its vitality, its capacity of discussing all the great problems of European civilisation, even under the strokes of the censor and the menaces of an omnipotent State's police. Tolstóy, with His wide humanitarianism, only summed up the aspirations which were kept alive in Russian literature since the times of Nóvikoff and Radísheff, by our best writers, without distinction of philosophical or religious creed.

There is now, in Western Europe and America, a widely spread desire of a better knowledge of Russian literature, and it surely will not be limited to an acquaintance with our great novelists. It will be extended, I hope, to our 'folk-novelists' and their ideals, as well as to some secondary novelists, mentioned in this book; to Russian art which worked hand in hand with our literature; and also to Russian history and science altogether. It is self-evident that in all these manifestations of intellectual life Russia owes a great deal to Western literature, art, and science. But a real artist always retains the stamp of his nationality, and, as the Western readers know, the Russian works of art have a specific Russian character.

A few words more.   In preparing this new edition
my first intention was to add to it a chapter dealing
with our contemporary authors.   However, such a
number of new writers belonging to a variety of new
literary schools came to the front during the last five-
and-twenty years that a new book would have been
required to deal with them in a proper way.   The new
schools of Decadents, Impressionists, Modernists, and
so on, count among their Russian adepts so many
writers of incontestable talent, such as Bálmont,
Andréeff, Sologúb, Veresáeff, and many others, and
the appearance of these innovators is so intimately
connected with the political life of Russia within the
last twenty-five years, that these new literary schools
cannot be dealt with otherwise than in connection with
the principal events of these years.   One has only to
consult the autobiographies of some of the representatives of these different schools, published in the work of
Professor V. S. Venguéroff, *Russian Twentieth Century
Literature*, 1890-1910 (its fourth part was published in
Moscow in 1915), to see how much the new currents
were originated in Russia, not only by Western influences, but still more by the events of Russian life itself.
Therefore I had to give up the idea of dealing with
this interesting subject in a few pages, and must refer
the reader, for general conceptions about the origin of
this modern literature, to the just mentioned work of
Professor Venguéroff, and to the works themselves of
this new pleiad of novelists and poets.

BRIGHTON,
   May 1916.

PREFACE

TO THE FIRST EDITION

THIS book originated in a series of eight lectures on Russian Literature during the Nineteenth Century which I delivered in March 1901, at the Lowell Institute, in Boston.

In accepting the invitation to deliver this course, I fully realised the difficulties which stood in my way. It is by no means an easy task to speak or to write about the literature of a country, when this literature is hardly known to the audience or to the readers. Only three or four Russian writers have been properly and at all completely translated into English; so that very often I had to speak *about* a poem or a novel, when it could have been readily characterised by simply reading a passage or two *from* it.

However, if the difficulties were great, the subject was well worth an effort. Russian literature is a rich mine of original poetic thought. It has a freshness and youthfulness which is not found to the same extent in older literatures. It has, moreover, a sincerity and simplicity of expression which render it all the more attractive to the mind that has grown sick of literary artificiality. And it has this distinctive feature, that it brings within the domain of art—the poem, the novel, the drama—nearly all those questions, social and political, which in Western Europe and America, at least in our present generation, are discussed chiefly in the political writings of the day, but seldom in literature.

In no other country does literature occupy so influential a position as it does in Russia. Nowhere else does it exercise so profound and so direct an influence upon the intellectual development of the younger generation. There are novels of Turguéneff, and even of the less-known writers, which have been real stepping-stones in the development of Russian youth within the last fifty years.

The reason why literature exercises such an influence in Russia is self-evident. There is no open political life, and with the exception of a few years at the time of the abolition of serfdom, the Russian people have never been called upon to take an active part in the framing of their country's institutions.

The consequence has been that the best minds of the country have chosen the poem, the novel, the satire, or literary criticism as the medium for expressing their aspirations, their conceptions of national life, or their ideals. It is not to blue-books, or to newspaper leaders, but to its works of art that one must go in Russia in order to understand the political, economical, and social ideals of the country—the aspirations of the history-making portions of Russian society.

As it would have been impossible to exhaust so wide a subject as Russian Literature within the limits of this book, I have concentrated my chief attention upon the modern literature. The early writers, down to Púshkin and Gógol—the founders of the modern literature—are dealt with in a short introductory sketch. The most representative writers in poetry, the novel, the drama, political literature, and art criticism, are considered

next, and round them I have grouped the less prominent writers, of whom the most important are mentioned
in short notes. I am fully aware that every one of the
latter presents something individual and well worth
knowing; and that some of the less-known authors
have even succeeded occasionally in better representing
a given current of thought than their more famous
colleagues; but in a book which is intended to give
only a broad, general idea of the subject, the plan I
have pursued was necessary.

Literary criticism has always been well represented
in Russia, and the views taken in this book must needs
bear traces of the work of our great critics—Byelínskiy,
Tchernyshévskiy, Dobrolúboff, and Písareff, and their
modern followers, Mihailóvskiy, Arsénieff, Skabitchévskiy, Venguéroff, and others. For biographical data
concerning contemporary writers I am indebted to the
excellent work on modern Russian literature by the
last-named author, and to the eighty volumes of the
admirable *Russian Encyclopædic Dictionary*.

I take this opportunity to express my hearty thanks
to my old friend, Mr. Richard Heath, who was kind
enough to read over all this book, both in manuscript
and in proof.

BROMLEY, KENT,
January 1905.

CONTENTS

PREFACE   v

THE PRONUNCIATION OF RUSSIAN NAMES   xvi

LIST OF WRITERS MENTIONED   xvii

AN INTRODUCTION by George Woodcock   xx

CHAPTER 1 : INTRODUCTION   1

The Russian Language—Early folk-literature: Folk-lore—
Songs—Sagas—*Lay of Igor's Raid*—Annals—The Mongol Invasion; its consequences—Correspondence between John IV and
Kúrbskiy—Split in the Church—Avvakúm's *Memoirs*—The
eighteenth century: Peter I and his contemporaries—Tretiakóvskiy—Lomonósoff—Sumarókoff—The times of Catherine II:
Derzhávin—Von Wízin—The Freemasons: Nóvikoff—Radíscheff—Early nineteenth century: Karamzín and Zhukóvskiy—
The Decembrists—Ryléeff.

CHAPTER II : PÚSHKIN AND LÉRMONTOFF   40

PÚSHKIN: Beauty and form—Púshkin and Schiller—His
youth; his exile; his later career and death—Fairy tales: *Ruslán
and Ludmíla*—His lyrics—'Byronism'—Drama—*Eughéniy Onyéghin*—LÉRMONTOFF: Púshkin or Lérmontoff?—His life—The
Caucasus—Poetry of Nature—Influence of Shelley—*The
Demon*—*Mtsyri*—Love of freedom—His death—Púshkin and
Lérmontoff as prosewriters—Other poets and novelists of the
same epoch.

CHAPTER III : GÓGOL   69

Little Russia—*Nights on a Farm near Dikánka, and Mírgorod*—Vil-
lage life and humour—*How Iván Ivánovitch quarrelled with Iván
Nikíforytch*—Historical novel: *Tarás Búlba*—*The Cloak*—Drama:
The Inspector-General—Its influence—*Dead Souls*: main types—
Realism in the Russian novel.

✓CHAPTER IV : TURGUÉNEFF—TOLSTÓY   92

TURGUÉNEFF: the main features of his art—*A Sportsman's
Notebook*—Pessimism of his early novels—His series of novels
representing the leading types of Russian society—Rúdin—
Lavrétskiy—Helen and Insároff—Bazároff—Why *Fathers and*

Sons was misunderstood—*Hamlet and Don Quixote*—*Virgin Soil*: movement towards the people—*Verses in Prose*. TOLSTÓY—*Childhood* and *Boyhood*—During and after the Crimean War—*Youth*: in search of an ideal—Small stories—*The Cossacks*—Educational work—*War and Peace*—*Anna Karénina*—Religious crisis—His interpretation of the Christian teaching—Main points of Christian ethics—Latest works of art—*Kreutzer Sonata* —*Resurrection*—Leaving his home.

CHAPTER V : GONTCHARÓFF—DOSTOYÉVSKIY—
NEKRÁSOFF   164

GONTCHARÓFF—*Oblómoff*—The Russian malady of Oblómovism—Is it exclusively Russian? *The Precipice*—DOSTOYÉVSKIY—His first novel—General character of his work—*Memoirs from a Dead-House*—*Downtrodden and Offended*—*Crime and Punishment*—*The Brothers Karamázoff*—NEKRÁSOFF—Discussions about his talent—His love of the people—Apotheosis of Woman—OTHER PROSE-WRITERS OF THE SAME EPOCH —Serghéi Akasákoff—Dal—Iván Panáeff—Hvóschinskaya (V. Krestóvskiy- pseudonym)—POETS OF THE SAME EPOCH—Kolstóff—Nikítin—Pleschéyeff—The admirers of pure art: Tyúttcheff—A. Máykoff—Scherbína—Polónskey—A. Fet—A.K. Tolstóy—THE TRANSLATORS.

CHAPTER VI : THE DRAMA   208

Its origin—The Tsars and Alexis and Peter I—Sumarókoff—Pseudo-classical tragedies: Knyahnín; Ozeroff—First comedies—The first years of the nineteenth century—Griboyédoff—The Moscow stage in the fifties—Ostróvskiy; his first dramas—*The Thunderstorm*—Ostróvskiy's later dramas—Historical dramas: A.K. Tostóy—Other dramatic writers.

CHAPTER VII : FOLK NOVELISTS   239

Their position in Russian literature—The early folk-novelists; Grigoróvitch—Márko Vovtchók—Danilévskiy—Intermediate period: Kókoreff—Písmskiy—Potyékhin—Ethnographical research—The realistic school: Pomyalóvskiy—Ryeshétnikoff—Levítoff—Gleb Uspénskiy—Zlatovrátskiy and other folk-novelists: Naúmoff—Zasódimskiy—Sáloff—Nefédoff—Modern Realism: MAXÍM GÓRKIY.

✓CHAPTER VIII : POLITICAL LITERATURE—SATIRE—ART
    CRITICISM—LATER PERIOD NOVELISTS   284
    POLITICAL LITERATURE—Difficulties due to censorship—
    The 'circles'—Westerners and Slavophiles—Political literature
    abroad: Hérzen—Ogaryóff—Bakúnin—Lavróff— Stepniák—
    Tchertkóff—*The Contemporary* and Tchernyshévskiy—SATIRE:
    Schedrín (Saltykóff)—ART CRITICISM: Its importance in Rus-
    sia—Byelínskiy—Dobrolúboff—Písareff —Mihailóvskiy—Tol-
    stóy's *What is Art?*—LATER PERIOD NOVELISTS: Oertel
    —Korolénko—Present drift of literature—Merezhkóvskiy—
    Boborykin—Potápenko—Tchéhoff.

BIBLIOGRAPHICAL NOTES   347

APPENDICES   351

INDEX   357

THE PRONUNCIATION OF RUSSIAN NAMES

THROUGHOUT this book the following transliteration of Russian names has been adopted. It is the transliteration which I have followed for more than thirty years in the *Encyclopædia Britannica*, *Chambers's Encyclopædia*, *Statesman's Yearbook*, and so on, and it only slightly differs from the transliteration adopted by the British Museum and the Geographical Society.

The pronunciation is as follows :—

a as in father	yo as in yoke
e „ net	yu „ yule
i „ in	tch „ Scotch
o „ not	sh „ shame
u „ rule	sch is a softened sh
ya „ yarn	(Schapoff = Shyapoff
ye „ yet	Schepkin = Shyepkin)

There are in Russian only four letters which have not their equivalents in English :

ж — a French *j*, is rendered by *zh*.

л — a rough *l*, similar to *ll* in rough Scotch *will*, *shall*.

ы — a rough *i*, as in *river* in broad Scotch. It is rendered by *y* (Pypin).

ь — after a consonant renders it soft.

The Spanish *ñ* is used to render a softened *n* : *ko* (horse) = French *cogne*.

LIST OF WRITERS MENTIONED

Modern transliteration	Kropotkin's transliteration
Ablesímov, A.O. (1742-83)	Ablesímoff
Aksákov, I.S. (1823-86)	Aksákoff, Ivan
Aksákov, K.S. (1817-60)	Aksákoff, Konstantin
Aksákov, S.T. (1791-1859)	Aksákoff, Serghei Tomofeevich
Ánnenkov, P.V. (1812-67)	Ánnenkoff, P.V.
Auerbach, Berthold (1812-82)	Auerbach, Bertold
Avvakúm, (c.1620-81)	Avvakúm
Bakúnin, M.A. (1814-76)	Bakúnin, Mikhail
Baratynsky, E.A. (1800-44)	Baratynskiy
Bayán (c. 12th century)	Bayán
Belínsky, V.G. (1811-48)	Byelínskiy
Bestúzhez, A.A. (Marlinsky) (1797-1837)	Bestúzheff, Alexander (Marlinskiy)
Biryukóv, P.I. (1860-1931)	Birókoff
Boborykin (P.D.) (1836-1822)	Boborykin
Bogdanóvich, I.F. (1743-1803)	Bogdanóvitch
Bylína (folk epics C. 19th century)	Bylíny
Chaadáyev, P.Y. (1794-1856)	Tchaadáeff
Chaikóvsky, P.I. (1840-93)	Tchaikóvsky, Piotr Ilyich
Chékhov, A.P. (1860-1904)	Tchéhoff, Anton P.
Chernyshévsky, N.G. (1828-89)	Tchernishévskiy
Chertkáv, V.G.(1954-1936)	Tchertkáff, V.
Dahl, V.I. (1801-72)	Dal, Dr. V. (Kosak Luganskiy)
Danilévky, G.P. (1829-90)	Danilévskiy
Délvig, A.A. (1798-1831)	Délwig
Derzhávin, G.R. (1743-1816)	Derzhávin
Dimitriev, I.I. (1760-1837)	Dmítrieff
Dobrolyúbov, N.A. (1836-61)	Dobrolúboff
Dolgorúky, I.M. (1764-1823)	Dolgorúkiy, Prince
Dostoyévsky, F.M. (1821-81)	Dostoévskiy
Druzhínin, A.V. (1824-64)	Druzhínin
Euler, Leonhard (1707-83)	Euler, Leonhard
Fet, A.A. (1920-92)	Shenshin, A. (A. Fet)
Fonvizin, D.I. (1745-92)	Wizin, von
Gógol, N.V. (1809-52)	Gógol, Nicolay Vasielevich
Goncharóv, I.A. (1812-91)	Gontcharóff
Górky, Maxim (1868-1936)	Gorkiy, Maxim A. (A. Pleskoff)
Grigoyédov, A.S. (1795-1829)	Griboyédoff
Grigóriev, A.A. (1822-64)	Grigórieff, A.
Hérzen, A.L. (1812-70)	Hérzen, Alexander (Iskander)
Kantémír, A.D. (1708-44)	Kantemír, son of a Moldavian prince

Kapníst, V.V. (1757-1823)   Kapníst
Karamzín, N.M. (1766-1826)   Karamzín
Katénin, P.A. (1792-1853)   Katénin
Katkóv, M.N. (1818-87)   Katkóff
Khmelnítsky, N.L. (1789-1846)   Hmelnítskiy
Khomyakóv, A.S. (1804-60)   Homyakóv
Kiréyefsky, Ivan (1806-56)
  and Peter (1808-56)   Kiréyevskiy, the brothers
Knyazhnín, Y.B. (1742-91)   Knyazhnín
Koltsóv, A.V. (1809-42)   Koltsoff
Korolénko, V.G. (1853-1921)   Korolénko, Vladimir
Kozlóv, I.I. (1799-1940)   Kozlóff
Kravchínsky S.M. (S. Stepniak) (1852-95)   S. Stepnyak
Krestóvsky, V.V. (1840-95)   Krestóvskiy
Krylóv, I.A. (1769-1844)   Krylóff, I.A.
Kúrbsky, Prince (c. 1520-83)   Kúrbskiy, Prince
Lavróv, P.L. (1823-1900)   Lavróff, Peter (Mirtoff)
Lazhéchnikov, I.I. (1792-1969)   Lazhétchnikoff
Lérmontov, M.Y. (1814-41)   Lérmontoff, Mikhail Yurievitch
Lomonósov, M.V. (1711-65)   Lomónosoff
Mámin-Sibiryák, D.N. (1852-1912)   Mámin
Márkovich, M.A. (née Veklenksy, pseud. Markóvitch, Madame Marie
  (Marko-Vovtchók) (1834-1907)
Máykov, A.N. (1821-97)   Máykoff, Apollon
Máykov, V.N. (1823-47)   Máykoff, Valerian
Mazéppa   Mazépa
Mélnikov (P.I.) (Péchersky) (1819-83)   Mélnikoff (Petcherakiy)
Mereshóvsky, D.D. (1865-1941)   Merezhkóvskiy, Dmitriy
Mey, L.A. (1822-62)   Mey, L.
Mickiévicz, Adam (1798-1855)   Mickiéwicz
Mikhaylóvsky, N.K. (1842-1904)   Mikhailóvskiy
Mordóvtsev, D.L. (1830-1905)   Mordóvtseff, D.L.
Nadézhdin, N.I. (1804-56)   Nadézkdin
Nádson, S.Y. (1862-87)   Nádson
Narézhny, V.T. (1780-1825)   Narézhnyi
Nekrásov, N.A. (1821-78)   Nekrássov, Nicholas
Nóvikov, N.I. (1744-1818)   Nóvikov
Novodvorsky, A.O. (1853-82)   Novodvórskiy
Odóyevsky, A.I. (1802-39)   Odóevsky, Prince
Ogarév, N.P. (1813-77)   Ogaryóff
Ostróvsky, A.N. (1823-86)   Ostróvskiy
Ózerov, V.A. (1769-1816)   Óveroff
Panáyev, I.I. (1812-62)   Panáeff, Ivan

Petrashévsky, M.V. (1621-66)	Petrashévskiy
Písarev, A.I. (1803-28)	Písareff, A.L.
Písarev, D.L. (1840-68)	Písareff, D.L.
Písemsky, A.F. (1820-81)	Písemskiy, A.
Pleschéyev, A.N. (1825-93)	Pleschéyeff, A.
Polevóy, N.A. (1796-1846)	Polevóy
Polezháyev, A.I. (1805-38)	Polezháyeff
Pomyalóvsky, N.G. (1835-63)	Pomyalórskiy
Prokopóvich, F. (1681-1736)	Procopóvitch
Púshkin, A.S. (1799-1837)	Púshkin, Alexander
Radíshev, A.N. (1749-1802)	Radíscheff
Ryléyev, KéF. (1795-1826)	Ryéeff
Saltykóv (Schedrin) (1826-89)	Saltykóff (Schedrin)
Samárin, Y.F. (1819-76)	Samárin
Scheller-Mikháylov, A.K. (1838-1900)	Scheller (A. Mikhaíloff)
Schépkin, M.S. (1788-1863)	Schépkin
Scherbátov, M.M. (1733-90)	Scherbátoff, Prince
Scherbína, N.F. (1821-69)	Scherbína
Shakhowskóy, A.A. (1777-1846)	Shahhovskíy
Schevchénko, T. (1814-1861)	Shevtchénko
Sleptsóv, V.A. (1836-78)	Slyeptsóff
Solovíev, V.S. (1853-1900)	Solovíoff, Vladimir
Stankívich, N.V. (1813-40)	Stankévitch
Stanyukóvich, K.M. (1844-1903)	Stanyukóvitch
Sukhovó-Kobylin, A.V. (1817-1903)	Sukhovó-Kobylin
Sumarókov, A.O. (1718-77)	Sumarókoff
Tatishév, V.N. (1686-1750)	Tatuschéff
Tolstóy, A.K. (1817-75)	Tolstóy, Count Alexei Konstantinovitch
Tolstóy, L.N. (1828-1910)	Tolstóy, Lyoff Nicolaevitch
Tretiakovsky, V.K. (1703-69)	Tretaikóvskiy
Turgénev, I.S. (1818-83)	Turguéneff, Ivan Sergeyevitch
Tyútchev, F.I. (1803-73)	Tyúttcheff
Uhland, Ludwig (1787-1862)	Uhland, Ludwig
Uspénsky, Gleb (1843-1902)	Uppénskiy, Gleb
Uspénsky, N. (1837-89)	Uspénskiy, Nicholas
Venevétinkov, D.V. (1805-27)	Venevétinkoff
Yazykov, N.M. (1803-46)	Yazykoff
Zagóskin, M.N. (1789-1852)	Zagóshkin
Zasodímsky, P.V. (1843-1912)	Zasodímskiy
Zhukóvsky, V.A. (1783-1852)	Zkukóvskiy
Zlatovrásky, N.N. (1845-1911)	Zlatovrátskiy

AN INTRODUCTION

Like most Russian intellectuals of his generation, Peter Kropotkin read widely in the contemporary literature of his country, which has now become its classical literature, for the culture of Russia was then going through its equivalent of the Elizabethan age in England, a time — from Pushkin onward, of extraordinary creative activity. Despite the difficulties that were imposed by an autocratic government and a rigorous but capricious censorship, Russia in the nineteenth century produced masters of fiction and drama which placed its literature on a level with those of the other European cultures. This outburst of original writing led to the emergence of critics who endeavoured to relate the creations of the great novelists to current political and social trends, so that major works like Turgenev's *Fathers and Sons* and Tolstoy's *War and Peace* initiated great debates on the nature and the destination of Russian society. And since avowedly political writing—even so moderate as Alexander Herzen's liberally radical essays — could reach Russians only thanks to the book-smuggling enterprises that developed after the death of Nicholas I, the texts of novels and the oblique statements of critics were as carefully examined for political implications as the oracle bones of ancient China. Thus it is not surprising that so many of the more prominent Russian intelligentsia were to be found on the borderland between literature and politics, including those best known as novelists, like

Tolstoy, Turgenev and even Dostoevsky, and those more generally associated with radical politics, like Herzen and Chernyshevsky and Kropotkin, with Maxim Gorki somewhere in the middle.

The literary men, like Tolstoy, often became involved in
writing tracts for the times, widely and illicitly distributed; even
Dosteovsky embarked on a kind of quasi-political journalism. On
the other hand, the political radicals often tried their hands at
something more literary. Herzen and Chernyshevsky each wrote
a novel, and Kropotkin, who had been an almost obsessive reader
since childhood, wrote at least two books that entitled him to a
place in the histories of Russian literature. One, of course, was the
Memoirs of a Revolutionist, which Tolstoy admired and which the
fine critic, D.S. Mirsky, in *A History of Russian Literature from Its
Beginnings to 1900,* described as "a first-class autobiography, the
most remarkable work of its kind since Herzen's *My Past and
Thoughts*". The other, of course, is the book I am at present introducing, *Russian Literature, Ideals and Realities,* which first appeared
in 1905, a year more eventful in Russian history than Kropotkin
can have imagined when he prepared his manuscript.

The two books are related in something more than their
place in Russian literature; they were originally written in English
in response to an interest in the United States at the turn of the
century in aspects of Russia and its culture. Herzen had long
before suggested that in the world of the future the old nation-
states of western and central Europe would be overshadowed by
the growth — rivalling each other across the oceans of the two
young giant powers of the United States and Russia, both vast
lands with immense resources and potential populations, and
both outside the moribund cultures — as Herzen saw them — of
the old Europe. The American revolution had already been
achieved, the Russian would soon follow, Herzen hoped, and then
these two young and vital civilizations would stand in confronta-
tion over an exhausted European Old World.

Many Americans, even if they did not express prophetic
insights equivalent to those of Herzen, regarded the potentialities
of Russia with an interest that was enhanced by the signs of

change shown by the great number of Russian emigrants reaching American ports at this period and also by the new availability of Russian literature which at last was being abundantly rendered into English by competent translators like Constance Garnett and, later, Aylmer Maude. Since the 1880s the Russian writers had been growing steadily in popularity abroad and generating an international interest in their own land.

That interest embraced Kropotkin, who, once Herzen had died in 1870 and Bakunin in 1876, became the most distinguished among the celebrated Russian exiles. Kropotkin, himself, meanwhile, was interested in North America, which he realized had much to contribute to the social studies that eventually resulted in *Mutual Aid* and *Fields, Factories and Workshops,* and in 1891, when an American lecture agency approached him with a proposal for a tour, he gladly accepted. All the arrangements were made, and a great farewell party, attended by hundreds of well-wishers, was held at the Athenaeum Hall, at the end of which, after the dancing and the revolutionary songs, Kropotkin gave a rousing speech denouncing the oppression that flourished in the United States and reminding his hearers of the judicial murder of the Chicago anarchists a few years before. Whether or not as a result of the speech, the agency decided the tour was impracticable, and Kropotkin was particularly put out, since he had made no plans to earn money over the winter of 1891-1892.

In 1897 another opportunity came when the British Association for the Advancement of Science held its annual meeting in Toronto. Kropotkin's old friend James Mavor, now Professor of Economics at the University of Toronto, persuaded him to take part, and he delivered two papers in the geographical section, one on glacial deposits in Finland and the other on his theories regarding the structure of Asian mountains. Then he went on the journey across Canada as a result of which he made his momentous suggestion that the Doukhobors, then being ferociously persecuted by the tsarist authorities, might find a refuge in the Canadian prairies. Afterwards he went on a brief lecture tour in the United States, where he spoke in Chicago, Philadelphia, New York, Boston and

Washington. At Boston he gave a group of lectures at the Lowell Institute on mutual aid, and later on, at Chickering Hall in New York, he gave a single lecture on Russian literature. But the most important event of this trip was his meeting with Walter Hines Page, of the *Atlantic Monthly*, who persuaded him to write the series of autobiographical essays which eventually were united in a book and published as *Memoirs of a Revolutionist*.

Kropotkin's lectures at the Lowell Institute had been so successful that in 1901 he was invited there again to give a series of eight lectures on Russian literature. He approached his task with a good deal of trepidation. Perhaps he felt he was stepping too far out of his main fields of interest, for just before his first lecture he wrote to Charles Eliot Norton:

> To tell the truth, I feel nervous for it. Such as I wrote it, it
> is too long, and may be too dull. So I rewrite it entirely,
> and so long as it is not done, I feel quite nervous. So I sit
> now and write, and will work till late at night.

In the event, the lectures were highly successful, largely because they told the American audiences so much about a subject of which they had little knowledge. Roger Baldwin, later a great civil libertarian, was there, and he remembered that Kropotkin "spoke from notes, in an English strongly accented, in a professorial but very earnest style." The press reports were friendly, and the audiences were large and actively interested, a feature which characterized the whole of Kropotkin's tour. It was these eight lectures given at the Lowell Institute that would later be turned into the eight chapters of *Russian Literature: Ideals and Realities*.

Afterwards he delivered a single lecture on Russian literature at Chickering Hall in New York, and on the 23rd April he reached the farthest point of his tour, at Madison, where he delivered a final lecture, on Tolstoy and Turgenev, at the University of Wisconsin. Returning through Ohio, he gathered information on American wheat growing practices which he used in the later editions of *Fields, Factories and Workshops*.

Unlike some of Kropotkin's other works, such as *The Conquest of Bread* and *The Great French Revolution, Russian Literature* — based on lectures that were written and delivered in English — did not have to be translated. Kropotkin, who immediately after his return from America was involved in preparing *Mutual Aid* for its first edition in 1902, was slow in completing *Russian Literature* and called for assistance and advice from his friend Richard Heath, an English journalist and amateur authority on the Anabaptists. The Heaths and the Kropotkins were family friends from the 1880s onwards, and Heath's daughter Emily, who later became a well-known painter and did the portrait of Kropotkin now in the possession of the Royal Geographical Society, wrote to me a delightful letter in the 1940s describing her visits as a child to Kropotkin's first frugal English home in Harrow.

Heath may have been a good journalist, and was obviously a good friend; he does not seem to have been a particularly good editor, for the text of *Russian Literature* is cluttered with imperfections. There is nothing wrong with the style, which is genial and inviting, as it should be in a book of this kind, but one is troubled, for example, by Kropotkin's slipshod way of dealing with the names of the writers he mentions or discusses. It is not a matter of the transliteration of Russian words, though this is done according to an old-fashioned system which forces one to look under the H's for Khomyakov, under the T's for Checkhov, and under the V's for Fonvizin. It is rather a tendency to follow neither the Russian custom of putting first name and patronymic before a surname, nor the British custom of putting merely the first name. Most of Kropotkin's writers appear by their surnames alone, and rarely are they dated when they are introduced. I have remedied this deficiency by following this introduction with a list which on the righthand side shows the name given to each writer by Kropotkin, and on the left-hand side the name of the same writer in a modern transliteration, with dates of birth and death, and with initials for surname and patronymic, a practice acceptable in Russia. There are also occasional absurdities caused by the too thorough transliterations of Russian names, as when one encounters the unfamiliar name of John the Terrible, only to realize that the monarch intended is the one we have grown used to calling Ivan.

Russian Literature: Ideals and Realities, could hardly count as criticism of any profound or penetrating kind; rather it must be considered as a literary history and an appreciation intended to introduce Russian writers to English readers likely to be relatively unfamiliar to them. His exposition is executed from the social standpoint of the veteran revolutionary, and this necessarily affects its character and the views Kropotkin offers on the various writers he discusses. Essentially he is propounding the thesis that in Russia literature occupies a unique position because it is the only way of reflecting the real currents of intellectual development and of underground political opinion. He puts the case for this viewpoint at an early stage in the book.

> *In no other country does literature occupy so influential a position as it does in Russia. Nowhere else does it exercise so profound and so direct an influence upon the intellectual development of the younger generation. There are the novels of Turgenev, and even of the less known writers, which have been real stepping-stones in the development of Russian youth within the last fifty years.*

> *The reason why literature exercises such an influence in Russia is self-evident. There is no open political life, and with the exception of a few years at the time of the abolition of serfdom, the Russian people have never been called upon to take an active part in the framing of their country's institutions.*

> *The consequence has been that the best minds of the country have chosen the poem, the novel, the satire, or literary criticism as the medium for expressing their aspirations, their conceptions of national life, of their ideals. It is not to blue-books, or to newspaper leaders, but to its works of art that one must go in Russia in order to*

understand the political, economical, and social ideals of
the country — the aspirations of the history-making
portion of Russian society.

Within his standpoint, Kropotkin's criteria of appreciation
are not narrow. He seeks to give credit not merely to anarchists, or
even to revolutionaries in general, but to any work that, however
obliquely presented, displays a form of resistance to or a criticism
of the prevalent authority. This gives his book its own catholicity,
but it has corresponding disadvantages, since it makes Kropotkin
concentrate on content rather than on form, on intention rather
than achievement, and also to ignore aspects of a writer's work
that are not broadly social. He tries to speak well of everybody,
which is in his nature and which also suits his purpose. And he
shows an almost complete failure to understand the religious
mind, so that his treatment of Tolstoy's Christianity, while quite
lengthy, is too elementary. In no way does he really appreciate the
spiritual duality of Dostoevsky or its effect on the social views he
expressed towards the end of his life. It may be that Kropotkin
himself was too secure and serene in his single-mindedness to
understand the intellectual torment that impelled these two great
masters of the Russian novel.

With men like Turgenev and Chekhov, whose attitude had
a clarity and coherence resembling his own, he is much more at
home, and there are both admirable conciseness and accuracy in
such a judgment as this of Chekhov.

Tchehoff's heroes are not people who have never heard
better words, or never conceived better ideas, than those
that circulate in the lowest circles of the Philistines. No,
they have heard such words and their hearts have beaten
once upon a time at the sound of such words. But the
commonplace everyday life has stifled all such aspira-
tions, apathy has taken their place, and now there re-
mains only a haphazard existence amidst a hopeless
meanness. The meanness which Tchehoff represents is

*one which begins with the loss of faith in one's forces and
the gradual loss of all those brighter hopes and illusions
which make the charm of all activity, and then, step by
step, this meanness destroys the very springs of life:
broken hopes, broken hearts, broken energies. Man
reaches a stage when he can only mechanically repeat
certain actions from day to day, and goes to bed, happy if
he has 'killed' his time in any way, gradually falling into
a complete intellectual apathy and a moral indifference.
The worst is that the very multiplicity of samples which
Tchehoff gives, without repeating himself, from so many
different layers of society, seems to tell the reader that it
is the rottenness of a whole civilization, of an epoch,
which the author divulges to us.*

Of Turgenev, Kropotkin claims that "for the artistic construction, the finish and the beauty of his novels, he was very
probably the greatest novel-writer of his century." Many will
debate this assertion in the name of either Dostoevsky or Tolstoy,
yet it can reasonably be admitted that, though Turgenev may not
have had the breadth or the intense passion of either of his
contemporaries, his novels are nearer formal and stylistic perfection, while his psychology, devoid of the moralism of Tolstoy or
the morbidity that so often surges in Dostoevsky, is more percep-
tive of true human character.

One must also bear in mind that Turgenev was the only
major Russian literary figure — if one counts out primarily political writers like Sergei Stepniak and Peter Lavrov — whom Kropotkin knew personally and directly. In England he was greatly
respected in literary circles; Bernard Shaw, William Morris, Oscar
Wilde, Frank Harris, William Rossetti, Patrick Geddes, Ford
Madox Ford, were all among his friends and admirers. But in
Russia, while in his boyhood his brother Alexander and his sister
Helen, as well as his tutors and some of his professors and fellow
students in the School of Pages, had encouraged him to read
widely in Russian literature, the circle he joined when he returned

from Siberia to St. Petersburg was not a literary one; it was the circle centring around Nicholas Chaikovsky, a populist group dedicated to learning the doctrines of western liberals and social- ists and finding ways to interpret them for Russian peasants and workers. When he visited western Europe in 1872, and later when he arrived there as a long-term sojourner after his prison escape in 1876, he made contact with his scientific associates connected with *Nature* and the Royal Geographic Society, and also with his fellow geographer and anarchist Elisée Reclus, but otherwise both his friendships and his writing activities were connected with the propaganda for anarchism he was trying to carry on in Switzer- land and southern France, and his only personal contact with a major Russian writer at this time was made in 1878 when Turge- nev, then in Paris, sent him an invitation through Peter Lavrov to dine in friendly celebration of his escape from prison.

The two men immediately took to each other and they met whenever Kropotkin was in Paris. Of these encounters the latter left an interesting account in his *Memoirs of a Revolutionist*, and the important points are worth quoting at length, since they give some guidance as to why Kropotkin seemed to understand Turgenev more easily than he did many other Russian writers.

> *His appearance is well known. Tall, strongly built, the head covered with soft and thick grey hair, he was cer- tainly beautiful; his eyes gleamed with intelligence, not devoid of a touch of humour, and his whole manner testified to that simplicity and absence of affectation which was characteristic of the best Russian writers...*

> *His talk was especially remarkable. He spoke, as he wrote, in images. What he wanted was to develop an idea he did not resort to arguments, although he was a master of philosophical discussion; he illustrated his idea by a scene presented in a form as beautiful as if it had been taken from a novel...*

He knew from Lavrov that I was an enthusiastic admirer of his writings; and one day, as we were returning in a carriage from a visit to Antokolski's studio, he asked me what I thought of Bazarov. I frankly replied, 'Bazarov is an admirable painting of the nihilist, but one feels that you did not love him as much as you did your other heroes.' 'On the contrary, I loved him, intensely loved him,' Turgenev replied, with unexpected vigour. 'When we get home I will show you my diary, in which I have noted how I wept when I had ended the novel with Bazarov's death.'

Turgenev certainly loved the intellectual aspect of Bazarov. He so identified himself with the nihilist philosophy of his hero that he even kept a diary in his name, appreciating the current events from Bazarov's point of view. But I think he admired him more than he loved him. In a brilliant lecture on Hamlet and Don Quixote, he divided the history-makers of mankind into two classes, represented by one or the other of these characters...He himself and several of his friends belonged more or less to the Hamlets. He loved Hamlet and admired Don Quixote. So he admired also Bazarov. He represented his superiority admirably well; he understood the tragic character of his isolated position; but he could not surround him with that tender, poetical love which he bestowed, as on a sick friend, when his heroes approached the Hamlet type. It would have been out of place...

I saw him for the last time in the autumn of 1881. He was very ill, and worried by the thought that it was his duty to write to Alexander III — who had just come to the throne and hesitated as to the policy he should follow — asking him to give Russia a constitution, and proving to him by solid arguments the necessity of that step. With evident grief he said to me: 'I feel that I must do it, but I feel I shall not be able to do it.' In fact, he was already suffering awful pains occasioned by a cancer in the spinal cord, and had the greatest difficulty even in sitting up and talking for a few moments. He did not write then, and a few weeks later it would have been useless. Alexander III had announced in a manifesto his intention to remain the absolute ruler of Russia.

These recollections suggest that personal knowledge had given Kropotkin a special insight into Turgenev's character, and this may explain the aptness with which he puts forward claims on Turgenev's behalf which the unbiassed reader cannot fail to find sympathetic. Kropotkin never actually met Tolstoy, yet their relationship, indirect as it was, was marked by strong mutual respect. Their ideas had much in common; both hated the State and any kind of institution that interfered with the freedom of individual conscience and actions; both denounced property; both believed that man's innate moral sense should be sufficient to prevent all those ills for the cure of which governments try to persuade us to accept the greater evils of police and armies, laws and punishments. They differed mainly on the matter of revolutionary violence, which Kropotkin accepted in extreme circumstances and Tolstoy not at all.

Tolstoy respected Kropotkin as a man of integrity who had sacrificed much for his opposition to Tsarism. Kropotkin regarded Tolstoy as a great writer who had thrown his life and prestige into the cause of the dispossessed and who had risked much by his fearless denunciations of Tsarist policy even within Russia.

Their first contact seems to have come with the arrival in England of Tolstoy's leading disciple, Vladimir Chertkov. This exiled Tolstoyan had, by coincidence, been an officer on duty in the St.Petersburg Military Hospital at the time of Kropotkin's escape. They became close friends,and Chertkov was a regular visitor at Kropotkin's Bromley home. Soon after their meeting, Kropotkin asked Chertkov to transmit a message of friendly esteem to Tolstoy. He seems to have made some reference to their difference of opinion on the question of violence, for Tolstoy wrote to Chertkov shortly afterwards:

> *Kropotkin's letter has pleased me very much. His arguments in favour of violence do not seem to me to be the expression of his opinions, but only of his fidelity to the banner under which he had served so honestly all his life. He cannot fail to see that the protest against violence, in order to be strong, must have a solid foundation. But a protest for violence has no foundation and for this very reason is destined to failure.*

Chertkov read these words to Kropotkin, who was very disturbed by what he regarded as a misunderstanding of his attitude, for he replied: *In order to understand how much I sympathise with the ideas of Tolstoy, it is sufficient to say that I have written a whole volume to demonstrate that life is created, not by the struggle for existence, but by mutual aid.*

Cordial feelings continued to flow between the age's two great opponents of government. Visitors to Tolstoy in Russia, like James Mavor and H.W. Nevinson, would be given special messages of friendly greeting for Kropotkin, and in January 1903 the old novelist wrote to Chertkov: "One has time to reflect when one is ill. During this illness I was particularly preoccupied with recollections, and my beautiful memories of Kropotkin were given special preference." A month later he wrote again: "Send my greetings to Kropotkin; I have recently read his *Memoirs* and I am delighted with them." In 1905 Nevinson found Tolstoy full of interest in *Fields, Factories and Workshops*, which he thought of using as a basis for starting a recovery of Russian agriculture. He transmitted his enthusiasm to his new Indian friend, Mohandas Gandhi, the future Mahatma, whose thoughts of a society of village communities were much influenced by Kropotkin's ideas.

It may be that, just as Kropotkin saw in Tolstoy the great writer inspired by an unbounded love of humanity, so Tolstoy saw in Kropotkin the man who had actually practiced the renunciation which he himself had been able to achieve only in thought and writing.

At last, in November 1910 when it was tragically too late, Tolstoy made the break with his old life which he had so long felt necessary. He disappeared from home, and a rumour circulated that he had entered a monastery and would probably recant his objections to the Orthodox Church. Kropotkin immediately went to his defence, writing to the *Times*:

> As to the possibility of 'recantation' by Tolstoy of his religious opinions, I can say it is absolutely improbable. It so happens that for the last two years I have been studying almost passionately and writing about the inner drama of Tolstoy's life as it appears from his novels, and other writings, and from the biographical material which he has himself permitted his friend, P.A. Biryukov, to publish; and I am sure that, having devoted the last thirty years of his life to the working out of a universal rationalist religion, divested of all the mystical elements of modern Christianity, a religion which, he says, would be equally acceptable to the Christian, the Buddhist, the Hebrew, the Musulman, the follower of Lao-tse and to every ethical philosopher, and after having so passionately proclaimed in his latest writings the supreme decisive right of reason in religious matters, Tolstoy will certainly not return to the teachings of the Greek Orthodox Church.

> I am not astonished to learn that Tolstoy had decided to retire to a peasant house where he might continue his teachings without having to rely upon anyone else's labour for supplying himself or his family with the luxuries of life. It is the necessary outcome of the terrible inner drama he had been living through the last thirty years — the drama, by the way, of thousands upon thousands of intellectuals in our present society. It is the accomplishment of what he was longing for a long time.

Kropotkin ended by expressing the hope that "our great, venerated, beloved writer's life" would not be poisoned by the Russian church authorities. At least this wish was granted, for a few days later came the news that Tolstoy had been seized with pneumonia on his last journey of escape, and had died, with a few friends and kin about him, in a remote stationmaster's house in Central Russia. Kropotkin was much afflicted by the news, and wrote several articles of appreciation, in which he referred to Tolstoy as "the most loved man, the most touchingly loved man, in the world."

Except for Chekhov, there is no other writer whom Kropotkin discusses with the same sympathy as he does Turgenev and Tolstoy, to both of whom he was drawn by such deep affinities. Yet, taken as a whole, *Russian Literature: Ideas and Realities* provides a fair and comprehensive introduction to Russian writing up to the end of the nineteenth century, as viewed by an exile who kept close touch with what was happening within the Russian literary world. As his particular interest is in the nineteenth century rebels, Kropotkin deals briefly with the older literature, from the early folk poems to Pushkin. But when he reaches the later writers of the nineteenth century, from Gogol onwards, his study becomes more comprehensive, and it was certainly sufficiently detailed for general purposes in his time, when readers in the west were just beginning to acquire a knowledge of and a taste for Russian writers. Almost every poet and prose-writer of any significance is discussed (the exceptions, as I shall suggest, tend to be interesting) and every class of literature is included, criticism as well as novels, and political writing as well as poetry. It is clear that, despite his other varied activities and his years of exile, Kropotkin always found time to continue that thorough reading of Russian literature which he began in childhood. He did not, like so many revolutionaries, allow social preoccupations to blunt his literary and artistic preoccupations, and *Russian Literature: Ideals and Realities,* is another proof that he always retained a wide and varied culture.

Yet there are some significant lacunae, which point, I suggest, to limitations of understanding as much as of tolerance.

Why, for instance, is there no mention of Nicholas Leskov, whose highly original books were all published during the period Kropotkin considers? Could he have failed to understand Leskov's unusual combination of Orthodox piety, shown in his Christian tales, and anger against the clergy, shown in his satirical pieces? Then there is the quite deliberate neglect, in the 1916 second edition, which we are told had been "revised and rewritten", of the highly interesting young writers who appeared around the turn of the century, and by this time were becoming well known, such as Andreyev, Blok and Balmont. Kropotkin in fact quite deliberately evades this issue of a rapidly changing literary scene by asserting, in the 1916 "Preface to the second edition", that "such a number of new writers belonging to a variety of new literary schools came to the front during the last five-and-twenty years that a new book would have been required to deal with them in a proper way." Was he perhaps tacitly admitting that he did not understand these younger men and women sufficiently to write about them sympathetically, for his was after all a descriptive literary talent and theirs were by and large allusive and elegiac ones? However that may be, Kropotkin's literary history of Russia can be taken as ending with the death of Chekhov, in the year before the book was published. It celebrates the golden age of Russian writing.

George Woodcock

CHAPTER I

INTRODUCTION

THE RUSSIAN LANGUAGE—Early folk-literature : Folk-lore—Songs—Sagas—*Lay of Igor's Raid*—Annals—The Mongol Invasion; its consequences—Correspondence between John IV. and Kúrbskiy—Split in the Church—Avvakúm's *Memoirs*—THE EIGHTEENTH CENTURY : Peter I. and his contemporaries — Tretiakóvskiy — Lomonósoff — Sumarókoff — The times of Catherine II. : Derzhávin—Von Wízin—The Freemasons : Nóvikoff—Radíscheff—EARLY NINETEENTH CENTURY : Karamzín and Zhukóvskiy—The Decembrists—Rýleeff.

ONE of the last messages which Turguéneff addressed to Russian writers from his death-bed was to implore them to keep in its purity 'that precious inheritance of ours—the Russian language.' He who knew in perfection most of the languages spoken in Western Europe had the highest opinion of Russian as an instrument for the expression of all possible shades of thought and feeling, and he had shown in his writings what depth and force of expression, and what melodiousness of prose, could be obtained in his native tongue. In his high appreciation of Russian, Turguéneff—as will often be seen in these pages—was perfectly right. The richness of the Russian language in words is astounding : many a word which stands alone for the expression of a given idea in the languages of Western Europe has in Russian three or four equivalents for the rendering of the various shades of the same idea. It is especially rich for rendering various shades of human feeling—tenderness and love, sadness and merriment—as also various degrees of the same action. Its pliability for translation is such that in no other language do we find an equal number of most beautiful, correct, and truly poetical renderings of foreign authors. Poets of the most diverse character, such as Heine and Béranger, Longfellow and Schiller, Shelley and Goethe—to say nothing of that favourite with Russian translators, Shakespeare—are equally well turned into Russian. The sarcasm of Voltaire, the rollicking humour of Dickens, the good-natured laughter of Cervantes are rendered with equal ease. Moreover, owing to the musical character of the Russian tongue, it is wonderfully adapted for rendering poetry in the same metres as those of the original. Longfellow's 'Hiawatha' (in two different translations, both admirable), Heine's capricious lyrics, Schiller's ballads, the melodious folk-songs of different nation-alities, and Béranger's playful *chansonnettes*, read in Russian with exactly the same rhythms as in the originals. The desperate vagueness of German meta-physics is quite as much at home in Russian as the matter-of-fact style of the eighteenth-century philo-sophers ; and the short, concrete and expressive, terse sentences of the best English writers offer no difficulty for the Russian translator.

Together with Czech and Polish, Serbian and Bulgarian, as also several minor tongues, the Russian belongs to the great Slavonian family of languages which, in its turn—together with the Scandinavo-Saxon and the Latin families, as also the Lithuanian, the Persian, the Armenian, the Georgian—belongs to the great Indo-European, or Aryan branch. Some day —soon, let us hope : the sooner the better—the treasures of both the folk-songs possessed by the South Slavonians and the many centuries old literature of the Czechs and the Poles will be revealed to Western readers. But in this work I have to concern myself only with the literature of the Eastern, *i.e.* the Russian, branch of the great Slavonian family ; and in this branch I shall have to omit both the South Russian or

Ukraïnian literature and the White or West Russian folk-lore and songs. I shall treat only of the literature of the Great Russians; or, simply, the Russians. Of all the Slavonian languages theirs is the most widely spoken. It is the language of Púshkin and Lérmontoff, Turguéneff and Tolstóy.

Like all other languages, the Russian has adopted many foreign words: Scandinavian, Turkish, Mongolian and, lately, Greek and Latin. But notwithstanding the assimilation of many nations and stems of the Ural-Altayan or Turanian stock which has been accomplished in the course of ages by the Russian nation, her language has remained remarkably pure. It is striking indeed to see how the translation of the Bible which was made in the ninth century into the language currently spoken then by the Bulgarians and other South Slavonians remains comprehensible, down to the present time, to the average Russian. Grammatical forms and the construction of sentences are of course quite different now. But the roots, as well as a very considerable number of words, remain the same as those which were used in current talk a thousand years ago.

It must be said that the South Slavonian had attained a high degree of perfection, even at that early time. Very few words of the Gospels had to be rendered in Greek—and these are names of things unknown to the South Slavonians; while for none of the abstract words, and for none of the poetical images of the original, had the translators any difficulty in finding the proper expressions. Some of the words they used are, moreover, of a remarkable beauty, and this beauty has not been lost even to-day. Every one remembers, for instance, the difficulty which the learned Dr. Faust, in Goethe's immortal tragedy, found in rendering the sentence: 'In the beginning was the Word.' 'Word,' in modern German, seemed to Dr. Faust to be too shallow an expression for the idea of 'the Word being God.' In the old Slavonian translation we have 'Slovo,' which also means 'Word,' but has at the same time, even for the modern Russian, a far deeper meaning than that of *das Wort*. In old Slavonian 'Slovo' included also the meaning of 'Intellect'—German *Vernunft*; and consequently it conveyed to the reader an idea which was deep enough not to clash with the second part of the Biblical sentence.

I wish that I could give here an idea of the beauty of the structure of the Russian language, such as it was spoken early in the eleventh century in North Russia, a sample of which has been preserved in the sermon of a Nóvgorod bishop (1035). The short sentences of this sermon, calculated to be understood by a newly christened flock, are really beautiful; while the bishop's conceptions of Christianity, utterly devoid of Byzantine gnosticism, are most characteristic of the manner in which Christianity was and is still understood by the masses of the Russian folk.

At the present time the Russian language (the Great Russian) is remarkably free from *patois*. Little Russian, or Ukraïnian,[1] which is spoken by nearly 15,000,000 people, and has its own literature—folk-lore and modern—is undoubtedly a separate language, in the same sense as Norwegian and Danish are separate from Swedish, or as Portuguese and Catalonian are separate from Castilian or Spanish. White Russian, which is spoken in some provinces of Western Russia, has also the characteristics of a separate branch of the Russian, rather than those of a local dialect. As to Great Russian, or Russian, it is spoken by a compact body of nearly eighty million people in Northern, Central, Eastern, and Southern Russia, as also in Northern Caucasia and Siberia. Its pronunciation slightly varies in different parts of this large territory; nevertheless the literary language of Púshkin, Gógol,

[1] Pronounce *Ook-ra-ee-nian.*

Turguéneff, and Tolstóy is understood by all this enormous mass of people. The Russian classics circulate in the villages by millions of copies, and when, in 1887, the literary property in Púshkin's works came to an end (fifty years after his death), complete editions of his works—some of them in ten volumes—were circulated by the hundred-thousand, at the almost incredibly low price of three shillings (75 cents) the ten volumes ; while millions of copies of his separate poems and tales are sold now by thousands of ambulant booksellers in the villages, at the price of from one to three farthings each. Even the complete works of Gógol, Turguéneff, and Gontcharóff, in twelve-volume editions, have sometimes sold to the number of 200,000 sets each, in the course of a single year. The advantages of this intellectual unity of the nation are self-evident.

EARLY FOLK-LITERATURE : FOLK-LORE— SONGS—SAGAS

The early folk-literature of Russia, part of which is still preserved in the memories of the people, is wonderfully rich and full of the deepest interest. No nation of Western Europe possesses such an astonishing wealth of traditions, tales, and lyric folk-songs—some of them of the greatest beauty—and such a rich cycle of archaic epic songs, as Russia does. Of course, all European nations have had, once upon a time, an equally rich folk-literature ; but the great bulk of it was lost before scientific explorers had understood its value or begun to collect it. In Russia this treasure was preserved in remote villages untouched by civilisation, especially in the region round Lake Onéga ; and when the folk-lorists began to collect it, in the eighteenth and nineteenth centuries, they found in Northern Russia and in Little Russia old bards still going about the villages with their primitive string instruments, and reciting poems of a very ancient origin.

Besides, a variety of very old songs are sung still by the village folk themselves. Every annual holiday—Christmas, Easter, Midsummer Day—has its own cycle of songs, which have been preserved, with their melodies, even from pagan times. At each marriage, which is accompanied by a very complicated ceremonial, and at each burial, similarly old songs are sung by the peasant women. Many of them have, of course, deteriorated in the course of ages; of many others mere fragments have survived; but, mindful of the popular saying that 'never a word must be cast out of a song,' the women in many localities continue to sing the most antique songs in full, even though the meaning of many of the words has already been lost.

There are, moreover, the *tales*. Many of them are certainly the same as we find among all nations of Aryan origin: one may read them in Grimm's collection of fairy tales; but others came also from the Mongols and the Turks; while some of them seem to have a purely Russian origin. And next come the songs recited by wandering singers—the *Kaliki*—also very ancient. They are entirely borrowed from the East, and deal with heroes and heroines of other nationalities than the Russian, such as 'Akib, the Assyrian King,' the beautiful Helen, Alexander the Great, or Rustem of Persia. The interest which these Russian versions of Eastern legends and tales offer to the explorer of folk-lore and mythology is self-evident.

Finally, there are the epic songs: the *byliny*, which correspond to the Icelandic *sagas*. Even at the present day they are sung in the villages of Northern Russia by special bards who accompany themselves with a special instrument, also of very ancient origin. The old singer utters in a sort of recitative one or two sentences, accompanying himself with his instrument; then follows a melody, into which each individual singer introduces modulations of his own, before he resumes next the quiet recitative of the epic narrative.

Unfortunately, these old bards are rapidly disappearing ;
but half a century ago a few of them were still alive in
the province of Olónets, to the north-east of St. Petersburg, and I once heard one of them, whom A. Hilferding
had brought to the capital, and who sang before the
Russian Geographical Society his wonderful ballads.
The collecting of the epic songs was happily begun in
good time—during the eighteenth century—and it has
been eagerly continued by specialists, so that Russia
possesses now perhaps the richest collection of such
songs—about four hundred—which have been saved
from oblivion.

The heroes of the Russian epic songs are knights-
errant, whom popular tradition unites round the table
of the Kíeff Prince, Vladímir the Fair Sun.   Endowed
with supernatural physical force, these knights, Iliyá
of Múrom, Dobrýnya Nikítich, Nicholas the Villager,
Alexéy the Priest's Son, and so on, are represented
going about Russia, clearing the country of giants, who
infested the land, or of Mongols and Turks.   Or else
they go to distant lands to fetch a bride for the chief
of their *schola*, the Prince Vladímir, or for themselves ;
and they meet, of course, on their journeys, with all
sorts of adventures, in which witchcraft plays an important part.   Each of the heroes of these sagas has
his own individuality.   For instance, Iliyá, the Peasant's
Son, does not care for gold or riches : he fights only to
clear the land of giants and strangers.   Nicholas the
Villager is the personification of the force with which
the tiller of the soil is endowed : nobody can pull out
of the ground his heavy plough, while he himself lifts it
with one hand and throws it above the clouds; Dobrýnya
embodies some of the features of the dragon-fighters,
to whom belongs St. George ; Sádko is the personification of the rich merchant, and Tchurílo of the refined,
handsome, urbane man with whom all women fall
in love.

At the same time, in each of these heroes, there are

doubtless mythological features. Consequently, the early Russian explorers of the *bylíny*, who worked under the influence of Grimm, endeavoured to explain them as fragments of an old Slavonian mythology, in which the forces of nature are personified in heroes. In Iliyá they found the features of the God of the Thunders. Dobrýnya the Dragon-Killer was supposed to represent the sun in its passive power—the active powers of fighting being left to Iliyá. Sádko was the personification of navigation, and the Sea-God whom he deals with was Neptune. Tchurílo was taken as a representative of the demoniacal element. And so on. Such was, at least, the interpretation put upon the sagas by the early explorers.

V. V. STÁSOFF, in his *Origin of the Russian Bylíny* (1868), entirely upset this theory. With a considerable wealth of argument he proved that these epic songs are not fragments of a Slavonic mythology, but represent borrowings from Eastern tales. Iliyá is the Rustem of the Iranian legends, placed in Russian surroundings. Dobrýnya is the Krishna of Indian folk-lore ; Sádko is the merchant of the Eastern tales, as also of a Norman tale. All the Russian epic heroes have an Eastern origin. Other explorers went still further than Stásoff. They saw in the heroes of Russian epics insignificant men who had lived in the fourteenth and fifteenth centuries (Iliyá of Múrom is really mentioned as a historic person in a Scandinavian chronicle), to whom the exploits of Eastern heroes, borrowed from Eastern tales, were attributed. Consequently, the heroes of the *bylíny* could have had nothing to do with the times of Vladímir, and still less with the earlier Slavonic mythology.

The gradual evolution and migration of myths, which are successively fastened upon new and local persons as they reach new countries, will aid, I believe, to explain these contradictions. That there are mythological features in the heroes of the Russian epics may be taken as certain ; only, the mythology they belong to is not Slavonian but Aryan. Out of these mythological representations of the forces of nature, human heroes were gradually evolved in the East.

At a later epoch, when these Eastern traditions began to spread in Russia, the exploits of their heroes were attributed to Russian men, who were made to act in Russian surroundings. Russian folk-lore assimilated them ; and, while it retained their deepest semi-mythological features and leading traits of character, it endowed, at the same time, the Iranian Rustem, the Indian dragon-killer, the Eastern merchant, and so on, with new features, purely Russian. It divested them, so to say, of the garb which had been put upon their mystical substances when they were first appropriated and humanised by the Iranians and the Indians, and dressed them now in a Russian garb—just as in the tales about Alexander the Great, which I heard in Transbaikália, the Greek hero is endowed with Buryate features and his exploits are located on such and such a Transbaikálian mountain. However, Russian folk-lore did not simply change the dress of the Persian prince, Rustem, into that of a Russian peasant, Iliyá. The Russian sagas, in their style, in the poetical images they resort to, and partly in the characteristics of their heroes, were new creations. Their heroes are thoroughly Russian : for instance, they never seek for blood-revenge, as Scandinavian heroes would do ; their actions, especially those of 'the elder heroes,' are not dictated by personal aims, but are imbued with a communal spirit, which is characteristic of Russian popular life. They are as much Russians as Rustem was Persian. As to the time of composition of these sagas, it is generally believed that they date from the tenth, eleventh, and twelfth centuries, but that they received their definite shape—the one that has reached us—in the fourteenth century. Since that time they have undergone but little alteration.

In these sagas Russia has thus a precious national inheritance of a rare poetical beauty, which has been fully appreciated in England by Ralston, and in France by the historian Rambaud.

LAY OF IGOR'S RAID

And yet Russia has not her Iliad. There has been no poet to inspire himself with the exploits of Iliyá, Dobrýnya, Sádko, Tchurílo, and the others, and to make out of them a poem similar to the epics of Homer, or the ' Kalevála ' of the Finns. This has been done with only one cycle of traditions : in the poem, *The Lay of Igor's Raid* (*Slóvo o Polkú Igoreve*).

This poem was composed at the end of the twelfth century, or early in the thirteenth (its full manuscript, destroyed during the conflagration of Moscow in 1812, dated from the fourteenth or the fifteenth century). It was undoubtedly the work of one author, and for its beauty and poetical form it stands by the side of the *Song of the Nibelungs* or the *Song of Roland.* It relates a real fact that did happen in 1185. Igor, a prince of Kíeff, starts with his *drúzhina (schloa)* of warriors to make a raid on the Pólovtsi, who occupied the prairies of South-eastern Russia, and continually raided the Russian villages. All sorts of bad omens are seen on the march through the prairies—the sun is darkened and casts its shadow on the band of Russian warriors ; the animals give different warnings ; but Igor exclaims : ' Brothers and friends : Better to fall dead than be prisoners of the Pólovtsi ! Let us march to the blue waters of the Don. Let us break our lances against those of the Pólovtsi. And either I leave there my head, or I will drink the water of the Don from my golden helmet.' The march is resumed, the Pólovtsi are met with, and a great battle is fought.

The description of the battle, in which all nature takes part—the eagles and the wolves, and the foxes that bark after the red shields of the Russians—is admirable. Igor's band is defeated. 'From sunrise to sunset, and from sunset to sunrise, the steel arrows flew, the swords clashed on the helmets, the lances were broken in a far-away land—the land of the Pólovtsi.' 'The black earth under the hoofs of the horses was strewn with bones, and out of this sowing affliction will rise in the land of the Russians.'

Then comes one of the best bits of early Russian poetry—the lamentations of Yaroslávna, Igor's wife, who waits for his return in the town of Putívl :

'The voice of Yaroslávna resounds as the complaint of a cuckoo ; it resounds at the rise of the sunlight.

'I will fly as a cuckoo down the river. I will wet my beaver sleeves in the Káyala ; I will wash with them the wounds of my prince—the deep wounds of my hero.

'Yaroslávna laments on the walls of Putívl.

'Oh, Wind, terrible Wind! Why dost thou, my master, blow so strong? Why didst thou carry on thy light wings the arrows of the Khan against the warriors of my hero? Is it not enough for thee to blow there, high up in the clouds? Not enough to rock the ships on the blue sea? Why didst thou lay down my beloved upon the grass of the Steppes?

'Yaroslávna laments upon the walls of Putívl.

'Oh, glorious Dniéper, thou hast pierced thy way through the rocky hills to the land of Pólovtsi. Thou hast carried the boats of Svyatosláv as they went to fight the Khan Kobyák. Bring, oh, my master, my husband back to me, and I will send no more tears through thy tide towards the sea.

'Yaroslávna laments upon the walls of Putívl.

'Brilliant Sun, thrice brilliant Sun! Thou givest heat to all, thou shinest for all. Why shouldest thou send thy burning rays upon my husband's warriors? Why didst thou, in the waterless steppe, dry up their bows in their hands? Why shouldest thou, making them suffer from thirst, cause their arrows to weigh so heavy upon their shoulders?'

This little fragment gives some idea of the general character and beauty of *The Lay of Igor's Raid*, which the composer Borodín took for his beautiful opera, *Prince Igor*.[1]

Surely this poem was not the only one that was composed and sung in those times. The introduction itself speaks of bards, and especially of one, Bayán, whose recitations and songs are compared to the wind that blows in the tops of the trees. Many such Bayáns surely went about and sang similar 'Sayings' during the festivals of the princes and their warriors. Unfortunately, only this one has reached us. The Russian Church, especially in the fifteenth, sixteenth, and seventeenth centuries, pitilessly proscribed the singing of all the epic songs which circulated among the people : it considered them 'pagan,' and inflicted the heaviest penalties upon the bards and those who sang old songs in their rings. Consequently, only small fragments of the early folk-lore have reached us.

And yet even these few relics of the past have exercised a powerful influence upon Russian literature, ever since it has taken the liberty of treating other subjects than purely religious ones. If Russian versification took the rhythmical form, as against the syllabic, it was because this form was imposed upon the Russian poets by the folk-song. Besides, down to quite recent times, folk-songs constituted such an important item in Russian country life, in the homes alike of the landlord and the peasant, that they could not but deeply influence the Russian poets ; and the first great poet of Russia, Púshkin, began his career by re-telling in verse his old nurse's tales to which he used to listen during the long winter nights. It is also

---

[1] English readers will find the translation of this poem in full in the excellent *Anthology of Russian Literature from the Earliest Period to the Present Time*, by Leo Wiener, published in two volumes, in 1902. Professor Wiener knows Russian literature perfectly well, and has made a happy choice of a great number of the most characteristic passages from Russian writers, beginning with the oldest period (911), and ending with our contemporaries, Górkiy and Merezhkóvskiy.

owing to our almost incredible wealth of most musical popular songs that we have had in Russia, since so early a date as 1835, an opera (Verstóvskiy's *Askóld's Grave*), based upon popular tradition, of which the purely Russian melodies at once catch the ear of the least musically educated Russian. This is also why the operas of Dargomýzhskiy and the younger composers are now successfully sung in the villages to peasant audiences and with local peasant choirs.

The folk-lore and the folk-song have thus rendered to Russia an immense service. They have maintained a certain unity of the spoken language all over Russia, as also a unity between the literary language and the language spoken by the masses ; between the music of Glínka, Tchaykóvskiy, Rímskiy Kórsakoff, Borodín, Musórgskiy, etc., and the music of the peasant choir— thus rendering both the poet and the composer accessible to the peasant.

THE ANNALS

And finally, whilst speaking of the early Russian literature, a few words, at least, must be said of the Annals.

No country has a richer collection of them. There were, in the tenth, eleventh, and twelfth centuries, several centres of development in Russia. Kíeff, Nóvgorod, Pskov, the land of Volhýnia, the land of Súzdal (Vladímir, Moscow),[1] Ryazán, etc., represented at that time independent republics, linked together only by the unity of language and religion, and by the fact that all of them elected their princes—military defenders and judges—from the house of Rúrik. Each of these centres had its own annals, bearing the stamp of local life and local character. The South Russian and

---

[1] The Russian name of the first capital of Russia is Moskvá. However, 'Moscow,' like 'Warsaw,' etc., is of so general a use that it would be affectation to use the Russian name.

Volhýnian annals—of which the so-called *Nestor's Annals* are the fullest and the best known, are not merely dry records of facts: they are imaginative and poetical in places. The annals of Nóvgorod bear the stamp of a city of rich merchants: they are very matter-of-fact, and the annalist warms to his subject only when he describes the victories of the Nóvgorod republic over the land of Súzdal. The annals of the sister-republic of Pskov, on the contrary, are imbued with a democratic spirit, and they relate with democratic sympathies and in a most picturesque manner the struggles between the poor of Pskov and the rich— the 'black people' and the 'white people.' Altogether, the annals are surely not the work of monks, as was supposed at the outset; they must have been written for the different cities by men fully informed about their political life, their treaties with other republics, their inner and outer conflicts.

Moreover, the annals, especially those of Kíeff,[1] or *Nestor's Annals*, are something more than mere records of events; they are, as may be seen from the very name of the latter (*From Whence and How came to be the Land of Russia*), attempts at writing a history of the country, under the inspiration of Greek models. Those manuscripts which have reached us—and especially is this true of the Kíeff annals—have thus a compound structure, and historians distinguish in them several superposed 'layers' dating from different periods. Old traditions; fragments of early historical knowledge, probably borrowed from the Byzantine historians; old treaties; complete poems relating certain episodes, such as Igor's raid; and local annals from different periods enter into their composition. Historical facts, relative to a very early period and fully confirmed by the Constantinople annalists and historians, are consequently mingled together with purely mythical traditions. But this is precisely what makes the high

[1] Pronounce Kíyeff.

literary value of the Russian annals, especially those of Southern and South-western Russia, which contain most precious fragments of early literature.

Such, then, were the treasuries of literature which Russia possessed at the beginning of the thirteenth century.

MEDIÆVAL LITERATURE

The Mongol invasion, which took place in 1223, destroyed all this young civilisation, and threw Russia into quite new channels.   The main cities of South and Middle Russia were laid waste.   Kíeff, which had been a populous city and a centre of learning, was reduced to the state of a straggling settlement, and disappeared from history for the next two centuries. Whole populations of large towns were either taken prisoners by the Mongols, or exterminated, if they had offered resistance to the invaders.   As if to add to the misfortunes of Russia, the Turks soon followed the Mongols, invading the Balkan peninsula, and by the end of the fifteenth century the two countries from which and through which learning used to come to Russia, namely Servia and Bulgaria, fell under the rule of the Osmanlis.   All the life of Russia underwent a deep transformation.

Before the invasion the land was covered with independent republics, similar to the mediæval city-republics of Western Europe.   Now, a centralised State, powerfully supported by the Church, began to be slowly built up at Moscow, which conquered, with the aid of the Mongol Khans, the independent principalities that surrounded it.   The main effort of the statesmen and the most active men of the Church was now directed towards the building up of a powerful kingdom which should be capable of throwing off the Mongol yoke.   State ideals were substituted for those of local autonomy and federation.   The Church, in its effort to constitute a Christian nationality, free

from all intellectual and moral contact with the
abhorred pagan Mongols, became a stern centralised
power which pitilessly persecuted everything that was
a reminder of a pagan past. It worked hard, at the
same time, to establish upon Byzantine ideals the
unlimited authority of the Moscow princes. Serfdom
was introduced in order to increase the military power
of the State. All independent local life was destroyed.
The idea of Moscow becoming a centre for Church and
State was powerfully supported by the Church, which
preached that Moscow was the heir to Constantinople
—'a third Rome,' where the only true Christianity was
now to develop. And at a later epoch, when the
Mongol yoke had been thrown off, the work of con-
solidating the Moscow monarchy was continued by
the Tsars and the Church, and the struggle was against
the intrusion of Western influences, in order to prevent
the 'Latin' Church from extending its authority over
Russia.

These new conditions necessarily exercised a deep
influence upon the further development of literature.
The freshness and vigorous youthfulness of the early
epic poetry was gone for ever. Sadness, melancholy,
resignation became the leading features of Russian
folk-lore. The continually repeated raids of the
Tartars, who carried away whole villages as prisoners
to their encampments in the South-eastern Steppes ;
the sufferings of the prisoners in slavery ; the visits of
the *baskáks*, who came to levy a high tribute and
behaved as conquerors in a conquered land ; the hardships inflicted upon the populations by the growing
military State—all this impressed the popular songs
with a deep note of sadness which they have never
since lost. At the same time the gay festival songs of
old and the epic songs of the wandering bards were
strictly forbidden, and those who dared to sing them
were cruelly persecuted by the Church, which saw
in these songs not only a reminiscence of a pagan

past, but also a possible link of union with the Tartars.

Learning was gradually concentrated in the monasteries, every one of which was a fortress built against the invaders; and it was limited, of course, to Christian literature. It became entirely scholastic. Knowledge of nature was 'unholy,' something of a witchcraft. Asceticism was preached as the highest virtue, and became the dominant feature of written literature. Legends about the saints were widely read and repeated verbally, and they found no balance in such learning as had been developed in Western Europe in the mediæval universities. The desire for a knowledge of nature was severely condemned by the Church, as a token of self-conceit. All poetry was a sin. The annals lost their animated character and became dry enumerations of the successes of the rising State, or merely related unimportant details concerning the local bishops and superiors of monasteries.

During the twelfth century there had been, in the northern republics of Nóvgorod and Pskov, a strong current of opinion leading, on the one side, to Protestant rationalism, and on the other side to the development of Christianity on the lines of the early Christian brotherhoods.[1] The apocryphal Gospels, the books of the Old Testament, and various books in which true Christianity was discussed, were eagerly copied and had a wide circulation. Now, the head of the Church in Central Russia violently antagonised all such tendencies towards reformed Christianity. A strict adherence to the very letter of the teachings of the Byzantine Church was exacted from the flock. Every kind of interpretation of the Gospels became heresy. All intellectual life in the domain of religion, as well as every criticism of the dignitaries of the Moscow Church, was treated as dangerous, and those

[1] See Kostomároff's *The Twelfth Century Rationalists*, in his *Works*.

B

who had ventured this way had to flee from Moscow, seeking refuge in the remote monasteries of the far North. As to the great movement of the Renaissance, which gave a new life to Western Europe, it did not reach Russia : the Church considered it a return to paganism, and cruelly exterminated its forerunners who came within her reach, burning them at the stake, or putting them to death on the racks of her torture-chambers.

I will not dwell upon this period, which covers nearly five centuries, because it offers very little interest for the student of Russian literature ; I will only mention the two or three works which must not be passed by in silence.

One of them is the letters exchanged between the Tsar John the Terrible (John IV.) and one of his chief vassals, Prince Kúrbskiy, who had left Moscow for Lithuania. From beyond the Lithuanian border he addressed to his cruel, half-lunatic ex-master long letters of reproach, which John answered, developing in his epistles the theory of the divine origin of the Tsar's authority. This correspondence is most characteristic of the political ideas that were current then, and of the learning of the period.

After the death of John the Terrible (who occupies in Russian history the same position as Louis XI. in French, since he destroyed by fire and sword—but with a truly Tartar cruelty—the power of the feudal princes), Russia passed, as is known, through years of great disturbance. The pretender Demetrius, who proclaimed himself a son of John, came from Poland and took possession of the throne at Moscow. The Poles invaded Russia, and were the masters of Moscow, Smolénsk, and all the western towns ; and when Demetrius was overthrown, a few months after his coronation, a general revolt of the peasants broke out, while all Central Russia was invaded by Cossack bands, and several new pretenders made their appearance.

These 'Disturbed Years' must have left traces in popular songs, but all such songs entirely disappeared in Russia during the dark period of serfdom which followed, and we know of them only through an Englishman, RICHARD JAMES, who was in Russia in 1619, and who wrote down some of the songs relating to this period.

The same must be said of the folk-literature, which must have come into existence during the later portion of the seventeenth century. The definite introduction of serfdom under the first Románoff (Mikhaíl, 1612-1640); the widespread revolts of the peasants which followed, culminating in the terrific uprising of Stepán Rázin, who has become since then a favourite hero with the oppressed peasants; and finally the stern and cruel persecution of the Nonconformists and their migrations eastward into the depths of the Uráls—all these events must have found their expression in folk-songs; but the State and the Church so cruelly hunted down everything that bore trace of a spirit of rebellion that no works of popular creation from that period have reached us. Only a few writings of a polemic character and the remarkable autobiography of an exiled priest have been preserved by the Nonconformists.

SPLIT IN THE CHURCH—MEMOIRS OF AVVAKÚM

The first Russian Bible was printed in Poland in 1580. A few years later a printing-office was established at Moscow, and the Russian Church authorities had now to decide which of the written texts then in circulation should be taken for the printing of the Holy Books. The handwritten copies which were in use at that time were full of errors, and it was evidently necessary to revise them by comparing them with the Greek texts, before committing any of them to print. This revision was undertaken at Moscow, with the aid of learned men brought over partly from Greece and partly from the Græco-Latin Academy of Kíeff; but for many different reasons this revision became the source of a widely spread discontent, and in the middle of the seventeenth century a formidable split (*raskól*) took place in the Church. It hardly need be said that this split was not a mere matter of theology, nor of Greek readings. The seventeenth century was a century when the Moscow Church had attained a formidable power in the State. The head of it, the Patriarch Níkon, was, moreover, a very ambitious man, who intended to play in the East the part which the Pope played in the West, and to that end he tried to impress the people by his grandeur and luxury—which meant, of course, heavy impositions upon the serfs of the Church and the lower clergy. He was hated by both, and was soon accused by the people of drifting into 'Latinism'; so that the split between the people and the clergy—especially the higher clergy—took the character of a widespread separation of the people from the Greek Church.

Most of the Nonconformist writings of the time are purely scholastic in character and consequently offer no literary interest. But the memoirs of a Nonconformist priest, AVVAKÚM (died 1681), who was exiled to Siberia and made his way on foot, with Cossack parties, as far as the banks of the Amúr, deserve to be mentioned. By their simplicity, their sincerity, and absence of all sensationalism, they have remained the prototype of Russian memoirs down to the present day. Here are a few quotations from this remarkable work :

'When I came to Yeniséisk,' Avvakúm wrote, 'another order came from Moscow to send me to Daúria, 2000 miles from Moscow, and to place me under the orders of Páshkoff. He had with him sixty men, and in punishment of my sins he proved to be a terrible man. Continually he burnt, and tortured, and flogged his men, and I had often spoken to him, remonstrating that what he did was not good, and now I fell myself into his hands. When we went along the Angará river he ordered me, "Get out of your boat, you are a heretic, that is why the boats don't get along. Go you on foot, across the mountains." It was hard to do. Mountains high, forests impenetrable, stony cliffs rising like walls—and we had to cross them, going about with wild beasts and birds; and I wrote him a little letter which began thus: "Man, be afraid of God. Even the heavenly forces and all animals and men are afraid of Him. Thou alone carest nought about Him." Much more was written in this letter, and I sent it to him. Presently I saw fifty men coming to me, and they took me before him. He had his sword in his hand and shook with fury. He asked me: "Art thou a priest, or a priest degraded?" I answered, "I am Avvakúm, a priest, what dost thou want from me?" And he began to beat me on the head and he threw me on the ground, and continued to beat me while I was lying on the ground, and then ordered them to give me seventy-two lashes with the knout, and I replied: "Jesus Christ, son of God, help me!" and he was only the more angered that I did not ask for mercy. Then they brought me to a small fort, and put me in a dungeon, giving me some straw, and all the winter I was kept in that tower, without fire. And the winter there is terribly cold; but God supported me, even though I had no furs. I lay there as a dog on the straw. One day they would feed me, another not. Rats were swarming all around. I used to kill them with my cap—the poor fools would not even give me a stick.'

Later on Avvakúm was taken to the Amúr, and when he and his wife had to march, in the winter, over the ice of the great river, she would often fall down from sheer exhaustion. 'Then I came,' Avvakúm writes, 'to lift her up, and she exclaimed in despair: "How long, priest, how long will these sufferings continue?" And I replied to her: "Until death even"; and then she would get up saying: "Well, then, priest; let us march on."' No sufferings could vanquish this great man. From the Amúr he was recalled to Moscow, and once more made the whole journey on foot. There he was accused of resistance to Church and State, and was burned at the stake in 1681.

THE EIGHTEENTH CENTURY

The violent reforms of Peter I., who created a military European state out of the semi-Byzantine and semi-Tartar state which Russia had been under his predecessors, gave a new turn to literature. It would be out of place to appreciate here the historical significance of the reforms of Peter I., but it must be mentioned that in Russian literature one finds, at least, two forerunners of Peter's work.

One of them was KOTOSHÍKHIN (1630-1667), a historian. He ran away from Moscow to Sweden, and wrote there, fifty years before Peter became Tsar, a history of Russia, in which he strenuously criticised the condition of ignorance prevailing at Moscow, and advocated wide reforms. His manuscript was unknown till the nineteenth century, when it was discovered at Upsala. Another writer, imbued with the same ideas, was a South Slavonian, KRYZHÁNITCH, who was called to Moscow in 1659, in order to revise the Holy Books, and wrote a most remarkable work, in which he also preached the necessity of thorough reforms. He was exiled two years later to Siberia, where he died.

Peter I., who fully realised the importance of literature, and was working hard to introduce European learning amongst his countrymen, understood that the Old Slavonian tongue, which was then in use among Russian writers, but was no longer the current language of the nation, could only hamper the development of literature and learning. Its forms, its expressions, and grammar were already quite strange to the Russians. It could be used still in religious writings, but a book on geometry, or algebra, or military art, written in the Biblical Old Slavonian, would have been simply ridiculous. Consequently, Peter removed the difficulty in his usual trenchant way. He established a new alphabet, to aid in the introduction into literature of the spoken but hitherto unwritten language. This alphabet, partly borrowed from the Old Slavonian, but very much simplified, is the one now in use.

Literature proper little interested Peter I.: he looked upon printed matter from the strictly utilitarian point of view, and his chief aim was to familiarise the Russians with the first elements of the exact sciences, as well as with the arts of navigation, warfare, and fortification. Accordingly, the writers of his time offer but little interest from the literary point of view, and I need mention but a very few of them.

The most interesting writer of the time of Peter I. and his immediate successors was perhaps PROCOPÓ-VITCH, a priest, without the slightest taint of religious fanaticism, a great admirer of West European learning, who founded a Græco-Slavonian academy. The courses of Russian literature also make mention of KANTEMÍR (1709-1744), the son of a Moldavian prince who had emigrated with his subjects to Russia. He wrote satires, in which he expressed himself with a freedom of thought that was quite remarkable for his time.[1] TRETIAKÓVSKIY (1703-1769) offers a certain melancholy interest. He was the son of a priest, and in his youth ran away from his father, in order to study at Moscow. Thence he went to Amsterdam and Paris, travelling mostly on foot. He studied at the Paris University and became an admirer of advanced ideas, about which he wrote in extremely clumsy verses. On his return to St. Petersburg he lived all his after-life in poverty and neglect, persecuted on all sides by sarcasms for his endeavours to reform Russian versification. He was himself entirely devoid of any poetical talent, and yet he rendered a great service to Russian poetry. Up to that date Russian verse was syllabic; but he understood that syllabic verse does not accord with the spirit of the Russian language, and he devoted his life to prove that Russian poetry should

---

[1] In the years 1730-1738 he was ambassador at London.

be written according to the laws of rhythmical versification. If he had had even a spark of talent, he would have found no difficulty in proving his thesis ; but he had none, and consequently resorted to the most ridiculous artifices. Some of his verses were lines of the most incongruous words strung together for the sole purpose of showing how rhythm and rhymes may be obtained. If he could not otherwise get his rhyme, he did not hesitate to split a word at the end of a verse, beginning the next one with what was left of it. In spite of his absurdities, he succeeded in persuading Russian poets to adopt rhythmical versification, and its rules have been followed ever since. In fact, this was only the natural development of the Russian popular song.

There was also a historian, TATÍSCHEFF (1686-1750), who wrote a history of Russia, and began a large work on the geography of the Empire—a hardworking man who studied a great deal in many sciences, as well as in Church matters, was superintendent of mines in the Uráls, and wrote a number of political works as well as history. He was the first to appreciate the value of the annals, which he collected and systematised, thus preparing materials for future historians, but he left no lasting trace in Russian literature. In fact, only one man of that period deserves more than a passing mention. It was LOMONÓSOFF (1712-1765). He was born in a village on the White Sea, near Archángel, in a fisherman's family. He also ran away from his parents, came on foot to Moscow, and entered a school in a monastery, living there in indescribable poverty. Later on he went to Kíeff, also on foot, and there he very nearly became a priest. It so happened, however, that at that time the St. Petersburg Academy of Sciences applied to the Moscow Theological Academy for twelve good students who might be sent to study abroad. Lomonósoff was chosen as one of them. He went to Germany, where he studied natural sciences under the best natural philosophers of the time, especially under Christian Wolff—always in terrible poverty, almost on the verge of starvation. In 1741 he came back to Russia, and was nominated a member of the Academy of Sciences at St. Petersburg.

The Academy was then in the hands of a few Germans who looked upon all Russian scholars with undisguised contempt, and consequently received Lomonósoff in a most unfriendly manner. It did not help him that the great mathematician, Euler, wrote that the work of Lomonósoff in natural philosophy and chemistry revealed a man of genius, and that any Academy might be happy to possess him. A bitter struggle soon began between the German members of the Academy and the Russian, who, it must be owned, was of a very violent character, especially when he was under the influence of drink. Poverty, his salary being confiscated as a punishment; detention at the police station; exclusion from the Senate of the Academy; and, worst of all, political persecution—such was the fate of Lomonósoff, who had joined the party of Elizabeth, and consequently was treated as an enemy when Catherine II. came to the throne. It was not until the nineteenth century that Lomonósoff was duly appreciated.

'Lomonósoff was himself a university,' was Púshkin's remark, and this remark was quite correct: so varied were the directions in which he worked. Not only was he a distinguished natural philosopher, chemist, physical geographer, and mineralogist: he laid also the foundations of the grammar of the Russian language, which he understood as part of a general grammar of all languages, considered in their natural evolution. He also worked out the different forms of Russian versification, and he created quite a new literary language, of which he could say that it was equally appropriate for rendering 'the powerful oratory of Cicero, the brilliant earnestness of Virgil, and the pleasant talk of Ovid, as well as the subtlest imaginary conceptions of philosophy, or discussing the various properties of matter and the changes which are always going on in the structure of the universe and in human affairs.' This he proved by his poetry, by his scientific writings, and by his 'Discourses,' in which he combined Huxley's readiness to defend science against blind faith with Humboldt's poetical conception of nature.

His odes were, it is true, written in the pompous style which was dear to the pseudo-classicism then reigning, and he retained Old Slavonian expressions 'for dealing with elevated subjects,' but in his scientific and other writings he used the commonly spoken language with great effect and force. Owing to the very variety of sciences which he had to acclimatise in Russia, he could not give much time to original research ; but when he took up the defence of the ideas of Copernicus, Newton, or Huyghens against the opposition which they met with on theological grounds, a true philosopher of natural science, in the modern sense of the term, was revealed in him. In his early boyhood he used to accompany his father—a sturdy northern fisherman—on his fishing expeditions, and there he got his love of nature and a fine comprehension of natural phenomena, which made of his 'Memoir on Arctic Exploration' a work that has not lost its value even now. It is well worthy of note that in this last work he had stated the mechanical theory of heat in such definite expressions that he undoubtedly anticipated by a full century this great discovery of our own time—a fact which has been entirely overlooked, even in Russia.

A contemporary of Lomonósoff, SUMARÓKOFF (1717-1777), who was described in those years as a 'Russian Racine,' must also be mentioned in this place. He belonged to the higher nobility, and had received an entirely French education. His dramas, of which he wrote a great number, were entirely imitated from the French pseudo-classical school ; but he contributed very much, as will be seen from a subsequent chapter, to the development of the Russian theatre. Sumarókoff wrote also lyrical verses, elegies, and satires—all of no great importance; but the remarkably good style of his letters, free of the Slavonic archaisms, which were habitual at that time, deserves to be mentioned.

THE TIMES OF CATHERINE II

With Catherine II., who reigned from 1752 till 1796, commenced a new era in Russian literature. It began to shake off its previous dullness, and although the Russian writers continued to imitate French models— chiefly pseudo-classical—they began also to introduce into their writings various subjects taken from direct observation of Russian life. There is, altogether, a frivolous youthfulness in the literature of the first years of Catherine's reign, when the Empress, being yet full of progressive ideas borrowed from her intercourse with French philosophers, composed—basing it on Montesquieu—her remarkable *Instruction* (*Nakáz*) to the deputies she convoked; wrote several comedies, in which she ridiculed the old-fashioned representatives of Russian nobility; and edited a monthly review, in which she entered into controversy both with some ultra-conservative writers and with the more advanced young reformers. An academy of belles-lettres was founded, and Princess VORONTSÓVA-DÁSHKOVA (1743-1819)—who had aided Catherine II. in her *coup d'état* against her husband, Peter III., and in taking possession of the throne—was nominated president of the Academy of Sciences. She assisted the Academy with real earnestness in compiling a dictionary of the Russian language, and she also edited a review which left a mark in Russian literature; while her memoirs, written in French (*Mon Histoire*), are a very valuable, though not always impartial, historical document.[1] Altogether

[1] In 1775-1782 she spent a few years at Edinburgh for the education of her son.

there began at that time quite a literary movement, which produced a remarkable poet, DERZHÁVIN (1743-1816); the writer of comedies, VON WÍZIN (1745-1792); the first philosopher, NÓVIKOFF (1742-1818); and a political writer, RADÍSCHEFF (1749-1802).

The poetry of Derzhávin certainly does not answer our modern requirements. He was the poet-laureate of Catherine, and sang in pompous odes the virtues of the ruler and the victories of her generals and favourites. Russia was then taking a firm hold on the shores of the Black Sea, and beginning to play a serious part in European affairs; so that occasions for the inflation of Derzhávin's patriotic feelings were not wanting. However, he had some of the marks of the true poet; he was open to the feeling of the poetry of nature, and capable of expressing it in verses that were positively good (*Ode to God, The Waterfall*). Nay, these really poetical verses, which are found side by side with un-natural, heavy lines stuffed with obsolete pompous words, are so evidently better than the latter, that they certainly were an admirable object-lesson for all subsequent Russian poets. They must have contributed to induce our poets to abandon mannerism. Púshkin, who in his youth admired Derzhávin, must have felt at once the disadvantages of a pompous style, illustrated by his predecessor, and with his wonderful command of his mother tongue he was necessarily brought to abandon the artificial language which formerly was considered 'poetical'— he began to write as we speak.

The comedies of VON WÍZIN (or FONVÍZIN) were quite a revelation for his contemporaries. His first comedy, *The Brigadier*, which he wrote at the age of twenty-two, created quite a sensation, and till now it has not lost its interest; while his second comedy, *Nédorosl* (1782), was received as an event in Russian literature, and is occasionally played even at the present day. Both deal with purely Russian subjects, taken from everyday life; and although Von Wízin too freely borrowed from foreign authors (the subject of *The Brigadier* is borrowed from a Danish comedy of Holberg, *Jean de France*), he managed nevertheless to make his chief personages truly Russian. In this sense he certainly was a creator of the Russian national drama, and he was also the first to introduce into our literature the realistic tendency which became so powerful with Púshkin, Gógol, and their followers. In his political opinions he remained true to the progressive opinions which Catherine II. patronised in the first years of her reign, and in his capacity of secretary to Count Pánin he boldly denounced serfdom, favouritism, and want of education in Russia.

I pass in silence several writers of the same epoch, namely, BOGDANÓVITCH (1743-1803), the author of a pretty and light poem, *Dushéñka*; HEMNITZER (1745-1784), a gifted writer of fables, who was a forerunner of Krylóff; KAPNÍST (1757-1829), who wrote rather superficial satires in good verse; Prince SCHERBÁTOFF (1733-1790), who began with several others the scientific collecting of old annals and folk-lore, and undertook to write a history of Russia, in which we find a scientific criticism of the annals and other sources of information; and several others. But I must say a few words upon the masonic movement which took place on the threshold of the nineteenth century.

THE FREEMASONS: FIRST MANIFESTATION OF POLITICAL THOUGHT

The looseness of habits which characterised Russian high society in the eighteenth century, the absence of ideals, the servility of the nobles, and the horrors of serfdom, necessarily produced a reaction amongst the better minds, and this reaction took the shape, partly of a widely spread masonic movement, and partly of Christian mysticism, which originated in the mystical teachings that had at that time widely spread in Germany. The freemasons and their Society of Friends undertook a serious effort for spreading moral education among the masses, and they found in NÓVIKOFF (1744-1818) a true apostle of renovation. He began his literary career very early, in one of those satirical reviews of which Catherine herself took the initiative at the beginning of her reign; and already in his amiable controversy with 'the grandmother' (Catherine) he showed that he would not remain satisfied with the superficial satire in which the empress delighted, but that, contrary to her wishes, he would go to the root of the evils of the time : namely, serfdom and its brutalising effects upon society at large. Nóvikoff was not only a well-educated man : he combined the deep moral convictions of an idealist with the capacities of an organiser and a business man; and although his review (from which the net income went entirely for philanthropic and educational purposes) was soon stopped by 'the grandmother,' he started in Moscow a most successful printing and book-selling business, for editing and spreading books of an ethical character. His immense printing-office, combined with a hospital for the workers and a chemist's shop, from which medicine was given free to all the poor of Moscow, was soon in business relations with booksellers all over Russia; while his influence upon educated society was growing rapidly, and working in an excellent direction. In 1787, during a famine, he organised relief for the starving peasants—quite a fortune having been put for this purpose at his disposal by one of his pupils. Of course, both the Church and the Government looked with suspicion upon the spreading of Christianity as it was understood by the freemason Friends; and although the metropolitan of Moscow testified that Nóvikoff was 'the best Christian he ever knew,' Nóvikoff was accused of political conspiracy.

He was arrested, and in accordance with the personal

wish of Catherine, though to the astonishment of all those who knew anything about him, was condemned to death in 1792. The death-sentence, however, was not fulfilled, but he was taken for fifteen years to the terrible fortress of Schlüsselburg, where he was put in the secret cell formerly occupied by the Grand Duke Ivan Antónovitch, and where his freemason friend, Doctor Bagryánskiy, volunteered to remain imprisoned with him. He remained there till the death of Catherine. Paul I. released him, in 1796, on the very day that he became emperor ; but Nóvikoff came out of the fortress a broken man, and fell entirely into mysticism, towards which there was already a marked tendency in several lodges of the freemasons.

The Christian mystics were not happier. One of them, LÁBZIN (1766-1825), who exercised a great influence upon society by his writings against corruption, was also denounced, and ended his days in exile. However, both the mystical Christians and the freemasons (some of whose lodges followed the Rosenkreuz teachings) exercised a deep influence on Russia. With the advent of Alexander I. to the throne the freemasons obtained more facilities for spreading their ideas ; and the growing conviction that serfdom must be abolished, and that the tribunals, as well as the whole system of administration, were in need of complete reform, was certainly to a great extent a result of their work. Besides, quite a number of remarkable men received their education at the Moscow Institute of the Friends— founded by Nóvikoff—including the historian Karamzín, the brothers Turguéneff, uncles of the great novelist, and several political men of mark.

RADÍSCHEFF (1749-1802), a political writer of the same epoch, had a still more tragic end. He received his education in the Corps of Pages, and was one of those young men whom the Russian Government had sent in 1766 to Germany to finish there their education. He followed the lectures of Hellert and Plattner at

Leipzig, and studied very earnestly the French philosophers. On his return he published, in 1790, a
Journey from St. Petersburg to Moscow, the idea of
which seems to have been suggested to him by Sterne's
Sentimental Journey. In this book he very ably intermingled his impressions of travel with various philosophical and moral discussions and with pictures from
Russian life.

He insisted especially upon the horrors of serfdom,
as also upon the bad organisation of the administration,
the venality of the law-courts, and so on, confirming his
general condemnations by concrete facts taken from
real life. Catherine, who already before the beginning
of the revolution in France, and especially since the
events of 1789, had come to regard with horror the
liberal ideas of her youth, ordered the book to be confiscated and destroyed at once. She described the
author as a revolutionist 'worse than Pugatchóff'; he
ventured to 'speak with approbation of Franklin' and
was infected with French ideas! Consequently, she
wrote herself a sharp criticism of the book, upon which
its prosecution had to be based. Radíscheff was
arrested, confined to the fortress, later on transported
to the remotest portions of Eastern Siberia, on the
Olenek. He was released only in 1801. Next year,
seeing that even the advent of Alexander I. did
not mean the coming of a new reformatory spirit, he
put an end to his life by suicide. As to his book, it
still remains forbidden in Russia. A new edition of it,
which was made in 1872, was confiscated and destroyed,
and in 1888 the permission was given to a publisher to
issue the work in editions of a hundred copies only,
which were to be distributed among a few men of
science and certain high functionaries.[1]

[1] Two free editions of it were made, one by Herzen at London:
Prince Scherbátoff and A. Radíscheff, 1858; and another at
Leipzig: *Journey*, in 1876. See A. Pypin's *History of Russian
Literature*, vol. iv.

THE FIRST YEARS OF THE NINETEENTH CENTURY

These were, then, the elements out of which Russian literature had to be evolved in the nineteenth century. The slow work of the last five hundred years had already prepared that admirable, pliable, and rich instrument—the literary language in which Púshkin would soon be enabled to write his melodious verses and Turguéneff his no less melodious prose. From the autobiography of the Nonconformist martyr, Avvakúm, one could already guess the value of the spoken language of the Russian people for literary purposes.

Tretiakóvskiy, by his clumsy verses, and especially Lomonósoff and Derzhávin by their odes, had definitely repelled the syllabic form that had been introduced from France and Poland, and had established the tonic, rhythmical form which was indicated by the popular song itself. Lomonósoff had created a popular scientific language; he had invented a number of new words, and had proved that the Latin and Old Slavonian constructions were hostile to the spirit of Russian, and quite unnecessary. The age of Catherine II. further introduced into written literature the forms of familiar everyday talk, borrowed even from the peasant class ; and Nóvikoff had created a Russian philosophical language—still heavy on account of its underlying mysticism, but splendidly adapted, as it appeared a few decades later, to abstract metaphysical discussions. The elements for a great and original literature were thus ready. They required only a vivifying spirit which should use them for higher purposes. This genius was Púshkin. But before speaking of him, the historian and novelist Karamzín and the poet Zhukóvskiy[1] must be mentioned, as they represent a link between the two epochs.

KARAMZÍN (1766-1826), by his monumental work, *The History of the Russian State*, did in literature what the great war of 1812 had done in national life. He

[1] Pronounce *Zh* as a French *j* (*Joukóvskiy* in French).

awakened the national consciousness and created a lasting interest in the history of the nation, in the making of the empire, in the evolution of national character and institutions. Karamzín's *History* was reactionary in spirit. He was the historian of the Russian State, not of the Russian people ; the poet of the virtues of monarchy and the wisdom of the rulers, but not an observer of the work that had been accomplished by the unknown masses of the nation. He was not the man to understand the federal principles which prevailed in Russia down to the fifteenth century, and still less the communal principles which pervaded Russian life and had permitted the nation to conquer and to colonise an immense continent. For him, the history of Russia was the regular, organic development of a monarchy, from the first appearance of the Scandinavian *varingiar* down to the present times, and he was chiefly concerned with describing the deeds of monarchs in their conquests and their building up of a state ; but, as it often happens with Russian writers, his foot-notes were a work of history in themselves. They contained a rich mine of information concerning the sources of Russia's history, and they suggested to the ordinary reader that the early centuries of mediæval Russia, with her independent city-republics, were far more interesting than they appeared in the book.[1] Karamzín was not the founder of a school, but he showed to Russia that she had a past worth knowing. Besides, his work was a work of art. It was written in a brilliant style, which accustomed the public to read historical works. The result was, that the first edition of his eight-volume *History*—3000 copies—was sold in twenty-five days.

---

[1] It is now known how much of the preparatory work which rendered Karamzín's *History* possible was done by the Academicians Schlötzer, Müller, and Stritter, as well as by the above-mentioned historian Scherbátoff, who had thoroughly studied the annals and whose views Karamzín closely followed in his work.

However, Karamzín's influence was not limited to his *History*: it was even greater through his novels and his *Letters of a Russian Traveller Abroad*. In the latter he made an attempt to bring the products of European thought, philosophy, and political life into circulation amidst a wide public; to spread broadly humanitarian views, at a time when they were most needed as a counterpoise to the sad realities of political and social life; and to establish a link of connection between the intellectual life of our country and that of Europe. As to Karamzín's novels, he appeared in them as a true follower of sentimental romanticism; but this was precisely what was required then, as a reaction against the would-be classical school. In one of his novels, *Poor Liza* (1792), he described the misfortunes of a peasant girl who fell in love with a nobleman, was abandoned by him, and finally drowned herself in a pond. This peasant girl surely would not answer to our present realistic requirements. She spoke in choice language and was not a peasant girl at all; but all reading Russia cried about the misfortune of ' poor Liza,' and the pond where the heroine was supposed to have been drowned became a place of pilgrimage for the sentimental youths of Moscow. The spirited protest against serfdom which we shall find later on in modern literature was thus already born in Karamzín's time.

ZHUKÓVSKIY (1783-1852) was a romantic poet in the true sense of the word, and a true worshipper of poetry, who fully understood its elevating power. His original productions were few. He was mainly a translator and rendered in excellent Russian verses the poems of Schiller, Uhland, Herder, Byron, Thomas Moore, and others, as well as the Odyssey, the Hindu poem of Nala and Damayanti, and the songs of the Western Slavonians. The beauty of these translations is such that I doubt whether there are in any other language, even in German, equally good renderings of foreign poets. However, Zhukóvskiy was not a mere translator : he took from other poets only what was agreeable to his own nature and what he would have liked to sing himself. Sad reflections about the unknown, aspirations towards distant lands, the sufferings of love, and the sadness of separation— all lived through by the poet—were the distinctive features of his poetry. They reflected his inner self. We may object now to his ultra-romanticism, but this direction, at that time, was an appeal to the broadly humanitarian feelings, and it was of first necessity for progress. By his poetry Zhukóvskiy appealed chiefly to women, and when we deal later on with the part that Russian women played half a century later in the general development of their country, we shall see that his appeal was not made in vain. Altogether, Zhukóvskiy appealed to the best sides of human nature. One note, however, was missing entirely in his poetry : it was the appeal to the sentiments of freedom and citizenship. This appeal came from the 'Decembrist' poet, Ryléeff.

THE DECEMBRISTS

The Tsar Alexander I. went through the same evolution as his grandmother, Catherine II. He was educated by the republican, La Harpe, and began his reign as a quite liberal sovereign, ready to grant to Russia a constitution. He did it in fact for Poland and Finland, and made a first step towards it in Russia. But he did not dare to touch serfdom, and gradually he fell under the influence of German mystics, became alarmed at liberal ideas, and surrendered his will to the worst reactionaries. The man who ruled Russia during the last ten or twelve years of his reign was General Arakchéeff, a maniac of cruelty and militarism, who maintained his influence by means of the crudest flattery and simulated religiousness.

A reaction against these conditions was sure to grow up, the more so as the Napoleonic wars had brought a great number of Russians in contact with Western Europe. The campaigns made in Germany, and the occupation of Paris by the Russian armies, had familiarised many officers with the ideas of liberty which reigned still in the French capital, while at home the endeavours of Nóvikoff were bearing fruit, and the freemason Friends continued his work. When Alexander I., having fallen under the influence of Madame Krüdener and other German mystics, concluded in 1815 the Holy Alliance with Germany and Austria, in order to combat all liberal ideas, secret societies began to be formed in Russia—chiefly among the officers—in order to promote the ideas of liberty, abolition of serfdom, and equality before the law, as the necessary steps towards the abolition of absolute rule. Every one who has read Tolstóy's *War and Peace* must remember ' Pierre ' and the impression produced upon this young man by his first meeting with an old freemason. ' Pierre ' is a true representative of many young men who later on became known as ' Decembrists.' Like ' Pierre,' they were imbued with humanitarian ideas ; many of them hated serfdom, and they wanted the introduction of constitutional guarantees ; while a few of them (Péstel, Ryléeff), despairing of monarchy, spoke of a return to the republican federalism of old Russia. With such ends in view they created their secret societies.

It is known how this conspiracy ended. After the sudden, mysterious death of Alexander I. in the south of Russia, the oath of allegiance was given at St. Petersburg to his brother Constantine, who was proclaimed his successor. But when, a few days later, it became known in the capital that Constantine had abdicated, and that his brother Nicholas was going to become emperor, and when the conspirators learned that they had been denounced in the meantime to the State

police, they saw nothing else to do but to proclaim
their programme openly in the streets and to fall in an
unequal fight.   They did so, on December 14 (26),
1825, in the Senate Square of St. Petersburg, followed
by a few hundred men from several regiments of the
Guard.   Five of the insurgents were hanged by
Nicholas I., and the remainder, about a hundred
young men who represented the flower of Russian
intelligence, were sent to hard labour in Siberia, where
they remained till 1856.   One can hardly imagine
what it meant, in a country which was not over-rich in
educated and well-intentioned men, when such a number
of the best representatives of a generation were taken
out of the ranks and reduced to silence.   Even in a
more civilised country of Western Europe the sudden
disappearance of so many men of thought and action
would have dealt a severe blow to progress.   In Russia
the effect was disastrous, the more so as the reign of
Nicholas I. lasted thirty years, during which every spark
of free thought was stifled as soon as it appeared.

One of the most brilliant literary representatives of
the 'Decembrists' was RYLÉEFF (1795-1826), one of
the five who were hanged by Nicholas I.   He had
received a good education, and in 1814 was already an
officer.   He was thus by a few years the elder of
Púshkin.   He twice visited France, in 1814 and 1815,
and after the conclusion of peace became a magistrate
at St. Petersburg.   His earlier productions were a series
of ballads dealing with the leading men of Russian
history.   Most of them were merely patriotic, but some
already revealed the sympathies of the poet for freedom.
Censorship did not allow these ballads to be printed,
but they circulated all over Russia in manuscript.   Their
poetical value was not great; but the next poem of
Ryléeff, *Voinaróvsky*, and especially some fragments of
unfinished poems, revealed in him a powerful poetical
gift, which Ryléeff's great friend, Púshkin, greeted with
effusion.   It is greatly to be regretted that the poem

Voinaróvsky has never been translated into English. Its subject is the struggle of Little Russia for the recovery of its independence under Peter I. When the Russian Tsar was engaged in a bitter struggle against the great northern warrior, Charles XII., the ruler of Little Russia, the *hétman* Mazépa, conceived the plan of joining Charles XII. against Peter I. for freeing his mother country from the Russian yoke. Charles XII., as is known, was defeated at Poltáva, and both he and the *hétman* had to flee to Turkey. As to Voinaróvsky, a young patriot friend of Mazépa, he was taken prisoner and transported to Siberia. There, at Yakútsk, he was visited by the historian Müller, and Ryléeff makes him tell his story to the German explorer. The scenes of nature in Siberia, at Yakútsk, with which the poem begins ; the preparations for the war in Little Russia and the war itself; the flight of Charles XII. and Mazépa ; then the sufferings of Voinaróvsky, when his young wife came to rejoin him in the land of exile, and died there—all these scenes are most beautiful, while in places the verses, by their simplicity and the beauty of their images, evoked the admiration even of Púshkin. Two or three generations have now read this poem, and it continues to inspire each new one with the same love of liberty and hatred of oppression.

CHAPTER II

PÚSHKIN AND LÉRMONTOFF

PÚSHKIN : Beauty of form—Púshkin and Schiller—His youth ;
his exile ; his later career and death—Fairy tales : *Ruslán
and Ludmíla*—His lyrics—'Byronism'—Drama—*Evghéniy
Onyéghin*—LÉRMONTOFF : Púshkin or Lérmontoff?—His
life—The Caucasus—Poetry of Nature—Influence of Shelley
—*The Demon*—*Mtsýri*—Love of freedom—His death—
Púshkin and Lérmontoff as prose-writers—Other poets and
novelists of the same epoch.

PÚSHKIN

PÚSHKIN is not quite a stranger to English readers.
In a valuable collection of review articles dealing with
Russian writers which Professor Coolidge, of Cambridge,
Massachusetts, put at my disposal, I found that in
1832, and later on in 1845, Púshkin was spoken of as
a writer more or less familiar in England, and translations of some of his lyrics were given in the reviews.
Later on Púshkin was rather neglected in Russia itself,
and the more so abroad, and up to the present time
there is no English translation, worthy of the great
poet, of any of his works.   In France, on the contrary
—owing to Turguéneff and Prosper Mérimée, who saw
in Púshkin one of the great poets of mankind—as well
as in Germany, all the chief works of the Russian poet
are known to literary men in good translations, of which
some are admirable.   To the great reading public the
Russian poet is, however, nowhere well known outside
his own mother country.

The reason why Púshkin has not become a favourite
with West European readers is easily understood.   His
lyric verse is certainly inimitable : it is that of a great

poet. His chief novel in verse, *Evghéniy Onyéghin*, is written with an easiness and a lightness of style, and a picturesqueness of detail, which makes it stand unique in European literature. His renderings in verses of Russian popular tales are delightful reading. But, apart from his very latest productions in the dramatic style, there is in whatever Púshkin wrote none of the depth and elevation of ideas which characterised Goethe and Schiller, Shelley, Byron and Browning, Victor Hugo and Barbier. The beauty of form, the happy ways of expression, the incomparable command of verse and rhyme are his main points—not the beauty of his *ideas*. And what we look for in poetry is always the higher inspiration, the noble ideas which can help to make us better. In reading Púshkin's verses the Russian reader is continually brought to exclaim: 'How beautifully this has been told! It could not, it ought not, to be told in a different way.' In this beauty of form Púshkin is inferior to none of the greatest poets. In his ways of expressing even the most insignificant remarks, and describing the most insignificant details of everyday life; in the variety of human feeling that he has expressed, and the delicate expression of love under a variety of aspects which is contained in his poetry; and finally, in the way he deeply impressed his own personality upon everything he wrote—he is certainly a great poet.

It is extremely interesting to compare Púshkin with Schiller, in their lyrics. Leaving aside the greatness and the variety of subjects touched upon by Schiller, and comparing only those pieces of poetry in which both poets speak of themselves, one feels at once that Schiller's personality is infinitely superior, in depth of thought and philosophical comprehension of life, to that of the bright, somewhat spoiled and rather superficial child that Púshkin was. But, at the same time, the individuality of Púshkin is more deeply impressed upon his writings than that of Schiller upon his.

Púshkin was full of vital intensity, and his own self is reflected in everything he wrote; a human heart, full of fire, is throbbing intensely in all his verses. This heart is far less sympathetic than that of Schiller, but it is more intimately revealed to the reader. In his best lyrics Schiller did not find either a better expression of feeling, or a greater variety of expression, than Púshkin did. In that respect the Russian poet decidedly stands by the side of Goethe.

Púshkin was born in an aristocratic family at Moscow. Through his mother he had African blood in his veins: she was a beautiful creole, the granddaughter of a negro who had been in the service of Peter I. His father was a typical representative of the noblemen of those times: squandering a large fortune, living all his life anyhow and anyway, amidst feasts, in a house half-furnished and half-empty; fond of the lighter French literature of the time, fond of entering into a discussion upon anything that he had just learned from the encyclopædists, and bringing together at his house all possible notabilities of literature, Russian and French, who happened to be at Moscow.

Púshkin's grandmother and his old nurse were the future poet's best friends in his childhood. From them he got his perfect mastership of the Russian language; and from his nurse, with whom he used to spend, later on, the long winter nights at his country house, when he was ordered by the State police to reside on his country estate, he borrowed that admirable knowledge of Russian folk-lore and Russian ways of expression which rendered his poetry and prose so wonderfully Russian. To these two women we thus owe some gratitude for the easy, pliable Russian language which Púshkin introduced into our literature.

He was educated at St. Petersburg, at the Tsárskoye Seló Lyceum, and even before he left school he became renowned as a most extraordinary poet, in whom Derzhávin recognised more than a mere successor, and whom Zhukóvskiy presented with his portrait bearing the following inscription : ' To a pupil, from his defeated teacher.' Unfortunately, Púshkin's passionate nature drew him away from both the literary circles and the circles of his best friends—the Decembrists Púschin and Küchelbecker—into the circles of the lazy, insignificant aristocrats, amongst whom he spent his vital energy. Something of the shallow, empty sort of life he lived then he has himself described in *Evghéniy Onyéghin*.

Being friendly with the political youth who appeared six or seven years later on the square of Peter I. at St. Petersburg, as insurgents against autocracy and serfdom, Púshkin wrote an *Ode to Liberty*, and numbers of small pieces of poetry expressing the most revolutionary ideas, as well as satires against the rulers of the time. The result was that in 1820, when he was only twenty years old, he was exiled to Kishinyóff, a very small town at that time, in newly annexed Bessarabia, where he led the most extravagant life, eventually joining a party of wandering gypsies. Happily enough he was permitted to leave for some time this dusty and uninteresting little spot, and to make, in company with the charming and educated family of the Rayévskys, a journey to the Crimea and the Caucasus, from which journey he brought back some of his finest lyrical works.

In 1824, when he had rendered himself quite impossible at Odessa (perhaps also from fear that he might escape to Greece, to join Byron), he was ordered to return to Central Russia and to reside at his small estate, Mikháilovskoye, in the province of Pskov, where he wrote his best things. On December 14, 1825, when the insurrection broke out at St. Petersburg, Púshkin was at Mikháilovskoye ; otherwise, like so many of his Decembrist friends, he would most certainly have ended his life in Siberia. He succeeded in burning all his papers before they could be seized by the secret police.

Shortly after that he was allowed to return to St. Petersburg, Nicholas I. undertaking to be himself the censor of his verses, and later on making Púshkin a chamberlain of his Court. Poor Púshkin had thus to live the futile life of a small functionary of the Winter Palace, and this life he certainly hated. The Court nobility and bureaucracy could never pardon him that he, who did not belong to their circle, was considered such a great man in Russia, and Púshkin's life was full of little stings to his self-respect, coming from these classes. He had also the misfortune to marry a lady who was very beautiful but did not in the least appreciate his genius. In 1837 he had to fight on her account a duel, in which he was killed, at the age of thirty-seven.

One of his earliest productions, written almost immediately after he left school, was *Ruslán and Ludmíla*, a fairy tale, which he put into beautiful verse. The dominating element of this poem is that wonderland where 'a green oak stands on the sea-beach, and a learned cat goes round the oak—to which it is attached by a golden chain—singing songs when it goes to the left, and telling tales when it goes to the right.' It is the wedding day of Ludmíla, the heroine; the long bridal feast comes at last to an end, and she retires with her husband; when all of a sudden comes darkness, thunder resounds, and in the storm Ludmíla disappears. She has been carried away by the terrible sorcerer from the Black Sea—a folk-lore allusion, of course, to the frequent raids of the nomads of Southern Russia. Now, the unhappy husband, as also three other young men, who were formerly suitors of Ludmíla, saddle their horses and go in search of the vanished bride. From their experiences the tale is made up, and it is full of both touching passages and humorous episodes. After many adventures Ruslán recovers his Ludmíla, and everything ends to the general satisfaction, as folk-tales always do.[1]

[1] The great composer Glínka has made of this fairy tale a most beautiful opera (*Ruslán i Ludmíla*), in which Russian, Finnish, Turkish, and Oriental music are intermingled in order to characterise the different heroes.

This was a most youthful production of Púshkin, but its effect in Russia was tremendous. Classicism, *i.e.* the pseudo-classicism which reigned then, was defeated for ever. Every one wanted to have the poem, every one retained in memory whole passages and even pages from it, and with this tale the modern Russian literature—simple, realistic in its descriptions, modest in its images and fable, earnest and slightly humoristic—was created. In fact, one could not imagine a greater simplicity in verse than that which Púshkin had already obtained in this poem. But to give an idea of this simplicity to English readers remains absolutely impossible so long as the poem is not translated by some very gifted English poet. Suffice it to say that, while its verses are wonderfully musical, it contains not one single passage in which the author has resorted to unusual or obsolete words—to any words, indeed, but those which every one uses in common conversation.

Thunders came upon Púshkin from the classical camp when this poem made its appearance. We have only to think of the Daphnes and the Chloes with which poetry used to be embellished at that time, and the sacerdotal attitude which the poet took towards his readers, to understand how the classical school was offended at the appearance of a poet who expressed his thoughts in beautiful images without resorting to any of these embellishments, who spoke the language which every one speaks, and related adventures fit for the nursery. With one cut of his sword Púshkin had freed literature from the ties which were keeping it enslaved.

The tales which he had heard from his old nurse gave him the matter, not only for *Ruslán and Ludmíla*, but also for a series of popular tales, of which the verses are so natural that as soon as you have pronounced one word that word calls up immediately the next, and this the following, because you cannot say the thing otherwise than in the way in which Púshkin has told it. ' Is it not exactly so that tales should be told ? ' was asked all over Russia ; and, the reply being in the affirmative, the fight against pseudo-classicism was won for ever.

This simplicity of expression characterised Púshkin in everything he afterwards wrote. He did not depart from it, even when he dealt with so-called elevated subjects, nor in the passionate or philosophical monologues of his latest dramas. It is what makes Púshkin so difficult to translate into English ; because, in the English literature of the nineteenth century, Wordsworth is the only poet who has written with the same simplicity. But, while Wordsworth applied this simplicity mainly to the description of the lovely and quiet English landscape, Púshkin spoke with the same simplicity of human life, and his verses continued to flow, as easy as prose, and as free from artificial expressions, even when he described the most violent human passions. In his contempt of everything exaggerated and theatrical, and in his determination to have nothing to do with ' the lurid tragic actor who wields a cardboard sword,' he was thoroughly Russian ; and he contributed towards establishing among his followers that taste for simplicity and honest expression of feeling of which so many examples will be given in the course of this book.[1]

Púshkin was at his best in his lyric poetry, and the chief note of his lyrics was love. The tragical contradictions between the ideals and real life, from which the deeper minds—Goethe, Byron, or Heine—had suffered, were strange to him. Púshkin was of a more superficial nature. It must also be said that a West European poet has an inheritance which the Russian has not. Every country of Western Europe has passed through periods of great national struggle, during which the great questions of human development were at stake. Great political conflicts have produced deep passions and resulted in tragical situations ; but in Russia the

---

[1] In Appendix A, as an example of this simplicity, I give a nearly verbal translation of one of Púshkin's best lyrical pieces.

great struggles and the religious movements which took place in the seventeenth century, and under Pugatchóff in the eighteenth, were uprisings of peasants, in which the educated classes took no part. The intellectual horizon of a Russian poet is thus necessarily limited. There is, however, something in human nature which always lives and appeals to every mind. This is love, and Púshkin, in his lyric poetry, represented love under so many aspects, in such beautiful forms, and with such a variety of shades, as one finds in no other poet. Besides, he often gave to love an expression so refined, so high, that his higher comprehension of love left as deep a stamp upon subsequent Russian literature as Goethe's refined types of women left in the world's literature. After Púshkin had written, it was impossible for Russian poets to speak of love in a lower sense than he did.

In Russia Púshkin has sometimes been described as a Russian Byron. This appreciation, however, is hardly correct. He certainly imitated Byron in some of his poems, although the imitation became, at least in *Evghéniy Onyéghin*, a brilliant original creation. He certainly was deeply impressed by Byron's spirited protest against the conventional life of European society, and there was a time when, if he only could have left Russia, he probably would have joined Byron in Greece.

But, with his light character, Púshkin could not fathom, and still less share, the depth of hatred and contempt towards post-revolutionary Europe which consumed Byron's heart. Púshkin's 'Byronism' was superficial; and, while he was ready to defy 'respectable' society, he knew neither the longings for freedom nor the hatred of hypocrisy which inspired Byron.

Altogether, Púshkin's force was not in his elevating or freedom-inspiring influence. His epicureanism, the education he received in his father's house, and his life amidst the frivolous classes of St. Petersburg society, prevented him from taking to heart the great problems which were already ripening in Russian life. This is why, towards the end of his short life, he was no longer in touch with those of his readers who felt that to glorify the military power of Russia, after the armies of Nicholas I. had crushed Poland, was not worthy of a poet ; and that to describe the attractions of a St. Petersburg winter-season for a rich and idle gentleman was not to describe Russian life, in which the horrors of serfdom and absolutism were being felt more and more heavily.

Púshkin's real force was in his having created in a few years a new literary language, freed from the theatrical, pompous style which was formerly considered necessary in whatever was printed in black and white. He was great in his stupendous powers of poetical creation, in his capacity of taking the commonest things of everyday life, or the commonest feelings of the most ordinary person, and of so relating them that the reader lived them through ; and, on the other side, constructing out of the scantiest materials, and calling to life, a whole historical epoch—a power of creation which, of those coming after him, only Tolstóy had to the same extent. Púshkin's power was next in his profound realism—that realism, understood in its best sense, which he was the first to introduce in Russia, and which, we shall see, became afterwards character-istic of the whole of Russian literature. And it is in the broadly humanitarian feelings with which his best writings are permeated, in his bright love of life, and his respect for women. As to beauty of form, his verses are so 'easy' that one knows them by heart after having read them twice or thrice. Now that they have penetrated into the villages, they are the delight of millions of peasant children, after having been the delight of such refined and philosophical poets as Turguéneff.

Púshkin also tried his hand at the drama ; and, so far as may be judged from his latest productions, *Don Juan* and *The Miser-Knight*, he surely would have

achieved great results had he lived to continue them.
His *Mermaid* (*Rusálka*) unfortunately remained unfinished, but its dramatic qualities can be judged from
what Dargomýzhskiy has made of it in his opera. His
historical drama, *Boris Godunóff*, taken from the times
of the pretender Demetrius, is enlivened here and there
by most beautiful scenes, some of them very amusing,
and some of them containing a delicate analysis of the
sentiments of love and ambition ; but it remains rather
a dramatic chronicle than a drama. As to *The Miser-
Knight*, it shows an extraordinary power of mature
talent, and contains passages undoubtedly worthy of
Shakespeare ; while his short drama, *Don Juan*, imbued
with a true Spanish atmosphere, gives a far better
comprehension of the Don Juan type than any other
representation of it in any literature, and has all the
qualities of a first-rate drama.

Towards the end of his very short life a note of
deeper comprehension of human affairs began to appear
in Púshkin's writings. He had had enough of the life
of the higher classes ; and, when he began to write a
history of the great peasant uprising which took place
under Pugatchóff during the reign of Catherine II., he
began also to understand and to feel the inner springs
of the life of the Russian peasant class. National life
appeared to him under a much broader aspect than
before. But at this stage of the development of his
genius his career came to a premature end. He was
killed, as already stated, in a duel with a society man.

The most popular work of Púshkin is his novel in
verse, *Evghéniy Onyéghin*. In its form it has much in
common with Byron's *Childe Harold*, but it is thoroughly
Russian, and contains perhaps the best description of
Russian life, both in the capitals and on the smaller
estates of noblemen in the country, that has ever been
written in Russian literature. Tchaykóvskiy, the
musician, has made of it an opera which enjoys
success on the Russian stage. The hero of the novel,

Onyéghin, is a typical representative of what society people were at that time. He has received a superficial education, partly from a French tutor, partly from a German teacher, and has learned 'something and anyhow.' At the age of nineteen he is the owner of a great fortune—consisting, of course, of serfs, about whom he does not care in the least—and he is engulfed in the 'high-life' of St. Petersburg. His day begins very late, with reading scores of invitations to tea-parties, evening-parties, and fancy balls. He is, of course, a visitor at the theatre, in which he prefers ballet to the clumsy productions of the Russian dramatists; and he spends a good deal of his day in fashionable restaurants, while his nights are given to balls, where he plays the part of a disillusioned young man, who is tired of life, and wraps himself in the mantle of Byronism. For some reason or other he is compelled to spend a summer on his estate, where he has for a neighbour a young poet, educated in Germany and full of German romanticism. They become great friends, and they make acquaintance with a squire's family in their neighbourhood. The head of the family—the old mother—is admirably described. Her two daughters, Tatiána and Olga, are very different in nature: Olga is a quite artless girl, full of the joy of living, who worries herself with no questions, and the young poet is madly in love with her; they are going to marry. As to Tatiána, she is a poetical girl, and Púshkin bestows on her all the wonderful powers of his talent, describing her as an ideal woman: intelligent, thoughtful, and inspired with vague aspirations towards something better than the prosaic life which she is compelled to live. Onyéghin produces upon her, from the first, a deep impression: she falls in love with him; but he, who has made so many conquests in the high circles of the capital, and now wears the mask of disgust of life, takes no notice of the naïve love of the poor country girl. She writes to him and tells him her love with

great frankness and in most pathetic words ; but the
young snob finds nothing better to do than to lecture
her about her rashness, and seems to take great pleasure
in turning the knife in her wound. At the same time,
at a small country ball Onyéghin, moved by some
spirit of mischief, begins to flirt in the most provoking
way with the other sister, Olga. The young girl seems
to be delighted with the attention paid to her by the
gloomy hero, and the result is that the poet provokes
his friend to a duel. An old retired officer, a true
duellist, is mixed up in the affair, and Onyéghin, who
cares very much about what the country gentlemen,
whom he pretends to despise, may say about him,
accepts the provocation and fights the duel. He kills
his poet friend and is compelled to leave the country.
Several years pass. Tatiána, recovered from an illness,
goes one day to the house where formerly Onyéghin
stayed and, making friends with an old keeper, spends
days and months reading in his library ; but life has
no attraction for her. After insistent supplication from
her mother she goes to Moscow, and there she marries
an old general. This marriage brings her to St.
Petersburg, where she plays a prominent part in the
Court circles. In these surroundings Onyéghin meets
her once more, and hardly recognises his Tánya in the
worldly lady whom he sees now ; he falls madly in love
with her. She takes no notice of him, and his letters
remain unanswered. At last one day he goes, at an
unseemly hour, into her house. He finds her reading
his letters, her eyes full of tears, and makes her a
passionate declaration of his love. To this Tatiána
replies by a monologue which is so beautiful that it
ought to be quoted here, if there existed an English
translation which rendered at least the touching simplicity of Tatiána's words, and consequently the beauty
of the verses. A whole generation of Russian women
have cried over this monologue, as they were reading
these lines :

'Onyéghin, I was younger then, and better looking,
I suppose; and I loved you'... but the love of a
country girl offered nothing new to Onyéghin. He
paid no attention to her.... Why then does he
follow her now at every step? Why such display of
his attention? Is it because she is now rich and
belongs to the high society, and is well received at Court?

> 'And that my fall, in these conditions,
> Would be commented ev'rywhere,
> And would in high society bring
> To you an envied reputation?'

And she continues:

> 'For me, Onyéghin, all that wealth,
> That showy tinsel of Court life,
> All my successes in the world,
> My well-appointed house and balls, ...
> For me, are nought!—I gladly would
> Give up these rags, this masquerade,
> And all this brilliancy and din,
> For a few books, a garden wild,
> Our weather-beaten house, so poor—
> Those very places where I met
> With you, Onyéghin, that first time;
> And for the churchyard of our village,
> Where now a cross and shady trees
> Stand on the grave of my poor nurse.
>
> .   .   .   .
> And happiness was possible then!
> It was so near!'...

She supplicates Onyéghin to leave her. 'I love you,'
she says:

> 'Why should I hide the truth from you?
> But I am given to another,
> And true to him I shall remain.'[1]

How many thousands of young Russian women have
later on repeated these same verses, and said to them-

---

[1] See Appendix A. For all translations, not otherwise mentioned,
it is myself who is responsible.

selves : 'I would gladly give up all these rags and all
this masquerade of luxurious life for a small shelf of
books, for life in the country, amidst the peasants, and
for the grave of my old nurse in our village'? How
many have done it? And we shall see how this same
type of Russian girl was developed still further in the
novels of Turguéneff—and in Russian life. Was not
Púshkin a great poet to have foreseen and predicted it?

LÉRMONTOFF

It is said that when Turguéneff and his great friend,
Kavélin, came together—Kavélin was a very sympathetic philosopher and a writer upon law—a favourite
theme of their discussions was : 'Púshkin or
Lérmontoff?' Turguéneff, as is known, considered
Púshkin one of the greatest poets, and especially one
of the greatest artists, among men ; while Kavélin
must have insisted upon the fact that in his best
productions Lérmontoff was but slightly inferior to
Púshkin as an artist, that his verses were real music,
while at the same time the inspiration of his poetry
was of a much higher standard than that of Púshkin.
When it is added that eight years was the entire limit
of Lérmontoff's literary career—he was killed in a duel
at the age of twenty-six—the powers and the potentialities of this poet will be seen at once.

Lérmontoff had Scottish blood in his veins. At least,
the founder of the family was a Scotsman, George
Learmonth, who, with sixty Scotsmen and Irishmen,
entered the service of Poland first, and afterwards, in
1613, of Russia. The inner biography of the poet
remains still but imperfectly known. It is certain that
his childhood and boyhood were anything but happy.
His mother was a lover of poetry—perhaps a poet
herself ; but he lost her when he was only three years
old—she was only twenty-one. His aristocratic grandmother on the maternal side took him from his father—

a poor army officer, whom the child worshipped—and educated him, preventing all intercourse between the father and the son. The boy was very gifted, and at the age of fourteen had already begun to write verses and poems—first in French (like Púshkin) and soon in Russian. Schiller and Shakespeare and, from the age of sixteen, Byron and Shelley were his favourites. At the age of sixteen Lérmontoff entered the Moscow University, from which he was, however, excluded next year for some offence against a very uninteresting professor. He then entered a military school at St. Petersburg, to become at the age of eighteen an officer of the hussars.

A young man of twenty-two, Lérmontoff suddenly became widely known for a piece of poetry which he wrote on the occasion of Púshkin's death (1837). A great poet, as well as a lover of liberty and a foe of oppression, was revealed at once in this passionate production of the young writer, of which the concluding verses were especially powerful. He wrote:

> And you, a haughty crowd around the throne,
> Of liberty, of genius the hangmen,
> You know, the Courts where Justice's lips are sealed
> Will shield you from the heavy sword of Law.
> But mind—there is a higher Tribunal,
> A higher Judge, not to be bought with gold,
> And before Him you will not wash away
> With all your blood the pure blood of the Poet!

In a few days all St. Petersburg, and very soon all educated Russia, knew these verses by heart; they circulated in thousands of manuscript copies.

For this passionate cry of his heart Lérmontoff was exiled at once. Only the intervention of his powerful friends prevented him from being marched straight to Siberia. He was transferred from the regiment of Guards to which he belonged to an army regiment in the Caucasus. Lérmontoff was already acquainted with the Caucasus: he had been taken there as a child of ten, and he had brought back from this sojourn an ineffaceable impression. Now the grandeur of the great mountain range impressed him still more forcibly. The Caucasus is one of the most beautiful regions on earth. It is a chain of mountains much greater than the Alps, surrounded by endless forests, gardens, and steppes, situated in a southern climate, in a dry region where the transparency of the air enhances immensely the natural beauty of the mountains. The snow-clad giants are seen from the Steppes scores of miles away, and the immensity of the chain produces an impression which is equalled nowhere in Europe. Moreover, a half-tropical vegetation clothes the mountain slopes, where the villages nestle, with their semi-military aspect and their turrets, basking in all the gorgeous sunshine of the East, or concealed in the dark shadows of the narrow gorges, and populated by a race of people among the most beautiful of Europe. Finally, at the time Lérmontoff was there the mountaineers were fighting against the Russian invaders with unabated courage and daring for each valley of their native mountains.

All these natural beauties of the Caucasus have been reflected in Lérmontoff's poetry, in such a way that in no other literature are there descriptions of nature so beautiful, or so impressive and correct. Bodenstedt, his German translator and personal friend, who knew the Caucasus well, was quite right in observing that they are worth volumes of geographical descriptions. The reading of many volumes about the Caucasus does not add any concrete features to those which are impressed upon the mind by reading the poems of Lérmontoff. Turguéneff quotes somewhere Shakespeare's description of the sea as seen from the cliffs of Dover (in *King Lear*) as a masterpiece of objective poetry dealing with nature. I must confess, however, that the concentration of attention upon small details in this description does not appeal to my mind. It gives no impression of the immensity of the sea as seen from the Dover cliffs, nor of the wonderful richness of colour displayed by the waters on a sunny day. No such reproach could ever be made against Lérmontoff's poetry of nature. Bodenstedt truly says that Lérmontoff has managed to satisfy at the same time both the naturalist and the lover of art. Whether he describes the gigantic chain, where the eye loses itself —here in snow clouds, there in the unfathomable depths of narrow gorges ; or whether he mentions some detail : a mountain stream, or the endless woods, or the smiling valleys of Georgia covered with flowers, or the strings of light clouds floating in the dry breezes of Northern Caucasia—he always remains so true to nature that his picture rises before the eye in life-colours, and yet it is imbued with a poetical atmosphere which makes one feel the freshness of these mountains, the balm of their forests and meadows, the purity of the air. And all this is written in verses wonderfully musical. Lérmontoff's verses, though not so 'easy' as Púshkin's, are very often even more musical. They sound like a beautiful melody. The Russian language is always rather melodious, but in the verses of Lérmontoff it becomes almost as melodious as Italian.

The intellectual aspect of Lérmontoff is nearer to Shelley than to any other poet. He was deeply impressed by the author of *Prometheus Unbound* ; but he did not try to imitate Shelley. In his earliest productions he did indeed imitate Púshkin and Púshkin's Byronism ; but he very soon struck a line of his own. All that can be said is, that the mind of Lérmontoff was disquieted by the same great problems of Good and Evil struggling in the human heart, as in the universe at large, which disquieted Shelley. Like Shelley among the poets, and like Schopenhauer among the philosophers, he felt the coming of that burning need of a revision of the moral principles now current, so characteristic of our own times. He embodied these ideas in two poems,

The Demon and *Mtsýri*, which complete each other.
The leading idea of the first is that of a fierce soul which
has broken with both earth and heaven, and looks with
contempt upon all who are moved by petty passions.
An exile from paradise and a hater of human virtues,
he knows these petty passions, and despises them with
all his superiority. The love of this demon towards
a Georgian girl who takes refuge from his love in a
convent, and dies there—what more unreal subject
could be chosen? And yet, on reading the poem, one
is struck at every line by its incredible wealth of purely
realistic, concrete descriptions of scenes and of human
feelings, all of the most exquisite beauty. The dance
of the girl at her Georgian castle before the wedding,
the encounter of the bridegroom with robbers and his
death, the galloping of his faithful horse, the sufferings
of the bride and her retirement to a convent, nay,
the love itself of the demon and every one of the
demon's movements—this is of the purest realism in the
highest sense of the word: that realism with which
Púshkin had stamped Russian literature once and
for all.

Mtsýri is the cry of a young soul longing for liberty.
A boy, taken from a Circassian village, from the mountains, is brought up in a small Russian monastery.
The monks think that they have killed in him all human
passions and longings; but the dream of his childhood
is—be it only once, be it only for a moment—to see his
native mountains where his sisters sang round his cradle,
and to press his burning bosom against the heart of one
who is not a stranger. One night, when a storm rages
and the monks are praying in fear in their church, he
escapes from the monastery, and wanders for three
days in the woods. For once in his life he enjoys a few
moments of liberty; he feels all the energy and all the
forces of his youth: 'As for me, I was like a wild
beast,' he says afterwards, 'and I was ready to fight
with the storm, the lightning, the tiger of the forest.'

But, being an exotic plant, weakened by education, he does not find his way to his native country. He is lost in the forests which spread for hundreds of miles round him, and is found a few days later, exhausted, not far from the monastery. He dies from the wounds which he has received in a fight with a leopard.

'The grave does not frighten me,' he says to the old monk who attends him. 'Suffering, they say, goes to sleep there in the eternal cold stillness. But I regret to part with life . . . I am young, still young . . . hast thou ever known the dreams of youth? Or hast thou forgotten how thou once lovedst and hatedst? Maybe this beautiful world has lost for thee its beauty. Thou art weak and grey; thou hast lost all desires. No matter! Thou hast lived once; thou hast something to forget in this world. Thou hast lived—I might have lived, too!' And he tells about the beauty of the nature which he saw when he had run away, his frantic joy at feeling free, his running after the lightning, his fight with a leopard.

> 'Thou askest me, what I have done
> While I was free?—I lived, old man!
> And were it not for these three days,
> Would not have been my life more gloomy
> Than even thine infirm old age?'

But it is impossible to *tell* all the beauties of this poem. It must be read, and let us hope that a good translation of it will be published some day.

Lérmontoff's demonism or pessimism was not the pessimism of despair, but a militant protest against all that is ignoble in life, and in this respect his poetry has deeply impressed itself upon all our subsequent literature. His pessimism was the irritation of a strong man at seeing others round him so weak and so base. With his inborn feeling of the Beautiful, which evidently can never exist without the True and the Good, and at the same time surrounded—especially in the worldly spheres he lived in, and on the Caucasus—by men and women who could not or did not dare to understand him, he might easily have arrived at a pessimistic contempt and hatred of mankind ; but he always maintained his faith in the higher qualities of man. It was quite natural that in his youth—especially in those years of universal reaction, the thirties—Lérmontoff should have expressed his discontent with the world in such a general and abstract creation as is *The Demon*. Something similar we find even with Schiller. But gradually his pessimism took a more concrete form. It was not mankind altogether, and still less heaven and earth, that he despised in his latter productions, but the negative features of his own generation. In his prose novel, *The Hero of our Own Time*, in his *Thoughts* (*Duma*), etc., he perceived higher ideals, and already in 1840—*i.e.* one year before his death—he seemed ready to open a new page in his creation, in which his powerfully constructive and critical mind would have been directed towards the real evils of actual life, and real, positive good would apparently have been his aim. But it was at this very moment that, like Púshkin, he fell in a duel.

Lérmontoff was, above all, a ' humanist '—a deeply humanitarian poet. Already at the age of twenty-three he had written a poem from the times of John the Terrible, *Song about the Merchant Kaláshnikoff*, which is rightly considered as one of the best gems of Russian literature, both for its powers, its artistic finish, and its wonderful epic style. The poem, which produced a great impression when it became known in Germany in Bodenstedt's translation, is imbued with the fiercest spirit of revolt against the courtiers of the Terrible Tsar.

Lérmontoff deeply loved Russia, but not the official Russia : not the crushing military power of a fatherland, which is so dear to the so-called patriots ; and he wrote :

> I love my fatherland ; but strange that love,
> In spite of all my reasoning may say ;
> Its glory, bought by shedding streams of blood,
> Its quietness, so full of fierce disdain,
> And the traditions of its gloomy past
> Do not awake in me a happy vision. . . .

What he loved in Russia was its country life, its plains, the life of its peasants. He was inspired at the same time with a deep love towards the natives of the Caucasus, who were waging their bitter fight against the Russians for their liberty. Himself a Russian, and a member of two military expeditions against the Circassians, his heart throbbed nevertheless in sympathy with that brave, warm-hearted people in their struggle for independence. One poem, *Izmail-Bey*, is an apotheosis of this struggle of the Circassians against the Russians ; in another, one of his best, a Circassian is described as fleeing from the field of battle to run home to his village, and there his mother herself repudiates him as a traitor. Another gem of poetry, one of his shorter poems, *Valérik*, is considered by those who know what real warfare is as the most correct description of it in poetry. And yet Lérmontoff disliked war, and he ends one of his admirable descriptions of fighting with these lines :

> I thought : ' How miserable is man !
> What does he want? There's room for all
> Beneath that sky, so blue, so pure.
> Why should, then, hatred fill his heart?'

He died in his twenty-seventh year. Exiled for a second time to the Caucasus (for a duel which he had fought at St. Petersburg with a Barrante, the son of the French Ambassador), he was staying at Pyatigórsk, frequenting the shallow society which usually comes together in such watering-places. His jokes and sarcasms addressed to an officer, Martýnoff, who used to drape himself in a Byronian mantle the better to capture the hearts of young girls, led to a duel. Lérmontoff, as he had already done in his first duel, shot sideways purposely ; but Martýnoff slowly and deliberately took his aim so as even to call forth the protests of the seconds—and killed Lérmontoff on the spot.

PÚSHKIN AND LÉRMONTOFF AS PROSE-WRITERS

Towards the end of his life Púshkin gave himself more and more to prose-writing. He began an extensive history of the peasant uprising of 1773 under Pugatchóff, and undertook for that purpose a journey to East Russia, where he collected, besides public documents, personal reminiscences and popular traditions relating to this uprising. At the same time he also wrote a novel, *The Captain's Daughter*, the scene of which was laid in that disturbed period. The novel is not very remarkable in itself. True, the portraits of Pugatchóff and of an old servant, as well as the description of the whole life in the small forts of East Russia, garrisoned at that time by only a few invalid soldiers, are true and brilliantly pictured ; but in the general construction of the novel Púshkin paid a tribute to the sentimentalism of the times. Nevertheless *The Captain's Daughter*, and especially the other prose novels of Púshkin, have played an important part in the history of Russian literature. Through them Púshkin introduced into Russia the realistic school, long before Balzac did so in France, and this school has since that time prevailed in Russian prose-literature. I do not mean, of course, realism in the sense of dwelling mainly upon the lowest instincts of man, as it was misunderstood by some French writers, but in the sense of treating both high and low manifestations of human nature in a way true to reality, and in their real proportions. Moreover, the *simplicity* of these novels, both as regards their plots and the way the plots are treated, is simply marvellous, and in this way they have traced the lines upon which the development of Russian novel-writing has ever since been pursued. The novels of Lérmontoff, of Hérzen (*Whose Fault ?*), and of Turguéneff and Tolstóy descend, I dare to say, in a much more direct line from Púshkin's novels than from those of Gógol.

Lérmontoff also wrote one novel in prose, *The Hero of Our Own Time*, of which the hero, Petchórin, was to some extent a real representative of a portion of the educated society in those years of romanticism. It is true that some critics saw in him the portraiture of the author himself and his acquaintances ; but, as Lérmontoff wrote in his preface to a second edition of this novel— ' The hero of our own time is indeed a portrait, but not of one single man : it is the portrait of the vices of our generation '—the book indicates ' the illness from which this generation suffers.'

Petchórin is an extremely clever, bold, enterprising man who regards his surroundings with cold contempt. He is undoubtedly a superior man, superior to Púshkin's Onyéghin ; but he is, above all, an egotist who finds no better application for his superior capacities than all sorts of mad adventures, always connected with love-making. He falls in love with a Circassian girl whom he sees at a native festival. The girl is also taken by the beauty and the gloomy aspect of the Russian. To marry her is evidently out of question, because her Moslem relatives would never give her to a Russian. Then Petchórin daringly kidnaps her, with the aid of her brother, and the girl is brought to the Russian fort where Petchórin is an officer. For several weeks she only cries and never speaks a word to the Russian, but by and by she feels love for him. That is the beginning of the tragedy. Petchórin soon has enough of the Circassian beauty ; he deserts her more and more for hunting adventures, and during one of them she is kidnapped by a Circassian who loves her, and who, on seeing that he cannot escape with her, kills her with his dagger. For Petchórin this solution is almost welcome.

A few years later the same Petchórin appears amidst

Russian society in one of the Caucasus watering-towns. There he meets with Princess Mary, who is courted by a young man—Grushnítsky—a sort of Caucasian caricature of Byron, draped in a mantle of contempt for mankind, but in reality a very shallow sort of personage. Petchórin, who cares but little for the Princess Mary, finds, however, a sort of wicked pleasure in rendering Grushnítsky ridiculous in her eyes, and uses all his wit to bring the girl to his feet. When this is done, he loses all interest in her. He makes a fool of Grushnítsky, and when the young man provokes him to a duel, he kills him. This was the hero of the time, and it must be owned that it was not a caricature. In a society free from care about the means of living—it was of course in serfdom times, under Nicholas I.—when there was no sort of political life in the country, a man of superior ability very often found no issue for his forces but in such adventures as Petchórin's.

It need not be said that the novel is admirably written—that it is full of living descriptions of Caucasus 'society'; that the characters are splendidly delineated, and that some of them, like the old Captain Maxím Maxímytch, have remained living types of some of the best specimens of mankind. Through these qualities *The Hero of Our Own Time*, like *Evghéniy Onyéghin*, became a model for quite a series of subsequent novels.

OTHER POETS AND NOVELISTS OF THE SAME EPOCH—KRYLÓFF

The fable-writer KRYLÓFF (1768-1844) is perhaps the Russian writer who is best known abroad. English readers know him through the excellent work and translations of so great a connoisseur of Russian literature and language as Ralston was, and little can be added to what Ralston has said of this eminently original writer.

He stands on the boundary between two centuries

and reflects both the end of the one and the beginning of the other. Up to 1807 he wrote comedies which, even more than the other comedies of the time, were mere imitations from the French. It was only in 1807-1809 that he found his true vocation and began writing fables, in which domain he attained the first rank, not only in Russia, but among the fable-writers in all modern literatures. Many of his fables—at any rate, the best known ones—are translations from Lafontaine; and yet they are entirely original productions. Lafontaine's animals are academically educated French gentlemen; even the peasants in his fables come from Versailles. There is nothing of the sort in Krylóff. Every animal in his fables is a character—true to life. Nay, even the cadence of his verses changes and takes a special aspect each time a new animal is introduced —that heavy simpleton, the Bear, or the fine and cunning Fox, or the versatile Monkey. Krylóff knew every one of them intimately; he knew all their movements, and above all he had noticed and enjoyed long since in his own self the humorous side of every one of the dwellers of the forests or the companions of Man, before he undertook to put them in his fables. This is why Krylóff is perhaps the greatest fable-writer, not only of Russia—where he had a not to be neglected rival in DMÍTRIEFF (1760-1837)—but also of all nations of modern times. True, there is no depth, no profound and cutting irony, in Krylóff's fables. Nothing but a good-natured, easy-going irony, which was the very essence of his heavy frame, his lazy habits, and his quiet contemplation. But is this not the true domain of fable, which must not be confounded with satire?

At the same time there is no writer who has better possessed and better understood the essence of the popular Russian language, the language spoken by the people. At a time when the Russian *littérateurs* hesitated between the elegant, Europeanised style of

Karamzín, and the clumsy, half-Slavonic style of the
nationalists of the old school, Krylóff, even in his very
first fables written in 1807, had already worked out a
style which at once gave him a quite unique position
in Russian literature, and which has not been surpassed
even by such masters of the popular Russian language
as was Ostróvskiy and some of the folk-novelists of a
later epoch.   For terseness, expressiveness, and strict
adherence to the true spirit of the popularly spoken
Russian, Krylóff has no rivals.

THE MINOR POETS

Several minor poets, contemporary of Púshkin and
Lérmontoff, and some of them their personal friends,
must be mentioned in this place.   The influence of
Púshkin was so great that he could not but call to life
a school of writers who should try to follow in his steps.
None of them reached such a height as to claim to be
considered a world poet ; but each of them has made
his contribution in one way or another to the development of Russian poetry, each one has had his humanising and elevating influence.

KOZLÓFF (1779-1840) has reflected in his poetry the
extremely sad character of his life.   At the age of
about forty he was stricken with paralysis, losing the
use of his legs, and soon after that his sight ; but his
poetical gift remained with him, and he dictated to his
daughter some of the saddest elegies which Russian
literature possesses, as also a great number of our most
perfect translations.   His *Monk* made every one of his
readers shed tears, and Púshkin hastened to acknow-
ledge the powers of the poem.   Endowed with a
most wonderful memory—he knew by heart all Byron,
all the poems of Walter Scott, all Racine, Tasso, and
Dante—Kozlóff, like Zhukóvskiy, with whom he had
much in common, made a great number of translations
from various languages, especially from the English

idealists ; and some of his translations from the Polish, such as *The Crimean Sonnets* of Mickiewicz, are real works of art.

DÉLWIG (1798-1831) was a great personal friend of Púshkin, whose comrade he had been at the Lyceum. He represented in Russian literature the tendency towards reviving ancient Greek forms of poetry, but happily enough he tried at the same time to write in the style of the Russian popular songs, and the lyrics which he wrote in this manner especially contributed to make of him in those years a favourite poet. Some of his romances have remained popular till now.

BARATÝNSKIY (1800-1844) was another poet of the same group of friends. Under the influence of the wild nature of Finland, where he spent several years in exile, he became a romantic poet, full of the love of nature, and also of melancholy, and deeply interested in philosophical questions, to which he could find no reply. He thus lacked a definite conception of life, but what he wrote was clothed in a beautiful form, and in very expressive, elegant verses.

YAZÝKOFF (1803-1846) belongs to the same circle. He was intimate with Púshkin, who much admired his verses. It must be said, however, that the poetry of Yazýkoff had chiefly a historical influence in the sense of perfecting the forms of poetical expression. Unfortunately, he had to struggle against almost continual illness, and he died just when he was reaching the full development of his talent.

VENEVÍTINOFF (1805-1827) died at a still younger age ; but there is no exaggeration in saying that he promised to become a great poet, endowed with the same depth of philosophical conception as was Goethe, and capable of attaining the same beauty of form. The few verses he wrote during the last year of his life revealed the suddenly attained maturity of a great poetical talent.

PRINCE ALEXANDER ODÓEVSKIY (1803-1839) and

POLEZHÁYEFF (1806-1838) are two other poets who died very young, and whose lives were entirely broken by political persecution. Odóevskiy was a friend of the Decembrists. After the 14th of December 1825 he was arrested, taken to the fortress of St. Peter and St. Paul, and then sentenced to hard labour in Siberia, whence he was not released till twelve years later, to be sent as a soldier to the Caucasus. There he became the friend of Lérmontoff, one of whose best elegies was written on Odóevskiy's death. The verses of Odóevskiy (they were not printed while he lived) lack finish, but he was a real poet and deeply loved his mother country, as is seen from his *Vision of a Poet* and his historical poem *Vasilkó*.

The fate of POLEZHÁYEFF was even more tragic. He was only twenty years old—a brilliant student of the Moscow University—when he wrote an autobiographical poem, *Sáshka*, where pictures of the life of the students were intermingled with irrespectful allusions to the higher authorities. This poem was shown to Nicholas I., who ordered the young poet to be sent as a soldier to an army regiment. The duration of service was then twenty-five years, and Polezháyeff saw not the slightest chance of release. More than that : for an unauthorised absence from his regiment (he had gone to Moscow with the intention of presenting a petition of release to the Tsar) he was condemned to receive one thousand strokes with the sticks, and only by mere luck escaped the punishment. He never succumbed to his fate, and in the horrible barracks of those times he remained what he was—a pupil of Byron, Lamartine, and Macpherson, never broken, protesting against tyranny in verses that were written in tears and blood. When he was dying from consumption in a military hospital at Moscow, Nicholas I. pardoned him : his promotion to the grade of officer came when he was dead. His lyrical verses had a certain originality, but even these were forbidden ; and some fifty pieces of his poetry, confiscated by the censor, were discovered in the archives of the Moscow Censorship Board only quite recently. They were published in 1915.

A similar fate befell the Little Russian poet SHEVT-CHÉNKO (1814-1861), who, for some of his poetry, was sent in 1847 to a battalion as a common soldier. His epical poems from the life of the free Cossacks in olden times, heart-rending poems from the life of the serfs, and lyrics, all written in Little Russian and thoroughly popular in both form and content, belong to the fine specimens of poetry of all nations.

Of prose-writers of the same epoch only a few can be mentioned in this book, and these in a few lines. ALEXANDER BESTÚZHEFF (1797-1837), who wrote under the *nom de plume* of MARLÍNSKIY—one of the 'Decembrists,' exiled to Siberia, and later on sent to the Caucasus as a soldier—was the author of very widely read novels. Like Púshkin and Lérmontoff he was under the influence of Byron, and described 'titanic passions' in Byron's style, as also striking adventures in the style of the French novelists of the Romantic school; but he deserves at the same time to be regarded as the first to write novels from Russian life in which matters of social interest were discussed.

Other favourite novelists of the same epoch were: ZAGÓSKIN (1789-1852), the author of extremely popular historical novels, *Yúriy Miloslávskiy*, *Róslavleff*, etc., all written in a sentimentally patriotic style; NARYÉZHNYI (1780-1825), who is considered by some Russian critics as a forerunner of Gógol, because he wrote already in the realistic style, describing, like Gógol, the dark sides of Russian life; and LAZHÉTCHNIKOFF (1792-1868), the author of a number of very popular historical novels from Russian life.

CHAPTER III

GÓGOL

LITTLE RUSSIA—*Nights on a Farm near Dikánka*, and *Mírgorod* —Village life and humour—*How Iván Ivánovitch quarrelled with Iván Nikíforytch*—Historical novel : *Tarás Búlba—The Cloak*—Drama : *The Inspector-General*—Its influence—*Dead Souls* : main types—Realism in the Russian novel.

WITH Gógol begins a new period of Russian literature, which is called by Russian literary critics 'the Gógol period,' and which lasts to the present date.

Gógol was not a Great Russian. He was born in 1809, in a Little Russian or Ukraïnian nobleman's family. His father had already displayed some literary talent and had written a few comedies in Little Russian, but Gógol lost him at an early age. The boy was educated in a small provincial town, which he left, however, while still young, and when he was only nineteen he was already at St. Petersburg. At that time the dream of his life was to become an actor, but the manager of the St. Petersburg Imperial theatres did not accept him, and Gógol had to look for another sphere of activity. The Civil Service, in which he obtained the position of a subordinate clerk, was evidently insufficient to interest him, and he soon entered upon his literary career.

Gógol's début was in 1829, with little novels taken from the village life of Little Russia. His *Nights on a Farm near Dikánka*, soon followed by another series of stories entitled *Mírgorod*, immediately won for him literary fame and introduced him into the circle of Zhukóvskiy and Púshkin. The two poets at once recognised Gógol's genius, and received him with open arms.

Little Russia differs considerably from the central parts of the empire, that is, from the country round Moscow, which is known as Great Russia. It has a more southern position, and everything southern has always a certain attraction for northerners. The villages in Little Russia are not disposed in streets as they are in Great Russia, but the white-washed houses are scattered, as in Western Europe, in separate little farms, surrounded by charming little gardens. The more genial climate, the warm nights, the musical language, the beauty of the race, which probably contains a mixture of South Slavonian with Turkish and Polish blood, the picturesque dress and the lyrical songs —all these render Little Russia especially attractive for the Great Russian. Besides, life in Little Russian villages is more poetical than it is in the villages of Great Russia. There is more freedom in the relations between the young men and the young girls, who freely meet before marriage ; the stamp of seclusion of the women which has been impressed by Byzantine habits upon Moscow does not exist in Little Russia, where the influence of Poland was prevalent. Little Russians have also maintained numerous traditions and epic poems and songs from the times when they were free Cossacks and used to fight against the Poles in the north and the Turks in the south. Having had to defend the Greek orthodox religion against these two nations, they strictly adhere now to the Russian Church, and one does not find in their villages the same passion for scholastic discussions about the letter of the Holy Books which is often met with in Great Russia among the Nonconformists. Their religion has altogether a more poetical aspect.

The Little Russian language is certainly more melodious than the Great Russian, and there is now a movement of some importance for its literary development ; but this evolution has yet to be accomplished, and Gógol very wisely wrote in Great Russian—that

is, in the language of Zhukóvskiy, Púshkin, and Lérmontoff. We have thus in Gógol a sort of union
between the two nationalities.

It would be impossible to give here an idea of the
humour and wit contained in Gógol's novels from Little
Russian life, without quoting whole pages. It is the
good-hearted laughter of a young man who himself
enjoys the fullness of life and himself laughs at the
comical positions into which he has put his heroes : a
village chanter, a wealthy peasant, a rural matron, or a
village smith. He is full of happiness ; no dark appre-
hension comes to disturb his joy of life. However,
those whom he depicts are not rendered comical in
obedience to the poet's whim : Gógol always remains
scrupulously true to reality. Every peasant, every
chanter, is taken from real life, and the truthfulness of
Gógol to reality is almost ethnographical, without ever
ceasing to be poetical. All the superstitions of a village
life on a Christmas Eve or during a midsummer night,
when the mischievous spirits and goblins get free till
the cock crows, are brought before the reader, and at
the same time we have all the wittiness which is inborn
in the Little Russian. It was only later on that Gógol's
comical vein became what can be truly described as
'humour '—that is, a sort of contrast between comical
surroundings and a sad substratum of life, which made
Púshkin say of Gógol's productions that 'behind his
laughter you feel the unseen tears.'

Not all the Little Russian tales of Gógol are taken
from peasant life. Some deal also with the upper class
of the small towns ; and one of them, *How Iván Ivánovitch quarrelled with Iván Nikíforytch*, is one of the
most humorous tales in existence. Iván Ivánovitch
and Iván Nikíforytch were two neighbours who lived
on excellent terms with each other ; but the inevitable-
ness of their quarrelling some day appears from the very
first lines of the novel. Iván Ivánovitch was a person
of fine behaviour. He would never offer snuff to an

acquaintance without saying : 'May I dare, sir, to ask you to be so kind as to oblige yourself.' He was a man of the most accurate habits ; and when he had eaten a melon he used to wrap its seeds in a bit of paper and to inscribe upon it, 'This melon was eaten on such a date,' and if there had been a friend at his table he would add, 'in the presence of Mr. So and So.' At the same time he was, after all, a miser, who appreciated very highly the comforts of his own life, but did not care to share them with others. His neighbour, Iván Nikíforytch, was quite the opposite. He was very stout and heavy, and fond of swearing. On a hot summer day he would take off all his clothes and sit in his garden, in the sunshine, warming his back. When he offered snuff to any one, he would simply produce his snuff-box saying, 'Oblige yourself.' He knew none of the refinements of his neighbour, and loudly expressed what he meant. It was inevitable that two men so different, whose yards were only separated by a low fence, should one day come to a quarrel ; and so it happened.

One day the stout and rough Iván Nikíforytch, seeing that his friend owned an old useless musket, was seized with the desire to possess the weapon. He had not the slightest need of it, but all the more he longed to have it, and this craving led to a feud which lasted for years. Iván Ivánovitch remarked very reasonably to his neighbour that he had no need of a rifle. The neighbour, stung by this remark, replied that this was precisely the thing he needed, and offered, if Iván Ivánovitch was not disposed to accept money for his musket, to give him in exchange—a pig. . . . This was understood by Iván Ivánovitch as a terrible offence : 'How could a musket, which is the symbol of hunting, of nobility, be exchanged by a gentleman for a pig ?' Hard words followed, and the offended neighbour called Iván Ivánovitch a gander. . . . A mortal feud, full of the most comical incidents, resulted from these rash

words. Their friends did everything to re-establish
peace, and one day their efforts seemed to be crowned
with success : the two enemies had been brought together, both pushed from behind by their friends ;
Iván Ivánovitch had already put his hand into his
pocket to take out his snuff-box and to offer it to his
enemy, when the latter made the unfortunate remark :
' There was nothing particular in being called a gander ;
no need to be offended by that.' . . . All the efforts
of the friends were brought to nought by these unfortunate words. The feud was renewed with even greater
acrimony than before ; and, tragedy always following
in the steps of comedy, the two enemies, by taking the
affair from one court to another, arrived at old age
totally ruined.

TARÁS BÚLBA—THE CLOAK

The pearl of Gógol's Little Russian novels is a
historical novel, *Tarás Búlba*, which recalls to life one
of the most interesting periods in the history of Little
Russia—the fifteenth century. Constantinople had
fallen into the hands of the Turks ; and although a
mighty Polish-Lithuanian state had grown in the
West, the Turks, nevertheless, menaced both Eastern
and Middle Europe. Then it was that the Little
Russians rose for the defence of Russia and Europe.
They lived in free communities of Cossacks, over whom
the Poles were beginning to establish feudal power.
In times of peace these Cossacks carried on agriculture
in the rich prairies, and fishing in the beautiful rivers
of South-west Russia, reaching at times the Black Sea ;
but every one of them was armed, and the whole
country was divided into regiments. As soon as there
was a military alarm they all rose to meet an invasion
of the Turks, or a raid of the Tartars, returning to their
fields and fisheries as soon as the war was over.

The whole nation was thus ready to resist the
invasions of the Mussulmans ; but a special vanguard

was kept in the lower course of the Dniéper, 'beyond the rapids,' on an island which soon became famous under the name of the Sécha. Men of all conditions, including runaways from their landlords, outlaws, and adventurers of all sorts, could come and settle in the Sécha without being asked any questions but whether they went to church. 'Well, then, make the sign of the cross,' the *hétman* of the Sécha said, 'and join the division you like.' The Sécha consisted of about sixty divisions, which were very similar to independent republics, or rather to schools of boys, who cared for nothing and lived in common. None of them had anything of his own, excepting his arms. No women were admitted, and absolute democracy prevailed.

The hero of the novel is an old Cossack, Tarás Búlba, who has himself spent many years in the Sécha, but is now peacefully settled inland on his farm. His two sons have been educated at the Academy of Kíeff and return home after several years of absence. Their first meeting with their father is very characteristic. As the father laughs at the sons' long clothes, which do not suit a Cossack, the elder son, Ostáp, challenges him to a good boxing fight. The father is delighted, and they fight until the old man, quite out of breath, exclaims : 'By God, this is a good fighter ; no need to test him further ; he will be a good Cossack !—Now, son, be welcome ; let us kiss each other.' On the very next day after their arrival, without letting the mother enjoy the sight of her sons, Tarás takes them to the Sécha, which—as often happened in those times—was going to begin war, in consequence of the exactions which the Polish landlords made upon the Little Russians.

The life of the free Cossacks in the republic 'beyond the rapids' and their ways of conducting war are wonderfully described ; but, paying a tribute to the then current romanticism, Gógol makes Tarás's younger son, a sentimentalist, fall in love with a noble Polish lady, during the siege of a Polish town, and go over to the enemy; while the father and the elder son continue fighting the Poles. The war lasts for a year or so, with varying success, till at length, in one of the desperate sorties of the besieged Poles, the younger son of Tarás is taken prisoner, and the father himself kills him for his treason. The elder son is next taken prisoner by the Poles and carried away to Warsaw, where he perishes on the rack; while Tarás, returning to Little Russia, raises a formidable army and makes one of those invasions into Poland with which the history of the two countries was filled for two centuries. Taken prisoner himself, Tarás perishes at the stake, with a disregard of life and suffering which were characteristic of this strong, fighting race of men. Such is, in brief, the theme of this novel, which is replete with admirable separate scenes.

Read in the light of modern requirements, *Tarás Búlba* certainly would not satisfy us. The influence of the Romantic school is too strongly felt. The younger son of Tarás is not a living being, and the Polish lady is entirely invented in order to answer the requirements of a novel, showing that Gógol never knew a single woman of that type. But the old Cossack and his son, as well as all the life of the Cossack camps, produces the illusion of real life. The reader is carried away in sympathy with old Tarás, while the ethnographer cannot but feel that he has before him a wonderful combination of an ethnographical document of the highest value, with a poetical reproduction—only the more real because it is poetical—of a bygone and most interesting epoch.

The Little Russian novels were followed by a few novels taken from the life of Great Russia, chiefly of St. Petersburg, and two of them, *The Memoirs of a Madman* and *The Cloak (Shinél)*, deserve a special mention. The psychology of the madman is strikingly drawn. As to *The Cloak*, it is in this novel that Gógol's laughter which conceals 'unseen tears' shows at its best. The poor life of a small functionary, who discovers with a sense of horror that his old cloak is so worn out as to be unfit to stand further repairs; his hesitation before he ventures to speak to a tailor about a new one; his nervous excitement on the day that it is ready and that he tries it on for the first time; and finally his despair, amidst general indifference, when night-robbers have robbed him of his cloak—every line of this work bears the stamp of one of the greatest artists. Sufficient to say that this novel produced at its appearance, and produces still, such an impression, that since the times of Gógol every Russian novel-writer has been aptly said to have rewritten *The Cloak*.

THE INSPECTOR-GENERAL

Gógol's prose-comedy, *The Inspector-General* (*Revizór*), has become, in its turn, a starting-point for the Russian drama—a model which every dramatic writer after Gógol has always kept before his eyes. 'Revizór,' in Russian, means some important functionary who has been sent by the ministry to some provincial town to inquire into the conditions of the local administration—an Inspector-General; and the comedy takes place in a small town, from which 'you may gallop for three years and yet arrive nowhere.' The little spot—we learn it at the rising of the curtain—is going to be visited by an Inspector-General. The local head of the police (in those times the head of the police was also the head of the town)—the Gorodníchiy or Governor—has convoked the chief functionaries of the place to communicate to them important news. He has had a bad dream; two rats came in, sniffed, and—went away; there must be something in that dream, and so there is; he has just got this morning a letter from a friend at St. Petersburg, announcing that an inspector-general is coming, and—what is still worse—is coming in-cog-ni-to! Now, the honourable Governor advises the functionaries to put some order in their respective offices. The patients in the hospital walk about in linen so dirty that you might take them for chimney-sweeps. The chief magistrate, who is a passionate lover of sport, has his hunting apparel hanging about in the court, and his attendants have made a poultry-yard of the entrance hall. In short, everything has to be put in order. The Governor feels very uncomfortable. Up to the present day he has freely levied tribute upon the merchants, pocketed the money destined for building a church, and within a fortnight he has flogged the wife of a non-commissioned officer, which he had no right to do ; and now, there's the Inspector-General coming! He asks the postmaster 'just to open a little' the letters which may be addressed from this town to St. Petersburg and, if he finds in them some reports about town matters, to keep them. The postmaster—a great student of human character—has always indulged, even without getting this advice, in the interesting pastime of reading the letters, and he falls in with the Governor's proposal.

At that very moment enter Petr Iványch Dóbchinsky and Petr Iványch Bóbchinsky. Every one knows them, you know them very well : they play the part of the town Gazette. They go about the town all day long, and as soon as they have learned something interesting they both hurry to spread the news, interrupting each other in telling it, and hurrying immediately to some other place to be the first to communicate the news to some one else. They have been at the only inn of the town, and there they saw a very suspicious person : a young man, 'who has something, you know, extra-ordinary about his face.' He is living there for a fortnight, never paying a penny, and does not journey any farther. 'What is his object in staying so long in a town like ours?' And then, when they were taking

their lunch he passed them by and looked so inquisitively in their plates—who may he be? Evidently,
the Governor and all present conclude, he must be the
Inspector-General who stays there incognito. . . . A
general confusion results from the suspicion. The
Governor starts immediately for the inn, to make
the necessary inquiries. The womenfolk are in a
tremendous excitement.

The stranger is simply a young man who is travelling
to rejoin his father. On some post-station he met with
a certain captain—a great master at cards—and lost all
he had in his pocket. Now he cannot proceed any
farther, and he cannot pay the landlord, who refuses to
credit him with any more meals. The young man feels
awfully hungry—no wonder he looked so inquisitively
into the plates of the two gentlemen—and resorts to all
sorts of tricks to induce the landlord to send him something for his dinner. Just as he is finishing some fossil-
like cutlet, enters the Gorodníchiy; and a most comic
scene follows, the young man thinking that the Governor
comes to arrest him, and the Governor thinking that he
is speaking to the Inspector-General who is trying to
conceal his identity. The Governor offers to remove
the young man to some more comfortable place. 'No,
thank you, I have no intent to go to a jail,' sharply
retorts the young man. . . . But it is to his own house
that the Governor takes the supposed Inspector, and
now an easy life begins for the adventurer. All the
functionaries appear in turn to introduce themselves, and
every one is only too happy to give him a bribe of a
hundred roubles or so. The merchants come to ask his
protection from the Governor; the widow who was flogged
comes to lodge a complaint. . . . In the meantime the
young man enters into a flirtation with both the wife and
the daughter of the Governor; and, finally, being caught
at a very pathetic moment when he is kneeling at the
feet of the daughter, without further thought he makes
a proposition of marriage. But, having gone so far, the

young man, well provided now with money, hastens to leave the town on the pretext of going to see an uncle ; he will be back in a couple of days. . . .

The delight of the Governor can easily be imagined. His Excellency, the Inspector-General, going to marry the Governor's daughter !   He and his wife are already making all sorts of plans.   They will remove to St. Petersburg, the Gorodníchiy will soon be a general, and you will see how he will keep the other Gorodníchiys at his door ! . . . The happy news spreads about the town, and all the functionaries and the society of the town hasten to offer their congratulations to the old man. There is a great gathering at his house—when the post-master comes in.   He has followed the advice of the Governor, and has opened a letter which the supposed Inspector-General had addressed to somebody at St. Petersburg.   He now brings this letter.   The young man is no inspector at all, and here is what he writes to a Bohemian friend of his about his adventures in the provincial town :

The Postmaster (reads) : 'I hasten to inform you, my dear friend, of the wonderful things which have happened to me.   On my way hither an infantry captain had cleared me out completely, so that the innkeeper here intended to send me to jail, when, all of a sudden, thanks to my St. Petersburg appearance and costume, all the town took me for a Governor-General.   Now I am staying at the Gorodníchiy's !   I have a splendid time, and flirt awfully with both his wife and his daughter. . . . Do you remember how hard up we were, taking our meals where we could get them, without paying for them, and how one day, in a tea-shop, the pastry-cook collared me for having eaten his pastry to the account of the king of England ?[1]   It is quite different now.   They all lend me money, as much as I care for.   They are an awful set of originals : you would split of laughter.   I know you write sometimes for the papers—put them into your literature.   To begin with, the Governor is as stupid as an old horse. . . .'

The Governor (interrupting) : That cannot be there ! There is no such thing in the letter.

Postmaster (showing the letter) : Read it, then, yourself.

Governor (reads) : 'As an old horse. . . .' Impossible ! You must have added that.

---

[1] This was in those times an expression which meant ' without paying.'

Postmaster : How could I ?

The Guests : Read ! read !

The Postmaster (continues to read) : 'The Governor is as stupid as an old horse. . . .'

Governor : The deuce ! Now he must repeat it—as if it were not standing there already !

Postmaster (continues reading) : Hm, hm, yes ! 'an old horse. The postmaster is also a good man. . . .' Well, he also makes an improper remark about me. . . .

Governor : Read it, then.

Postmaster : Is it necessary ?

Governor : The deuce ! once we have begun to read it, we must read it all through.

Artémy Filípovitch (head of the philanthropic institutions) : Permit me, please, I shall read (*puts on his spectacles and reads*) : 'The postmaster is quite like the old porter in our office, and the rascal must drink equally hard. . . .'

Postmaster : A naughty boy, who ought to be flogged—that's all !

Art. Fil. (continues reading) : 'The head of the philanthropic in—in . . .'

Koróbkin : Why do you stop now ?

Art. Fil. : Bad writing. But, after all, it is quite evident that he is a scoundrel.

Koróbkin : Give me the letter, please. I think I have better eyes (*tries to take the letter*).

Art. Fil. (does not give it) : No use at all. This passage can be omitted. Further on everything is quite readable.

Koróbkin : Let me have it. I shall see all about it.

Art. Fil. : I also can read it. I tell you that after that passage everything is readable.

Postm. : No, no, read it all. Everything was read so far.

The Guests : Artémy Filípovitch, pass the letter over. (*To Koróbkin*) : Read it, read it !

Art. Fil. : All right, all right. (*He passes the letter.*) There it is ; but wait a moment (*he covers a part of it with his finger*). Begin here (*all surround him*).

Postm. : Go on. Nonsense, read it all.

Koróbkin (reads) : 'The head of the philanthropic institutions resembles a pig that wears a cap. . . .'

Art. Fil. (to the audience) : Not witty at all ! A pig that wears a cap ! Have you ever seen a pig wearing a cap ?

Koróbkin (continues reading) : 'The inspector of the schools smells of onions all through !'

The Inspector (to the audience) : Upon my honour, I never touch onions.

The Judge (apart) : Thank God, there is nothing about me.

Koróbkin (reading) : 'The judge . . .'

The Judge : There ! . . . (*aloud*) : Well, gentlemen, I think the letter is much too long, and quite uninteresting—why the deuce should we go on reading that nonsense?

Insp. of Schools : No ! no !

Postm. : No !—go on !

Art. Fil. : No, it must be read.

Koróbkin (continues) : ' The judge Lyápkin-Tyápkin is extremely *mauvais ton.'* (*Stops.*) That must be a French word ?

The Judge : The deuce knows what it means. If it were only ' a robber,' then it would be all right, but it may be something worse.

In short, the letter produces a great sensation. The friends of the Governor are delighted to see him and his family in such straits, all accuse each other, and finally fall upon the two gentlemen, when a police soldier enters the room and announces in a loud voice : ' A functionary from St. Petersburg, with Imperial orders, wants to see you all immediately. He stays at the hotel.' Thereupon the curtain drops over a living picture of which Gógol himself had made a striking sketch in pencil, and which is usually reproduced in his works ; it shows how admirably well, with what a fine artistic sense, he represented to himself his characters.

The Inspector-General marks a new era in the development of dramatic art in Russia. The comedies and dramas which were being played in Russia at that time (Griboyédoff's *Misfortune from Intelligence* would have been an exception, but it was not allowed to appear on the stage) hardly deserved the name of dramatic literature, so imperfect and puerile they were. *The Inspector-General*, on the contrary, would have marked, at the time of its appearance (1835), an epoch in any language. Its stage qualities, which will be appreciated by every good actor ; its sound and hearty humour ; the natural character of the comical scenes, which result from the very characters of those who appear in this comedy ; the sense of measure which pervades it —all these make it one of the best comedies in existence. If the conditions of life which are depicted here were not so exclusively Russian, and did not so exclusively belong to a bygone stage of life which is unknown outside Russia, it would have been generally recognised as a pearl of the world's literature. This is why, when it was played a few years ago in Germany, by actors who properly understood Russian life, it achieved a great success.

The Inspector-General provoked such a storm of hostile criticism on the part of all reactionary Russia that it was hopeless to expect that the comedy which Gógol began next, concerning the life of the St. Petersburg functionaries (*The Vladimir Cross*), could ever be admitted on the stage, and Gógol never finished it, only publishing a few striking scenes from it : *The Morning of a Busy Man, The Law Suit*, etc. Another comedy, *Marriage*, in which he represented the hesitation and terror through which an inveterate bachelor goes before a marriage, which he finally eludes by jumping out of a window a few moments before the beginning of the ceremony, has not lost its interest even now. It is so full of comical situations, which fine actors cannot but highly appreciate, that it is still a part of the current *répertoire* of the Russian stage.

DEAD SOULS

Gógol's main work was *Dead Souls*. This is a novel almost without a plot, or rather with a plot of the utmost simplicity. Like the plot of *The Inspector-General*, it was suggested to Gógol by Púshkin. In those times, when serfdom was flourishing in Russia, the ambition of every nobleman was to become the owner of at least a couple of hundred serfs. The serfs used to be sold like slaves and could be bought separately. A needy nobleman, Tchítchikoff, conceives accordingly a very clever plan. A census of the population being made only every ten or twenty years, and every serf-owner having in the interval to pay taxes for every male soul which he owned at the time of the last census, even though part of his 'souls' be dead since, Tchítchikoff conceives the idea of taking advantage of this anomaly. He will buy the dead souls at a very small expense : the landlords will be only too pleased to get rid of this burden and surely will sell them for anything ; and after Tchítchikoff has bought two or three hundred of these imaginary serfs, he will buy cheap land somewhere in the southern prairies, transfer the dead souls, on paper, to that land, register them as if they were really settled there, and mortgage that new sort of estate to the State Landlords' Bank. In this way he can easily make the beginnings of a fortune. With this plan Tchítchikoff comes to a provincial town and begins his operations. He makes, first of all, the necessary visits.

'The newcomer made visits to all the functionaries of the town. He went to testify his respects to the Governor, who like Tchítchikoff himself, was neither stout nor thin. He was decorated with a cross and was spoken of as a person who would soon get a star; but was, after all, a very good fellow and was fond of making embroideries upon fine muslin. Tchítchikoff's next visits were to the Vice-Governor, to the Chief Magistrate, to the Chief of Police, the Head of the Crown Factories . . . but it is so difficult to remember all the powerful persons in this world . . . sufficient to say that the newcomer showed a wonderful activity as regards visits. He even went to testify his respects to. the Sanitary Inspector, and to the Town Surveyor, and after that he sat for a long time in his carriage trying to remember to whom else he might pay a visit; but he could think of no more functionaries in the town. In his conversations with all these influential persons he managed to say something to flatter every one of them. In talking with the Governor he accidentally dropped the remark that when one enters this province one thinks of paradise—all the roads being quite like velvet; and that "governments which nominate wise functionaries surely deserve universal gratitude." To the Chief of the Police he said something very gratifying about the police force, and while he was talking to the Vice-Governor and to the presiding Magistrate, who were only State-Councillors, he twice made the mistake of calling them " Your Excellency," with which

mistake they were both immensely pleased. The result of all
this was that the Governor asked Tchítchikoff to come that
same day to an evening-party, and the other functionaries
invited him, some to dine with them, others to a cup of tea,
and others again to a party of whist.

'About himself Tchítchikoff avoided talking, and if he
spoke at all it was in vague sentences only, with a remarkable
modesty, his conversation taking in such cases a rather
bookish turn. He said that he was a mere nobody in this
world and did not wish people to take any particular interest
in him ; that he had had varied experiences in his life, suffered
in the service of the State for the sake of truth, had had many
enemies, some of whom had even attempted his life, but that
now, wishing to lead a quiet existence, he intended to find at
last some corner to live in, and, having come to this town, he
considered it his imperative duty to testify his respect to the
chief functionaries of the place. This was all they could
learn about the new person who soon made his appearance at
the Governor's evening-party.

' Here, the newcomer once more produced the most favourable impression. . . . He always found out what he ought
to do on every occasion ; and he proved himself an experienced man of the world. Whatsoever the conversation
might be about, he always knew how to support it. If people
talked about horses, he spoke about horses ; if they began
talking about the best hunting dogs, here also Tchítchikoff
would make remarks to the point. If the conversation related
to some inquest which was being made by the Government,
he would show that he also knew something about the tricks
of the Civil Service functionaries. When the talk was about
billiards, he showed that in billiards he could keep his own ;
if people talked about virtue, he also spoke about virtue, even
with tears in his eyes ; and if the conversation turned on
making brandy, he knew all about brandy ; as to Custom
officers, he knew everything about them, as though he had
himself been a Custom officer, or a detective ; but the most
remarkable thing was that he knew how to cover all this with
a certain sense of propriety, and in every circumstance knew
how to behave. He never spoke too loudly, and never in
too subdued a tone, but exactly as one ought to speak. In
short, take him from any side you like, he was a very respectable man. All the functionaries were delighted with the
arrival of such a person in their town.'

It has often been said that Gógol's Tchítchikoff is a truly Russian type. But—is it so? Has not every one of us met Tchítchikoff?—middle-aged; not too thick and not too thin; moving about with the lightness almost of a military man. . . . The subject he wishes to speak to you about may offer many difficulties, but he knows how to approach it and to interest you in it in a thousand different ways. When he talks to an old general he rises to the understanding of the greatness of the country and her military glory. He is not a jingo—surely not—but he has, just in the proper measure, the love of war and victories which is required in a man who wishes to be described as a patriot. When he meets with a sentimental reformer, he is sentimental and desirous of reforms, and so on, and he always will keep in view the object he aims at at a given moment, and will try to interest you in it. Tchítchikoff may buy dead souls, or railway shares, or he may collect funds for some charitable institution, or look for a position in a bank, but he is an immortal international type; we meet him everywhere; he is of all lands and of all times; he but takes different forms to suit the requirements of nationality and time.

One of the first landlords to whom Tchítchikoff spoke of his intention of buying dead souls was Maníloff —also a universal type, with the addition of those special features which the quiet life of a serf-owner could add to such a character. 'A very nice man to look at,' as Gógol says; his features possessed something very pleasant—only it seemed as if too much sugar had been put into them. 'When you meet him for the first time you cannot but exclaim after the first few minutes of conversation: "What a nice and pleasant man he is." The next moment you say nothing, but the next but one moment you say to yourself: "The deuce knows what he is," and you go away; but if you don't, you feel mortally bored.' You could never hear from him a lively or animated word.

Every one has some point of interest and enthusiasm.
Maníloff had nothing of the kind; he was always in
the same mild temper. He seemed to be lost in reflection; but what about, no one knew. Sometimes,
as he looked from his window on his wide courtyard
and the pond behind, he would say to himself: 'How
nice it would be to have there an underground passage
leading from the mansion to the pond, and to have
across the pond a stone bridge, with pretty shops on
both its sides, in which shops all sorts of things useful
for the poor people could be bought.' His eyes became
in this case wonderfully soft, and his face took on a
most contented expression. However, even less strange
intentions remained mere intentions. In his house
something was always missing; his drawing-room had
excellent furniture covered with fine silk stuff, which
probably had cost much money; but for two of the
chairs there was not sufficient of the stuff, and so they
remained covered with plain sack-cloth; and for many
years in succession the proprietor used to stop his
guests with these words: 'Please do not take that
chair; it is not yet ready.' 'His wife . . . But they
were quite satisfied with each other. Although more
than eight years had passed since they had married,
one of them would still occasionally bring to the other
a piece of apple or a tiny sweet, or a nut, saying in a
touchingly sweet voice which expressed infinite love:
"Open, my dearest, your little mouth—I will put into
it this little sweet." Evidently the mouth was opened
in a very charming way. For her husband's birthday
the wife always prepared some surprise—for instance,
an embroidered sheath for his tooth-pick, and very
often, sitting on the sofa, all of a sudden, no one knows
for what reason, one of them would leave his pipe and
the other her work, and impress on each other such a
sweet and long kiss that during it one might easily
smoke a little cigarette. In short, they were what
people call quite happy.'

It is evident that of his estate and of the condition of his peasants Maníloff never thought. He knew absolutely nothing about such matters, and left everything in the hands of a very sharp manager, under whose rule Maníloff's serfs were worse off than under a brutal landlord. Thousands of such Maníloffs peopled Russia about the middle of the last century, and I think that if we look closer round we shall find such would-be 'sentimental' persons under every latitude.

It is easy to conceive what a gallery of portraits Gógol was enabled to produce as he followed Tchítchikoff in his wanderings from one landlord to another, while his hero tried to buy as many 'dead souls' as he could. Every one of the landlords described in *Dead Souls*—the sentimentalist Maníloff, the heavy and cunning Sobakévitch, the arch-liar and cheat Nózdreff, the fossilised, antediluvian lady Koróbotchka, the miser Plyúshkin—have become common names in Russian conversation. Some of them, as for instance the miser Plyúshkin, are depicted with such a depth of psychological insight that one may ask whether a better and more humane portrait of a miser can be found in any literature?

Towards the end of his life Gógol, who was suffering from a nervous disease, fell under the influence of 'pietists,' especially of Madame O. A. Smirnóff (born Rossett), and began to consider all his writings as a sin of his life. Twice, in a paroxysm of religious self-accusation, he burned the manuscript of the second volume of *Dead Souls*, of which only some parts have been preserved, and were circulated in his lifetime in manuscript. The last ten years of his life were extremely painful. He repented with reference to all his writings, and published a very unwholesome book, *Correspondence with Friends*, in which, under the mask of Christian humility, he took a most arrogant position with respect to all literature, his own writings included. He died at Moscow in 1852.

It hardly need be added that the Government of Nicholas I. considered Gógol's writings extremely dangerous. The author had the utmost difficulties in getting permission for *The Inspector-General* to be played at all on the stage, and the permission was only obtained by Zhukóvskiy, at the express will of the Tsar himself. Before the authorisation was given to print the first volume of *Dead Souls*, Gógol had to undergo most incredible trouble ; and when the volume was out of print a second edition was never permitted to be published during his lifetime. When Gógol died, and Turguéneff published in a Moscow paper a short obituary notice, which really contained absolutely nothing (' any tradesman might have had a better one,' as Turguéneff himself said), the young novelist was arrested, and it was only because of the influence of his friends in high position that the punishment which Nicholas I. inflicted upon him was limited to exile from Moscow and a forced residence on his estate in the country.

The police of Nicholas I. were not wrong when they attributed to Gógol a great influence upon the minds of Russians. His works circulated immensely in manuscript copies. In my childhood we used to copy the second volume of *Dead Souls*, the whole book from beginning to end, as well as parts from the first volume. Every one considered then this work as a formidable indictment against serfdom and its consequences. In this respect Gógol was the forerunner of the literary movement against serfdom which began in Russia with such force, a very few years later, during and especially after the Crimean War. Gógol never expressed his personal ideas about this subject, but the life-pictures of serf-owners which he gave and their relations to their serfs—especially the waste of the labour of the serfs—were a stronger indictment than if Gógol had related facts of brutal behaviour of landlords towards their men. In fact, it is impossible to read

Dead Souls without being impressed by the fact that serfdom was an institution which had produced its own doom. Drinking, gluttony, waste of the serfs' labour in order to keep hundreds of retainers, or for things as useless as the sentimentalist Maníloff's bridges, were characteristic of the landlords ; and when Gógol wanted to represent one landlord who, at least, obtained some pecuniary advantage from the forced labour of his serfs and enriched himself, he had to produce a landlord who was not a pure Russian : in fact, among the Russian landlords such a man would have been a most extraordinary occurrence.

As to the literary influence of Gógol, it was immense, and it is felt down to the present day. Gógol was not a deep thinker, but he was a great artist. His art was pure realism, but it was imbued with the desire of making for mankind something good and great. When he wrote the most comical things, it was not merely for the pleasure of laughing at human weaknesses, but he also tried to awaken the desire of something better and greater, and he always achieved that aim. Art, in Gógol's conception, is a torch-bearer which indicates a higher ideal ; and it was certainly this high conception of art which induced him to give such an incredible amount of time to the working out of the schemes of his works, and afterwards, to the elaboration of every line which he published.

The generation of the Decembrists surely would have introduced social and political ideas in the novel. But that generation had perished, and Gógol was now the first to introduce the social element into Russian literature, so as to give it its prominent and dominating position. While it remains an open question whether realism in the Russian novel does not date from Púshkin, rather than from Gógol—this, in fact, is the view of both Turguéneff and Tolstóy—there is yet no doubt that it was Gógol's writings which introduced into Russian literature the social element, and social criticism based upon the analysis of the conditions within Russia itself. The peasant novels of Grigoróvitch, Turguéneff's *Sportsman's Notebook*, and the first works of Dostoyévskiy were a direct outcome of Gógol's initiative.

Realism in art was much discussed some time ago, in connection chiefly with the first writings of Zola; but we Russians, who had had Gógol and knew realism in its best form, could not fall in with the views of the French realists. We saw in Zola a tremendous amount of the same romanticism which he combated; and in his realism, such as it appeared in his writings of the first period, we saw a step backwards from the realism of Balzac. For us, realism could not be limited to a mere anatomy of society: it had to have a higher background; the realistic description had to be made subservient to an idealistic aim. Still less could we understand realism as a description only of the lowest aspects of life, because to limit one's observations to the lowest aspects only, is *not* to be a realist. Real life has beside and even within its lowest manifestations its highest ones as well. Degeneracy is not the sole nor dominant feature of modern society, if we look at it as a whole. Consequently, the artist who limits his observations to the lowest and most degenerate aspects only, and, if he does that for a special purpose, does not make us understand that he explores only one small corner of life—such an artist does not conceive life *as it is*: he knows but one aspect of it, and this is not the most interesting one.

Realism in France was certainly a necessary protest, partly against unbridled romanticism, but chiefly against the elegant art which glided on the surface and refused to glance at the often most inelegant motives of the so-called correct and elegant life. For Russia this protest was not necessary. Since Gógol, art could not be limited to any class of society. It was bound to embody them all, to treat them all realistically, and to penetrate beneath the surface of social relations.

Therefore there was no need of the exaggeration which in France was a necessary and sound reaction. There was no need, moreover, to fall into extremes in order to free art from dull moralisation. Our great realist, Gógol, had already shown to his followers how realism can be put to the service of higher aims, without losing anything of its penetration or ceasing to be a true reproduction of life.

CHAPTER IV

TURGUÉNEFF—TOLSTÓY

TURGUÉNEFF: the main features of his art—*A Sportsman's Notebook*—Pessimism of his early novels—His series of novels representing the leading types of Russian society—Rúdin—Lavrétskiy—Helen and Insároff—Bazároff—Why *Fathers and Sons* was misunderstood—*Hamlet and Don Quixote*—*Virgin Soil*: movement towards the people—*Verses in Prose.* TOLSTÓY: *Childhood* and *Boyhood*—During and after the Crimean War—*Youth*: in search of an ideal—Small stories—*The Cossacks*—Educational work—*War and Peace*—*Anna Karénina*—Religious crisis—His interpretation of the Christian teaching—Main points of Christian ethics—Latest works of art—*Kreutzer Sonata*—*Resurrection*—Leaving his home.

TURGUÉNEFF

PÚSHKIN, Lérmontoff, and Gógol were the real creators of Russian literature; but to Western Europe they remained nearly total strangers. It was only Turguéneff and Tolstóy—the two greatest novelists of Russia, if not of their century altogether—and, to some extent, Dostoyévskiy, who broke down the barrier of language which had kept Russian writers unknown to West Europeans. They have made Russian literature familiar and popular outside Russia; they have exercised and still exercise their share of influence upon West European thought and art; and owing to them, we may be sure that henceforward the best productions of the Russian mind will be part of the general intellectual belongings of civilised mankind.

For the artistic construction, the finish and the beauty of his novels, Turguéneff was very probably the greatest novel-writer of his century. However, the chief characteristic of his poetical genius lay not only in that sense of the beautiful which he possessed to so high a degree, but also in the highly *intellectual* contents of his creations. His novels are not mere stories dealing at random with this or that type of men, or with some particular current of life, or accident happening to fall under the author's observation. They are intimately connected with each other, and they give the succession of the leading intellectual types of Russia which have impressed their own stamp upon each successive generation. The novels of Turguéneff, of which the first appeared in 1845, cover a period of more than thirty years, and during these three decades Russian society underwent one of the deepest and the most rapid modifications ever witnessed in European history. The leading types of the educated classes went through successive changes with a rapidity which was only possible in a society suddenly awakening from a long slumber, casting away an institution which hitherto had permeated its whole existence (I mean serfdom), and rushing towards a new life. And this succession of 'history-making' types was represented by Turguéneff with a depth of conception, a fullness of philosophical and humanitarian understanding, and an artistic insight, almost equal to foresight, which are found in none of the modern writers to the same extent and in that happy combination.

Not that he would follow a preconceived plan. 'All these discussions about "tendency" and "unconsciousness" in art,' he wrote, 'are nothing but a debased coin of rhetorics. . . . Those only who cannot do better will submit to a preconceived programme, because a truly talented writer is the condensed expression of life itself, and he cannot write either a panegyric or a pamphlet : either would be too mean for him.' But as soon as a new leading type of men or women appeared amidst the educated classes of Russia, it took possession of Turguéneff. He was haunted by it, and haunted until he had succeeded in representing it to the best of his understanding in a work of art, just as for years Murillo was haunted by the image of a Virgin in the ecstasy of purest love, until he finally succeeded in rendering on the canvas his full conception.

When some human problem had thus taken possession of Turguéneff's mind, he evidently could not discuss it in terms of logic—this would have been the manner of the political writer—he conceived it in the shape of images and scenes. Even in his conversation, when he intended to give you an idea of some problem which worried his mind, he used to do it by describing a scene so vividly that it would for ever engrave itself in the memory. This was also a marked trait in his writings. His novels are a succession of scenes—some of them of the most exquisite beauty—each of which helps him further to characterise his heroes. Therefore all his novels are short, and need no plot to sustain the reader's attention. Those who have been perverted by sensational novel-reading may, of course, be disappointed with a want of sensational episode; but the ordinary intelligent reader feels from the very first pages that he has *real* and interesting men and women before him, with really human hearts throbbing in them, and he cannot part with the book before he has reached the end and grasped the characters in full. Simplicity of means for accomplishing far-reaching ends—that chief feature of truly good art—is felt in everything Turguéneff wrote.

George Brandes, in his admirable study of Turguéneff (in *Moderne Geister*), the best, the deepest, and the most poetical of all that has been written about the great novelist, makes the following remark :

'It is not easy to say quite definitely what makes of Turguéneff an artist of the first rank. . . . That he has in the highest degree the capacity which makes a true poet, of producing living human beings, does not, after all, comprise everything. What makes the reader feel so much his artistic superiority is the concordance one feels between the interest taken by the poet in the person whom he depicts, or the poet's judgment about this person, and the impression which the reader himself gets ; because it is in this point—the relation of the artist to his own creations—that every weakness of either the man or the poet must necessarily appear.'

The reader feels every such mistake at once and keeps the remembrance of it, notwithstanding all the efforts of the author to dissipate its impression.

'What reader of Balzac, or of Dickens, or of Auerbach—to speak of the great dead only—does not know this feeling?' Brandes continues. 'When Balzac swims in warmed-up excitement, or when Dickens becomes childishly touching, and Auerbach intentionally naïve, the reader feels repulsed by the untrue, the unpleasant. Never do we meet with anything artistically repulsive in Turguéneff.'

This remark of the great critic is absolutely true, and only a few words need be added to it, with reference to the wonderful architecture of all Turguéneff's novels. Be it a small novel, or a large one, the proportion of the parts is wonderfully held ; not a single episode of a merely 'ethnographical' character comes in to disturb or to slacken the development of the inner human drama ; not one feature, and certainly not one single scene, can be omitted without destroying the impression of the whole ; and the final accord, which seals the usually touching general impression, is always worked out with wonderful finish.[1]

And then the beauty of the chief scenes. Every one of them could be made the subject of a most artistic and telling picture. Take, for instance, the final scenes of Helen and Insároff in Venice : their visit to the picture gallery, which made the keeper exclaim, as he looked at them, *Poveretti!* or the scene in the theatre, where in response to the imitated cough of the actress

---

[1] The only exception to be made is the scene with the two old people in *Virgin Soil.* It is useless and out of place. To have introduced it was simply 'a literary whim.'

(who played Violetta in *Traviata*) resounded the deep, real cough of the dying Insároff. The actress herself, with her poor dress and bony shoulders, who yet took possession of the audience by the warmth and reality of her feeling, and created a storm of enthusiasm by her cry of dying joy on the return of Alfred ; nay, I should even say, the dark harbour where one sees the gull drop from rosy light into the deep blackness of the night—each of these scenes comes to the imagination on canvas. In his lecture, *Hamlet and Don Quixote*, where he speaks of Shakespeare and Cervantes being contemporaries, and mentions that the romance of Cervantes was translated into English in Shakespeare's lifetime, so that he might have read it, Turguéneff exclaims : ' What a picture, worthy of the brush of a thoughtful painter : Shakespeare reading Don Quixote ! ' It would seem as if in these lines he betrayed the secret of the wonderful beauty—the pictorial beauty—of such a number of his scenes. He must have imagined them, not only with the music of the feeling that speaks in them, but also as *pictures*, full of a fine psychological meaning and in which all the surroundings of the main figures—the Russian birch wood, or the German town on the Rhine, or the harbour of Venice—are in harmony with the feeling.

Turguéneff knew the human heart deeply, especially the heart of a young, thoroughly honest, and reasoning girl when she awakes to higher feelings and ideas, and that awakening takes, without her realising it, the shape of love. In the description of that moment of life Turguéneff stands quite unrivalled. On the whole, love is the leading motive of all his novels ; and the moment of its full development is the moment when his hero —he may be a political agitator or a modest squire— appears in full light. The great poet knew that a human type cannot be characterised by the daily work in which such a man is engaged—however important that work may be—and still less by a flow of words.

Consequently, when he draws, for instance, the picture of an agitator in *Dmitri Rúdin*, he does not report his fiery speeches—for the simple reason that the agitator's words would not have characterised him. Many have pronounced the same appeals to Equality and Liberty before him, and many more will pronounce them after his death. But that special type of apostle of equality and liberty—the 'man of the word and of no action' which he intended to represent in Rúdin—is characterised by the hero's relations to different persons, and particularly, above all, by his love. By his love—because it is in love that the human being appears in full, with its individual features. Thousands of men have made 'propaganda by word,' all very much in the same expressions, but each of them has loved in a different way. Mazzini and Lassalle did similar work; but how different they were in their loves! You do not know Lassalle unless you know his relations to the Countess of Hatzfeld.

In common with all great writers, Turguéneff combined the qualities of a pessimist and a lover of mankind.

'There flows a deep and broad stream of melancholy in Turguéneff's mind,' remarks Brandes, 'and therefore it flows also through all his works. Though his description be objective and impersonal, and although he hardly ever introduces into his novels lyric poetry, nevertheless they produce on the whole the impression of lyrics. There is so much of Turguéneff's own personality expressed in them, and this personality is always sadness—a specific sadness without a touch of sentimentality. Never does Turguéneff give himself up entirely to his feelings: he impresses by restraint ; but no West European novelist is so sad as he is. The great melancholists of the Latin race, such as Leopardi and Flaubert, have hard, fast outlines in their style; the German sadness is of a caustic humour, or it is pathetic, or sentimental; but Turguéneff's melancholy is, in its substance, the melancholy of the Slavonian races in its weakness and tragical aspect, it is a descendant in a straight line from the melancholy of the Slavonian folk-song. . . . When Gógol is melancholy, it is from de-

spair.   When Dostoyévskiy expresses the same feeling, it is because his heart bleeds with sympathy for the down-trodden,
and especially for great sinners.   Tolstóy's melancholy has its
foundation in his religious fatalism.   Turguéneff alone is a
philosopher. . . . He loves man, even though he does not
think much of him and does not trust him very much.'

The full force of Turguéneff's talent appeared already
in his earlier productions—that is, in the series of short
sketches from village life, to which the misleading title
of *A Sportsman's Notebook* was given in order to avoid
the rigours of censorship.   Notwithstanding the simplicity of their contents and the total absence of the
satirical element, these sketches gave a decided blow to
serfdom.   Turguéneff did not describe in them such
atrocities of serfdom as might have been considered
mere exceptions to the rule ; nor did he idealise the
Russian peasant ; but by giving life-portraits of sensible,
reasoning, and loving beings, bent down under the yoke
of serfdom, together with life-pictures of the shallowness
and meanness of the life of the serf-owners—even the
best of them—he awakened the consciousness of the
wrong done by the system.   The social influence of
these sketches was profound.   As to their artistic qualities, suffice it to say that in these short sketches we
find in a few pages vivid pictures of a great variety of
human characters, together with most beautiful sketches
of nature.   Contempt, admiration, sympathy, or deep
sadness are impressed in turns on the reader at the will
of the young author—each time, however, in such a
form and by such vivid scenes that each of these short
sketches is worth a good novel.

In the series of short novels, *A Quiet Corner, Correspondence, Yákov Pásynkov, Faust,* and *Asya,* all dated
1854 and 1855, the genius of Turguéneff revealed itself
fully : his manner, his inner self, his powers.   A deep
sadness pervades these novels.   A sort of despair in the
educated Russian, who, even in his love, appears utterly
incapable of a strong feeling which would carry away all

obstacles, and always manages, even when circumstances favour him, to bring the woman who loves him to grief and despair. The following lines from *Correspondence* characterise best the leading idea of three of these novels : *A Quiet Corner, Correspondence,* and *Asya.* It is a girl of twenty-six who writes to a friend of her childhood :

'Again I repeat that I do not speak of the girl who finds it difficult and hard to think. . . . She looks round, she expects, and asks herself, when the one whom her soul is longing for will come. . . . At last he appears : she is carried away by him ; she is like soft wax in his hands. Happiness, love, thought—all these come now in streams ; all her unrest is settled, all doubts resolved by him ; truth itself seems to speak through his lips. She worships him, she feels ashamed of her own happiness, she learns, she loves. Great is his power over her at that time ! . . . If he were a hero he could have fired her, taught her how to sacrifice herself, and all sacrifices would have been easy for her ! But there are no heroes nowadays. . . . Still, he leads her wherever he likes ; she takes to what interests him ; each of his words penetrates into her soul—she does not know yet how insignificant and empty, how false, words can be, how little they cost the one who pronounces them, how little they can be trusted. Then, following these first moments of happiness and hopes, comes usually— owing to circumstances (circumstances are always the fault)— comes usually the separation. I have heard it said that there have been cases when the two kindred souls have united immediately ; I have also heard that they did not always find happiness in that . . . however, I will not speak of what I have not seen myself. But—the fact that calculation of the pettiest sort and the most miserable prudence can live in a young heart by the side of the most passionate exaltation, this I have unfortunately learned from experience. So the separation comes. . . . Happy the girl who at once sees that this is the end of all, and will not soothe herself by expectations ! But you, brave and just men, you mostly have not the courage, nor the desire, to tell us the truth . . . it is easier for you to deceive us . . . or, after all, I am ready to believe that, together with us, you deceive yourselves.'

A complete despair in the capacity for action of the educated man in Russia runs through all the novels of this period. Those few men who seem to be an exception—those who have energy, or stimulate it for a short time—generally end their lives in the billiard-room of the public-house, or spoil their existences in some other way. The years 1854 and 1855, when these novels were written, fully explain the pessimism of Turguéneff. In Russia they were perhaps the darkest years of that dark period of Russian history, the reign of Nicholas I.; and in Western Europe, too, the years closely following the *coup d'état* of Napoleon III. were years of a general reaction after the great unrealised hopes of 1848.

Turguéneff, who came very near being marched to Siberia in 1852 for having printed at Moscow his innocent necrological note about Gógol, after it had been forbidden by the St. Petersburg censorship, was compelled to live now on his estate, beholding round him the servile submissiveness of all those who had formerly shown some signs of revolt. Seeing all round the triumph of the supporters of serfdom and despotism, he might easily have been brought to despair. But the sadness which pervades the novels of this period was not a cry of despair; it was not a satire either; it was the gentle touch of a loving friend, and that constitutes their main charm. From the artistic point of view, *Asya* and *Correspondence* are perhaps the finest gems which we owe to Turguéneff.

To judge of the importance of Turguéneff's work one must read in succession—so he himself desired—his six novels: *Dmitri Rúdin, A Nobleman's Retreat* (*Une Nichée de Gentilshommes,* or *Líza,* in Mr. Ralston's version), *On the Eve, Fathers and Sons, Smoke,* and *Virgin Soil.* In them one sees his poetical powers in full; at the same time one gets an insight into the different aspects which intellectual life took in Russia from 1848 to 1876, and one understands the poet's attitude towards the best representatives of advanced thought in Russia during that most interesting period of her development. In some of his earlier short tales Turguéneff had already touched upon Hamletism in Russian life. In his *Hamlet of the Schigróvsky District* and his *Diary of a Useless Man* he had already given admirable sketches of that sort of man. But it was in *Rúdin* (1855) that he achieved the full artistic representation of that type which had grown upon Russian soil with especial profusion at a time when our best men were condemned to inactivity and— words. Turguéneff did not spare men of that type ; he represented them with their worst features, as well as with their best, and yet he treated them with tenderness. He loved Rúdin, with all his defects, and in this love he was at one with the best men of his generation, and of ours too.

Rúdin was a man of the forties, nurtured upon Hegel's philosophy, and developed under the conditions which prevailed under Nicholas I., when there was no possibility whatever for a thinking man to apply his energy, unless he chose to become an obedient functionary of an autocratic, slave-owning state. The scene is laid in one of the estates in Middle Russia, in the family of a lady who takes a superficial interest in all sorts of novelties, reads books that are prohibited by the censorship, such as Tocqueville's *Democracy in America*, and must always have round her, in her *salon*, whether it be in the capital or on her estate, all sorts of men of mark. It is in her drawing-room that Rúdin makes his first appearance. In a few moments he becomes master of the conversation, and by his intelligent remarks to the point wins the ad- miration of the hostess and the sympathy of the younger generation. The latter is represented by the daughter of the lady and by a young student who is the tutor of her boys. Both are entirely captivated by Rúdin. When he speaks, later on in the evening, of his student years, and touches upon such taking subjects as liberty, free thought, and the struggles in Western Europe for free- dom, his words are full of so much fire, so much poetry and enthusiasm, that the two younger people listen to him with a feeling which approaches worship. The result is evident : Natásha, the daughter, falls in love with him. Rúdin is much older than Natásha—silver streaks already appear in his beautiful hair, and he speaks of love as of something which, for him, belongs to the past. 'Look at this oak,' he says ; 'the last autumn's leaves still cover it, and they will never fall off until the young green leaves have made their appearance.' Natásha understands this in the sense that Rúdin's old love can only fade away when a new one has taken its place—and gives him her love. Breaking with all the traditions of the strictly correct house of her mother, she gives an interview to Rúdin in the early morning on the banks of a remote pond. She is ready to follow him anywhere, anyhow, without making any conditions ; but he, whose love is more in his brain than in his heart, finds nothing to say to her but to talk about the impossibility of obtaining the permission of her mother for this marriage. Natásha hardly listens to his words. She would follow him with or without the consent of her mother, and asks : 'What is then to be done ?'—'To submit,' is Rúdin's reply.

The hero who spoke so beautifully about fighting against all possible obstacles has broken down before the first obstacle that appeared in his way. Words, words, and no actions, was indeed the characteristic of these men, who in the forties represented the best thinking element of Russian society.

Later on we meet Rúdin once more. He has still found no work for himself, neither has he made peace with the conditions of life at that time. He remains poor, exiled by the government from one town to another, till at last he goes abroad, and during the insurrection of June 1848 he is killed on a barricade in Paris. There is an epilogue to the novel, and that epilogue is so beautiful that a few passages from it must be produced here. It is Lézhneff, formerly Rúdin's enemy, who speaks.

'I know him well,' continued Lézhneff, 'I am aware of his faults. They are the more conspicuous because he is not to be regarded on a small scale.'[1]

'His is a character of genius!' cried Bassístoff.[2]

'Genius very likely he has!' replied Lézhneff, 'but as for character, . . . That's just his misfortune: there's no force of character in him.[2] . . . But I want to speak of what is good, of what is rare in him. He has enthusiasm; and, believe me, who am a phlegmatic person enough, that is the most precious quality in our times. We have all become insufferably reasonable, indifferent, and slothful; we are asleep and cold, and thanks to any one who will wake us up and warm us! It is high time! Do you remember, Sásha, once when I was talking to you about him, I blamed him for coldness? I was right, and wrong too, then. The coldness is in his blood—that is not his fault—and not in his head. He is not an actor, as I called him, nor a cheat, nor a scoundrel; he lives at other people's expense, not like a swindler, but like a child. . . . Yes; no doubt he will die somewhere in poverty and want; but are we to throw stones at him for that? He never does anything himself precisely, he has no vital force, no blood; but who has the right to say that he has not been of use, that his words have not scattered good seeds in young hearts, to whom nature has not denied, as she has to him, powers for action, and the faculty of carrying out their own ideas? Indeed, I myself, to begin with, have gained all that I have from him. Sásha knows what Rúdin did for me in my youth. I also maintained, I recollect, that Rúdin's words could not produce an effect on men; but I was speaking then of men like myself, at my present age, of men who have already lived and been broken in by life. One false note in a man's eloquence, and the whole harmony is spoiled for us; but a young man's ear, happily, is not so over-fine, not so trained. If the substance of what he hears seems fine to him, what does he care about the intonation? The intonation he will supply for himself!'

'Bravo, bravo!' cried Bassístoff, 'that is justly spoken! And as regards Rúdin's influence, I swear to you, that man not only knows how to move you, he lifts you up; he does not let you stand still, he stirs you to the depths and sets you on fire!'

---

[1] Taken from the excellent translation by Mrs. Constance Garnett, in Heinemann's edition of Turguéneff's Works.

[2] I slightly alter Mrs. Garnett's rendering of this difficult passage.

However, with such men as Rúdin further progress in Russia would have been impossible : new men had to appear. And so they did : we find them in the subsequent novels of Turguéneff—but what difficulties they meet with, what pains they undergo ! This we see in Lavrétskiy and Líza (*A Nobleman's Retreat*), who belonged to the intermediate period. Lavrétskiy could not be satisfied with Rúdin's rôle of an errant apostle ; he tried his hands at practical activity ; but he also could not find his way amidst the new currents of life. He had the same artistic and philosophical development as Rúdin ; he had the necessary will ; but his powers of action were palsied—not by his power of analysis in this case, but by the mediocrity of his surroundings and by his unfortunate marriage. Lavrétskiy ends also in wreck.

A Nobleman's Retreat was an immense success. It was said that, together with the autobiographic tale, *First Love*, it was the most artistic of Turguéneff's works. This, however, is hardly so. Its great success was surely due, first of all, to the wide circle of readers to whom it appealed. Lavrétskiy has married most unfortunately —a lady who soon becomes a sort of second-rate Parisian lioness. They separate ; and then he meets with a girl, Líza, in whom Turguéneff has given the best impersonation imaginable of the average, thoroughly good and honest Russian girl of those times. She and Lavrétskiy fall in love with each other. For a moment both she and Lavrétskiy think that the latter's wife is dead—so it stood, at least, in a Paris *feuilleton* ; but the lady reappears bringing with her all her abominable atmosphere, and Líza goes to a convent. Unlike Rúdin or Bazároff, all the persons of this drama, as well as the drama itself, are quite familiar to the average reader, and for merely that reason the novel appealed to an extremely wide circle of sympathisers. Of course, the artistic powers of Turguéneff appear with a wonderful force in the representation of such types as Líza and Lavrétskiy's wife, Líza's old aunt, and Lavrétskiy himself. Altogether, the artistic finish and the fine chiselling of both the main characters and the secondary ones, as well as the note of poetry and sadness which pervade this novel, make of it one of the finest works of art. And yet, I venture to say, the following novel, *On the Eve*, superseded the former in the depth of its conception and hardly remained behind it in the beauty of its workmanship.

Already, in Natásha, Turguéneff had given a life-picture of a Russian girl who has grown up in the quietness of village life, but has in her heart, and mind, and will, the germs of that which moves human beings to higher action. Rúdin's spirited words, his appeals to what is grand and worth living for, inflamed her. She was ready to follow him, to support him in the great work which he so eagerly and uselessly searched for, but it was he who proved to be her inferior. Turguéneff thus foresaw, since 1855, the coming of that type of woman who later on played so prominent a part in the revival of Young Russia. Four years later, in *On the Eve*, he gave, in Helen, a further and fuller development of the same type. Helen is not satisfied with the dull, trifling life in her own family, and she longs for a wider sphere of action. 'To be good is not enough ; to do good—yes ; that is the great thing in life,' she writes in her diary. But whom does she meet in her surroundings ? Shúbin, a talented artist, a spoiled child, 'a butterfly which admires itself' ; Berséneff, a future professor, a true Russian nature—an excellent man, most unselfish and modest, but wanting inspiration, totally lacking in vigour and initiative. These two are the best. There is a moment when Shúbin, as he rambles on a summer night with his friend Berséneff, says to him : ' I love Helen, but Helen loves you. . . . Sing, sing louder, if you can ; and if you cannot, then take off your hat, look above, and smile to the stars. They all look upon you, upon you alone : they always look on those who are in love.' But Berséneff returns to his small room, and—opens Raumer's ' History of the

Hohenstauffens,' on the same page where he had left it the last time. . . .

Thereupon appears Insároff, a Bulgarian patriot, entirely absorbed by *one* idea—the liberation of his mother country ; a man of steel, rude to the touch, who has cast away all melancholy philosophical dreaming, and marches straight forward, towards the aim of his life—and the choice of Helen is settled. The pages given to the awakening of her feeling and to its growth are among the best ever written by Turguéneff. When Insároff suddenly becomes aware of his own love for Helen, his first decision is to leave at once the suburb of Moscow, where they are all staying, and Russia as well. He goes to Helen's house to announce there his departure. Helen asks him to promise that he will see her again to-morrow before he leaves, but he does not promise. Helen waits for him, and when he has not come in the afternoon, she herself goes to him. Rain and thunder overtake her on the road, and she steps into an old chapel by the roadside. There she meets Insároff, and the explanation between the shy, modest girl who perceives that Insároff loves her, and the patriot, who discovers in her the force which, far from standing in his way, would only double his own energy, terminates by Insároff exclaiming : ' Well, then, welcome, my wife, before God and men ! '

In Helen we have the true type of that Russian woman who a few years later joined heart and soul in all movements for Russian freedom : the woman who conquered her right to knowledge, totally reformed the education of children, fought for the liberation of the toiling masses, endured unbroken in the snows and gaols of Siberia, died if necessary on the scaffold, and at the present moment continues with unabated energy the same struggle. The high artistic beauty of this novel has already been incidentally mentioned. Only one reproach can be made to it : the hero, Insároff, the man of action, is not sufficiently living. But both for the general architecture of the novel and the beauty of its separate scenes, beginning with the very first and ending with the last, *On the Eve* stands among the highest productions of the sort in all literatures.

The next novel of Turguéneff was *Fathers and Sons.* It was written in 1859 when, instead of the sentimentalists and 'æsthetical' people of old, quite a new type of man was making its appearance in the educated portion of Russian society—the nihilist. Those who have not read Turguéneff's works will perhaps associate the word 'nihilist' with the struggle which took place in Russia in 1879-1881 between the autocratic power and the terrorists ; but this would be a great mistake. 'Nihilism' is not 'terrorism,' and the type of the nihilist is infinitely deeper and wider than that of a terrorist. Turguéneff's *Fathers and Sons* must be read in order to understand it. The representative of this type in the novel is a young doctor, Bazároff—'a man who bows before no authority, however venerated it may be, and accepts of no principle unproved.' Consequently he takes a negative attitude towards all the institutions of the present time, and he throws overboard all the conventionalities and the petty lies of ordinary society life. He comes on a visit to his old parents and stays also at the country-house of a young friend of his, whose father and uncle are two typical representatives of the old generation. This gives to Turguéneff the possibility of illustrating in a series of masterly scenes the conflict between the two generations—'the fathers' and 'the sons.' The same conflict was going on in those years with bitter acrimony all over Russia.

One of the two brothers, Nikolái Petróvitch, is an excellent, slightly enthusiastic dreamer who in his youth was fond of Schiller and Púshkin, but never took great interest in practical matters ; he now lives, on his estate, the lazy life of a landowner. He would like, however, to show to the young people that he, too, can go a long way with them : he tries to read the materialistic books which his son and Bazároff read, and even to speak their language ; but his entire education stands in the way of a true 'realistic' comprehension of the real state of affairs.

The elder brother, Pável Petróvitch, is, on the contrary, a direct descendant from Lérmontoff's Petchórin —that is, a thorough, well-bred egotist. Having spent his youth in high society circles, he, even now in the dullness of the small country estate, considers it as a 'duty' to be always properly dressed 'as a perfect gentleman,' strictly to obey the rules of 'Society,' to remain faithful to Church and State, and never to abandon his attitude of extreme reserve—which he abandons, however, every time that he enters into a discussion about 'principles' with Bazároff. The 'nihilist' inspires him with hatred.

The nihilist is, of course, the out-and-out negation of all the 'principles' of Pável Petróvitch. He does not believe in the established principles of Church and State, and openly professes a profound contempt for all the established forms of society life. He does not see that the wearing of a clean collar and a perfect necktie should be described as the performance of a duty. When he speaks, he says what he thinks. Absolute sincerity—not only in what he says, but also towards himself—and a common-sense standard of judgments, without the old prejudices, are the ruling features of his character. This leads, evidently, to a certain assumed roughness of expression, and the conflict between the two generations must necessarily take a tragical aspect. So it was everywhere in Russia at that time. The novel expressed the real tendency of the time and accentuated it, so that—as has been remarked by a gifted Russian critic, S. Venguéroff—the novel and the reality mutually influenced each other.

Fathers and Sons produced a tremendous impression. Turguéneff was assailed on all sides : by the old generation, which reproached him with being 'a nihilist himself,' and by the youth, which was discontented at being identified with Bazároff. The truth is that, with a very few exceptions, among whom was the great critic, Písareff, the young generation did not properly understand Bazároff. Turguéneff had so much accustomed us to a certain poetical halo which surrounded his heroes, and to his own tender love which followed them, even when he condemned them, that finding nothing of the sort in his attitude towards Bazároff, we saw in the absence of these features a hostility of the author towards the hero. Moreover, certain features of Bazároff decidedly displeased us. Why should a man of his powers display such a harshness towards his old parents, his loving mother and his father—the poor old village doctor who has retained, to old age, faith in his science? Why should Bazároff fall in love with that most uninteresting, self-admiring lady, Madame Odintsóff, and fail to be loved, even by her? And then why, at a time when in the young generation the seeds of a great movement towards freeing the masses were already ripening, why make Bazároff say that he is ready to work for the peasant, but if somebody comes and says to him that he is bound to do so, he will hate that peasant? To which Bazároff adds, in a moment of reflection: 'And what of that? Grass will grow out of me when this peasant acquires well-being!' We did not understand this attitude of Turguéneff's Nihilist, and it was only on rereading *Fathers and Sons* much later on that we noticed, in the very words that so offended us, the germs of a realistic philosophy of solidarity and duty which only now begins to take a more or less definite shape. In 1860 we, the young generation, looked on it as Turguéneff's desire to throw a stone at a new type with which he did not sympathise.

And yet, as Písareff understood at once, Bazároff *was* a real representative of the young generation. Turguéneff, as he himself wrote later on, merely did not 'add syrup' to make his hero appear somewhat sweeter.

'Bazároff,' he wrote, 'puts all the other personalities of my novel in the shade. He is honest, straightforward, and a democrat of the purest water, and you find no good qualities in him! The duel with Pável Petróvitch is only introduced to show the intellectual emptiness of the elegant, noble knighthood; in fact, I even exaggerated and made it ridiculous. My conception of Bazároff is such as to make him appear throughout much superior to Pável Petróvitch. Nevertheless, when he calls himself nihilist you must read *revolutionist*. To draw on one side a functionary who takes bribes, and on the other an ideal youth—I leave it to others to make such pictures. My aim was much higher than that. I conclude with one remark: If the reader is not won by Bazároff, notwithstanding his roughness, absence of heart, pitiless dryness and terseness, then the fault is with me—I have missed my aim; but to sweeten him with syrup (to use Bazároff's own language), this I did not want to do, although perhaps through that I would have won Russian youth at once to my side.'

The true key to the understanding of *Fathers and Sons*, and, in fact, of whatever Turguéneff wrote, is given, I will permit myself to suggest, in his admirable lecture, *Hamlet and Don Quixote* (1860). I have already elsewhere intimated this; but I am bound to repeat it here, as I think that, better than any other of Turguéneff's writings, this lecture enables us to look into the very philosophy of the great novelist.

Hamlet and Don Quixote—Turguéneff wrote—personify the two opposite particularities of human nature. All men belong more or less to the one or to the other of these two types. And, with his powers of analysis, he thus characterised the two heroes:

'Don Quixote is imbued with devotion towards his ideal, for which he is ready to suffer all possible privations, to sacrifice his life; life itself he values only so far as it can serve for the incarnation of the ideal, for the promotion of truth, of justice on Earth. . . . He lives for his brothers, for opposing the forces hostile to mankind: the witches, the giants—that is, the oppressors. . . . Therefore he is fearless, patient ; he is satisfied with the most modest food, the poorest cloth : he has other things to think of. Humble in his heart, he is great and daring in his mind. . . .' 'And who is Hamlet? Analysis, first of all, and egotism, and therefore no faith. He lives entirely for himself, he is an egotist ; but to believe in one's self—even an egotist cannot do that : we can believe only in something which is outside us and above us. . . . As he has doubts of everything, Hamlet evidently does not spare himself ; his intellect is too developed to remain satisfied with what he finds in himself : he feels his weakness, but each self-consciousness is a force ;—and therefrom his irony, the opposite of the enthusiasm of Don Quixote. . . .' 'Don Quixote—a poor man, almost a beggar, without means and relations, old, isolated—undertakes to redress all the evils and to protect oppressed strangers all over the earth. What does it matter to him that his first attempt at freeing the innocent from his oppressor falls twice as heavy upon the head of the innocent himself? . . . What does it matter that, thinking that he has to deal with noxious giants, Don Quixote attacks useful windmills? . . . Nothing of the sort can ever happen with Hamlet : how could he, with his perspicacious, refined, sceptical mind, ever commit such a mistake! No, he will not fight with windmills, he does not believe in giants . . . but he would not have attacked them even if they did exist. . . . And yet, although Hamlet is a sceptic, although he disbelieves in good, he does not believe in evil. Evil and deceit are his inveterate enemies. His scepticism is not indifferentism. . . .' 'But in negation, as in fire, there is a destructive power, and how to keep it in bounds, how to tell it where to stop, when that which it must destroy, and that which it must spare, are often inseparably welded together? Here it is that the often-noticed tragical aspect of human life comes in : for action we require will, and for action we require thought ; but thought and will have parted from each other, and separate every day more and more. . . .

> 'And thus the native hue of resolution
> Is sicklied o'er with the pale cast of thought. . . .'

This lecture fully explains, I believe, the attitude of Turguéneff towards Bazároff. He himself belonged to a great extent to the Hamlets. Among them he had his best friends. He loved Hamlet; yet he admired Don Quixote—the man of action. He felt his superiority; but, while describing this second type of men, he never could surround it with that tender poetical love for a sick friend which makes the irresistible attraction of those of his novels which deal with one or other of the Hamlet type. He admired Bazároff—his roughness as well as his power; Bazároff overpowered him; but he could by no means have for him the tender feelings which he had had for men of his own generation and his own refinement. In fact, with Bazároff they would have been out of place.

This we did not notice at that time, and therefore we did not understand Turguéneff's intention of representing the *tragic* position of Bazároff amidst his surroundings. 'I entirely share Bazároff's ideas,' he wrote, later on. 'All of them, with the exception of his negation of art.' 'I *loved* Bazároff; I will prove it to you by my diary,' he told me once in Paris. Certainly he loved him—but with an intellectually admiring love, quite different from the compassionate love which he had bestowed upon Rúdin and Lavrétskiy. This difference escaped us, and was the chief cause of the misunderstanding which was so painful to the great poet.

Turguéneff's next novel, *Smoke* (1867), need not be dwelt upon. One object he had in it was to represent the powerful type of a Russian society lioness, which had haunted him for years, and to which he returned several times, until he finally succeeded in finding for it, in *Spring Flood*, the fullest and the most perfect artistic expression. His other object was to picture in its true colours the shallowness—nay, the silliness—of that society of bureaucrats into whose hands Russia fell for the next twenty years. Deep despair in the future of Russia after the wreck of that great reform movement which had given to us the abolition of serfdom pervades the novel; a despair which can by no means be attributed entirely, or even chiefly, to the hostile reception of *Fathers and Sons* by the Russian youth, but must be sought for in the wreck of the great hopes which Turguéneff and his best friends had laid in the representatives of the reform movement of 1859-1863. This same despair made Turguéneff write *'Enough; from the Memoirs of a Dead Artist'* (1865), and the fantastic sketch, *'Ghosts'* (1867). He recovered from it only when he saw the birth in Russia of a new movement, 'towards the people!' which took place amongst our youth in the early seventies.

This movement he represented in his last novel of the above-mentioned series, *Virgin Soil* (1876). That he was fully sympathetic with it is self-evident; but the question, whether his novel gives a correct idea of the movement, must be answered to some extent in the negative—even though Turguéneff had, with his wonderful intuition, caught some of the most striking features of the movement. The novel was finished in 1876 (we read it, in a full set of proofs, at the house of P. L. Lavróff, in London, in the autumn of that year) —that means, two years before the great trial of those who were arrested for this agitation took place. And in 1876 no one could possibly have known the youth of our circles unless he had himself belonged to them. Consequently, *Virgin Soil* could only refer to the very beginnings of the movement. Besides, Turguéneff did not meet with any of the best representatives of it. Much of the novel is true, but the general impression it conveys is not precisely the impression which Turguéneff himself would have received if he had better known the Russian youth at that time.

With all the force of his immense talent, he could not supply by intuition the lack of knowledge. And yet he understood two characteristic features of the earliest part of the movement: misconception of the peasantry, the peculiar incapacity of most of the early promoters of the movement to understand the Russian peasant, on account of the bias of their false literary, historical, and social education ; and the Hamletism : the want of resolution, or rather 'resolution sicklied o'er with the pale cast of thought,' which really charac- terised the movement at its outset.   If Turguéneff had lived a few years more he surely would have noticed coming into the arena the new type of men of action —the new modification of the Insároff and Bazároff type, which grew up in proportion as the movement was taking firm root.   He had already perceived them through the dryness of official records of the trial of the ' Hundred-and-Ninety-Three,' and in 1878 he asked me to tell him all I knew about Mýshkin, one of the powerful individualities of that trial.

He did not live to accomplish this.   A disease which nobody understood and was mistaken for 'gout,' but which was in reality a cancer of the spinal cord, kept him for the last few years of his life an invalid, riveted to his couch.   Only his letters, full of thought and life, where sadness and merriment go on in turn, are what remains from his pen during that period of life, when he seems to have meditated upon several novels which he left unfinished or perhaps unwritten.   He died at Paris in 1883 at the age of sixty-five.

In conclusion, a few words, at least, must be said about his *Poems in Prose*, or *Senilia* (1882).   These are ' flying remarks, thoughts, images ' which he wrote down from 1878 onwards under the impression of this or that fact of his own personal life, or of public life.   Though written in prose, they are true pieces of excellent poetry, some of them real gems ; some deeply touching and as impressive as the best verses of the best poets (*Old Woman ; The Beggar ; Másha ; How Beautiful, how Fresh were the Roses*) ; while others (*Nature, The Dog*) are more characteristic of Turguéneff's philosophical conceptions than anything else he has written.   And finally, in *On the Threshold*, written a few months before his death, he expressed in most poetical accents his admiration of those women who gave their lives for the revolutionary movement and went on the scaffold, without being even understood at the time by those for whom they died.

TOLSTÓY—*CHILDHOOD* AND *BOYHOOD*

More than half a century ago, *i.e.* in 1852, the first story of Tolstóy, *Childhood*, soon followed by *Boyhood*, made its appearance in the monthly review, *The Contemporary*, with the modest signature, 'L. N. T.' The little story was a great success. It was imbued with such a charm; it had such freshness, and was so free of all the mannerism of the literary trade, that the unknown author at once became a favourite, and was placed by the side of Turguéneff and Gontcharóff.

There are excellent children stories in all languages. Childhood is the period of life with which many authors have best succeeded in dealing. And yet no one, perhaps, has so well described the life of children from within, from their own point of view, as Tolstóy did. With him, it is the child itself which expresses its childish feelings, and it does this so as to compel the reader to judge full-grown people from the child's point of view. Such is the realism of *Childhood* and *Boyhood*—that is, their richness in facts caught from real life—that a Russian critic, Písareff, developed quite a theory of education chiefly on the basis of the data contained in these two stories of Tolstóy's.

It is related somewhere that one day, during their rambles in the country, Turguéneff and Tolstóy came across an old hack of a horse which was finishing its days in a lonely field. Tolstóy entered at once into the feelings of the horse and began to describe its sad reflections so vividly, that Turguéneff, alluding to the then new ideas of Darwinism, could not help exclaiming, 'I am sure, Lyov Nikoláevitch, that you *must* have had horses among your ancestors!' In the capacity of entirely identifying himself with the feelings and the thoughts of the beings of whom he speaks, Tolstóy has but few rivals ; but with children this power of identification attains its highest degree.   The moment he speaks of children, Tolstóy becomes himself a child.

Childhood and *Boyhood* are, it is now known, autobiographical stories, in which only small details are altered, and in the boy Irténeff we have a glimpse of what L. N. Tolstóy was in his childhood.   He was born in 1828, in the estate of Yásnaya Polyána, which now enjoys universal fame, and for the first fifteen years of his life he remained, almost without interruption, an inhabitant of the country.   His father and grandfather—we know it now from Biryukóff's ' Biography '—are described in *War and Peace*, in Nicholas Róstoff and the old Count Róstoff respectively ; while his mother, who was born a Princess Volkhónskaya, is represented as Mary Bolkónskaya.   Leo Tolstóy lost his mother at the age of two and his father at the age of nine, and after that time his education was taken care of by a woman relative, T.A. Yergólskaya, in Yásnaya Polyána, and after 1840, at Kazáñ, by his aunt P. I. Yúshkova, whose house, we are told, must have been very much the same as the house of the Róstoffs in *War and Peace*.

Leo Tolstóy was only fifteen when he entered the Kazáñ University, where he spent two years in the Oriental faculty and two years in the faculty of Law. However, the teaching staff of both faculties was so feeble at that time that only a single professor was able to awaken in the young man some passing interest in his subject.   Four years later, that is in 1847, when he was only nineteen, Leo Tolstóy had already left the University and was making at Yásnaya Polyána some attempts at improving the conditions of his peasant serfs, of which attempts he has told us later on, with such a striking sincerity, in *The Morning of a Landed Proprietor*.

The next four years of his life he spent, externally, like most young men of his aristocratic circle, but internally, in a continual reaction against the life he was leading. An insight into what he was then—slightly exaggerated, of course, and dramatised—we can get from the *Notes of a Billiard Marker*. Happily he could not put up with such paltry surroundings, and in 1851 he suddenly renounced the life he had hitherto led— that of an idle aristocratic youth—and following his brother Nicholas, he went to the Caucasus in order to enter military service. There he stayed first at Pyati-górsk—the place so full of reminiscences of Lérmontoff —until, having passed the necessary examinations, he was received as a non-commissioned officer (*junker*) in the artillery and went to serve in a Cossack village on the banks of the Térek.

His experiences and reflections in these new surround-ings we know from his *Cossacks*. But it was there also that, in the face of the beautiful nature which had so powerfully inspired Púshkin and Lérmontoff, he found his true vocation. He sent to the *Contemporary* his first literary experiment, *Childhood*, and this first story, as he soon learned from a letter of the poet Nekrásoff, editor of the review, and from the critical notes of Grigórieff, Annenkoff, Druzhínin, and Tchernyshévskiy (they belonged to four different æsthetical schools), proved to be a *chef-d'œuvre*.

DURING AND AFTER THE CRIMEAN WAR

However, the great Crimean war began towards the end of the next year (1853), and L. N. Tolstóy did not want to remain inactive in the Caucasus army. He obtained his transfer to the Danube army, took part in the siege of Silistria, and later on in the battle of Balakláva, and from November 1854 till August 1855 remained besieged in Sebastopol—partly in the terrible 'Fourth Bastion,' where he lived through all the dread-ful experiences of the heroic defenders of that fortress. He has therefore the right to speak of War : he knows it from within. He knows what it is, even under its best aspects, in such a significant and inspired phase as was the defence of these forts and bastions that had grown up under the enemy's shells. He obstinately refused during the siege to become an officer of the staff, and remained with his battery in the most dangerous spots.

I perfectly well remember, although I was only twelve or thirteen, the profound impression which his sketch, *Sebastopol in December* (1854)—followed, after the fall of the fortress, by two more Sebastopol sketches—produced in Russia. The very character of these sketches was original. They were not leaves from a diary, and yet they were as true to reality as such leaves could be ; in fact, even more true, because they were not representing one corner only of real life—the corner which accidentally fell under the writer's observations—but the whole life, the prevailing modes of thought and the habits of life in the besieged fortress. They represented —and this is characteristic of all subsequent works of Tolstóy—an interweaving of *Dichtung* and *Wahrheit*, of poetry and truth, truth and poetry, containing much more truth than is usually found in a novel, and more poetry, more poetical creation, than occurs in most works of pure fiction.

Tolstóy apparently never wrote in verse ; but during the siege of Sebastopol he composed, in the usual metre and language of soldiers' songs, a satirical song in which he described the blunders of the commanders which ended in the Balakláva disaster. The song, written in an admirable popular style, could not be printed, but it spread over Russia in thousands of copies, and was widely sung, both during and immediately after the campaign. The name of the author also leaked out, but there was some uncertainty as to whether it was the author of the Sebastopol sketches or some other Tolstóy.

On his return from Sebastopol and the conclusion of peace (1856) Tolstóy stayed partly at St. Petersburg and partly at Yásnaya Polyána. In the capital he was received with open arms by all classes of society, both literary and worldly, as a 'Sebastopol hero' and as a rising great writer. But of the life he lived then he could not speak later on otherwise than with disgust : it was the life of hundreds of young men—officers of the Guard and *jeunesse dorée* of his own class—which was passed in the restaurants and *cafés chantants* of the Russian capital, amidst gamblers, horse dealers, Tsigane choirs, and French adventuresses. He became at that time friendly with Turguéneff and saw much of him, both at St. Petersburg and at Yásnaya Polyána—the estates of the two great writers being not very far from each other ; but, although his friend Turguéneff was taking then a lively part in co-editing with Hérzen the famous revolutionary paper, *The Bell* (see chapter viii.), Tolstóy seems to have taken no interest in it ; and while he was well acquainted with the editing staff of the then famous review, *The Contemporary*, which was fighting the good fight for the liberation of the peasants and for freedom in general, Tolstóy, for one reason or another, never became friendly with the Radical leaders of that review—Tchernyshévskiy, Dobrolúboff, Mikháiloff, and their friends.

Altogether, the great intellectual and reform movement which was going on then in Russia seems to have left him cold. He did not join the party of reforms. Still less was he inclined to join those young Nihilists whom Turguéneff had portrayed to the best of his ability in *Fathers and Sons*, or, later on in the seventies, the youth whose watchword became 'Be the people,' and with whom Tolstóy had so much in common during the last twenty years of his life. What was the reason of that estrangement we are unable to say. Was it that a deep chasm separated the young epicurean aristocrat from the ultra-democratic writers, like Dobrolúboff, who worked at spreading socialistic and democratic ideas in Russia, and still more from those who, like Rakhmétoff in Tchernyshévskiy's novel *What is to be done*, lived the life of the peasant, thus practising then what Tolstóy began to preach twenty years later?

Or was it the difference between the two generations —the man of thirty or more, which Tolstóy was, and the young people in their early twenties, possessed of all the haughty intolerance of youth—which kept them aloof from each other? And was it not, in addition to all this, the result of theories? namely, a fundamental difference between the conceptions of the advanced Russian Radicals, who at that time were mostly admirers of Governmental Jacobinism, and the Rousseau-type Populist, which Tolstóy must have already then been—this tendency distinctly appearing in his negative attitude towards Western civilisation, and especially in the educational work which he began in 1861 in the Yásnaya Polyána school?

The novels which Tolstóy·brought out during these years, 1856-1862, do not throw much light upon his state of mind, because, even though they are to a great extent autobiographical, they mostly relate to earlier periods of his life. Thus he published two more of his Sebastopol war-sketches. All his powers of observation and war-psychology, all his deep comprehension of the Russian soldier, and especially of the plain, un-theatrical hero who really wins the battles, and a profound understanding of that inner spirit of an army upon which depend success and failure : everything, in short, which developed into the beauty and the truth-fulness of *War and Peace* was already manifested in these sketches, which undoubtedly represented a new departure in war-literature the world over.

YOUTH—IN SEARCH OF AN IDEAL

Youth, The Morning of a Landed Proprietor, and *Lucerne* appeared during the same years, but they produced upon us readers, as well as upon the literary critics, a strange and rather unfavourable impression. The great writer remained; his talent was showing evident signs of growth; and the problems of life which he touched upon were deepening and widening; but the heroes who seemed to represent the ideas of the author himself could not win our sympathies. In *Childhood* and *Boyhood* we had had before us the boy Irténeff. Now, in *Youth*, Irténeff makes the acquaintance of Prince Neklúdoff; they become great friends, and promise, without the slightest reservation, to confess to each other their moral failings. Of course, they do not always keep this promise; but it leads them to continual self-probing, to a repentance one moment which is forgotten the next, and to an unavoidable duality of mind which has the most debilitating effect upon the two young men's character. The ill results of these moral endeavours Tolstóy did not conceal. He detailed them with the greatest imaginable sincerity, but he seemed nevertheless to keep them before his readers as something desirable; and with this we could not agree.

Youth is certainly the age when higher moral ideals find their way into the mind of the future man or woman; the years when one strives to get rid of the imperfections of boyhood or girlhood; but this aim is never attained in the ways recommended at monasteries and Jesuit schools. The only proper way is to open before the young mind new, broad horizons; to free it from superstitions and fears; to grasp man's position amidst nature and mankind; and especially to feel at one with some great cause and to nurture one's forces with the view of being able some day to struggle for that cause. Idealism—that is, the capacity of conceiving a poetical love towards something great, and to prepare for it—is the only sure preservation from all that destroys the vital forces of man: vice, dissipation, and so on. This inspiration, this love of an ideal, the

Russian youth used to find in the student circles, of which Turguéneff has left us such spirited descriptions. Instead of that, Irténeff and Neklúdoff, remaining during their university years in their splendid aristocratic isolation, are unable to conceive a higher ideal worth living for, and spend their forces in vain endeavours of semi-religious moral improvement, on a plan that may perhaps succeed in the isolation of a monastery, but usually ends in failure amidst the attractions lying round a young man of the world. These failures Tolstóy relates, as usual, with absolute earnestness and sincerity.

The Morning of a Landed Proprietor produced, again, a strange impression. The story deals with the unsuccessful philanthropic endeavours of a serf-owner who tries to make his serfs happy and wealthy—without ever thinking of beginning where he ought to begin: namely, of setting his slaves free. In those years of liberation of the serfs and enthusiastic hopes, such a story sounded as an anachronism—the more so as it was not known at the time of its appearance that it was a page from Tolstóy's earlier autobiography relating to the year 1847, when he settled in Yásnaya Polyána, immediately after having left the University, and when extremely few were those who thought of liberating their serfs. It was one of those sketches of which Brandes has so truly said that in them Tolstóy 'thinks aloud' about some page of his own life. It thus produced a certain mixed, undefined feeling. And yet one could not but admire in it the same great objective talent that was so striking in *Childhood* and the Sebastopol sketches. In speaking of peasants who received with distrust the measures with which their lord was going to benefit them, it would have been so easy, so humanly natural, for an educated man to throw upon their ignorance their unwillingness to accept the threshing-machine (which, by the way, did not work), or the refusal of a peasant to accept the free gift of a stone house (which was far from the village). . . . But not a shade of that sort of pleading in favour of the landlord is to be found in the story, and the thinking reader necessarily concludes in favour of the common sense of the peasants.

Then came *Lucerne*. It is told in that story how the same Neklúdoff, bitterly struck by the indifference of a party of English tourists who sat on the balcony of a rich Swiss hotel and refused to throw even a few pennies to a poor singer to whose songs they had listened with evident emotion, brings the singer to the hotel, takes him to the dining-hall, to the great scandal of the English visitors, and treats him there to a bottle of champagne. The feelings of Neklúdoff are certainly very just; but while reading this story one suffers all the while for the poor musician, and experiences a sense of anger against the Russian nobleman who uses him as a rod to chastise the tourists, without even noticing how he makes the old man miserable during this lesson in morals. The worst of it is that the author, too, seems not to remark the false note which rings in the conduct of Neklúdoff, nor to realise how a man with really humane feelings would have taken the singer to some small wine-shop and would have had with him a friendly talk over a *picholette* of common wine. Yet we see again all Tolstóy's force of talent. He so honestly, so fully, and so truly describes the uneasiness of the singer during the whole scene that the reader's unavoidable conclusion is that although the young aristocrat was right in protesting against stone-heartedness, his ways were as unsympathetic as those of the self-contented Englishmen at the hotel. Tolstóy's artistic power carries him beyond and above his theories.

This is not the only case where such a remark may be made concerning Tolstóy's work. His appreciation of this or that action, of this or that of his heroes, may be wrong; his own 'philosophy' may be open to controversy;

but the force of his descriptive talent and his literary honesty are always so great, that he will often make the feelings and actions of his heroes speak against their creator, and prove something very different from what he intended to prove.[1] This is probably why Turgué-neff, and apparently other literary friends, too, told him : 'Don't put your " philosophy into your art." Trust to your artistic feeling, and you will create great things.' In fact, notwithstanding Tolstóy's distrust of science, I must say that I always feel in reading his works the likeness which exists between his mind and the mind of that most conscientious man of science, Darwin, who always tried to find out the weak points of his own hypotheses and to state them himself. True science and true art are not hostile to each other, they can work in harmony.

SMALL STORIES—*THE COSSACKS*

More novels and stories of Tolstóy appeared in the years 1857-1862 (*The Snow-storm, The Two Hussars, Three Deaths, The Cossacks*), and each one of them won new admiration for his talent. The first is a mere trifle, and yet it is a gem of art ; it concerns the wanderings of a traveller during a snow-storm, in the plains of Central Russia. The same remark is true of *The Two Hussars*, in which two generations are sketched on a few pages in striking contrast. As to the deeply pantheistic *Three Deaths*, in which the death of a rich lady, a poor horse-driver, and a birch-tree are contrasted, it is a piece of poetry in prose that deserves a place beside Goethe's best pieces of pantheistic poetry, while for its social signifi-

---

[1] This has struck most critics. Thus, speaking of *War and Peace*, Písareff wrote : ' The images he has created have their own life, independently of the intentions of the author ; they enter into direct relations with the reader, speak for themselves, and unavoidably bring the reader to such thoughts and conclusions as the author never had in view and of which he, perhaps, would not approve ' (*Works*, vi. p. 420).

cance it is already a forerunner of the Tolstóy of the later epoch.

The Cossacks is an autobiographical novel, and relates to the time, already mentioned on a previous page, when Tolstóy, at twenty-four, running away from the meaningless life he was living, went to Pyatigórsk, and then to a lonely Cossack village on the Térek, hunted there in company with the old Cossack Yeróshka and the young Lukáshka, and found in the poetical enjoyment of a beautiful nature, in the plain life of these squatters, and in the mute adoration of a Cossack girl, the awakening of his wonderful literary genius.

The appearance of this novel, in which one feels a most genuine touch of genius, provoked violent discussions. It was begun in 1852, but was not published till 1860, when Russia was awaiting with anxiety the results of the work of the Abolition of Serfdom Committees, foreseeing that when serfdom should be done away with, a complete destruction of all other rotten, obsolete, and barbarous institutions of past ages would have to begin. For this great work of reform Russia looked to Western civilisation for inspiration and for teachings. And there came a young writer who, following in the steps of Rousseau, revolted against that civilisation and preached a return to nature and the throwing off of the artificialities we call civilised life, which are in reality a poor substitute for the happiness of free work amidst a free nature. Every one knows by this time the dominant idea of *The Cossacks*. It is the contrast between the natural life of these sons of the prairies and the artificial life of the young officer thrown in their midst. He tells of strong men who are similar to the American squatters, and have been developed in the Steppes at the foot of the Caucasus Mountains, by a perilous life in which force, endurance, and calm courage are a first necessity. Into their midst comes one of the sickly products of our semi-intellectual town life, and at every step he feels himself the inferior of the Cossack Lukáshka. He wishes to do something on a grand scale, but has neither the intellectual nor the physical force to accomplish it.   Even his love is not the strong healthy love of the prairie man, but a sort of slight excitement of the nerves, which evidently will not last, and which only produces a similar restlessness in the Cossack girl, but cannot carry her away.   And when he talks to her of love, in the force of which he himself does not believe, she sends him off with the words : ' Go away, you weakling ! '

Some saw in that novel a glorification of the semi-savage state, similar to that in which writers of the eighteenth century, and especially Rousseau, are supposed to have indulged.   There is in Tolstóy nothing of the sort, as there was nothing of the sort in Rousseau. But Tolstóy saw that in the life of the Cossacks there is more *vitality*, more vigour, more power, than in his well-born hero's life—and he told it in an impressive form. His hero—like whom there are thousands upon thousands—has none of the powers that come from manual work and struggle with nature ; and neither has he those powers which knowledge and true civilisation might have given him.   A real intellectual power is not asking itself at every moment, ' Am I right, or am I wrong ? ' It feels that there are principles in which it is *not* wrong.   The same is true of a moral force : it knows that to such an extent it can trust to itself.   But, like so many thousands of men in the so-called educated classes, Neklúdoff has neither of these powers.   He is a weakling, and Tolstóy brought out his intellectual and moral frailty with a distinctness that was bound to produce a deep impression.

EDUCATIONAL WORK

In the years 1859-1862 the struggle between the ' fathers ' and the ' sons ' which called forth violent attacks against the young generation, even from such an ' objective ' writer as Gontcharóff—to say nothing of Písemskiy and several others—was going on all over Russia.   But we do not know which side had Tolstóy's sympathy. It must be said, though, that most of this time he was abroad, with his elder brother Nicholas, who died of consumption in the south of France. All we know is that the failure of Western civilisation in attaining any approach to well-being and equality for the great masses of the people struck Tolstóy deeply ; and we are told that the only men of mark, besides Hérzen, whom he went to see during this journey abroad were Auerbach, who wrote at that time his Schwarzwald stories from the life of the peasants and edited popular almanacks, and Proudhon, who was then in exile at Brussels. Tolstóy returned to Russia at the moment when the serfs were freed, accepted the position of a *mirovóy posrédnik*, or arbitrator of peace between the landlords and the freed serfs, and, settling at Yásnaya Polyána, began there his work of education of peasant children. This he started on entirely independent lines—that is, on purely anarchistic principles, totally free from the artificial methods of education which had been worked out by German pedagogists, and were then greatly admired in Russia. There was no sort of discipline in his school. Instead of working out programmes according to which the children are to be taught, the teacher, Tolstóy said, must learn from the children themselves what to teach them, and must adapt his teaching to the individual tastes and capacities of each child. Tolstóy carried this out with his pupils, and obtained excellent results. His methods, however, have as yet received but little attention ; and only one great writer—another poet, William Morris—has advocated (in *News from Nowhere*) the same freedom in education. But we may be sure that some day Tolstóy's Yásnaya Polyána papers, studied by some gifted teacher, as Rousseau's *Emile* was studied by Froebel, will become the starting-point of an educational reform much deeper than the reforms of Pestalozzi and Froebel.

It is now known that a violent end to this educational experiment was put by the Russian Government. During Tolstóy's absence from his estate a search was made by the gendarmes, who not only frightened to death Tolstóy's old aunt (she fell ill after that), but visited every corner of the house and read aloud, with cynical comments, the most intimate diary which the great writer had kept since his youth. More searches were promised, so that Tolstóy intended to emigrate for ever to London, and warned Alexander II., through the Countess A. A. Tolstáya, that he kept a loaded revolver by his side and would shoot down the first police-officer who would dare to enter his house. The school had evidently to be closed.

WAR AND PEACE

In the year 1862 Tolstóy married the young daughter of a Moscow doctor, Bers ; and, staying nearly without interruption on his Túla estate, he gave his time, for the next fifteen or sixteen years, to his great work, *War and Peace*, and next to *Anna Karénina*. His first intention was to write (probably utilising some family traditions and documents) a great historical novel, *The Decembrists* (see chapter i.), and he finished in 1863 the first chapters of this novel (vol. iii. of his *Works*, in Russian ; Moscow, 10th edition). But in trying to create the types of the Decembrists he must have been taken back in his thoughts to the great war of 1812. He had heard so much about it in the family traditions of the Tolstóys and Volkhónskys, and that war had so much in common with the Crimean war through which he himself had lived, that he came to write this great epopee, *War and Peace*, which has no parallel in any literature.

A whole epoch, from 1805 to 1812, is reconstituted in these volumes, and its meaning appears, not from the conventional historian's point of view, but as it was understood then by those who lived and acted in those years. All the society of those times passes before the reader, from its highest spheres, with their heart-rending levity, conventional ways of thinking, and superficiality, down to the simplest soldier in the army, who bore the hardships of that terrible conflict as a sort of ordeal that was sent by a supreme power upon the Russians, and who forgot himself and his own sufferings in the life and sufferings of the nation. A fashionable drawing-room at St. Petersburg, the *salon* of a person who is admitted into the intimacy of the dowager-empress ; the quarters of the Russian diplomatists in Austria and the Austrian Court ; the thoughtless life of the Róstoff family at Moscow and on their estate ; the austere house of the old general, Prince Bolkónskiy ; then the camp life of the Russian General Staff and of Napoleon on the one hand, and on the other, the inner life of a simple regiment of the hussars or of a field-battery ; then such world-battles as Schöngraben, the disaster of Austerlitz, Smolénsk, and Borodinó ; the abandonment and the burning of Moscow ; the life of those Russian prisoners who had been arrested pell-mell during the conflagration and were executed in batches ; and finally the horrors of the retreat of Napoleon from Moscow, and the guerilla warfare—all this immense variety of scenes, events, and small episodes, interwoven with romance of the deepest interest, is unrolled before us as we read the pages of this epopee of Russia's great conflict with Western Europe.

We make acquaintance with more than a hundred different persons, and each of them is so well depicted, each has his or her own *human* physiognomy so well determined, that each one appears with his or her own individuality, distinct amongst the scores of actors in the same great drama. It is not so easy to forget even the least important of these figures, be it one of the ministers of Alexander I. or any one of the orderlies of the cavalry officers. Nay, every anonymous soldier of various rank—the infantryman, the hussar, or the artilleryman—has his own physiognomy ; even the different chargers of Róstoff, or of Denísoff, stand out with individual features. When you think of the variety of human characters which pass under your eyes on these pages, you have the real sensation of a vast crowd —of historical events that you seem to have lived through—of a whole nation roused by a calamity; while the impression you retain of human beings whom you have loved in *War and Peace*, or for whom you have suffered when misfortune befell them, or when they themselves have wronged others (as, for instance, the old Countess Róstoff and Sónitchka)—the impression left by these persons, when they emerge in your memory from the crowd, gives to that crowd the same illusion of reality which little details give to the personality of a hero.

The great difficulty in a historical novel lies not so much in the representation of secondary figures as in painting the great historical personalities—the chief actors of the historical drama—so as to make of them real, living beings. But this is exactly where Tolstóy has succeeded most wonderfully. His Bagratión, his Alexander I., his Napoleon, and his Kutúzoff are living men, so realistically represented that one *sees* them and is tempted to seize the brush and paint them, or to imitate their movements and ways of talking.

The ' philosophy of war' which Tolstóy had developed in *War and Peace* has provoked, as is well known, passionate discussion and bitter criticism ; and yet its correctness cannot but be recognised. In fact, it *is* recognised by such as know war from within, or have witnessed popular movements. Of course, those who know war from newspaper reports, especially such officers as, after having recited many times over an ' improved ' report of a battle as *they* would have liked it to be, giving themselves a leading rôle—such men will not agree with Tolstóy's ways of dealing with ' heroes ' ; but it is sufficient to read, for instance, what Moltke and Bismarck wrote in their private letters about the war of 1870-71, or the plain, honest descriptions of some historical event with which we occasionally meet, to understand Tolstóy's views of war and his conceptions of the extremely limited part played by 'heroes' in historical events. Tolstóy did not invent the artillery officer Túshin who had been forgotten by his superiors in the centre of the Schöngraben position, and who, continuing all day long to use his four guns with initiative and discernment, prevented the battle from ending in disaster for the Russian rearguard : he knew only too well of such Túshins in Sebastopol. They compose the real vital force of every army in the world ; and the success of an army depends infinitely more upon its number of Túshins than upon the genius of its high commander. This is where Tolstóy and Moltke are of one mind, and where they entirely disagree with the 'war-correspondent' and with the General Staff historians.

In the hands of a writer possessed of less genius than Tolstóy, such a thesis might have failed to appear convincing ; but in *War and Peace* it appears almost with the force of self-evidence. Tolstóy's Kutúzoff is—as he was in reality—quite an ordinary man ; but he was a great man for the precise reason that, foreseeing the unavoidable and almost fatal drift of events, instead of pretending that he directed them, he simply did his best to utilise the vital forces of his army in order to avoid still greater disasters.

It hardly need be said that *War and Peace* is a powerful indictment against war. The effect which the great writer has exercised in this direction upon his generation could be actually seen in Russia. It was quite apparent during the great Turkish war of 1877-78, when it was absolutely impossible to find in Russia a correspondent who would have described how 'we have peppered the enemy with grape-shot' or how 'we shot them down like nine-pins.' If a man could have been found to use in his letters such survivals of savagery, no paper would have dared to print them. The general character of the Russian war-correspondent had grown totally different; and during the same war there came to the front such a novelist as Gárshin and such a painter as Vereschágin, with whom to combat war became a life work.

Every one who has read *War and Peace* remembers, of course, the hard experiences of Pierre, and his friendship with the soldier Karatáeff. One feels that Tolstóy is full of admiration for the quiet philosophy of this man of the people—a typical representative of the ordinary, common-sense Russian peasant. Some literary critics concluded that Tolstóy was preaching in Karatáeff a sort of Oriental fatalism. In the present writer's opinion there is nothing of the sort. Karatáeff, who is a consistent pantheist, simply knows that there are natural calamities which it is impossible to resist; and he knows that the miseries which befall him—his personal sufferings, and eventually the shooting of a number of prisoners among whom to-morrow he may or may not be included—are the unavoidable consequences of a much greater event: the armed conflict between nations, which, once it has begun, must unroll itself with all its revolting but absolutely ungovernable consequences. Karatáeff acts as one of those cows on the slope of an Alpine mountain, mentioned by the philosopher Guyau. When it feels that it begins to slip down a steep mountain slope, it makes at first desperate efforts to hold its ground, but when it sees that no effort can arrest the fatal gliding, it lets itself quietly be dragged down into the abyss. Karatáeff accepts the inevitable; but he is not a fatalist. If he had felt that his efforts could prevent war, he would have exerted them. In fact, towards the end of the work, when Pierre tells his wife Natásha that he is going to join the Decembrists (it is told in veiled words, on account of censorship, but a Russian reader understands nevertheless), and she asks him, 'Would Platón Karatáeff approve of it?' Pierre, after a moment's reflection, answers decidedly, 'Yes, he would.'

I don't know what a Frenchman, an Englishman, or a German feels when he reads *War and Peace*—I have heard educated Englishmen say that they found it dull—but I know that for educated Russians the reading of nearly every scene in *War and Peace* is a source of indescribable æsthetic pleasure. Having, like so many Russians, read the work many times, I could not, if I were asked, name the scenes which delight me most : the romances among the children, the mass-effects in the war scenes, the regimental life, the inimitable scenes from the life of the Court aristocracy, the tiny details concerning Napoleon or Kutúzoff, or the life of the Róstoffs—the dinner, the hunt, the departure from Moscow, and so on.

Many felt offended, in reading this epopee, to see their hero, Napoleon, reduced to such small proportions, and even ridiculed. But the Napoleon who came to Russia was no longer the man who had inspired the armies of the *sans-culottes* in their first steps eastwards for the abolition of serfdom, absolutism, and inquisition. All men in high positions are actors to a great extent —as Tolstóy so wonderfully shows in so many places of his great work—and Napoleon surely was not the least actor among them. And by the time he came to Russia, an emperor, spoiled by the adulation of the courtiers of all Europe and the worship of the masses, who attributed to him what was attributable to the vast stir of minds produced by the Great Revolution, and consequently saw in him a half-god—by the time he came to Russia, the actor in him had got the upper hand over the man in whom there had been formerly incarnated the youthful energy of the suddenly awakened French nation, and through whom its force had been further increased. To these original characteristics was due the fascination which the name of Napoleon exercised upon his contemporaries. At Smolénsk, Kutúzoff himself must have experienced that fascination when, rather than rouse the lion to a desperate battle, he opened before him the way to retreat.

ANNA KARÉNINA

Of all the Tolstóy novels *Anna Karénina* is the one which has been the most widely read in all languages. As a work of art it is a masterpiece. From the very first appearance of the heroine you feel that this woman must bring with her a drama ; from the very outset her tragical end is as inevitable as it is in a drama of Shakespeare. In that sense the novel is true to life throughout. It is a corner of real life that we have before us. As a rule, Tolstóy is not at his best in picturing women—with the exception of very young girls—and I don't think that Anna Karénina herself is as deep, as psychologically complete, and as living a creation as she might have been ; but the more ordinary woman, Dolly, is simply teeming with life. As to the various scenes of the novel—the ball scenes, the races of the officers, the inner family life of Dolly, the country scenes on Lévin's estate, the death of his brother, and so on—all these are pages taken from Tolstóy's real surroundings, and they are depicted in such a way that for its artistic qualities *Anna Karénina* stands foremost even amongst the many beautiful things Tolstóy has written.

And yet, notwithstanding all that, the novel produced in Russia a decidedly unfavourable impression, which brought to Tolstóy congratulations from the reactionary camp and a very cool reception from the advanced portion of society. The fact is, that the question of marriage and of an eventual separation between husband and wife had been most earnestly debated in Russia by the best men and women, both in literature and in life. It is self-evident that such indifferent levity towards marriage as is continually unveiled before the courts in 'Society' divorce cases was absolutely and unconditionally condemned ; and that any form of deceit, such as makes the subject of countless French novels and dramas, was ruled out of question in any honest discussion of the matter. But after the above levity and deceit had been severely branded, the rights of a new love, serious and deep, appearing after years of happy married life, had only been the more seriously analysed. Tchernyshévskiy's novel, *What is to be Done?* can be taken as the best expression of the opinions upon marriage which had become current amongst the better portion of the young generation. Once you are married, it was said, don't take lightly to love affairs, or so-called flirtation. Every fit of passion does not deserve the name of a new love; and what is sometimes described as love is in a very great number of cases nothing but temporary desire. Even if it were real love, in most cases, before a real and deep love has grown up, there is a period when one has time to reflect upon the consequences that would follow if his or her new sympathy should attain the depth of such a love. But, with all that, there are cases when a new love does come, and there are cases when such an event must happen almost fatally, when, for instance, a girl has been married almost against her will, under the continued insistence of her lover, or when the two have married without properly understanding each other, or when one of the two has continued to progress in his or her development towards a higher ideal, while the other, after having worn for some time the mask of idealism, falls into the Philistine happiness of warmed slippers. In such cases separation not only becomes inevitable, but it often is to the interest of both. It would be much better for both to live through the sufferings which a separation would involve (honest natures are by such sufferings made better) than to spoil the entire subsequent existence of the one—in most cases, of both—and to face moreover the fatal results that living together under such circumstances would necessarily mean for the children. This was, at least, the conclusion to which both Russian literature and the best all-round portion of our society had come.

And now came Tolstóy with *Anna Karénina*, which bears the menacing biblical epigraph, 'Vengeance is mine, I will repay,' and in which the biblical revenge falls upon the unfortunate Karénina, who puts an end by suicide to her sufferings after her separation from her husband. Russian critics evidently could not accept Tolstóy's views. The case of Karénina was one of those where there could be no question of ' vengeance.' She was married as a young girl to an old and un-attractive man. At that time she did not know exactly what she was doing, and nobody had explained it to her. She had never known love, and learned it for the first time when she saw Vrónskiy. Deceit, for her, was absolutely out of the question ; and to keep up a merely conventional marriage would have been a sacri-fice which would not have made her husband and child any happier. Separation, and a new life with Vrónskiy, who seriously loved her, was the only possible outcome. At any rate, if the story of Anna Karénina had to end in tragedy, it was not in the least in consequence of an act of supreme justice. As always, the honest artistic genius of Tolstóy had itself indicated another cause— the real one. It was the inconsistency of Vrónskiy and Karénina. After having separated from her husband and defied 'public opinion'—that is, the opinion of women who, as Tolstóy shows it himself, were not honest enough to be allowed any voice in the matter —neither she nor Vrónskiy had the courage of breaking entirely with that society, the futility of which Tolstóy knows and describes so exquisitely. Instead of that, when Anna returned with Vrónskiy to St. Petersburg, her own and Vrónskiy's chief preoccupation was—How Betsey and other such women would receive her, if she made her appearance among them. And it was the opinion of the Betseys—surely not superhuman justice —which brought Karénina to suicide.

RELIGIOUS CRISIS

Every one knows the profound change which took place in Tolstóy's fundamental conceptions of life in the years 1875-78, when he had reached the age of about fifty. I do not think that one has the right to discuss publicly what has been going on in the very depths of another's mind ; but, by telling us himself the inner drama and the struggles which he has lived through, the great writer has, so to say, invited us to verify whether he was correct in his reasonings and conclusions ; and limiting ourselves to the psychological material which he has given us, we may discuss it without undue intrusion into the motives of his actions.

It is most striking to find, on rereading the earlier works of Tolstóy, how the ideas which he advocated in the later years of his life were always cropping up in his earlier writings. Philosophical questions and questions concerning the moral foundations of life interested him from his early youth. At the age of sixteen he used to read philosophical works, and during his university years, and even through ' the stormy days of passion,' questions as to how we ought to live rose with their full importance before him. His autobiographical novels, especially *Youth*, bear deep traces of that inner work of his mind, even though, as he says in *Confession*, he has never said all he might have said on this subject. Nay, it is evident that although he describes his frame of mind in those years as that of ' a philosophical Nihilist,' he had never parted, in reality, with the beliefs of his childhood.[1] He always was an admirer and follower of Rousseau. In his papers on education (collected in vol. iv. of the tenth Moscow edition of his *Works*) one

[1] *Introduction to the Criticism of Dogmatic Theology and to an Analysis of the Christian Teaching*, or *Confession* ; vol. i. of Tchertkóff's edition of *Works prohibited by the Russian Censorship* (in Russian), Christchurch, 1902, p. 13. Also Birukóff's *Biography of Tolstóy*.

finds, treated in a very radical way, most of the burning social questions which he has discussed in his later years. These questions even then worried him so much that, while he was carrying on his school work in Yásnaya Polyána and was a Peace Mediator—that is, in the years 1861-62—he grew so disgusted with the unavoidable dualism of his position as a benevolent landlord, that—to quote his own words—'I should have come then, perhaps, to the crisis which I reached fifteen years later, if there had not remained one aspect of life which promised me salvation—namely, married life.' In other words, Tolstóy was already very near to breaking with the privileged class point of view on Property and Labour, and to joining the great 'populist' movement which was already beginning in Russia. This he probably would have done, had not a new world of love, family life, and family interests, which he embraced with the usual intensity of his passionate nature, fastened the ties that kept him attached to his own class.

Art, too, must have contributed to divert his attention from the social problem—at least, from its economic aspects. In *War and Peace* he developed the philosophy of *the masses versus the heroes*, a philosophy which in those years would have found among the educated men of all Europe very few persons ready to accept it. Was it his poetical genius which revealed to him the part played by the masses in the great war of 1812, and taught him that they—the masses, and not the heroes —had accomplished all the great things in history? Or was it but a further development of the ideas which inspired him in his Yásnaya Polyána school, in opposition to all the educational theories that had been elaborated by Church and State in the interest of the privileged classes? At any rate, *War and Peace* must have offered him a problem great enough to absorb his thoughts for a number of years; and in writing this monumental work, in which he strove to promote a new conception of history, he must have felt that he was working in the right way. As to *Anna Karénina*, which had no such reformatory or philosophical purpose, it must have offered to Tolstóy the possibility of living through once more, with all the intensity of poetical creation, the shallow life of the leisured classes, and to contrast it with the life of the peasants and their work. And it was while he was finishing this novel that he began to fully realise how much his own life was in opposition to the ideals of his earlier years.

A terrible conflict must have been going on then in the mind of the great writer. The communistic feeling which had induced him to put in italics the fact about the singer in *Lucerne*, and to add to it a hot indictment against the civilisation of the moneyed classes; the trend of thought which had dictated his severe criticisms against private property in *Holstomyér: the History of a Horse*; the anarchistic ideas which had brought him, in his Yásnaya Polyána educational articles, to a negation of a civilisation based on Capitalism and State; and, on the other hand, his individual property conceptions, which he tried to conciliate with his communistic leanings (see the conversation between the two brothers Lévin in *Anna Karénina*); his want of sympathy with the parties which stood in opposition to the Russian Government and, at the same time, his profound, deeply rooted dislike of that Government—all these tendencies must have been in an irreconcilable conflict in the mind of the great writer, with all the passionate intensity which is characteristic of Tolstóy, as with all men of genius. These constant contradictions were so apparent that while less perspicacious Russian critics and the *Moscow Gazette* defenders of serfdom considered Tolstóy as having joined their reactionary camp, a gifted Russian critic, Mihailóvskiy, published in 1875 a series of remarkable articles, entitled *The Right Hand and the Left Hand of Count Tolstóy*, in which he pointed out the two men who constantly were in conflict in the great writer.

In these articles the young critic, a great admirer of Tolstóy, analysed the advanced ideas which he had developed in his educational articles, which were almost quite unknown at that time, and contrasted them with the strangely conservative ideas which he had expressed in his later writings. As a consequence, Mihailóvskiy predicted a crisis to which the great writer was inevitably coming:

'I will not speak,' he wrote, 'of *Anna Karénina*, first of all because it is not yet terminated, and second, because one must speak of it very much, or not at all. I shall only remark that in this novel—much more superficially, but for that very reason perhaps even more distinctly than anywhere else— one sees the traces of the drama which is going on in the soul of the author. One asks oneself what such a man is to do, how can he live, how shall he avoid that poisoning of his consciousness which at every step intrudes into the pleasures of a satisfied need? Most certainly he must, even though it may be instinctively, seek for a means to put an end to the inner drama of his soul, to drop the curtain; but how to do it? I think that if an ordinary man were in such a position, he would have ended in suicide or in drunkenness. A man of value will, on the contrary, seek for other issues, and of such issues there are several' (*Otechestvennyia Zapiski*, a review, June 1875; also Mihailóvskiy's *Works*, vol. iii. p. 491).

One of these issues—Mihailóvskiy continued—would be to write for the people. Of course, very few are so happy as to possess the talent and the faculties which are necessary for that:

'But once he (Tolstóy) is persuaded that the nation consists of two halves, and that even the "innocent" pleasures of the one half are to the disadvantage of the other half—why should he not devote his formidable forces to this immense task? It is even difficult to imagine that any other theme could interest the writer who carries in his soul such a terrible drama as the one that Count Tolstóy carries. So deep and so serious is it, so deeply does it go to the root of all literary activity, that it must presumably destroy all other interests, just as the creeper suffocates all other plants. And, Is it not a sufficiently high aim in life, always to remind "Society" that its pleasures and amusements are not the pleasures and the amusements of all mankind, to explain to "Society" the true sense of the phenomena of progress, to wake up, be it only in the few, the more impressionable, the conscience and the feeling of justice? And is not this field wide enough for poetical creation? . . .

'The drama which is going on in Count Tolstóy's soul is my hypothesis,' Mihailóvskiy concluded, 'but it is a legitimate hypothesis without which it is impossible to understand his writings' (*Works*, vol. iii. p. 496).

It is now known how much Mihailóvskiy's hypothesis was a prevision. In the years 1875-76, as Tolstóy was finishing *Anna Karénina*, he began fully to realise the shallowness and the duality of the life that he had hitherto led. 'Something strange,' he says, 'began to happen within me : I began to experience minutes of bewilderment, of arrest of life, as if I did not know how to live and what to do.' 'What for? What next?' were the questions which began to rise before him. 'Well,' he said to himself, 'you will have 15,000 acres of land in Samara, 3000 horses—but what of that? And I was bewildered, and did not know what to think next.' Literary fame had lost for him its attraction, now that he had reached the great heights to which *War and Peace* had brought him. The little picture of Philistine family-happiness which he had pictured in a novel before his marriage (*Family Happiness*) he had now lived through, but it no longer satisfied him. The life of epicureanism which he had led hitherto had lost all sense for him. 'I felt,' he writes in *Confession*, 'that what I had stood upon had broken down ; that there was nothing for me to stand upon ; that what I had lived by was no more, and that there was nothing left me to live by. My life had come to a stop.' The so-called 'family duties' had lost their interest. When he thought of the education of his children, he asked himself, 'What for?' and very probably he felt that in his landlord's surroundings he never would be able to give

them a better education than his own, which he condemned ; and when he began thinking of the well-being
of the masses he would all of a sudden ask himself:
' What business have I to think of it ? '

He felt that he had nothing to live for.   He even
had no wishes which he could recognise as reasonable.
' If a fairy had come to me, and offered to satisfy my
wish, I should not have known what to wish. . . . I
even could not wish to know Truth, because I had
guessed of what it would consist.   The Truth was, that
life is nonsense.'   He had no aim in life, no purpose,
and he realised that without a purpose, and with its
unavoidable sufferings, life is not worth living (*Confession*, vi., vii.).

He had not—to use his own expression—' the moral
bluntness of imagination' which would be required not
to have his epicureanism poisoned by the surrounding
misery ; and yet, like Schopenhauer, he had not the will
that was necessary for adjusting his actions in accordance
with the dictates of his reason.   Self-annihilation, death,
appeared therefore as a welcome solution.

However, Tolstóy was too strong a man to end his
life in suicide.   He found an outcome, and that outcome was indicated to him by a return to the love
which he had cherished in his youth: *the love of the
peasant masses*.   ' Was it in consequence of a strange,
so to say a physical, love of the truly working people,'
he writes—or of some other cause ? but he understood
at last that he must seek the sense of life among the
millions who toil all their life long.   He began to
examine with more attention than before the life of
these millions.   ' And I began,' he says, ' to love these
people.'   And the more he penetrated into their lives,
past and present, the more he loved them, and ' the
easier it was for me to live.'   As to the life of the men
of his own circle—the wealthy and cultured, ' I not only
felt disgust for it : it lost all sense in my eyes.'   He
understood that if he did not see what life was worth

living for, it was his own life 'in exclusive conditions of epicureanism' which had obscured the truth.

'I understood,' he continues, 'that my question, "What is life?" and my reply to it, "Evil," were quite correct. I was only wrong in applying them to life altogether. To the question, "What is life?" I had got the reply, "Evil and nonsense!" And so it was. My own life—a life of indulgence in passions—was void of sense and full of evil, but this was true of my life only, not of the life of all men. Beginning with the birds and the lowest animals, all live to maintain life and to secure it for others besides themselves, while I not only did not secure it for others: I did not secure it even for myself. I lived as a parasite, and, having put to myself the question, "What do I live for?" I got the reply, "For no purpose."'

The conviction, then, that he must live as the millions live, earning his own livelihood; that he must toil as the millions toil; and that such a life is the *only* possible reply to the questions which had brought him to despair —the only way to escape the terrible contradictions which had made Schopenhauer preach self-annihilation, and Solomon, Sakiamuni, and so many others preach their gospel of despairing pessimism; this conviction, then, saved him and restored to him lost energy and the will to live. But that same idea had inspired thousands of the Russian youth, in those same years, and had induced them to start the great movement '*V narod!*' 'Towards the people; be the people!'

Tolstóy has told us in an admirable book, *What is then to be Done?* the impressions which the slums of Moscow produced upon him in 1881, and the influence they had upon the ulterior development of his thoughts. But we do not yet know what facts and impressions made him so vividly realise in 1875-81 the emptiness of the life which he had been hitherto leading. Is it then presuming too much if I suggest that it was this very same movement, 'towards the people,' which had inspired so many of the Russian youth to go to the villages and the factories, and to live there the life of the people, which finally brought Tolstóy, also, to reconsider his position as a rich landlord?

That he knew of this movement there is not the slightest doubt. The trial of the Netcháyeff groups in 1871 was printed in full in the Russian newspapers, and one could easily read through all the youthful immaturity of the speeches of the accused the high motives and the love of the people which inspired them. The trial of the Dolgúshin groups, in 1875, produced a still deeper impression in the same direction; but especially the trial, in March 1877, of those girls of transcendent worth, Bárdina, Lubatóvitch, the sisters Subbótin, 'the Moscow Fifty' as they were named in the circles, who, all from wealthy families, had led the life of factory girls, in the horrible factory-barracks, working fourteen and sixteen hours a day, in order to be with the working people and to teach them. . . . And then—the trial of the 'Hundred-and-Ninety-Three' and of Véra Zasúlitch in 1878. However great Tolstóy's dislike of revolutionists might have been, he must have felt, as he read the reports of these trials, or heard what was said about them at Moscow and in his province of Túla, and witnessed round him the impression they had produced—he, the great artist, must have felt that this youth was much nearer to what he himself was in his earlier days, in 1861-62, than to those among whom he lived now—Katkóff, the poet 'Fet,' and the like. And then, even if he knew nothing about these trials and had heard nothing about the 'Moscow Fifty,' he knew, at least, Turguéneff's *Virgin Soil*, which was published in January 1877, and he must have felt, even from that imperfect picture, so warmly greeted by young Russia, what this young Russia was.

I leave these pages as they were written in 1904, and will only add that Tolstóy's acquaintance with members of the 'populist' movement, and their influence upon him, are now fully confirmed. In 1878 he made the acquaintance of V. Alexéyeff, an active member of our circles, who spent a couple of years in Kanzas with Frey, Málikoff, and N. Tchaykóvskiy, working on the land in a colony of 'populists.' Alexéyeff was invited as a tutor to Tolstóy's children; he lived in Yásnaya Polyána, and became intimate with the great writer. As to the influence he exercised upon him, it is best seen from the following extracts from a letter of Tolstóy to Alexéyeff, published by Biryukóff:

'Thanks for your good letter, dear Vasíliy Ivánovitch. We, as it were, forget that we love each other. I do not wish to forget it—or that I am much indebted to you for the tranquillity and clearness of the outlook on life that I have attained. You were the first man (touched by education) whom I knew, who not in words but in spirit confessed the faith that has become for him a clear and steadfast light. That made me believe in the possibility of what had always dimly stirred in my soul. And therefore, as you have been, so you will always remain dear to me' (Birukóff, l.c.; also Aylmer Maude's *The Life of Tolstóy*, vol. ii. 'The Later Years,' London (Constable), 1910, p. 94).

Besides, Tolstóy met also a member of the Netcháyeff populist circles—Orlóff—who had been kept two years in prison for his ideas, and Fyódoroff, another man of mark of the same faith, and he became friendly with both. He also made the acquaintance of a populist of renown in literature, Prugávin, who fought all his life for the cause of the Russian Nonconformists, and brought Tolstóy into contact with that remarkable peasant, Syutáeff, about whom Tolstóy speaks with such respect in one of his ethical writings.

All of them certainly told him about the hundreds of men and women who lived in accordance with their socialist conceptions of life, and went by the hundred to prison and to Siberia for preaching the socialist gospel among the peasants and the factory workers. And one easily understands the impression that this movement produced upon Tolstóy, who himself had shared the same ideals in the sixties, had tried then to spread them in the Russian villages, and now returned to them.

If Tolstóy had been in his twenties, he might possibly have joined the movement, in one form or another, notwithstanding all the obstacles. Such as he was, in his surroundings, and especially with his mind already preoccupied by the problem, 'Where is the lever which would move human hearts at large, and become the source of the deep moral reform of every individual?' with such a question on his mind, he had to live through many a struggle before he was brought consciously to take the very same step. For our young men and women, the mere statement that one who had got an education thanks to the toil of the masses, owed it therefore to these masses to work in their behalf—this simple hint was sufficient. They left their wealthy houses, took to the simplest life, hardly different from that of a working-man, and devoted their lives to the people. But for many reasons—such as education, habits, surroundings, age, and, perhaps, the great philosophical question he had in his mind—Tolstóy had to live through the most painful struggles before he came to the very same conclusion, but in a different way: that is to say, before he concluded that he, being the bearer of a portion of the divine Unknown, had to fulfil the will of that Unknown, which will was, that every one should work for universal welfare.[1]

---

[1] 'That which some people told me, and of which I sometimes had tried to persuade myself—namely, that a man should desire happiness, not for himself only, but for others, his neighbours, and for all men as well: this did not satisfy me. Firstly, I could not sincerely desire happiness for others as much as for myself; secondly, and chiefly, others, in like manner as myself, were doomed to unhappiness and death, and therefore all my efforts for other people's happiness were useless. I despaired.' The understanding that personal happiness is best found in the happiness of all did not appeal to him; and the very striving towards the happiness of all, and an advance towards it, he thus found insufficient as a purpose in life.

The moment, however, that he came to such a conclusion, he did not hesitate to act in accordance with it.
The difficulties he met in his way, before he could follow
the injunction of his conscience, must have been immense.
We have only to look at the letters of his wife, published
by Mr. Maude, or read his drama, *And Light Shines in
the Dark*, published in vol. ii. of his *Posthumous Works*,
to realise these difficulties. The sophisms he had to
combat—especially when all the admirers of his talent
protested against his condemnation of his previous
writings—we can easily imagine. And one can but
admire the force of his convictions, when he finally
succeeded in reforming the life he had hitherto led.

The small room he took in his rich mansion is well
known through a world-renowned photograph. Tolstóy
behind the plough, painted by Ryépin, has gone the
round of the world, and is considered by the Russian
Government so dangerous an image that it has been
taken from the public gallery where it was exhibited.
Limiting his own living to the strictly necessary
minimum of the plainest sort of food, he did his best,
so long as his physical forces lasted, to earn that little
by physical work. And for the last years of his life he
wrote even more than he ever did in the years of his
greatest literary productivity.

The effects of this example which Tolstóy has given
mankind, every one knows. He understood, however,
that he was bound to give also the philosophical and
religious reasons for his conduct, and this he did in a
series of remarkable works.

Guided by the idea that millions of plain working
people realised the sense of life, and found it in life
itself, which they considered as the accomplishment of
' the will of the Creator of the universe,' he accepted
the simple creed of the masses of the Russian peasants,
and followed with them the rites of the Greek Orthodox
Church, even though his mind was reluctant to do so.
There was a limit, however, to such a concession, and

there were beliefs which he positively could not accept. He felt that when he was, for instance, solemnly declaring during the mass, before communion, that he took the latter in the literal sense of the words—not figuratively—he was affirming something which he could not say in full conscience. Besides, he soon made the acquaintance of the Nonconformist peasants, Syutáeff and Bondaryóff, whom he deeply respected, and he saw, from his intercourse with them, that by joining the Greek Orthodox Church he was lending a hand to all its abominable prosecutions of the Nonconformists—that he was a party to the hatred which Churches profess towards each other.

Consequently, he undertook a complete study of Christianity, irrespective of the teachings of the different Churches, including a careful revision of the translations of the gospels, with the intention of finding out what was the real meaning of the Great Teacher's precepts, and what had been added to it by his followers. In a remarkable, most elaborate work (*Criticism of Dogmatic Theology*) he demonstrated how fundamentally the interpretations of the Churches differed from what was in his opinion the true sense of the words of the Christ. And then he worked out, quite independently, an interpretation of the Christian teaching which is quite similar to the interpretations that have been given to it by all the great popular movements—in the ninth century in Armenia, later on by Wycliff, and by the early Anabaptists, such as Hans Denck [1]—laying, however, like the Quakers, especial stress on the doctrine of non-resistance.

HIS INTERPRETATION OF THE CHRISTIAN TEACHING

The ideas which Tolstóy thus slowly worked out are explained in a succession of three separate works:

[1] See *Anabaptism from its Rise at Zwickau to its Fall at Münster*, 1521-1536, by Richard Heath (*Baptist Manuals*, i. 1895).

(1) *Dogmatic Theology*, of which the Introduction is better known as *Confession* and was written in 1882 ; (2) *What is my Faith?* (1884); and (3) *What is then to be Done?* (1886), to which must be added *The Kingdom of God in Yourselves, or Christianity, not as a mystic Teaching but as a new Understanding of Life* (1900), and, above all, a small book, *The Christian Teaching* (1902), which is written in short, concise, numbered paragraphs, like a catechism, and contains a full and definite exposition of Tolstóy's views. A number of other works dealing with the same subject —such as *The Life and the Teaching of Jesus, My Reply to the Synod's Edict of Excommunication, What is Religion? On Life*, etc., were published during the same year. These books represent the work of Tolstóy for the last twenty years, and at least four of them (*Confession, My Faith, What is then to be Done?* and *Christian Teaching*) must be read in the indicated succession, in correct translations, by every one who wishes to know the religious and moral conceptions of Tolstóy and to extricate himself from the confused ideas which are sometimes represented as Tolstóyism. As to the short work, *The Life and the Teaching of Jesus*, it is, so to speak, the four gospels in one, told in a language easy to be understood, and free of all mystical and meta-phorical elements ; it contains Tolstóy's reading of the gospels.

These works represent the most remarkable attempt at a rationalistic interpretation of Christianity that has ever been ventured upon. Christianity appears in them devoid of all gnosticism and mysticism, as a purely spiritual teaching about the universal spirit which guides man to a higher life—a life of equality and of friendly relations with all men. If Tolstóy accepts Christianity as the foundation of his faith, it is not because he considers it as a revelation, but because its teaching, purified of all the additions that have been made to it by the Churches, contains 'the very same solution of the problem of life as has been given more or less explicitly by the best of men, both before and since the gospel was given to us—a succession which goes on from Moses, Isaiah, and Confucius, to the early Greeks, Buddha, and Socrates, down to Pascal, Spinoza, Fichte, Feuerbach, and all others, often unnoticed and unknown, who, taking no teachings on mere trust, have taught us, and spoken to us with sincerity, about the meaning of life';[1] because it gives 'an explanation of the meaning of life' and 'a solution of this contradiction between the aspiration after welfare and life, and the consciousness of their being unattainable' (*Christian Teaching*, § 13)—'between the desire for happiness and life on the one hand, and the increasingly clear perception of the certainty of calamity and death on the other' (*ibid.*, § 10).

As to the dogmatic and mystical elements of Christianity, which he treats as mere additions to the real teaching of Christ, he considers them so noxious that even he makes the following remark: 'It is terrible to say so (but sometimes I have this thought): if the teaching of Christ, together with the teaching of the Church that has grown upon it, did not exist at all— those who now call themselves Christians would have been nearer to the teachings of Christ—that is, to an intelligent teaching about the good of life—than they are now. The moral teachings of all the prophets of mankind would not have been closed for them.'[2]

Putting aside all the mystical and metaphysical con-

---

[1] *The Christian Teaching*, Introduction, p. vi. In another similar passage he adds Marcus Aurelius and Lao-tse to the above-mentioned teachers.

[2] *What is my Belief?* ch. x. p. 145 of Tchertkóff's edition of *Works prohibited by the Russian Censorship.* On pp. 18 and 19 of the little work, *What is Religion and What is its Substance?* Tolstóy expresses himself even more severely about 'Church Christianity.' He also gives us in this remarkable little work his ideas about the substance of religion altogether, from which one can deduct its desirable relations to science, to synthetic philosophy, and to philosophical ethics.

ceptions which have been interwoven with Christianity, he concentrates his main attention upon the moral aspects of the Christian teaching. One of the most powerful means—he says—by which men are prevented from living a life in accordance with this teaching is 'religious deception.' 'Humanity moves slowly but unceasingly onward, towards an ever higher development of consciousness of the true meaning of life, and towards the organisation of life in conformity with this development of consciousness'; but in this ascendant march all men do not move at an equal pace, and 'the less sensitive continue to adhere to the previous understanding and order of life, and try to uphold it.' This they achieve mainly by means of the religious deception which consists 'in the intentional confusion of faith with superstition, and the substitution of the one for the other' (*Christian Teaching*, §§ 181, 180). The only means to free one's self from this deception is— he says—'to understand and to remember that the only instrument which man possesses for the acquisition of knowledge is reason, and that therefore every teaching which affirms that which is contrary to reason is a delusion.' Altogether, Tolstóy is especially emphatic upon this point of the importance of reason (see *Christian Teaching*, §§ 206, 214).

Another great obstacle to the spreading of the Christian teaching he sees in the current belief in the immortality of the soul—such as it is understood now. (*My Belief*, p. 134 of Tchertkóff's Russ. ed.) In this form he repudiates it; but we can—he says—give a deeper meaning to our life by making it to be a service to men—to mankind—by merging our life into the life of the universe; and although this idea may seem less attractive than the idea of individual immortality, 'though little, it is sure' (*Christian Teaching*).

In speaking of God he takes sometimes a pantheistic position, and describes God as Life, or as Love, or else as the Ideal which man is conscious of in himself

(*Thoughts about God*, collected by V. and A. Tchertkóff);
but in his last work (*Christian Teaching*, ch. vii. and
viii.) he prefers to identify God with 'the universal desire for welfare which is the source of all life.' 'So that,
according to the Christian teaching, God is that Essence
of life which man recognises both within himself and in
the whole universe as the desire for welfare; it being at
the same time the cause by which this Essence is en-
closed and conditioned in individual and corporal life'
(§ 36). Every reasoning man—Tolstóy adds—comes
to a similar conclusion. A desire for *universal* welfare
appears in every reasoning man, after his rational consciousness has been awakened at a certain age; and in
the world around man the same desire is manifest in all
separate beings, each of whom strives for his own welfare
(§ 37). These two desires 'converge towards one distinct purpose—definite, attainable, and joyful for man.'
Consequently, he concludes, Observation, Tradition (religious), and Reason, all three, show him 'that the greatest welfare of man, towards which all men aspire, can
only be obtained by perfect union and concord among
men.' All three show that the immediate work of the
world's development, in which he is called upon to take
part, is 'the substitution of union and harmony for
division and discord.' 'The inner tendency of that
spiritual being—love—which is in the process of birth
within him, impels him in the same direction.'

Union and harmony; and a steady, relentless effort to
promote them, which means not only *all* the work required for supporting one's life, but work also for increas-
ing universal welfare—these are, then, the two final ac-
cords in which all the discords, all the storms, which for
more than twenty years had raged in the distraught mind
of the great artist, all the religious ecstasies and the
rationalistic doubts which had agitated his superior intelligence in its insistent search for truth, finally found
their solution. On the highest metaphysical heights the
striving of every living being for its own welfare, which

is Egoism and Love at the same time, because it is Self-Love, and rational Self-Love must embrace all congeners of the same species—this striving for individual welfare by its very nature tends to comprise all that exists. 'It expands its limits naturally by love, first for one's family—one's wife and children—then for friends, then for one's fellow-countrymen ; but Love is not satisfied with this, and tends to embrace all' (*Christian Teaching*, § 46).

MAIN POINTS OF THE CHRISTIAN ETHICS

The central point of the Christian teaching Tolstóy sees in non-resistance. During the first years after his crisis he preached absolute 'non-resistance to evil'—in full conformity with the verbal and definite sense of the words of the gospel, which words, taken in connection with the sentence about the right and the left cheek, evidently mean complete humility and resignation. However, he soon realised that such a teaching not only was not in conformity with his above-mentioned conception of God, but that it amounted simply to abetting evil. Consequently, in 1898, he wrote in his *Diary* (now published) : 'I say that we must not resist evil by evil. They say against me that I advise not to struggle against evil.' He tells us how he once met in a train the Governor of the Túla province at the head of a detachment of soldiers who were armed with rifles and provided with a cart-load of birch-rods. They were going to flog the peasants of a village in order to enforce an act of sheer robbery passed by the Administration in favour of the landlord, in open breach of the law. He describes with his well-known graphical powers how, in their presence, a 'Liberal lady' openly, loudly, and in strong terms condemned the Governor and the officers, and how they were ashamed. Then he describes how, when this 'expedition' began its work, the peasants, with truly Christian resignation, would cross themselves with trembling hand and lie down on the ground, to be martyrised

and flogged till the heart of the victim stopped beating,
without the officers having been touched in the least by
that Christian humility. What Tolstóy did when he
met the expedition, we don't know : he does not tell
us. Maybe he remonstrated with the chiefs and ad-
vised the soldiers not to obey them—that is, to revolt.
At any rate, he must have felt that a passive attitude in
the face of this evil—the non-resistance to it—would
have meant a tacit approval of the evil ; it would have
meant giving support to it. Moreover, a passive attitude
of resignation in the face of evil is so contrary to the very
nature of Tolstóy, that he could not remain for a long
time a follower of such a doctrine, and he soon altered
his interpretation of the text of the gospel in the sense
of ' Don't resist evil by violence.' All his later writings
have consequently been *a passionate resistance against
the different forms of evil* which he has seen round about
himself in the world. Continually he made his mighty
voice resound against evil and evil-doers ; he only objected to physical force in resisting evil, because he believed that this would work harm.

The other four points of the Christian teaching, always
according to Tolstóy's interpretation of it, are : Do not
be angry, or, at least, abstain from anger as much as you
can. Remain true to the one woman with whom you
have united your life, and avoid all that excites passion.
Do not take oaths, which in Tolstóy's opinion means :
Never tie your hands with an oath ; oath-taking is the
means resorted to by all governments to bind men in
their *consciences* to do whatever they bid them do. And
finally, Love your enemies ; or, as Tolstóy points it out
in several of his writings : Never judge, and never pro-
secute another before a tribunal.

To these four rules Tolstóy gives the widest possible
interpretation, and he deducts from them all the teachings
of free communism. He proves with a wealth of arguments that to live upon the work of others, and not to
earn one's own living, is to break the very law of all

nature ; it is the main cause of all social evils, as also of nearly all personal unhappiness and discomforts. He shows how the present capitalistic organisation of labour is as bad as slavery or serfdom has ever been.

He insists upon the simplification of life—in food, dress, and dwelling—which results from one's taking to manual work, especially on the land, and he shows the advantages that even the rich and idle of to-day would find in such labour. He points out that all the evils of present misgovernment result from the fact that the very men who protest against bad government make every effort to become a part of that government.

As emphatically as he protests against the Church, he protests against the State—the getting rid of the State being the only real means for bringing to an end the present slavery, imposed upon men by this institution. He advises men to refuse having anything to do with the State. And finally he proves, with a wealth of illustrations in which his artistic powers appear in full, that the lust of the rich classes for wealth and luxury—a lust which has no limits, and can have none—is what maintains all this slavery, all these abnormal conditions of life, and all the prejudices and teachings now disseminated by Church and State in the interest of the ruling classes.

On the other hand, whenever he speaks of God, or of immortality, his constant desire is to show that he needs none of the mystical conceptions and metaphysical words which are usually resorted to. And while his language is borrowed from religious writings, he brings forward, again and again, the rationalistic interpretation of religious conceptions. He carefully sifts from the Christian teaching all that cannot be accepted by followers of other religions, and brings into relief all that is common to Christianity as well as to other positive religions—all that is simply humane in them and thus might be approved by reason, and therefore be accepted by disbelievers as well as by believers.

In other words, in proportion as he studied the teachings of different founders of religions and those of moral
philosophers, he tried to determine and to state *the elements of a universal religion* in which all men could unite
—a religion, however, which would have nothing supernatural in it, nothing that reason and knowledge would
have to reject, but would contain a moral guidance for
all men, at whatever stage of intellectual development
they may halt.   Having thus begun, in 1875-77, by
joining the Greek Orthodox religion—in the sense in
which Russian peasants understand it—he came finally
in *The Christian Teaching* to the construction of a moral
philosophy which, in his opinion, might be accepted by
the Christian, the Jew, the Mussulman, the Buddhist, and
so on, and the naturalist philosopher as well—a religion
which would retain the only substantial elements of
all religions : namely, a determination of one's *relation
towards the universe*, in accordance with present knowledge, and *a recognition of the equality of all men.*

Whether these two elements, one of which belongs to
the domain of knowledge and science and the other
(Justice) to the domain of ethics, are sufficient to constitute a *religion*, and need no substratum of mysticism,
is a question which lies beyond the scope of this book.

Let me only add that Tolstóy thus returned in his
old age to the idea which he had cherished at the age
of twenty-six and had inscribed (on March 5, 1855) in
the diary he kept during the siege of Sebastopol, in the
terrible Fourth Bastion.   It was worded as follows :

'A conversation about divinity and faith suggested to me a
great, a stupendous idea, to the realisation of which I feel
myself capable of devoting my life.   This idea is the foundation of a new religion, corresponding to the present state of
mankind—the religion of Jesus, but purified from dogma and
mysticism, a practical religion, not promising future bliss, but
giving bliss upon earth.   I feel that this idea can be realised
only by generations consciously looking towards it as a goal.
One generation will hand on the idea to the next and, some

day, enthusiasm or reason will bring it into being. To act with a deliberate view to the religious union of mankind, this is the leading principle of the idea which I hope will command my enthusiasm.'[1]

That this idea was suggested to Tolstóy by Rousseau seems highly probable. He was so great an admirer of Rousseau that during his stay in Caucasia he used to carry with him a copy of the *Contrat Social* even during the raids in which he took part with his battery, and which he described so artistically in *A Raid* and *Cutting Wood.*

LATEST WORKS OF ART

The disturbed conditions of the civilised world, and especially of Russia, evidently more than once attracted the attention of Tolstóy, and induced him to publish a considerable number of letters, papers, and appeals on various subjects. In all of them he advocated, first of all, and above all, an attitude of negation towards Church and State. Never enter the service of the State, even in the provincial and urban institutions, which are granted by the State only as a snare. Refuse to support exploitation in any form. Refuse to perform military service, whatever the consequences may be: for this is the only method of being truly anti-militarist. Never have anything to do with courts, even if you are offended or assailed ;—nothing but evil results from them. Such a negative and eminently sincere attitude, he maintains, would better promote the cause of true progress than any revolutionary means. As a first

---

[1] I take these lines from the most interesting book, *Lyov Nikolái-vitch Tolstóy: a Biography, based on Unpublished Materials (Reminiscences and Letters of L. N. Tolstóy)*, by P. Birukóff, 2nd edition, in 3 vols., Moscow, 1913,—of which, I am sorry to say, only the first volume, dealing with childhood and early manhood, was translated into English and published by Mr. Heinemann in 1906. A short abstract from the whole work, made by the author himself and translated into English, was published in 1911 by Cassel, under the title *The Life of Tolstóy*, by Paul Birukóff.

step, however, towards the abolition of modern slavery, he also recommends the nationalisation, or rather the municipalisation, of land.

It is manifest that the works of art which he wrote after 1876 must bear deep traces of his new point of view. He began, first, by writing for the people, and although most of his small stories for popular reading are spoiled to some extent by the too obvious desire of drawing a certain moral, and a consequent distortion of facts, there are a few among them—especially *How much Land is required for a Man* and *The Master and the Labourer*—which are wonderfully artistic. *The Death of Iván Ilyítch* need only be named to recall the profound impression produced at its appearance. It ranks amongst the most artistic works of Tolstóy.

In order to speak to a still wider audience in the theatres for the people, which began to be started in Russia about that time, he wrote *The Power of Darkness*, a most terrible drama from the life of the peasants, in which he aimed at producing a deep impression by means of a Shakespearian or rather Marlowian realism. His other play, *The Fruits of Civilisation*, written to be played at Yásnaya Polyána by his family and friends, is in a comical vein. The superstitions of the 'upper classes' as regards spiritualism are ridiculed in it. Both plays (the former with alterations in the final scene) are played with success on the Russian stage.

However, it is not only the novels and dramas of this period which are works of art. The five religious works which have been named on a preceding page are also works of art in the best sense of the word, as they contain descriptive pages of a high artistic value; while the very ways in which Tolstóy explains the economical principles of Socialism, or the No-Government principles of Anarchism, are masterpieces like the best socialistic and anarchistic pages of William Morris, but still surpassing the latter in simplicity and artistic power.

Kreutzer Sonata is surely, after *Anna Karénina*, the work of Tolstóy which has been the most widely read. However, the theme of this novel, and the crusade against marriage altogether which it contains, so much attract the attention of the reader and usually become the subject of so passionate a discussion among those who have read it, that the analysis of life and the high artistic qualities of this novel have hardly received the recognition they deserve. The moral teaching that Tolstóy has put in *Kreutzer Sonata* hardly need be mentioned, the more so as the author himself withdrew it to a very great extent. But for the appreciation of Tolstóy's work and for the comprehension of the artist's inner life this novel has a deep meaning. No stronger accusation against marriage for mere outer attraction, without intellectual union or sympathy of purpose between husband and wife, has ever been written; and the struggle that goes on between Kóznysheff and his wife is one of the most deeply dramatic pages of married life that we possess in any literature.

Tolstóy's *What is Art?* will be mentioned in chapter viii. of this book. His greatest production of the latest period is, however, *Resurrection.* It is not enough to say that the energy and youthfulness of the septuagenarian author shown in this novel are simply marvellous. Its absolute artistic qualities are so high that if Tolstóy had written nothing else but *Resurrection* he would have been recognised as one of the great writers. All those parts of the novel which deal with society, beginning with the letter of ' Missie,' and Missie herself, her father, and so on, are of the same high standard as the best pages of the first volume of *War and Peace.* Everything which deals with the court, the jurymen, and the prisons is again of the same high standard. It may be said, of course, that the principal hero, Nehlyúdoff, is not sufficiently living ; but this is quite unavoidable for a figure which is meant to represent, if not the author himself, at least his ideas or his experience: this is a drawback of all novels containing so much of an autobiographical element. As to all the other figures, of which an immense number pass before our eyes, each of them has its own character in striking relief, even if the figure (like one of the judges or of the jurymen, or the daughter of a jailer) appears only on a single page, never to reappear again.

The number of questions which are raised in this novel—social, political, party questions, and so on—is so great, that a whole society, such as it is, living and throbbing with all its problems and contradictions, appears before the reader; and this is not Russian society only, but society the civilised world over. In fact, apart from the scenes which deal with the political prisoners, *Resurrection* applies to all nations. It is the most international of all works of Tolstóy. At the same time the main question: 'Has society the right to judge? Is it reasonable in maintaining a system of tribunals and prisons?' this terrible question, which the coming century is bound to solve, is so forcibly impressed upon the reader that it is impossible to read the book without, at least, conceiving serious doubts about our system of punishments. *Ce livre pèsera sur la conscience du siècle* ('This book will weigh upon the conscience of the century') was the remark of a French critic; and of the justice of this remark I have had the opportunity of convincing myself during my numerous conversations in America with persons having anything to do with prisons. The book weighs already on their consciences.

The same remark applies to the whole activity of Tolstóy. Whether his attempt at impressing upon men the elements of a universal religion which—he believes —reason trained by science might accept, and which man might take as guidance for his moral life, working at the same time for the solution of the great social

problem and all questions connected with it—whether
this bold attempt be successful or not, can only be
decided by time. But it is absolutely certain that no
man since the times of Rousseau has so profoundly
stirred the human conscience as Tolstóy has by his
moral writings. He has fearlessly stated the moral
aspects of all the burning questions of the day, in a
form so deeply impressive that whoever has read any
one of his writings can no longer forget these questions
or set them aside ; one feels the necessity of finding, in
one way or another, some solution. Tolstóy's influence,
consequently, is not one which may be measured by
mere years or decades of years : it will last long. Nor
is it limited to one country only. In millions of copies
his works are read in all languages, appealing equally
to men and women of all classes and all nations, and
everywhere producing the same result. Towards the
end of his life Tolstóy was the most loved man, the
most touchingly loved man, in the world.

Most of the readers must remember the sensation
which was produced in the civilised world, in November
1910, when it became known that Tolstóy had secretly
left his home, in the night, for an unknown destination.
For a day or two it was not even known where the
great writer was—his daughter Alexandra and his
doctor friend Makovítskiy being the only two persons
who were in the secret of his departure. It was
suggested that he probably intended to join a small
communist settlement in Caucasia, where a few educated
people had settled to work upon the land, when the
news came that Tolstóy fell ill on his journey and was
laid up with a serious attack of pneumonia in the small
house of the station-master of Astápovo, a little railway-
station of Central Russia. There he was joined by a
few intimate friends, who took care not to admit to him
those who intended to say that in his last moments he
joined the Greek Orthodox Church, which had excom-
municated him for his conception of Christianity. The

L

illness rapidly developed, and a few days later he quietly
passed away.

His burial became a national event.   Thousands of
people—of the educated classes and peasants, students
and factory hands—came from all sides to the railway-
station nearest to Yásnaya Polyána to carry on their
shoulders the remains of ' The Great Writer of Russia '
to the spot where he had desired to be buried.   It was
a coppice on his estate where he and his brother
Nicholas used to say in their childhood that there was
buried a green magic wand, upon which the means of
rendering all men happy had been inscribed.   The spot
has been since a place of pilgrimage for thousands of
people of all classes.

For many admirers of Tolstóy his sudden departure
from his house was a surprise ; but not so for those
who knew his intimate life.   Already in 1900-1902 he
had written a drama, *And Light Shines in the Dark*
(now published in his *Posthumous Works*), where he
told the struggle he had to sustain in his house for the
right of living in accordance with his principles.   In
this drama Nikoláy Ivánovitch, who personifies Tolstóy
himself, after having vainly tried to convert his wife and
his children to his Socialist ideas, transfers to them all
his fortune, which at first he had intended to transfer to
the peasants.   He loves too much his wife and children
to abandon them, and he tries for some time to live, in a
poorly furnished room of his rich house, a life of manual
work and propaganda of his ideas.   But soon he can
stand no longer the duality which is unavoidable in
such conditions, and one night, while a dancing soirée
is in full swing in his house, he, accompanied by a co-
religionary, is on the point of leaving his house for ever.
His wife rushes to him, and her tears, as well as her
menace to throw herself under the train which he is
going to take, compel Nikoláy Ivánovitch to abandon
his plan.   It may also be added that Birukóff has
published in his biography of Tolstóy a letter which

the great writer had written to his wife in 1897, from which it appears that even then the idea of abandoning his rich house and the life that was going on in it was cherished by Tolstóy. In July 1910 he actually left his home; but after a few weeks he was prevailed upon to return. Now, in November 1910, he left it with the firm resolution of finding a spot where he could finish his days in accordance with his principles—when illness overcame him.

The inner drama of his life, which he had described so powerfully in a succession of works of art, was thus brought to an end by an act of revolt against the so-called civilisation of the present times. The great Rousseau of the nineteenth century indicated by this act what those who were revolted, like him, by the turn civilisation had taken, ought to do.

CHAPTER V

GONTCHARÓFF—DOSTOYÉVSKIY—NEKRÁSOFF

GONTCHARÓFF—*Oblómoff*—The Russian malady of Oblómovism
—Is it exclusively Russian?—*The Precipice*—DOSTOYÉVSKIY
—His first novel—General character of his work—*Memoirs from a Dead-House*—*Downtrodden and Offended*—*Crime and Punishment*—*The Brothers Karamázoff*—NEKRÁSOFF
—Discussions about his talent—His love of the people—
Apotheosis of Woman—OTHER PROSE-WRITERS OF THE SAME EPOCH—Serghéi Aksákoff—Dal—Iván Panáeff—Hvóschinskaya (V. Krestóvskiy-pseudonym)— POETS OF THE SAME EPOCH — Koltsóff—Nikítin—Pleschéyeff—The admirers of pure art : Tyúttcheff—A. Máykoff—Scherbína—Polónskiy—A. Fet—A. K. Tolstóy—THE TRANSLATORS.

GONTCHARÓFF

GONTCHARÓFF occupies in Russian literature the next place after Turguéneff and Tolstóy, but this extremely interesting writer remained till quite lately almost entirely unknown to English readers. He was not a prolific writer, and apart from small sketches and a book of travel (*The Frigate Pallas*), he has left only three novels : *A Common Story* (translated into English by Constance Garnett), *Oblómoff*, and *The Precipice* (translated only in 1915), of which the second, *Oblómoff*, has conquered for him a position by the side of the two great writers just named.

In Russia Gontcharóff is always described as a writer of an eminently objective talent, but this qualification must evidently be taken with a certain restriction. A writer is never entirely objective—he has his sympathies and antipathies, and do what he may, they will appear even through his most objective descriptions. On the other hand, a good writer seldom introduces his own individual emotions to speak for his heroes. However, with Turguéneff and Tolstóy you feel that they live with their heroes, that they suffer and feel happy with them—that they are in love when the hero is in love, and that they feel miserable when misfortunes befall him ; but you do not feel that to the same extent with Gontcharóff. It is certain that these three novels are to a great extent autobiographical, but he tries to conceal it, and to preserve towards his heroes an attitude of strict impartiality—an attitude, I hardly need say, which a writer can never maintain. An epic profusion of details certainly characterises Gontcharóff's novels ; but these details are not obtrusive, they do not diminish the impression, and the reader's interest in the hero is not distracted by all these minutiæ, because, under Gontcharóff's pen, they never appear insignificant. One feels, however, that the author, whatever his inner storms may be at times, is a person who takes human life quietly, and will never give way to a burst of passion, whatsoever may happen to his heroes.

The most popular of the novels of Gontcharóff is *Oblómoff*, which, like Turguéneff's *Fathers and Sons*, and Tolstóy's *War and Peace* and *Resurrection*, is, I venture to say, one of the profoundest productions of the last half of the nineteenth century. It is thoroughly Russian, so Russian indeed that only a Russian can fully appreciate it ; but it is at the same time universally human, as it introduces a type which is almost as universal as that of Hamlet or Don Quixote.

Oblómoff is a Russian nobleman, of moderate means— the owner of six or seven hundred serfs—and the time of action is, let us say, in the fifties of the nineteenth century. All the early childhood of Oblómoff was such as to destroy in him any capacity of initiative. Imagine a spacious, well-kept nobleman's estate in the middle of Russia, somewhere on the picturesque banks of the Vólga, at a time when there were no railways to disturb a peaceful patriarchal life, and no 'questions' to worry the minds of its inhabitants. A 'reign of plenty,' both for the owners of the estate and the scores of their servants and retainers, characterises their life. Nurses, servants, serving boys and maids surround the child from its earliest days, their only thoughts being how to feed it, make it grow, render it strong, and never bore it with either much learning or, in fact, with any sort of work. 'From my earliest childhood have I myself ever put on my socks?' Oblómoff asks later on. In the morning the coming midday meal is the main question for all the household; and when the dinner is over at an early hour of the day, sleep—a reign of sleep, sleep rising to an epical degree, which implies full loss of consciousness for all the inhabitants of the mansion and its dependencies—spreads its wings for several hours from the bedchamber of the landlord even as far as the remotest corner of the retainers' dwellings.

In these surroundings Oblómoff's childhood and youth were passed. Later on he enters the University; but his trustworthy servants follow him to the capital, and the lazy, sleepy atmosphere of his native 'Oblómovka' (the estate) holds him even there in its enchanted arms. A few lectures at the University, some elevating talk with a young friend in the evening, some vague aspiration towards the ideal, occasionally stir the young man's heart; and a beautiful vision begins to rise before his eyes—these things are certainly a necessary accompaniment of the years spent at the University; but the soothing, soporific influence of Oblómovka, its quietness and laziness, its feeling of a fully guaranteed, undisturbed existence, deaden even these impressions of youth. Other students grow hot in their discussions, and join 'circles.' Oblómoff looks quietly at all that and asks himself: 'What is it for?' And then, the moment that the young student has returned home after his University years, the same atmosphere again envelops him.

'Why should you think and worry yourself with this or that?' Leave that to 'others.' Have you not there your old nurse, thinking whether there is anything else she might do for your comfort?

'My people did not let me have even a wish,' Gontcharóff wrote in his short autobiography, from which we learned the close connection between the author and his hero; 'all had been foreseen and attended to long since. The old servants, with my nurse at their head, looked into my eyes to guess my wishes, trying to remember what I liked best when I was with them, where my writing-table ought to be put, which chair I preferred to the others, how to make my bed. The cook tried to remember which dishes I had liked in my childhood—and all could not admire me enough.'

Such was Oblómoff's youth, and such was to a very great extent Gontcharóff's youth and character as well.

The novel begins with Oblómoff's morning in his lodgings at St. Petersburg. It is late, but he is still in bed; several times already he has tried to get up, several times his foot was in the slipper; but, after a moment's reflection, he has returned under his blankets. His trusty Zakhár—his old faithful servant who formerly had carried him as a baby in his arms—is by his side, and brings him his glass of tea. Visitors come in; they try to induce Oblómoff to go out, to take a drive to the yearly First of May promenade; but—'What for?' he asks. 'For what should I take all this trouble, and do all this moving about?' And he remains in bed.

His only trouble is that the landlord wants him to leave the lodgings which he occupies. The rooms are dull, dusty—Zakhár is no great admirer of cleanliness; but to change lodgings is such a calamity for Oblómoff that he tries to avoid it by all possible means, or at least to postpone it.

Oblómoff is very well educated, well-bred, he has a refined taste, and in matters of art he is a fine judge. Everything that is vulgar is repulsive to him. He never will commit a dishonest act; he cannot. He also

shares the highest and noblest aspirations of his contemporaries. Like many others, he is ashamed of being
a serf-owner, and he has in his head a certain scheme
which he is going to put some day into writing—a
scheme which, if it only is carried out, will surely improve
the condition of his peasants and eventually free them.

'The joy of higher inspirations was accessible to him,'
Gontcharóff writes; 'the miseries of mankind were not strange
to him. Sometimes he cried bitterly in the depths of his
heart about human sorrows. He felt unnamed, unknown
sufferings and sadness, and a desire of going somewhere far
away—probably into that world towards which his friend
Stoltz had tried to take him in his younger days. Sweet tears
would then flow upon his cheeks. It would also happen that
he would himself feel hatred towards human vices, towards
deceit, towards the evil which is spread all over the world;
and he would then feel the desire to show mankind its diseases.
Thoughts would then burn within him, rolling in his head like
waves in the sea; they would grow into decisions which would
make all his blood boil; his muscles would be ready to move,
his sinews would be strained, intentions would be on the point
of transforming themselves into decisions. . . . Moved by a
moral force, he would rapidly change over and over again his
position in his bed; with a fixed stare he would half lift himself from it, move his hand, look about with inspired eyes . . .
the inspiration would seem ready to realise itself, to transform
itself into an act of heroism, and then, What miracles, what
admirable results might one not expect from so great an effort!
But—the morning would pass away, the shades of evening
would take the place of the broad daylight, and with them
the strained forces of Oblómoff would incline towards rest—
the storms in his soul would subside—his head would shake
off the worrying thoughts—his blood would circulate more
slowly in his veins—and Oblómoff would slowly turn over,
and recline on his back; looking sadly through his window
upon the sky, following sadly with his eyes the sun which was
setting gloriously behind the neighbouring house—and how
many times had he thus followed with his eyes that sunset!'

In such lines as these Gontcharóff depicts the state of
inactivity into which Oblómoff had fallen at the age

of about thirty-five. It is the supreme poetry of laziness—a laziness created by a whole life of old-time landlordism.

Oblómoff, as I just said, is very uncomfortable in his lodgings ; moreover, the landlord, who intends to make some repairs in the house, wants him to leave ; but for Oblómoff to change his lodgings is something so terrific, so extraordinary, that he tries by all sorts of artifices to postpone the undesirable moment. His old Zakhár tries to convince him that they cannot remain any longer in that house, and ventures the unfortunate word that, after all, 'others' move when they have to.

'I thought,' he said, 'that others are not worse than we are, and that they move sometimes ; so we could move, too.'

'What, what?' exclaimed Oblómoff, rising from his easy-chair, 'what is it that you say?'

Zakhár felt very ashamed. He could not understand what had provoked the reproachful exclamation of his master, and did not reply.

'Others are not worse than we are!' repeated Iliyá Ilyích (Oblómoff) with a sense of horror. 'That is what you have come to. Now I shall know henceforth that I am for you the same as "the others."'

After a time Oblómoff calls Zakhár back and has with him an explanation which is worth reproducing.

'Have you ever thought what it meant—"the others"?' Oblómoff began. 'Must I tell you what this means?'

Poor Zakhár shifted about uneasily, like a bear in his den, and sighed aloud.

'"Another"—that means a wild, uneducated man ; he lives poorly, dirtily, in an attic ; he can sleep on a piece of felt stretched somewhere on the floor—what does that matter to him?—Nothing ! He will feed on potatoes and herrings ; misery compels him continuously to shift from one place to another. He runs about all day long—*he*, he may, of course, go to new lodgings. There is Lagáeff ; he takes under his arm his ruler and his two shirts wrapped in a handkerchief, and he is off. "Where are you going?"

you ask him.—"I am moving," he says. That is what "the others" means.—Am I one of those others, do you mean?'

Zakhár threw a glance upon his master, shifted from one foot to the other, but said nothing.

'Do you understand now what "another" means?' continued Oblómoff. '"Another," that is the man who cleans his own boots, who himself puts on his clothes—without any help! Of course, he may sometimes look like a gentleman, but that is mere deceit: he does not know what it means to have a servant—he has nobody to send to the shop to make his purchases; he makes them himself—he will even poke his own fire, and occasionally use a duster.'

'Yes,' replied Zakhár sternly, 'there are many such people among the Germans.'

'That's it, that's it! And I? do you think that I am one of them?'

'No, you are different,' Zakhár said, still unable to understand what his master was driving at. . . . 'But God knows what is coming upon you. . . .'

'Ah! I am different! Most certainly I am. Do I run about? do I work? don't I eat whenever I am hungry? Look at me—am I thin? am I sickly to look at? Is there anything I lack? Thank God, I have people to do things for me. I have never put on my own socks since I was born, thank God! Must I also be restless like the others?—What for?— And to whom am I saying all this? Have you not been with me from childhood? . . . You have seen it all. You know that I have received a delicate education; that I have never suffered from cold or from hunger—never knew want—never worked for my own bread—have never done any sort of dirty work. . . . Well, how dare you put me on the same level as the "others"?'

Later on, when Zakhár brought him a glass of water, 'No, wait a moment,' Oblómoff said. 'I ask you, How did you dare to so deeply offend your master, whom you carried in your arms when he was a baby, whom you have served all your life, and who has always been a benefactor to you?' Zakhár could not stand it any longer—the word benefactor broke him down—he began to blink. The less he understood the speech of Iliyá Ilyích, the more sad he felt. Finally, the reproachful words of his master made him break into tears, while Iliyá Ilyích, seizing this pretext for postponing his letter-writing till to-morrow, tells Zakhár, 'You had better pull the blinds down and cover me nicely, and see that nobody disturbs me. Perhaps I may sleep for an hour or so, and at half-past five wake me for dinner.'

About this time Oblómoff meets a young girl, Olga, who is perhaps one of the finest representatives of Russian women in our novels. A mutual friend, Stoltz, has said much to her about Oblómoff—about his talents and possibilities, and also about the laziness of his life, which would surely ruin him if it continued. Women are always ready to undertake rescue work, and Olga tries to draw Oblómoff out of his sleepy, vegetative existence. She sings beautifully, and Oblómoff, who is a great lover of music, is deeply moved by her songs.

Gradually Olga and Oblómoff fall in love with each other, and she tries to shake off his laziness, to arouse him to higher interests in life. She insists that he shall finish the great scheme for the improvement of his peasant serfs upon which he is supposed to have been working for years. She tries to awaken in him an interest for art and literature, to create for him a life in which his gifted nature shall find a field of activity. It seems at first as if the vigour and charm of Olga are going to renovate Oblómoff by insensible steps. He wakes up, he returns to life. The love of Olga for Oblómoff, which is depicted in its development with a mastery almost equalling that of Turguéneff, grows deeper and deeper, and the inevitable next step—marriage—is approaching. . . . But this is enough to frighten away Oblómoff. To take this step he would have to bestir himself, to go to his estate, to break the lazy monotony of his life, and this is too much for him. He lingers and hesitates to make the first necessary steps. He postpones them from day to day, and finally he falls back into his Oblómoffdom, and returns to his sofa, his dressing-gown, and his slippers. Olga is ready to do the impossible ; she tries to carry him away by her love and her energy ; but she is forced to realise that all her endeavours are useless, and that she has trusted too much to her own strength: the disease of Oblómoff is incurable. She has to abandon him, and Gontcharóff describes their parting in a most beautiful scene, from which I will translate here a few of the concluding passages.

'Then we must part?' she said. . . . 'If we married, what would come next?' He replied nothing. 'You would fall asleep, deeper and deeper every day—is it not so? And I— you see what I am—I shall not grow old, I shall never be tired of life. We should live from day to day and year to year, looking forward to Christmas, and then to the Carnival; we should go to parties, dance, and think about nothing at all. We should lie down at night thanking God that one day has passed, and next morning we should wake up with the desire that to-day may be like yesterday; that would be our future, is it not so? But is that life? I should wither under it—I should die. And for what, Iliyá? Could I make you happy?'

He cast his eyes around and tried to move, to run away, but his feet would not obey him. He wanted to say something, but his mouth was dry, his tongue motionless, his voice would not come out of his throat. He moved his hand towards her, then he began something, with lowered voice, but could not finish it, and with his look he said to her, 'Good-bye—farewell.'

She also wanted to say something, but could not—moved her hand in his direction, but before it had reached his it dropped. She wanted to say 'Farewell,' but her voice broke in the middle of the word and took a false accent. Then her face quivered, she put her hand and her head on his shoulder and cried. It seemed now as if all her weapons had been taken out of her hand—reasoning had gone—there remained only the woman, helpless against her sorrow. 'Farewell, Farewell' came out of her sobbings. . . .

'No,' said Olga, trying to look upon him through her tears, 'it is only now that I see that I loved in you what I wanted you to be, I loved the future Oblómoff. You are good, honest, Iliyá, you are tender as a dove, you put your head under your wing and want nothing more, you are ready all your life to coo under a roof . . . but I am not so, that would be too little for me. I want something more—what, I do not know; can you tell me what it is that I want? give me it, that I should. . . . As to sweetness, there is plenty of it everywhere.'

They part. Olga passes through a severe illness, and a few months later we see Oblómoff married to the landlady of his rooms, a very respectable person with beautiful elbows, and a great master in kitchen affairs and household work generally. As to Olga, she marries Stoltz later on. But this Stoltz is rather a symbol of intelligent industrial activity than a living man. He is invented, and I pass him by.

The impression which this novel produced in Russia, on its appearance in 1859, was indescribable. It was a far greater event than the appearance of a new work by Turguéneff. All educated Russia read *Oblómoff* and discussed 'Oblómovism.' Every one recognised something of himself in Oblómoff, felt the disease of Oblómoff in his own veins. As to Olga, thousands of young people fell in love with her: her favourite song, the 'Casta Diva,' became their favourite melody. And even now one can read and reread *Oblómoff* with the same pleasure as half a century ago. It has lost nothing of its meaning, while it has acquired many new ones : there are always living Oblómoffs.

At the time of the appearance of this novel 'Oblómoffdom' became a current word to designate the state of Russia. All Russian life, all Russian history, bears traces of the malady—that laziness of mind and heart, that right to laziness proclaimed as a virtue, that conservatism and inertia, that contempt of feverish activity, which characterise Oblómoff and were so much cultivated in serfdom times, even amongst the best men in Russia —and even among the malcontents. 'A sad result of serfdom'—it was said then. But, as we live further away from serfdom times, we begin to realise that Oblómoff is not dead amongst us : that serfdom is not the only thing which creates this type of men, but that the very conditions of wealthy life, the routine of civilised life, contribute to maintain it.

'A racial feature, distinctive of the Russian race,' others said ; and they were right, too, to a great extent. The absence of a love for struggle ; the 'let me alone' attitude, the want of 'aggressive virtue' ; non-resistance and passive submission—these are to a great extent distinctive features of the Russian race. And this is probably why a Russian writer has so well pictured the type. But with all that the Oblómoff type is not limited to Russia : it is a universal type—a type which is nurtured by our present civilisation, amidst its opulent, self-satisfied life. It is the conservative type. Not in the political sense, but in the sense of the conservatism of well-being. A man who has reached a certain welfare, or has got it by inheritance, is not willingly moved to undertake anything new, because it might mean introducing something unpleasant and full of worries into his quiet and smooth existence. Therefore he lingers in a life devoid of the true impulses of real life, from fear that these might disturb the quietness of his vegetative existence.

Oblómoff knows the value of art and its impulses ; he knows the higher enthusiasms of poetical love : he has felt both. But—'What is the use ?' he asks again. 'Why all this trouble of going about and seeing people ? What is it for ?' He is not a Diogenes who has no needs. Far from that. If his meat be served too dry and his fowl be burned, he resents it. It is the higher interests which he thinks not worth the trouble they occasion. When he was young he thought of setting his serfs free—in such a way that the step should not much diminish his income. But gradually he has forgotten all about that, and now his main thought is, how to shake off all the worries of the management of his estate. 'I don't know'—he says—'what obligatory work is, what is farmer's work, what ownership means, what a poor peasant is and what a rich one ; what

makes a quarter of wheat, when wheat has to be sown
and reaped, or when it has to be sold.' And when he
dreams of country life on his estate he thinks of pretty
greenhouses, of picnics in the woods, of idyllic walks in
company with a goodly submissive and plump wife, who
looks into his eyes and worships him. The question of
why and how all this wealth comes to him, and why all
these people must work for him, never worries his mind.
But how many of those all over the world, who own
factories, wheat-fields, and coal-mines, or hold shares in
them, ever think of mines, wheat-fields, and factories
otherwise than in the way Oblómoff thought of his
country seat—that is, in an idyllic contemplation of how
others work, without the slightest intention of sharing
their burdens ?

The city-bred Oblómoffs may take the place of the
country-bred, but the type remains. And then comes
the long succession of Oblómoffs in intellectual, social,
nay even in personal, life. Everything new in the
domain of the intellect makes them restless, and they
are only satisfied when all men have accepted the same
ideas. They are suspicious of social reform, because the
very suggestion of a change frightens them. Love itself
frightens them. Oblómoff is loved by Olga ; he, too,
loves her ; but to take that step—marriage—frightens
him. She is too restless. She wants him to go about
and to see pictures ; to read and to discuss this and that ;
to throw him into the whirl of life. She loves him so
much that she is ready to follow him without asking any
questions. But this very power of love, this very intensity of life, frightens an Oblómoff.

He tries to find pretexts for avoiding this irruption of
life into his vegetative existence ; he prizes so much his
little material comfort that he dares not love—dares not
take love with all its consequences—'its tears, its impulses, its life,' and soon falls back into his cosy Oblómovism.

Decidedly, Oblómovism is not a racial disease. It

exists on both continents and in all latitudes. And besides the Oblómovism which Gontcharóff has so well depicted, and which even Olga was powerless to break through, there is the squire's Oblómovism, the red-tape Oblómovism of the Government offices, the scientist's Oblómovism, and, above all, the family-life Oblómovism, to which all of us readily pay so large a tribute.

THE PRECIPICE

The last and longest novel of Gontcharóff, *The Precipice,* has not the unity of conception and workmanship which characterise *Oblómoff.* It contains wonderful pages, worthy of a writer of genius ; but, all said, it is a failure. It took Gontcharóff full ten years to write it, and having begun to depict in it types of one generation, he remodelled later on these types into types from the next generation—at a time when the sons differed totally from their fathers : he has told this himself in a very interesting critical sketch of his own work. As a result there is no wholeness, so to speak, in the main personages of the novel. The woman upon whom he has bestowed all his admiration, Vyéra, and whom he tries to represent as most sympathetic, is certainly interesting, but not sympathetic at all. One would say that Gontcharóff's mind was haunted by two women of two totally different types when he pictured his Vyéra : the one whom he tried—and failed—to picture in Sophie Byelovódova, and the other—the coming woman of the sixties, of whom he saw some features, and whom he admired, without fully understanding her. Vyéra's cruelty towards her grandmother, and towards Ráyskiy, the hero, render her most unsympathetic, although you feel that the author adores her. As to the Nihilist, Vólokhoff, he is simply a caricature—taken perhaps from real life— maybe from among the author's personal acquaintances —but certainly not representative of the Nihilist type. Gontcharóff's first sketch of Vólokhoff was, as he wrote himself, some sort of Bohemian Radical of the forties who had retained in full the Don Juanesque features of the ' Byronists ' of the preceding generation. Gradually, however, Gontcharóff, who had not yet finished his novel by the end of the fifties, transformed the figure into a Nihilist of the sixties, and the result is that one has the sensation of the double origin of Vólokhoff, as one feels the double origin of Vyéra.

Of the main figures of the novel the best and really true to life is the grandmother of Vyéra. This is an admirably painted figure of the simple, common-sense, independent woman of old Russia, while Martha, the sister of Vyéra, is an excellent picture of the common-place girl, full of life, respectful of old traditions, who will be one day an honest and reliable mother of a family. These two figures, as well as that of the artist Ráyskiy and several secondary figures, are the work of a great artist ; and yet, even in the grandmother, there is much exaggeration in the tragical way in which she takes Vyéra's fall. As to the background of the novel—the estate on a precipice leading to the Vólga—it is one of the most beautiful landscapes in Russian literature.

DOSTOYÉVSKIY

Few authors have been so well received, from their very first appearance in literature, as Dostoyévskiy was. In 1845 he arrived in St. Petersburg, a quite unknown young man who only two years before had finished his education in a school of military engineers, and after having spent two years in the engineering service had then abandoned it with the intention of devoting himself to literature. He was only twenty-four when he wrote his first novel, *Poor People*, which his school-comrade, Grigoróvitch, gave to the poet Nekrásoff, offering it for a literary almanac. Dostoyévskiy had inwardly doubted whether the novel would even be read by the editor. He was living then in a poor,

M

miserable room, and was fast asleep when at four o'clock in the morning Nekrásoff and Grigoróvitch knocked at his door. They threw themselves on Dostoyévskiy's neck, congratulating him with tears in their eyes. Nekrásoff and his friend had begun to read the novel late in the evening; they could not stop reading till they came to the end, and they were both so deeply impressed by it that they could not help going on this nocturnal expedition, to see the author and tell him what they felt. A few days later Dostoyévskiy was introduced to the great critic of the time, Byelínskiy, and from him he received the same warm reception. As to the reading public, the novel produced quite a sensation. The same must be said about all subsequent novels of Dostoyévskiy. They had an immense sale all over Russia.

The life of Dostoyévskiy was extremely sad. In the year 1849, four years after he had won his first success with *Poor People*, he became mixed up in the affairs of some Fourierists (members of the circles of Petra-shévskiy), who used to meet together to read the works of Fourier, commenting on them, and talking about the necessity of a Socialistic movement in Russia. At one of these gatherings Dostoyévskiy read a certain letter from Byelínskiy to Gógol, in which the great critic spoke in rather sharp language about the Russian Church and the State; he also took part in a meeting at which the starting of a secret printing-office was discussed. He was arrested, tried (of course with closed doors), and, with several others, was condemned to death. In December 1849 he was taken to a public square, placed on the scaffold, under a gibbet, to listen there to a profusely worded death-sentence, and only at the last moment came a messenger from Nicholas I. bringing a pardon. Three days later he was trans-ported to Siberia and locked up in a hard-labour prison at Omsk. There he remained for four years, when owing to some influence at St. Petersburg he was liberated, only to be made a soldier. It was said that during his detention in the hard-labour prison he was submitted, for some minor offence, to the terrible punishment of the cat-o'-nine-tails, and from that time dates his disease—epilepsy—which he never quite got rid of during all his life; but this is considered now as a mere legend. The coronation amnesty of Alexander II. did not improve Dostoyévskiy's fate. Not until 1859—four years after the advent of Alexander II. to the throne—was the great writer pardoned and allowed to return to Russia. He died in 1883.

Dostoyévskiy was a rapid writer, and even before his arrest he had published ten novels, of which *The Double* was already a forerunner of his later psycho-pathological novels, and *Nétochka Nezvánova* showed a rapidly maturing literary talent of the highest quality. On his return from Siberia he began publishing a series of novels which produced a deep impression on the reading public. He opened the series by a great novel, *The Downtrodden and Offended*, which was soon followed by *Memoirs from a Dead-House*, in which he described his hard-labour experience. Then came a novel, *Crime and Punishment*, which lately was widely read all over Europe and America, and was put on the English stage in a very much modified form. *The Idiot*, *The Youth*, and *The Devils* deal partly with psycho-pathological and partly with social problems ; while *The Brothers Karamázoff* is considered his profoundest work and is much admired in certain literary circles.

If Dostoyévskiy's work had been judged from the purely æsthetic point of view, the verdict of critics concerning its literary value could have been very severe. He wrote with such rapidity that, as Dobrolúboff has shown, the literary form is in many places almost below criticism. His heroes speak in a slipshod way, continually repeating themselves, and whatever the hero says in the novel (especially is this so in *The Downtrodden*), you feel it is the author who speaks. Besides, to these serious defects one must add the extremely romantic and obsolete forms of the plots of his novels, the disorder of their construction, and the unnatural succession of their events—to say nothing of the atmosphere of the lunatic asylum with which the later ones are permeated. And yet, with all this, the works of Dostoyévskiy are penetrated with such a deep feeling of reality, and by the side of the most unreal characters one finds characters so well known to every one of us, and so real, that all these defects are redeemed. Even when you think that Dostoyévskiy's record of the conversations of his heroes is not correct, you feel that the men whom he describes —at least some of them—were exactly such as he wanted to describe them.

The *Memoirs from a Dead-House* is the only production of Dostoyévskiy which can be recognised as truly artistic : its leading idea is beautiful, and the form is worked out in conformity with the idea ; but in his later productions the author is so much oppressed by his ideas, all very vague, and he grows so nervously excited over them, that he cannot find the proper form. The favourite themes of Dostoyévskiy are the men who have been brought so low by the circumstances of their lives that they have not even a conception of there being a possibility of rising above these conditions. You feel, moreover, that Dostoyévskiy finds a real pleasure in describing the sufferings, moral and physical, of the downtrodden—that he revels in representing that misery of mind, that absolute hopelessness of redress, and that completely broken-down condition of human nature which is characteristic of neuro-pathological cases. By the side of such sufferers you find a few others who are so deeply human that all your sympathies go with them ; but the favourite heroes of Dostoyévskiy are the man and the woman who consider themselves as not having either the force to compel respect, or even the right of being treated as human beings. They once have made some timid attempt at defending their personalities, but they have succumbed, and never will try it again. They will sink deeper and deeper in their wretchedness, and die, either from consumption or from exposure, or they will become the victims of some mental affection—a sort of half-lucid lunacy, during which man occasionally rises to the highest conceptions of human philosophy—while some will conceive an embitterment which will bring them to commit some crime, followed by repentance the very next instant after it has been done.

In *Downtrodden and Offended* we see a young man madly in love with a girl from a moderately poor family. This girl falls in love with a very aristocratic prince—a man without principles, but charming in his childish egotism—extremely attractive by his sincerity, and with a full capacity for quite unconsciously committing the worst crimes towards those with whom life brings him into contact. The psychology of both the girl and the young aristocrat is very good, but where Dostoyévskiy appears at his best is in representing how the other young man, rejected by the girl, devotes the whole of his existence to being the humble servant of that girl, and against his own will becomes instrumental in throwing her into the hands of the young aristocrat. All this is quite possible, all this exists in life, and it is all told by Dostoyévskiy so as to make one feel the deepest commiseration with the poor and the downtrodden; but even in this novel the pleasure which the author finds in representing the unfathomable submission and servitude of his heroes, and the pleasure they find in the very sufferings and the ill-treatment that has been inflicted upon them, is repulsive to a sound mind.

The next great novel of Dostoyévskiy, *Crime and Punishment*, produced quite a sensation. Its hero is a young student, Raskólnikoff, who deeply loves his mother and his sister—both extremely poor, like himself—and who, haunted by the desire of finding some money in order to finish his studies and to become a support to his dear ones, comes to the idea of killing an old woman, a private money-lender whom he knows and who is said to possess a few thousand roubles. A series of more or less fortuitous circumstances confirms him in this idea and pushes him this way. Thus, his sister, who sees no escape from their poverty, is going at last to sacrifice herself for her family, and to marry a certain despicable, elderly man with much money, and Raskólnikoff is firmly decided to prevent this marriage. At the same time he meets with an old man—a small civil service clerk and a drunkard who has a most sympathetic daughter from the first marriage, Sónya. The family are at the lowest imaginable depths of destitution—such as can only be found in a large city like St. Petersburg—and Raskólnikoff is brought to take an interest in them. Owing to all these circumstances, while he himself sinks deeper and deeper into the darkest misery, and realises the depths of hopeless poverty and misery which surround him, the idea of killing the old money-lending woman takes a firm hold of him. He accomplishes the crime and, of course, as might have been foreseen, does not take advantage of the money: he hardly finds it in his excitement; and, after having lived for a few days haunted by remorse and shame—again under the pressure of a series of various circumstances which add to the feeling of remorse—he goes to surrender himself, denouncing himself as the murderer of the old woman and her sister.

This is, of course, only the framework of the novel; in reality it is full of the most thrilling scenes of poverty on the one hand and of moral degradation on the other, while a number of secondary characters—an elderly gentleman in whose family Raskólnikoff's sister has been a governess, the examining magistrate, and so on—are introduced. Besides, Dostoyévskiy, after having accumulated so many reasons which might have brought a Raskólnikoff to commit such a murder, found it necessary to introduce, moreover, a theoretical motive. One learns in the midst of the novel that Raskólnikoff, captivated by the modern, current ideas of materialist philosophy, has written and published a newspaper article to prove that men are divided into superior and inferior beings, and that for the former—Napoleon being a sample of them—the current rules of morality are not obligatory.

Most of the readers of this novel and most of the literary critics speak very highly of the psychological analysis of Raskólnikoff's soul and of the motives which brought him to his desperate step. However, I will permit myself to remark that the very profusion of accidental causes accumulated by Dostoyévskiy shows how difficult he felt it himself to prove that the propaganda of materialistic ideas could in reality bring an honest young man to act as Raskólnikoff did. Raskólnikoffs do not become murderers under the influence of such theoretical considerations, while those who murder and invoke such motives, like Lebiès at Paris, are not in the least of the Raskólnikoff type.[1] Behind Raskólnikoff I feel Dostoyévskiy trying to decide whether he himself, or a man like him, might have been brought to act as Raskólnikoff did, and what would be the psychological explanation if he had been driven to do so. But such men do *not* murder. Besides, men like the examining magistrate and M. Svidrigailoff are purely romantic inventions.

However, with all its faults, the novel produces a most powerful effect by its real pictures of slum life, and inspires every honest reader with the deepest commiseration towards even the lowest sunken inhabitants of the slums. The fact is, that when Dostoyévskiy

---

[1] Lebiès was a French student who murdered an old money-lender woman, under the influence—it was said—of the theory which represents individual struggle for life as a law of nature.

comes to them, he becomes a realist writer in the best sense of the word, like Turguéneff or Tolstóy. Marmeládoff—the old drunken official—his drunken talk and his death, his family, and the incidents which happen after his burial, his wife and his daughter Sónya—all these are living beings and real incidents of the life of the poorest ones, and the pages that Dostoyévskiy gave to them belong to the most impressive and the most moving pages in any literature. They have the touch of genius. But after these pages comes the romantic writer (a follower of Eugène Sue in his best works), and the novel which combines these two moods loses its unity.

The Brothers Karamázoff is the most artistically worked out of Dostoyévskiy's novels, but it is also the novel in which all the inner defects of the author's mind and imagination have found their fullest expression. The philosophy of this novel—incredulous Western Europe; wildly passionate, drunken, unreformed Russia; and Russia reformed by creed and monks—the three represented by the three brothers Karamázoff—only faintly appears in the background. But there is certainly not in any literature such a collection of the most repulsive types of mankind—lunatics, half-lunatics, criminals in germ and in reality, in all possible gradations—as one finds in this novel. A Russian specialist in brain and nervous diseases finds representatives of all sorts of such diseases in Dostoyévskiy's novels, and especially in *The Brothers Karamázoff*—the whole being set in a frame which represents the strangest mixture of realism and romanticism run wild. Whatsoever a certain portion of contemporary critics, fond of all sorts of morbid literature, may have written about this novel, the present writer can only say that he finds it, all through, so unnatural, so much fabricated for the purpose of introducing—here, a bit of morals, there, some abominable character taken from a psycho-pathological hospital; or again, in order to analyse the feelings of some purely imaginary criminal, that a few good pages scattered here and there do not compensate the reader for the hard task of reading these two volumes.

Some critics represent *The Brothers Karamázoff* as an 'essentially Russian' novel, but an exactly identical collection of psycho-pathological types can be found in every large city. Even the passionate discussions about God, which are said to be typical of Russian 'intellectuals,' were equally passionate in the intellectuals in those years, 'the sixties,' in Western Europe.

Dostoyévskiy is still very much read in Russia; and when his novels were first translated into French, German, and English, they were received by certain critics as a revelation. He was praised as one of the greatest writers of our own time, and as undoubtedly the one who 'had best expressed the mystic Slavonic soul'—whatever that expression may mean! Turguéneff was eclipsed by Dostoyévskiy, and Tolstóy was forgotten for a time. There was, of course, a great deal of hysterical exaggeration in all this, and at the present time sound literary critics do not venture to indulge in such praises. The fact is, that there is certainly a great deal of power in whatever Dostoyévskiy wrote: his powers of creation suggest those of Eugène Sue and Hoffmann; and his sympathy with the most downtrodden and downcast products of the civilisation of our large towns is so deep that it carries away the most indifferent reader and exercises a powerful impression in the right direction upon young readers. His analysis of the most varied specimens of incipient psychical disease is said to be thoroughly correct.

Altogether, the artistic qualities of his novels are far below those of the three great Russian masters: Tolstóy, Turguéneff, or Gontcharóff. Pages of consummate realism are interwoven with the most fantastical incidents worthy only of the most incorrigible romantics.

Scenes of thrilling interest are interrupted in order to
introduce a score of pages of the most unnatural theoretical discussions. Besides, the author is in such a
hurry that he seems never to have had the time himself
to read over his novels before sending them to the
printer. And, worst of all, every one of the heroes of
Dostoyévskiy, especially in his novels of the later period,
is a person suffering from some psychical disease or from
moral perversion. As a result, while one may read
some of the novels of Dostoyévskiy with the greatest
interest, one is never tempted to reread them, as one
rereads the novels of Tolstóy and Turguéneff, and even
those of many secondary novel writers ; and the present
writer must confess that he had the greatest pain lately
in reading through, for instance, *The Brothers Karamázoff*, and never could pull himself through such a novel
as *The Idiot*.

And yet, with all that, one pardons Dostoyévskiy
everything, because when he speaks of the ill-treated
and forgotten children of our town civilisation he becomes truly great through his wide, infinite love of
mankind—of man, even in his worst manifestations.
Through his love of those drunkards, beggars, petty
thieves, and so on, whom we usually pass by without
even bestowing upon them a pitying glance ; through
hispower of discovering what is human and often great
in the lowest sunken being ; through the love which he
inspires in us, even for the least interesting types of
mankind, even for those who never will make an effort
to get out of the low and miserable position into which
life has thrown them—through this faculty Dostoyévskiy
has certainly won a unique position among the Russian
writers of modern times ; and he will be read, not for
the artistic finish of his writings, but for the good
thoughts which are scattered through them, for their
real reproduction of slum life in the great cities, and
for the infinite sympathy which a being like Sónya can
inspire in the reader.

Even in the lowest types of man which he depicted he found the means of introducing at times truly sympathetic features.

Besides, if in his later-period novels the unsound psychiatric element takes in some of his heroes a more and more repulsive form, the inner struggles going on in men between their higher social conceptions and their low, and sometimes lowest, instincts take a more and more tragic character. And these struggles between the higher and the lower part of human nature are depicted with such a psychological insight that the reader is kept in their grip, even though he fails to be in sympathy with the author.

NEKRÁSOFF

With Nekrásoff we come to a poet whose work has been the subject of a lively controversy in Russia. He was born in 1821, his father being a poor army officer who married a Polish lady for love. This lady must have been most remarkable, because in his poems Nekrásoff continually refers to his mother in accents of love and respect, such as perhaps have no parallel in any other poet. His mother, however, died very early, and their large family, which consisted of thirteen brothers and sisters, must have been in great straits. No sooner had Nicholas Nekrásoff, the future poet, attained his sixteenth year than he left the provincial town where the family were staying and went to St. Petersburg, to enter the University, where he joined the philological faculty. Most Russian students live very poorly—chiefly by lessons, or entering as tutors in families where they are paid very little, but have at least lodging and food. But Nekrásoff experienced simply black misery : ' For full three years,' he said at a later period, ' I felt continually hungry every day.' ' It often happened that I entered one of the great restaurants where people may go to read newspapers, even without ordering anything to eat, and while I read my paper I would draw the bread-plate towards myself and eat the bread, and that was my only food.' At last he fell ill, and during his convalescence the old soldier from whom he rented a tiny room, and to whom he had already run into debt, one cold November night refused to admit his lodger to his room. Nekrásoff would have had to spend the night out of doors, but a passing beggar took pity on him and took him to some slums on the outskirts of the town, to a 'doss-house,' where the young poet found also the possibility of earning fifteen farthings for some petition that he wrote for one of the inmates. Such was the youth of Nekrásoff; but during it he had the opportunity of making acquaintance with the poorest and lowest classes of St. Petersburg, and the love towards them which he acquired during these peregrinations he retained all his life. Gradually, by means of relentless work, and by editing all sorts of almanacs, he improved his material conditions. He became a regular contributor to the chief review of the time, for which Turguéneff, Dostoyévskiy, Hérzen, and all our best writers wrote, and in 1846 he even became a co-editor of this review, *The Contemporary*, which soon had the best forces of Russia as its contributors, and for the next fifteen years played so important a part in Russian literature. In *The Contemporary* he came, in the sixties, into close contact and friendship with two remarkable men, Tchernyshévskiy and Dobrolúboff, and about this time he wrote his best verses. In 1875 he fell seriously ill, and for the next two years his life was simply agony. He died in December 1877, and thousands of people, especially the University students, followed his body to the grave.

Here, over his grave, began the passionate discussion, which has not yet ended, about the merits of Nekrásoff as a poet. While speaking over his grave Dostoyévskiy put Nekrásoff by the side of Púshkin and Lérmontoff ('higher still than Púshkin and Lérmontoff,' exclaimed some young enthusiast in the crowd), and the question, 'Is Nekrásoff a great poet, like Púshkin and Lérmontoff?' has been discussed ever since.

Nekrásoff's poetry played such an important part in my own development, during my youth, that I did not dare trust my own high appreciation of it ; and therefore to verify and support my impressions and appreciations I have compared them with those of the Russian critics, Arsénieff, Skabitchévskiy, and Venguéroff (the author of a great biographical dictionary of Russian authors).

When we enter the period of adolescence, from sixteen years to twenty, we need to find words to express the aspirations and the higher ideas which begin to wake up in our minds. It is not enough to have these aspirations : we want *words* to express them. Some will find these words in those of the prayers which they hear in the church ; others—and I belonged to their number—will not be satisfied with this expression of their feelings : it will strike them as too vague, and they will look for something else to express in more concrete terms their growing sympathies with mankind and the philosophical questions about the life of the universe which preoccupy them. They will look for poetry. For me, Goethe on the one side, by his philosophical poetry, and Nekrásoff on the other, by the concrete images in which he expressed his love of the peasant masses, supplied the words which the heart wanted for the expression of its poetical feelings. But this is only a personal remark. The question is, whether Nekrásoff can really be put by the side of Púshkin and Lérmontoff as a great poet.

Some people repudiate such a comparison. He was not a poet, they say, because he always wrote with a purpose. However, this reasoning, which is often defended by the pure æsthetics, is evidently incorrect. Shelley also had a purpose, which did not prevent him from being a great poet ; Browning had a purpose in a number of his poems, and this did not prevent him from being a great poet. Every great poet has a purpose in most of his poems, and the question is only whether he has found a beautiful form for expressing this purpose, or not. The poet who shall succeed in combining a really beautiful form, that is, impressive images and sonorous verses, with a grand purpose, will be the greatest poet.

Now, one certainly feels, on reading Nekrásoff, that he had difficulty in writing his verses. There is nothing in his poetry similar to the easiness with which Púshkin used the forms of versification for expressing his thoughts, nor is there any approach to the musical harmony of Lérmontoff's verse or A. K. Tolstóy's. Even in his best poems there are lines which are not agreeable to the ear on account of their wooden and clumsy form ; but you feel that these unhappy verses could be improved by the change of a few words, without the beauty of the images in which the feelings are expressed being altered by that. One certainly feels that Nekrásoff was not master enough of his words and his rhymes ; but there is not one single poetical image which does not suit the whole idea of the poem, or which strikes the reader as a dissonance, or is not beautiful ; while in some of his verses Nekrásoff has certainly succeeded in combining a very high degree of poetical inspiration with great beauty of form. It must not be forgotten that the *Yambes* of Barbier and the *Châtiments* of Victor Hugo also leave, here and there, much to be desired as regards form.

Nekrásoff was a most unequal writer, but one of the above-named critics has pointed out that even amidst his most unpoetical 'poem'—the one in which he describes in very poor verses the printing-office of a newspaper—the moment that he touches upon the sufferings of the working-man there come in twelve lines which for the beauty of poetical images and musicalness, connected with their inner force, have few equals in the whole of Russian literature.

When we estimate a poet, there is something general in his poetry which we either love or pass by indifferently, and to reduce literary criticism exclusively to the analysis of the beauty of the poet's verses or to the correspondence between 'idea and form' is surely to reduce immensely its value. Every one will recognise that Tennyson possessed a wonderful beauty of form, and yet he cannot be considered as superior to Shelley, for the simple reason that the general tenor of the latter's ideas was so much superior to the general tenor of Tennyson's. It is on the general contents of his poetry that Nekrásoff's superiority rests.

We have had in Russia—S. Venguéroff remarks— several poets who also wrote upon social subjects or the duties of a citizen, such as Pleschéyeff and Mináyeff, and they attained sometimes, from the versifier's point of view, a higher beauty of form than Nekrásoff. But in whatever Nekrásoff wrote there is an inner force which you do not find in either of these poets, and this force suggests to him images which are rightly considered as pearls of Russian poetry. Nekrásoff called his Muse, 'A Muse of Vengeance and of Sadness,' and this was true. Nekrásoff was a pessimist, but his pessimism had an original character. Although his poetry contains so many depressing pictures representing the misery of the Russian masses, nevertheless the fundamental impression which it leaves upon the reader is an elevating feeling. The poet does not bow his head before the sad reality : he enters into a struggle with it, and he is sure of victory. The reading of Nekrásoff wakes up that discontent which bears in itself the seeds of recovery.

The mass of the Russian people, the peasants and their sufferings, are the main themes of our poet's verses. His love for the people passes as a red thread through all his works ; he remained true to it all his life. In his younger years that love saved him from squandering his talent in the sort of life which so many of his contemporaries have led ; later on it inspired him in his struggle against serfdom ; and when serfdom was abolished he did not consider his work terminated, as so many of his friends did : he became the poet of the dark masses oppressed by the economical and political yoke. He wrote :

> From those whose lives are feast and talking,
> From those whose hands are steeped in blood,
> Lead me into the camp of those
> Who perish for the Cause of Love !

Towards the end of his life he did not say, ' Well, I have done what I could,' but till his last breath his verses were a complaint about not having been enough of a fighter. He wrote : ' Struggle stood in the way of my becoming a poet, and songs prevented me from becoming a fighter' ; and again :

> Only he, who was serving the aims of his time,
> Who was giving his life for his brother men's good,
> Only he will survive in the hearts of mankind.

Sometimes he sounded a note of despair ; however, such a note was not frequent in Nekrásoff. His Russian peasant is not a man who only sheds tears. He is serene, sometimes humorous, and sometimes an extremely gay worker. Very seldom does Nekrásoff idealise the peasant : for the most part he takes him just as he is, from life itself ; and the poet's faith in the forces of that Russian peasant is deep and vigorous. ' A little more freedom to breathe,' he says, ' and Russia will show that she has men, and that she has a future.' This is an idea which frequently recurs in his poetry.

The best poem of Nekrásoff is *Red-nosed Frost*. It is the apotheosis of the Russian peasant woman. The poem has nothing sentimental in it. It is written, on the contrary, in a sort of elevated epic style, and the second part, where Frost personified passes on his way through the wood, and where the peasant woman is slowly freezing to death, while bright pictures of past happiness fly through her brain—all this is admirable, even from the point of view of the most æsthetic critics, because it is written in good verses and in a succession of beautiful images and pictures.

The Peasant Children is a charming village idyll. The 'Muse of Vengeance and Sadness'—one of our critics remarks—becomes wonderfully mild and gentle as soon as she begins to speak of women and children. In fact, none of the Russian poets has ever done so much for the apotheosis of women, and especially of the mother-woman, as this supposedly severe poet of Vengeance and Sadness. As soon as Nekrásoff begins to speak of a mother he grows powerful; and the strophes he devoted to his own mother—a woman lost in a squire's house, amidst men thinking only of hunting, drinking, and exercising their powers as slave-owners in their full brutality—these strophes are real pearls in the poetry of all nations.

His poem devoted to the exiles in Siberia and to the Russian women—that is, to the wives of the Decembrists—in exile, is excellent and contains really beautiful passages, but it is inferior to either his poems dealing with the peasants or to his pretty poem, *Sasha*, in which he described, contemporaneously with Turguéneff, the very same two types as Rúdin and Natásha. And yet, the concluding scene of the former, relating the interview of Princess Volkónsky with her husband at the bottom of a mine in Siberia, is one of the beautiful pages of the world's poetry.

It is quite true that Nekrásoff's verses often bear traces of a painful struggle with rhyme, and that there are lines in his poems which are decidedly inferior; but he is certainly one of our most popular poets amidst the masses of the people. Part of his poetry has already become

the inheritance of all the Russian nation.   He is immensely read, not only by the educated classes, but by
the poorest peasants as well.   In fact, as has been remarked by one of our critics, to understand Púshkin a
certain more or less artificial literary development is required ; while to understand Nekrásoff it is sufficient for
the peasant simply to know reading ; and it is difficult
to imagine, without having seen it, the delight with which
Russian children in the poorest village schools are now
reading Nekrásoff and learning full pages from his verses
by heart.

OTHER PROSE-WRITERS OF THE SAME EPOCH

Having analysed the work of those writers who may
be considered as the true founders of modern Russian
literature, I ought now to review a number of prose-
writers and poets of less renown, belonging to the same
epoch.   However, following the plan of this book, only
some of the most remarkable among them will be mentioned in a few words.

A writer of great power, very little known in Western
Europe, who occupies a quite unique position in Russian
literature, is SERGHÉI TIMOFÉEVITCH AKSÁKOFF (1791-
1859), the father of the two Slavophile writers, Konstantín and Iván Aksákoff.   He was in reality a contemporary of Púshkin and Lérmontoff, but during the first
part of his career he displayed no originality whatever,
and lingered in the fields of pseudo-classicism.   It was
only after Gógol had written—that is, after 1846—that
he struck a quite new vein, and attained the full development of his by no means ordinary talent.   In the years
1847-1855 he published his *Memoirs of Angling, Memoirs
of a Hunter with his Fowling Piece in the Government of
Orenbúrg*, and *Stories and Remembrances of a Sportsman* ; and these three works would have been sufficient
to establish his reputation as a first-rate writer.   The
Orenbúrg region, in the Southern Uráls, was very thinly

inhabited at that time, and its nature and physiognomy are so well described in these books that Aksákoff's work reminds one of the *Natural History of Selbourne.* It has the same accuracy ; but Aksákoff is moreover a poet and a first-rate poetical landscape painter. Besides, he so admirably knew the life of the animals, and so well *understood* them, that in this respect his rivals could only be Krylóff among the fable-writers, and Brehm and Audubon among the naturalists.

The influence of Gógol induced S. T. Aksákoff entirely to abandon the domain of pseudo-classical fiction. In 1846 he began to describe real life, and the result was a large work, *A Family Chronicle and Remembrances* (1856), soon followed by *The Early Years of Bagróff-the-Grandchild* (1858), which put him in the first ranks among the writers of his century. ˙ Slavophile enthusiasts described him even as a Shakespeare, nay, as a Homer ; but all exaggeration apart, S. T. Aksákoff has really succeeded not only in reproducing a whole epoch in his *Memoirs*, but also in creating real types of men of that time, which have served as models for all our subsequent writers. If the leading idea of these *Memoirs* had not been so much in favour of the ' good old times ' of serfdom, they would have been even more widely read than they are now.

V. DAL (1801-1872) cannot be omitted even from this short sketch. He was born in South-eastern Russia, of a Danish father (a linguist) and a Franco-German mother, and received his education at the Dorpat University. He was a naturalist and a doctor by profession, but his favourite study was ethnography, and he became a remarkable ethnographer, as well as one of the best connoisseurs of the Russian spoken language and its provincial dialects. His sketches from the life of the people, signed KOZÁK LUGÁNSKIY (about a hundred of them are embodied in a volume, *Pictures from Russian Life*, 1861), were very widely read in the forties and the fifties, and were highly praised by Turguéneff and Byelínskiy. Although they are mere sketches and leaflets from a diary, without real poetical creation, they are delightful reading. As to the ethnographical work of Dal, it was immense. During his continual peregrinations over Russia, in his capacity of a military doctor attached to his regiment, he made most wonderful collections of words, expressions, riddles, proverbs, and so on, and embodied them in two large works. His main work is *An Explanatory Dictionary of the Russian Language*, in four quarto volumes (first edition in 1861-1868, second in 1880-1882). This is a monumental work and contains the first and very successful attempt at a lexicology of the Russian language, which, notwithstanding some occasional mistakes, is of the greatest value for the understanding and the etymology of the Russian tongue as it is spoken in different provinces. It contains at the same time a precious and extremely rich collection of linguistic material for future research, part of which would have been lost by now if Dal had not collected it, fifty years ago, before the advent of railways. Another great work of Dal, only second to the one just mentioned, is a collection of proverbs, entitled *The Proverbs of the Russian People* (second edition in 1879).

A writer who occupies a prominent place in the evolution of the Russian novel, but has not yet been sufficiently appreciated, is IVÁN PANÁEFF (1812-1862), who was a great friend of all the literary circle of the *Sovreménnik* (*Contemporary*). Of this review he was co-editor with Nekrásoff, and he wrote for it a mass of literary notes and *feuilletons* upon all sorts of subjects, interesting for the characteristics of those times. In his novels Panáeff, like Turguéneff, took his types chiefly from the educated classes, both at St. Petersburg and in the provinces. His collection of ' Swaggerers ' (*hlyschí*), both from the highest classes in the capitals and from provincials, is not inferior to Thackeray's collection of ' snobs.' In fact, the ' swaggerer,' as Panáeff understood him, is even a much broader and much more complicated type of man than the snob, and cannot easily be described in a few words. The greatest service rendered by Panáeff was, however, the creation in his novels of a series of such exquisite types of Russian women that they were truly described by some critics as ' the spiritual mothers of the heroines of Turguéneff.'

A. HÉRZEN (1812-1870) also belongs to the same epoch, but he will be spoken of in a subsequent chapter.

A very sympathetic woman writer, who belongs to the same group and would deserve much more than a brief notice, is N. D. HVÓSCHINSKAYA (1825-1889; Zaionchkóvskaya after her marriage). She wrote under the masculine *nom de plume* of V. KRESTÓVSKIY, and in order not to confound her with a very prolific writer of novels in the style of the French detective novel— the author of *St. Petersburg Slums*, whose name was VSEVOLOD KRESTÓVSKIY—she is usually known in Russia as ' V. Krestóvskiy-pseudonym.'

N. D. Hvóschinskaya began to write very early, in 1847, and her novels were endowed with such an inner charm that they were always admired by the general public and were widely read. It must, however, be said that during the first part of her literary career the full value of her work was not appreciated, and that down to the end of the seventies literary criticism remained hostile to her. It was only towards the end of her career (in 1878-1880) that our best literary critics— Mihailóvskiy, Arsénieff, and the novelist Boborýkin— recognised the full value of this writer, who deserves being placed by the side of George Eliot and the author of *Jane Eyre*.

N. D. Hvóschinskaya certainly was not one of those who attain recognition at once ; but the cause of the rather hostile attitude of Russian critics towards her was that, having been born in a poor nobleman's family of Ryazán, and having spent all her life in the province, her novels of the first period, in which she dealt with provincial life and provincial types only, suffered from a certain narrowness of view. This last defect was especially evident in those types of men for whom the young author tried to win sympathy, but who, after all, had no claims to it, and simply proved that the author felt the need of idealising somebody, at least, in her dull surroundings.

Apart from this defect N. D. Hvóschinskaya knew provincial life very well and pictured it admirably. She represented it exactly in the same pessimistic light in which Turguéneff saw it in those same years—the last years of the reign of Nicholas I. She excelled especially in representing the sad and hopeless existence of the girl in most of the families of those times.

In her own family she met the bigoted tyranny of her mother and the 'let-me-alone' egotism of her father, and among her admirers she found only a collection of good-for-nothings who covered their shallowness with empty, sonorous phrases. Every novel written by our author during this period contains the drama of a girl whose best self is crushed in such surroundings, or it relates the still more heart-rending drama of an old maid compelled to live under the tyranny, the petty persecutions, and the pin-prickings of her relations.

When Russia entered into a better period, in the early sixties, the novels of Miss Hvóschinskaya also took a different, much more hopeful character, and among them *The Great Bear* (1870-71) is the most prominent. At the time of its appearance it produced quite a sensation amidst our youth, and it had upon them a deep influence, in the very best sense of the word. The heroine Kátya meets in Verhóvskiy a man of the weakling type which we know from Turguéneff's *Correspondence*, but dressed this time in the garb of a social reformer, prevented only by 'circumstances' and 'misfortunes' from accomplishing greater things. Verhóvskiy, whom Kátya

loves and who falls in love with her—so far, at least, as
such men can fall in love—is admirably pictured.   It is
one of the best representatives in the already rich gallery
of such types in Russian literature.   It must be owned
that there are in *The Great Bear* one or two characters
which are not quite real, or, at least, are not correctly
appreciated by the author (for instance, the old Bagryánskiy) ; but we find also a fine collection of admirably
painted characters ; while Kátya stands higher, is more
alive, and is more fully pictured than Turguéneff's
Natásha or even his Helen.   She has had enough of all
the talk about heroic deeds which ' circumstances ' prevent the would-be heroes from accomplishing, and she
takes to a much smaller task : she becomes a loving
schoolmistress in a village school, and undertakes to
bring into the village darkness her higher ideals and
her hopes of a better future.   The appearance of this
novel, just at the time when that great movement of the
youth ' towards the people ' was beginning in Russia,
made it favourite reading among the young people of
both sexes, by the side of D. L. MORDÓVTSEFF'S *Signs
of the Times* and Spielhagen's *Amboss und Hammer*
and *In Reih und Glied.*   The warm tone of the novel
and the refined, deeply humane, poetical touches of
which it is full—all these added immensely to the inner
merits of *The Great Bear.*   In Russia it has sown many
a good idea, and there is no doubt that if it were known
in Western Europe, it would have been here as well a
favourite with the thinking and well-inspired young
women and men.

A third period may be distinguished in the art of
Miss Hvóschinskaya, after the end of the seventies.
The novels of this period—among which the series
entitled *The Album : Groups and Portraits* is the best—
have a new character.   When the great liberal movement which Russia had lived through in the early
sixties came to an end, and reaction had got the upper
hand, after 1864, hundreds and hundreds of those who

had been prominent in this movement as representatives of advanced thought and reform, abandoned the faith and the ideals of their best years. Under a thousand various pretexts they now tried to persuade themselves —and, of course, those women who had trusted them— that new times had come and new requirements had grown up ; that they had only become 'practical' when they deserted the old banner and ranged themselves under a new one—that of personal enrichment ; that to do this was on their part a necessary self-sacrifice, a manifestation of 'virile citizenship,' which requires from every man that he should not stop even before the sacrifice of his ideals in the interest of his 'cause.' Miss Hvóschinskaya, as a woman who had loved the ideals, understood better than any man the real sense of these sophisms. She must have bitterly suffered from them in her personal life ; and I doubt whether in any litera-ture there is a collection of such 'groups and portraits' of deserters as we see in *The Album*, and especially in *At the Photographer's*. In reading these stories we are conscious of a loving heart which bleeds as it describes these deserters, and this makes of *Groups and Portraits* one of the finest pieces of 'subjective realism' we possess in our literature.[1]

POETS OF THE SAME EPOCH

Several poets of the epoch described in the last two chapters ought to be analysed at some length in this place, if this book pretended to be a course in Russian literature. I shall have, however, to limit myself to very short notes, although most of the poets could not have failed to be favourites with other nations if they had written in a language better known abroad than Russian.

[1] Two sisters of N. D. Hvóschinskaya, who wrote under the *noms de plume* of ZIMÁROFF and VESÉNIEFF, were also novelists. The former wrote a biography of her sister Nathalie.

Such was undoubtedly KOLTSÓFF (1808-1842), a poet from the people, who has sung in his songs, so deeply appealing to every poetical mind, the borderless steppes of Southern Russia, the poor life of the tiller of the soil, the sad existence of the Russian peasant woman, that love which is for the loving soul only a source of acute suffering, that fate which is not a mother but a step-mother, and that happiness which has been so short and has left behind only tears and sadness.

The style, the contents, the form—all were original in this poet of the Steppes. Even the form of his verse is not the form established in Russian prosody : it is something as musical as the Russian folk-song and in places is equally irregular. However, every line of the poetry of the Koltsóff of his second period—when he had freed himself from imitation and had become a true poet of the people—every expression and every thought appeal to the heart and fill it with poetical love for nature and men. Like all the best Russian poets he died very young, just at the age when he was reaching the full maturity of his talent and deeper questions were beginning to inspire his poetry.

NIKÍTIN (1824-1861) was another poet who originated from a similar class of traders. He was born in a poor artisan's family, also in South Russia. His life in this family, of which the head was continually under the influence of drink, and which the young man had to maintain, was terrible. He also died young, but he left some very fine and most touching pieces of poetry, in which, with a simplicity that we shall find only with the later folk-novelists, he described scenes from popular life, coloured with the deep sadness impressed upon him by his own unhappy life.

A. PLESCHÉYEFF (1825-1893) has been for the last thirty years of his life one of the favourite Russian poets. Like so many other gifted men of his generation, he was arrested in 1849 in connection with the affair of the ' Petrashévskiy circles,' for which Dostoyévskiy was sent to hard labour. He was found even less 'guilty' than the great novelist, and was marched as a soldier to the Orenbúrg region, where he probably would have died a soldier, if Nicholas I. had not himself died in 1855. He was pardoned by Alexander II., and permitted to settle at Moscow.

Unlike so many of his contemporaries, Pleschéyeff never let himself be crushed by persecution or by the dark years which Russia has lately lived through. On the contrary, he always retained that same note of vigour, freshness, and faith in his humanitarian, though perhaps too abstract ideals, which characterised his first poetical productions in the forties. Only towards his very latest years, under the influence of ill-health, did a pessimistic note begin to creep into his verses. Besides writing original poetry he translated very much, and very well, from the German, English, French, and Italian poets.

Besides these three poets, who sought their inspiration in the realities of life or in higher humanitarian ideals, we have a group of poets who are usually described as admirers of 'pure beauty' and 'art for art's sake.' TH. TYÚTTCHEFF (1803-1873)[1] may be taken as the best representative of this group. Turguéneff spoke of him very highly—in 1854—praising his fine and true feeling for nature and his fine taste. The influence of the epoch of Púshkin upon him was evident, but his development went on his own original lines. His literary legacy was small, but it contained some of the finest pieces of Russian poetry—partly descriptions of nature (Russian nature, even though he spent most of his life abroad), but especially philosophical, pantheistic poetry, dealing with nature's primitive, wild forces. In this last direction he sometimes attained great heights. He also wrote political verses, but they were so reactionary that they rendered him unsympathetic to

[1] Pronounce Tyút-cheff.

those generations which had to sustain a hard struggle against the autocratic power and its bureaucracy.

APOLLON MÁYKOFF (1821-1897) is often described as a poet of pure art for art's sake ; at any rate, this is what he preached in theory ; but in reality his poetry belonged to three distinct domains. In his youth he was a pure admirer of antique Greece and Rome, and his chief work, *Three Deaths* (written in 1852 it received its final development thirty years later in *Two Worlds*), was devoted to the conflict between antique paganism and natureism and Christianity—the best types in his poem being representatives of the former. During these same years he wrote several very good pieces of poetry devoted to the history of the Church in mediæval times (*Savonarola*, *The Council of Constance*). In the sixties he was carried away by the liberal movement in Russia and in Western Europe, and his poems were imbued with its spirit of freedom. He wrote during those years his best poems, and made numbers of excellent translations from Heine. And finally, after the liberal period had come to an end in Russia, he also changed his opinions and began to write in the opposite direction, losing more and more both the sympathy of his readers and his talent. Apart from some of the productions of this last period of decay, the verses of Máykoff are as a rule very musical, poetical, and not devoid of force. In his earlier productions, and in some pieces of his third period, he attained real beauty.

N. SCHERBÍNA (1821-1869), also an admirer of classical Greece, may be mentioned for his anthological poetry from the life of Greek antiquity, in which he even excelled Máykoff.

POLÓNSKIY (1820-1898), a contemporary and a great friend of Turguéneff, displayed all the elements of a great artist. His verses are full of true melody, his poetical images are rich, and yet natural and simple, and the subjects he took were not devoid of originality.

This is why his verses were always read with interest. But he had none of that force, or of that depth of conception, or of that intensity of passion which might have made of him a great poet. His best piece, *A Musical Cricket*, is written in a jocose mood, and his most popular verses are those which he wrote in the style of folk-poetry. One may say that they have become the property of the people. Altogether Polónskiy appealed chiefly to the quiet, moderate 'intellectual,' who does not much care about going to the bottom of the great problems of life. If he touched upon some of these, it was owing to a passing, rather than to a life, interest in them.

One more poet of this group, perhaps the most characteristic of it, was A. SHENSHÍN (1820-1892), much better known under his *nom de plume* of A. FET. He remained all his life a poet of ' pure art for art's sake.' He wrote a good deal about economical and social matters, always in the reactionary sense, but—in prose. As to verses, he never resorted to them for anything but the worship of beauty for beauty's sake. In this direction he succeeded very well. His short verses are especially pretty and sometimes almost beautiful. Nature, in its quiet, lovely aspects, which lead to a gentle, aimless sadness, he depicted sometimes to perfection, as also those moods of the mind which can be best described as indefinite sensations, slightly erotic. However, taken as a whole, his poetry appears monotonous. His *Reminiscences*, published lately in two volumes, are very interesting. Having been a personal friend of both Tolstóy and Turguéneff, he gave valuable data for the biography of these two writers, as well as about a hundred of their letters.

To the same group one might add A. K. TOLSTÓY, whose verses attain sometimes a rare perfection and sound like the best music. The feelings expressed in them may not be very deep, but the form and the music of the verses are delightful. They have, moreover, the stamp of originality, because nobody could write poems in the style of Russian folk-poetry better than Alexéi Tolstóy. Theoretically, he preached art for art's sake. But he never remained true to this canon, and, taking either the life of old epical Russia, or the period of the struggle between the Moscow Tsars and the feudal boyars, he developed his admiration of the olden times in very melodic verses. He also wrote a novel, *Prince Serébryanyi*, from the times of John the Terrible, which was very widely read; but his main work was a trilogy of dramas from the same interesting period of Russian history (see chapter vi.).

Almost all the poets just mentioned have translated a great deal, and they have enriched Russian literature with such a number of translations from all languages —so admirably done, as a rule—that no other literature of the world, not even the German, can claim to possess an equally great treasury. Some translations, beginning with Zhukóvskiy's rendering of the *Prisoner of Chillon*, or the translations of *Hiawatha*, are simply classical. All Schiller, most of Goethe, nearly all Byron, a great deal of Shelley, all that is worth knowing in Tennyson, Wordsworth, Crabbe, all that could be translated from Browning, Barbier, Victor Hugo, and so on, are as familiar in Russia as in the mother countries of these poets, and occasionally even more so. As to such favourites as Heine, I really don't know whether his best poems lose anything in those splendid translations which we owe to our best poets; while the songs of Béranger, in the free translation of Kúrotchkin, are not in the least inferor to the originals.

We have moreover some good poets who are chiefly known for their translations. Such are: N. Gérbel (1827-1883), who made his reputation by an admirable rendering of the *Lay of Igor's Raid* (see chapter i.), and later on by his versions of a great number of West European poets. His edition of *Schiller, trans-*

lated by Russian Poets (1857), followed by similar editions of Shakespeare, Byron, and Goethe, was epoch-making.

MIKHAIL MIKHÁILOFF (1826-1865), one of the most brilliant writers of the *Contemporary*, condemned in 1861 to hard labour in Siberia, where he died four years later, was especially renowned for his translations from Heine, as also for those from Longfellow, Hood, Tennyson, Lenan, and others.

P. WEINBERG (born 1830) made his reputation by his excellent translations from Shakespeare, Byron (*Sardanapal*), Shelley (*Cenci*), Sheridan, Coppe, Gutzkow, Heine, etc., and for his editions of the work of Goethe and Heine in Russian translations. He still continues to enrich Russian literature with excellent versions of the masterpieces of foreign literatures.

L. MÉY (1822-1862), the author of a number of poems from popular life, written in a very picturesque language, and of several dramas, of which those from old Russian life are especially valuable ; one of them, *The Girl of Pskov*, was taken by RÍMSKIY KÓRSAKOFF as the subject of his opera, *John the Terrible*. He has also made a great number of translations, not only from the modern West European poets—English, French, German, Italian, and Polish—but also from Greek, Latin, and Old Hebrew, all of which languages he knew to perfection. Besides excellent translations of Anacreon and the idylls of Theocritus, he wrote also poetical versions of the *Song of Songs* and of various other portions of the Bible.

D. MINÁYEFF (1835-1889), the author of a great number of satirical verses, also belongs to this group of translators. His renderings from Byron, Burns, Cornwall, and Moore, Goethe and Heine, Leopardi, Dante, and several others, were, as a rule, very fine.

A. A. SOKOLÓVSKIY (born 1837) translated a great deal, both in prose and in verse, from Goethe and Byron, for the Russian editions of these two poets ; but his life-work was a complete translation of Shakespeare, which he published in 1898, with copious historical notes and annotations, and for which he received the Púshkin prize of the Academy of Sciences.

And finally I must mention one, at least, of the prose-translators, VVEDÉNSKIY (1813-1855), for his fine translations of the chief novels of Dickens. His renderings were the result of such an assimilation of the genius of Dickens that the translator almost identified himself with the original author.

The translations of Madame L. P. SHELGUNÓFF from Spielhagen, Auerbach, Schlosser, and so on, are also worthy of notice.

CHAPTER VI

THE DRAMA

Its origin—The Tsars Alexis and Peter I.—Sumarókoff—Pseudo-classical tragedies: Knyazhnín; Ozeroff—First comedies—The first years of the nineteenth century—Griboyédoff—The Moscow stage in the fifties — Ostróvskiy; his first dramas — *The Thunderstorm* — Ostróvskiy's later dramas—Historical dramas: A. K. Tolstóy—Other dramatic writers.

THE Drama in Russia, as everywhere else, had a double origin. It developed out of the religious ' mysteries ' on the one hand and the popular comedy on the other, witty interludes being introduced into the grave, moral representations, the subjects of which were borrowed from the Old or the New Testament. Several such mysteries were adapted in the seventeenth century by the teachers of the Græco-Latin Theological Academy at Kíeff for representation in Little Russian by the students of the Academy, and later on these adaptations found their way to Moscow.

Towards the end of the seventeenth century—on the eve, so to speak, of the reforms of Peter I.—a strong desire to introduce Western habits of life was felt in certain small circles at Moscow, and the father of Peter, the Tsar Alexis, was not hostile to it. He took a liking to theatrical representations, and induced some foreigners residing at Moscow to write pieces for representation at the palace. A certain GREGORY undertook this task, and, taking German versions of plays, which used to be called at that time ' English Plays,' he adapted them to Russian tastes. *The Comedy of Queen Esther and the Haughty Haman, Tobias, Judith,* etc., were represented before the Tsar. A high functionary of the Church, SIMEÓN PÓLOTSKIY, did not disdain to write such mysteries, and several of them have come down to us; while a daughter of Alexis, the Princess Sophie (a pupil of Simeón), breaking with the strict habits of isolation which were then obligatory for women, had theatrical representations given at the palace in her presence.

This was too much for the old Moscow Conservatives, and after the death of Alexis the theatre was closed; and so it remained a quarter of a century, *i.e.* until 1702, when Peter I., who was very fond of the drama, opened a theatre in the old capital. He had a company of actors brought for the purpose from Danzig, and a special house was built for them within the holy precincts of the Kremlin. More than that, another sister of Peter I., Nathalie, who was as fond of dramatic performances as the great reformer himself, a few years later took all the properties of this theatre to her own palace, and had the representations given there—first in German, and later on in Russian. It is also very probable that she herself wrote a few dramas—perhaps in collaboration with one of the pupils of a certain Doctor Bidlo, who had opened another theatre at the Moscow Hospital, the actors being the students. Later on the theatre of Princess Nathalie was transferred to the new capital founded by her brother on the Neva.

The *répertoire* of this theatre was pretty varied, and included, besides German dramas, like *Scipio the African, Don Juan and Don Pedro*, and the like, free translations from Molière, as also German farces of a very coarse character. A few original Russian dramas (partly contributed, apparently, by Nathalie), drawn from the lives of the saints, and from some Polish novels, widely read at that time in Russian manuscript translations, were also acted in this theatre.

It was out of these elements and out of West European

O

models that the Russian drama evolved, when the theatre became, in the middle of the eighteenth century, a permanent institution. It is most interesting to note, that it was not in either of the capitals, but in a provincial town, Yaroslàv, under the patronage of the local tradesmen, that the first permanent Russian theatre was founded, in 1750, by the private enterprise of a few actors : the two brothers Vólkoff, Dmitrévsky, and several others. The Empress Elisabeth — probably following the advice of Sumarókoff, who himself began about that time to write dramas—ordered these actors to move to St. Petersburg, where they became ' artists of the Imperial Theatre,' in the service of the Crown. Thus the Russian theatre became, in 1756, an institution of the Government.

SUMARÓKOFF (1718-1777), who wrote, besides verses and fables (the latter of a certain value), a considerable number of tragedies and comedies, played an important part in the development of the Russian drama. In his tragedies he imitated Racine and Voltaire. He followed strictly their rules of ' unity,' and cared even less than they did for historical truth ; but as he had not the great talent of his French masters, he made of his heroes mere personifications of certain virtues or vices, figures quite devoid of life, and indulging in endless pompous monologues. Several of his tragedies (*Hórev*, written in 1747, *Sináv and Trúvor, Yaropólk and Dílitza, Dmítri the Impostor*) were taken from Russian history ; but, after all, their heroes were as little Slavonian as Racine's heroes were Greek and Roman. This, however, must be said in favour of Sumarókoff, that he never failed to express in his tragedies the more advanced humanitarian ideas of the times—sometimes with real feeling, which pierced through even the conventional forms of speech of his heroes. As to his comedies, although they had not the same success as his serious dramas, they were much nearer to life. They contained touches of the life of Russia, especially of the life of the

Moscow nobility, and their satirical character undoubtedly influenced Sumarókoff's followers.

KNYAZHNÍN (1742-1791) followed on the same lines. Like Sumarókoff he translated tragedies from the French, and also wrote imitations of French tragedies, taking his subjects partly from Russian history (*Rossláv*, 1784; *Vadím of Nóvgorod*, which was printed after his death and was immediately destroyed by the Government on account of its tendencies towards freedom).

OZEROFF (1769-1816) continued the work of Knyazhnín, but introduced the sentimental and the romantic elements into his pseudo-classical tragedies (*Oedipus in Athens, Death of Olèg*). With all their defects these tragedies enjoyed a lasting success, and powerfully contributed to the development of both the stage and a public of serious playgoers.

At the same time comedies also began to be written by the same authors and their followers (*The Brawler*, *Strange People*, by Knyazhnín), and although they were for the most part imitations of the French, nevertheless subjects taken from Russian everyday life began to be introduced. Sumarókoff had already done something in this direction, and he had been seconded by CATHERINE II., who contributed a couple of satirical comedies, taken from her surroundings, such as *The Fête of Mrs. Grumbler*, and a comic opera from Russian popular life. She was perhaps the first to introduce Russian peasants on the stage; and it is worthy of note that the taste for a popular vein on the stage rapidly developed—the comedies, *The Miller*, by ABLESÍMOFF, *Zbítenshik (The Hawker)*, by Knyazhnín, and so on, all taken from the life of the people, being for some time great favourites with the playgoers.

VON WÍZIN has already been mentioned in a previous chapter, and it is sufficient here to recall the fact, that by his two comedies, *The Brigadier* (1768) and *Nédorosl* (1782), which continued to be played up to the middle of the nineteenth century, he became the father of the realistic satirical comedy in Russia. *Denunciation* (*Yábeda*), by KAPNÍST, and a few comedies contributed by the great fable-writer KRYLÓFF, belong to the same category.

THE FIRST YEARS OF THE NINETEENTH CENTURY

During the first thirty years of the nineteenth century the Russian theatre developed remarkably. The stage produced, at St. Petersburg and at Moscow, a number of gifted and original actors and actresses, both in tragedy and in comedy. The number of writers for the stage became so considerable that all the forms of dramatic art were able to develop at the same time. During the Napoleonic wars patriotic tragedies, full of allusions to current events, such as *Dmítri Donskóy* (1807), by Ozeroff, invaded the stage. However, the pseudo-classical tragedy continued to hold its own. Better translations and imitations of Racine were produced (KATÉNIN, KOKÓSHKIN) and enjoyed a certain success, especially at St. Petersburg, owing to good tragic actors of the declamatory school. At the same time translations of KOTZEBUE had an enormous success, as also the Russian productions of his sentimental imitators.

Romanticism and pseudo-classicism were, of course, at war with each other for the possession of the stage, as they were in the domains of poetry and the novel; but, owing to the spirit of the time, and patronised as it was by KARAMZÍN and ZHUKÓVSKIY, romanticism triumphed. It was aided especially by the energetic efforts of Prince SHAHOVSKÓY, who wrote, with a good knowledge of the stage, more than a hundred varied pieces—tragedies, comedies, operas, vaudevilles, and ballets—taking the subjects for his dramas from Walter Scott, Ossian, Shakespeare, and Púshkin. At the same time comedy, and especially satirical comedy, as also the vaudeville (which approached comedy by a rather more careful treatment of characters than is usual in that sort of literature on the French stage), were represented by a very great number of more or less original productions. Besides the excellent translations of HMELNÍTSKIY from Molière, the public enjoyed also the pieces of ZAGÓSKIN, full of good-hearted merriment, the sometimes brilliant and always animated comedies and vaudevilles of Shahovskóy, the vaudevilles of A. I. PÍSAREFF, and so on. True, all the comedies were either directly inspired by Molière or were adaptations from the French into which Russian characters and Russian manners had been introduced. But as there was still some original creation in these adaptions, which was carried a step further on the stage by gifted actors of the natural, realist school, it all prepared the way for the truly Russian comedy, which found its embodiment in Griboyédoff, Gógol, and Ostróvskiy.

GRIBOYÉDOFF

GRIBOYÉDOFF (1795-1829) died very young, and all that he left was one comedy, *Misfortune from Intelligence (Góre ot Umá)*, and a couple of scenes from an unfinished tragedy in the Shakespearian style. However, his comedy is a work of genius, and owing to it alone Griboyédoff may be described as having done for the Russian stage what Púshkin has done for Russian poetry.

Griboyédoff was born at Moscow, and received a good education at home before he entered the Moscow University, at the age of fifteen. Here he was fortunate enough to fall under the influence of the historian Schlötzer and Professor Buhle, who developed in him the desire for a thorough acquaintance with the world-literature, together with habits of serious work. It was consequently during his stay at the University (1810-1812) that Griboyédoff wrote the first sketch of his comedy, at which he worked for the next twelve years.

In 1812, during the invasion of Napoleon, he entered

the military service, and for four years remained an officer of the hussars, chiefly in Western Russia. The spirit of the army was quite different then from what it became later on under Nicholas I. : it was in the army that the 'Decembrists' made their chief propaganda, and Griboyédoff met among his comrades men of high humanitarian tendencies. In 1816 he left the military service, and, obeying the desire of his mother, entered the diplomatic service at St. Petersburg (now Petrograd), where he became friendly with the 'Decembrists' Tchaadáeff (see chapter viii.), Ryléeff, and Odóevskiy (see chapters i. and ii.).

A duel, in which Griboyédoff took part as a second, was the cause of the future dramatist's removal from St. Petersburg. His mother insisted upon his being sent as far as possible from the capital, and he was accordingly despatched to Teheran. He travelled a good deal in Persia, and, with his wonderful activity and liveliness, took a prominent part in the diplomatic work of the Russian Embassy. Later on, staying at Tiflís, and acting as a secretary to the Lieutenant of the Caucasus, he worked hard in the same diplomatic domain ; but he worked also all the time at his comedy, and in 1824 he finished it while he was for a few months in Central Russia. Owing to a mere accident the manuscript of *Misfortune from Intelligence* became known to a few friends, and the comedy produced a tremendous sensation among them. In a few months it was being widely read in manuscript copies, raising storms of indignation amongst the old generation, and provoking the greatest admiration among the young. All efforts, however, to obtain its production on the stage, or even to have it represented once in private, were thwarted by the censorship, and Griboyédoff returned to the Caucasus without having seen his comedy played at a theatre.

There, at Tiflís, he was arrested a few days after the 14th of December 1825 (see chapter i.), and taken in all speed to the St. Petersburg fortress, where his best friends were already imprisoned. It is said in the Memoirs of one of the Decembrists that even in the gloomy surroundings of the fortress the habitual brightness of Griboyédoff did not leave him. He used to tell his unfortunate friends such amusing stories by means of taps on the walls that they rolled on their beds, laughing like children.

In June 1826 he was set free, and sent back to Tiflís. But after the execution of some of his friends —Ryléeff was among them—and the harsh sentence to hard labour for life in Siberian mines, which was passed upon all the others, his old gaiety was gone for ever.

At Tiflís he worked harder than ever at spreading seeds of a better civilisation in the newly conquered territory ; but next year he had to take part in the war of 1827-1828 against Persia, accompanying the army as a diplomatic agent, and after a crushing defeat of the Shah, Abbas Mirza, it was he who concluded the well-known Turkmancháy treaty, by which Russia obtained rich provinces from Persia and gained such an influence over her inner affairs. After a flying visit to St. Petersburg, Griboyédoff was sent once more to Teheran —this time as an ambassador. Before leaving, he married at Tiflís a Georgian princess of remarkable beauty, but he felt, as he left the Caucasus for Persia, that his chances of returning alive were few : ' Abbas Mirza,' he wrote, ' will never pardon me the Turkmancháy treaty '—and so it happened. A few months after his arrival at Teheran a crowd of Persians fell upon the Russian embassy, and Griboyédoff was killed.

For the last few years of his life Griboyédoff had not much time nor taste for literary work. He knew that nothing he desired to write could ever see the light. Even *Misfortune from Intelligence* had been so mutilated by censorship that many of its best passages had lost all sense. He wrote, however, a tragedy in the romantic style, *A Georgian Night*, and those of his friends who had read it in full rated high its poetic and dramatic qualities; but only two scenes from this tragedy and the outline of its contents have reached us. The manuscript was lost—perhaps at Teheran.

Misfortune from Intelligence is a most powerful satire, directed against the high society of Moscow in the years 1820-1830. Griboyédoff knew this society from the inside, and his types are not invented. Real men gave him the foundations for such immortal types as Fámusoff, the aged nobleman, and Skalozúb, the fanatic of militarism, as well as for all the secondary personages. As to the language in which Griboyédoff's personages speak, it has often been remarked that up to his time only three writers had been such great masters of the truly Russian spoken language: Púshkin, Krylóff, and Griboyédoff. Later on Ostróvskiy could be added to these three. It is the true language of Moscow. Besides, the comedy is full of verses so strikingly satirical and so well said that scores of them became proverbs known all over Russia.

The idea of the comedy must have been suggested by Molière's *Misanthrope*, and the hero, Tchátskiy, has certainly much in common with Alceste. But Tchátskiy is, at the same time, so much Griboyédoff himself, and his cutting sarcasms are so much the sarcasms which Griboyédoff and his Decembrist friends must have launched against their Moscow acquaintances, while all the other persons of the comedy are so truly Moscow people—so exclusively Moscow nobles—that apart from its leading motive, the comedy is entirely original and most thoroughly Russian.

Tchátskiy is a young man who returns from a long journey abroad, and hastens to the house of an old gentleman, Fámusoff, whose daughter Sophie was his playmate in childhood, and is loved by him now. However, the object of his vows has meanwhile made the acquaintance of her father's secretary—a most insignificant and repulsive young man, Moltchálin, whose rules of life are : first, 'moderation and punctuality,' and next, to please every one in the house of his superiors, down to the gatekeeper and his dog, 'that even the dog may be kind to me.' Following his rules, Moltchálin courts at the same time the daughter of his principal and her maid : the former, to make himself agreeable in his master's house, and the latter, because she pleases him. Tchátskiy is received in a very cold way. Sophie is afraid of his intelligence and his sarcasm, and her father has already found a partner for her in Colonel Skalozúb—a military man full six feet high in his socks, who speaks in a deep bass voice, exclusively about military matters, but has a fortune and will soon be a general.

Tchátskiy behaves just as an enamoured young man would do. He sees nothing but Sophie, whom he pursues with his adoration, making in her presence stinging remarks about Moltchálin, and bringing her father to despair by his free criticism of Moscow manners—the cruelty of the old serf-owners, the platitudes of the old courtiers, and so on ; and as a climax, at a ball which Fámusoff gives that night, he indulges in long monologues against the adoration of the Moscow ladies for everything French. Sophie, in the meantime, offended by his remarks about Moltchálin, retaliates by setting afloat the rumour that Tchátskiy is not quite right in his mind, a rumour which is taken up with delight by society at the ball, and spreads like wildfire.

It has often been said in Russia that the satirical remarks of Tchátskiy at the ball, being directed against such a trifling matter as the adoration of foreigners, are rather superficial and irrelevant. But it is more than probable that Griboyédoff limited himself to such innocent remarks because he knew that no others would be tolerated by the censorship ; he must have hoped that these, at least, would not be wiped out by the censor's red ink. From what Tchátskiy says during his morning call in Fámusoff's study, and from what is dropped by other personages, it is evident that Griboyédoff had far more serious criticisms to put into his hero's mouth.

Altogether, a Russian satirical writer is necessarily placed under a serious disadvantage with foreigners. When Molière gives a satirical description of Parisian society, this satire is not strange to the readers of other nations : we all know something about life in Paris ; but when Griboyédoff describes Moscow society in the same satirical vein, and reproduces in easily flowing verses purely Moscow types—not even typical Russians, but Moscow types ('On all the Moscow people,' he says, 'there is a special stamp')—they are so strange to the Western mind that the translator ought to be half-Russian himself, and a poet, in order to render Griboyédoff's comedy in another language.   If such a translation were made, I am sure that this comedy would become a favourite on the stages of Western Europe.   In Russia it has been played over and over again up to the present time, and although it is now seventy years old, it has lost nothing of its interest and attractiveness.[1]

THE MOSCOW STAGE

In the forties of the nineteenth century the theatre was treated everywhere with great respect—and more than anywhere else was this the case in Russia.   Italian opera had not yet reached the development it attained at St. Petersburg some twenty years later, and Russian opera, represented by poor singers, and treated as a step-daughter by the directors of the Imperial Theatres, offered but little attraction.   It was the drama and occasionally the ballet, when Fanny Elsler, or a local star, appeared on the horizon, which brought together the best elements of educated society and aroused the youth

---

[1] In Appendix B I give the attempt I have made to translate in blank verses one of the most striking scenes of *Misfortune from Intelligence*—the scene during the ball, when Sophie, half accidentally, launches the rumour of Tchátskiy having gone mad.

of all classes, including the University students. The dramatic stage was looked upon—to speak in the style of those years—as 'a temple of art,' a centre of far-reaching educational influence. As to the actors and actresses, they endeavoured, in their turn, not merely to render on the stage the characters created by the dramatist; they did their best to contribute themselves, like Cruikshank in his illustrations of Dickens's novels, to the final creation of the character, by finding its true personification.

It was especially at Moscow that this intellectual intercourse between the stage and society was going on, and a superior conception of dramatic art was developed. The intercourse which Gógol established with the actors who played his *Inspector-General*, and especially with SCHÉPKIN; the influence of the literary and philosophical circles which had then their seat at Moscow; and the intelligent appreciation and criticism of their work which the actors found in the Press—all this concurred in making of the Moscow Máliy Teátr (Small Theatre) the cradle of a superior dramatic art. While St. Petersburg patronised the so-called 'French' school of acting —declamatory and unnaturally refined—the Moscow stage attained a high degree of perfection in the development of the naturalistic school. I mean the school of which Duse is now such a great representative, and to which Lena Ashwell owed her success in *Resurrection*; that is, the school in which the actor parts with the routine of conventional stage tradition, and provokes the deepest emotions in his audience by the depth of his own real feeling and by the natural truth and simplicity of its expression.

In the forties and the early fifties this school had attained its highest perfection at Moscow, and had in its ranks such first-class actors and actresses as Schépkin— the real soul of this stage—MOTCHÁLOFF, SADÓVSKIY, S. VASÍLIEFF, and MME. NIKÚLINA-KOSSÍTSKAYA, supported by quite a pleiad of good secondary aids. Their

répertoire was not very rich ; but the two comedies of
Gógol (*Inspector-General* and *Marriage*), occasionally
Griboyédoff's great satire ; a comedy, *The Marriage of
Kretchínskiy*, by SUKHOVÓ-KOBÝLIN, which gave excellent opportunities for displaying the best qualities of the
artists just named ; now and then a drama of Shakespeare,[1] plenty of melodramas adapted from the French,
and vaudevilles which came nearer to light comedy than
to farce—this was the ever-varied programme of the
Small Theatre.　Some plays were played to perfection
—combining the *ensemble* and the 'go' which characterise the Odéon with the simplicity and naturalness
already mentioned.

The mutual influence which the stage and dramatic
authors necessarily exercise upon each other was admirably illustrated at Moscow.　Several dramatists wrote
specially for this stage—not in order that this or that
actress might eclipse all others, as happens nowadays in
those theatres where one play is played scores of nights
in succession, but for this given *stage* and its actors as a
whole.　OSTRÓVSKIY (1823-1886) was the one who best
realised this mutual relation between the dramatic author
and the stage, and thus he came to hold with regard to
the Russian drama the same position that Turguéneff
and Tolstóy hold with regard to the Russian novel.

OSTRÓVSKIY : *POVERTY—NO VICE*

Ostróvskiy was born at Moscow in the family of a
small civil functionary, and, like the best of the younger
generation of his time, he was from the age of seventeen
an enthusiastic visitor of the Moscow theatre.　At that
age, we are told, his favourite talk with his comrades was
the stage.　He went to the University, but two years

---

[1] Shakespeare has always been a great favourite in Russia, both
in the two capitals and the provinces, but his dramas require a
certain wealth of scenery not always at the disposal of the Small
Theatre.

later he was compelled to leave, in consequence of a quarrel with a professor, and he became an under-clerk in one of the old Commercial tribunals. There he had the very best opportunities of making acquaintance with the world of Moscow merchants—a quite separate class which remained in its isolation the keeper of the traditions of old Russia. It was from this class that Ostróvskiy took nearly all the types of his first and best dramas. Only later on did he begin to widen the circle of his observations, taking in various classes of educated society.

His first comedy, *Pictures of Family Happiness*, was written in 1847, and three years later appeared his first drama, *We shall settle it among Ourselves*, or *The Bankrupt*, which at once gave him the reputation of a great dramatic writer. It was printed in a review, and had a great vogue all over Russia (the actor Sadóvskiy read it widely in private houses at Moscow), but it was not allowed to be put on the stage. The Moscow merchants even lodged a complaint with Nicholas I. against the author, and Ostróvskiy was dismissed from the civil service and placed under police supervision as a suspect. Only many years later, four years after Alexander II. had succeeded his father—that is, in 1860—was the drama played at Moscow, and even then the censorship insisted upon introducing at the end of it a police-officer to represent the triumph of justice over the wickedness of the bankrupt.

In the years 1853 and 1854 Ostróvskiy brought out in close succession two dramas of remarkable power— *Don't take a Seat in Other People's Sledges*, and *Poverty —no Vice*. The subject of the former was not new : a girl from a tradesman's family runs away with a nobleman, who abandons and ill-treats her when he realises that she will get from her father neither pardon nor money. But this subject was treated with such freshness, and the characters were depicted in positions so well chosen, that for its literary and stage qualities the drama is one of the best Ostróvskiy has written. As to *Poverty—no Vice*, it produced a tremendous impression all over Russia. We see in it a family of the old type, the head of which is a rich merchant—a man who is wont to impose his will upon all his surroundings and has no other conception of life. He has, however, taken outwardly to 'civilisation'—that is, to restaurant civilisation: he dresses in the fashions of Western Europe and tries to follow Western customs in his house—at least in the presence of the acquaintances he makes in the fashionable restaurants. Nevertheless, his wife is his slave, and his household trembles at his voice. He has a daughter who loves, and is loved by, one of her father's clerks, Mítya, a most timid but honest young man, and the mother would like her daughter to marry this clerk; but the father has made the acquaintance of a more or less wealthy aged manufacturer, who dresses according to the latest fashion, drinks champagne instead of rye-whisky, and therefore plays among Moscow merchants a certain rôle of authority in questions of fashion and rules of propriety. To this man the girl must be married. She is saved, however, by the interference of her uncle, Lubím Tortsóff. Lubím was once rich, like his brother, but he was not satisfied with the dull Philistine life of his surroundings, and seeing no way out of it and into a better social atmosphere, he took to drink—to unmitigated drunkenness, such as was to be seen in olden times at Moscow. His wealthy brother has helped him to get rid of his fortune, and now in a ragged mantle he goes about the lower-class taverns, making of himself a sort of jester for a chance glass of gin. Penniless, dressed in his rags, cold and hungry, he comes to the young clerk's room, asking permission to stay there overnight.

The drama goes on at Christmas time, and this gives Ostróvskiy the opportunity for introducing all sorts of songs and Christmas masquerades, in true Russian style. In the midst of all this merriment, which has been going on in his absence, Tortsóff, the father, comes in with the

bridegroom of his choice.   All the 'vulgar' pleasures
must now come to an end, and the father, full of venera-
tion for his fashionable friend, curtly orders his daughter
to marry the man he has chosen for her.   The tears of
the girl and her mother are of no avail: the father's
orders must be obeyed.   But there enters Lubím
Tortsóff, in his rags and with his jester's antics—terrible
in his degradation, and yet a man.   The father's terror
at such a sight can easily be imagined, and Lubím
Tortsóff, who during his wanderings has heard all about
the manufacturer's past, and who knows of his brother's
scheme, begins to tell before the guests what sort of
man the would-be bridegroom is.   The latter, holding
himself insulted in his friend's house, affects great anger
and leaves the room, whereupon Lubím Tortsóff tells
his brother what a crime he is going to commit by
giving his daughter to the old man.   He is ordered to
leave the room, but he persists, and, standing in the
rear of the crowd, he begins piteously to beg: 'Brother,
give your daughter to Mítya' (the young clerk): 'he,
at least, will give me a corner in his house.   I have
suffered enough from cold and hunger.   My years are
passing: it becomes hard for me to get my piece of bread
by performing my antics in the bitter frost.   Mítya will
let me live honestly in my old age.'   The mother and
daughter join with the uncle, and finally the father, who
resents the insults of his friend, exclaims: 'Well, do
you take me, then, for a wild beast? I won't give my
daughter to that man.   Mítya, marry her!'

The drama has a happy end, but the audience feels
that it might have been as well the other way.   The
father's whim might have ended in the life-long misery
and misfortune of the daughter, and this would probably
have been the outcome in most such cases.

Like Griboyédoff's comedy, like Gontcharóff's
Oblómoff, and many other good things in Russian
literature, this drama is so typically Russian that one is
apt to overlook its broadly human signification.   It

seems to be typically Moscovite; but, change names and customs, change a few details and rise a bit higher or sink a bit lower in the strata of society; put, instead of the drunkard Lubím Tortsóff, a poor relation or an honest friend who has retained his common sense—and the drama applies to any nation and to any class of society. It is deeply human. This is what caused its tremendous success and made it a favourite on every Russian stage for fifty years. I do not speak, of course, of the foolishly exaggerated enthusiasm with which it was received by the so-called nationalists, and especially the Slavophiles, who saw in Lubím Tortsóff the personification of a 'truly Russian soul'—a man who, even though he has sunk so deep, retains virtues which 'the rotten West' can never possess! The more sensible of Russians did not go to such lengths; but they understood what wonderful material of observation, drawn from real life, this and the other dramas of Ostróvskiy were offering. The leading review of the time was *The Contemporary*, and its leading critic, Dobrolúboff, wrote two long articles to analyse Ostróvskiy's dramas, under the significant title of *The Kingdom of Darkness*; and when he had passed in review all the darkness which then prevailed in Russian life as represented by Ostróvskiy, he produced something which has been one of the most powerful inflences in the whole subsequent intellectual development of the Russian youth.

THE THUNDERSTORM

One of the best dramas of Ostróvskiy is *The Thunderstorm* (translated by Mrs. Constance Garnett as *The Storm*). The scene is laid in a small provincial town, somewhere on the upper Vólga, where the manners of the local tradespeople have retained the stamp of primitive wildness. There is, for instance, one old merchant, Dikóy, very much respected by the inhabitants, who

represents a special type of those tyrants whom Ostróvskiy has so well depicted. Whenever Dikóy has a
payment to make, even though he knows perfectly well
that pay he must, he stirs up a quarrel with the man to
whom he is in debt. He has an old friend, Madame
Kabanóva, and when he is the worse for drink, and in
a bad temper, he always goes to her : ' I have no business
with you,' he declares, 'but I have been drinking.'
Following is a scene which takes place between them :

Kabanóva : I really wonder at you ; with all the crowd of
folks in your house, not a single one can do anything to your
liking.

Dikóy : That 's so !

Kabanóva : Come, what do you want of me ?

Dikóy : Well, talk me out of my temper. You 're the
only person in the whole town who knows how to talk to me.

Kabanóva : How have they put you into such a rage ?

Dikóy : I 've been so all day since the morning.

Kabanóva : I suppose they 've been asking for money.

Dikóy : As if they were in league together, damn them !
One after another, the whole day long they 've been at me.

Kabanóva : No doubt you 'll have to give it them, or they
wouldn't persist.

Dikóy : I know that ; but what would you have me do, since
I 've a temper like that ? Why, I know that I must pay, still I
can't do it with a good will. You 're a friend of mine, and
I 've to pay you something, and you come and ask me for it—
I 'm bound to swear at you ! Pay I will, if pay I must, but I
must swear too. For you 've only to hint at money to me, and
I feel hot all over in a minute ; red-hot all over, and that 's all
about it. You may be sure at such times I 'd swear at any one
for nothing at all.

Kabanóva : You have no one over you, and so you think
you can do as you like.

Dikóy : No, you hold your tongue ! Listen to me ! I 'll tell
you the sort of troubles that happen to me. I had fasted in
Lent, and was all ready for Communion, and then the Evil
One thrusts a wretched peasant under my nose. He had
come for money, for wood he had supplied us. And, for my
sins, he must needs show himself at a time like that ! I fell
into sin, of course ; I pitched into him, pitched into him

P

finely, I did, all but thrashed him. There you have it, my temper! Afterwards I asked his pardon, bowed down to his feet, upon my word I did. It's the truth I'm telling you, I bowed down to a peasant's feet. That's what my temper brings me to: on the spot there, in the mud I bowed down to his feet; before every one, I did.[1]

Madame Kabanóva is well matched with Dikóy. She may be less primitive than her friend, but she is an infinitely more tyrannical oppressor. Her son is married and loves, more or less, his young wife; but he is kept under his mother's rule just as if he were a boy. The mother hates, of course, her young daughter-in-law, Katerína, and tyrannises over her as much as she can; and the husband has no energy to step in and defend her. He is only too happy when he can slip away from the house. He might have shown more love to his wife if they had been living apart from his mother; but being in this house, always under its tyrannical rule, he looks upon his wife as part of it all. Katerína, on the contrary, is a poetical being. She was brought up in a very good family, where she enjoyed full liberty, before she married the young Kabanóff, and now she feels very unhappy under the yoke of her terrible mother-in-law, having nobody but a weakling husband to say occasionally a word in her favour. There is also a little detail—she has a mortal fear of thunderstorms. This is a feature which is quite characteristic in the small towns on the upper Vólga: I have myself known well-educated ladies who, having once been frightened by one of these sudden storms—they are of a terrific grandeur—retained a life-long fear of thunder.

It so happens that Katerína's husband has to leave his town for a fortnight. Katerína, in the meantime, who has met occasionally on the promenade a young man, Borís, a nephew of Dikóy, and has received some attention from him, partly driven to it by her husband's

[1] Taken from the excellent translation of Mrs. C. Garnett (*The Storm*, London, Duckworth and Co., 1899).

sister—a very flighty girl, who is wont to steal from
the back garden to meet her sweethearts—has during
these few days one or two interviews with the young
man, and falls in love with him. Borís is the first man
who, since her marriage, has treated her with respect;
he himself suffers from the oppression of Dikóy, and she
feels half-sympathy, half-love towards him. But Borís
is also of weak, irresolute character, and as soon as his
uncle Dikóy orders him to leave the town he obeys, and
has only the usual words of regret that 'circumstances'
so soon separate him from Katerína. The husband
returns, and when he, his wife, and the old mother
Kabanóva are caught by a terrific thunderstorm on the
promenade along the Vólga, Katerína, in mortal fear of
sudden death, tells, in the presence of the crowd which
has taken refuge in a shelter on the promenade, what
has happened during her husband's absence. The consequences will best be learned from the following scene,
which I quote from the same translation. It also takes
place on the high bank of the Vólga. After having
wandered for some time in the dusk on the solitary
bank, Katerína at last perceives Borís and runs up
to him.

Katerína: At last I see you again! (*Weeps on his breast.
Silence.*)
Borís: Well, God has granted us to weep together.
Katerína: You have not forgotten me?
Borís: How can you speak of forgetting?
Katerína: Oh no, it was not that, not that! You are not
angry?
Borís: Angry for what?
Katerína: Forgive me! I did not mean to do you any harm.
I was not free myself. I did not know what I said, what I did.
Borís: Don't speak of it! Don't.
Katerína: Well, how is it with you? What are you going
to do?
Borís: I am going away.
Katerína: Where are you going?
Borís: Far away, Kátya, to Siberia.

Katerína : Take me with you, away from here.

Borís : I cannot, Kátya. I am not going of my free will; my uncle is sending me, he has the horses waiting for me already; I only begged for a minute, I wanted to take a last farewell of the spot where we used to see each other.

Katerína : Go, and God be with you! Don't grieve over me. At first your heart will be heavy, perhaps, poor boy, but then you will begin to forget.

Borís : Why talk of me! I am free at least; how about you? what of your husband's mother?

Katerína : She tortures me, she locks me up. She tells every one, even my husband : ' Don't trust her, she is sly and deceitful.' They all follow me about all day long, and laugh at me before my face. At every word they reproach me with you.

Borís : And your husband ?

Katerína : One minute he's kind, one minute he's angry, but he's drinking all the while. He is loathsome to me, loathsome; his kindness is worse than his blows.

Borís : You are wretched, Kátya ?

Katerína : So wretched, so wretched, that it were better to die!

Borís : Who could have dreamed that we should have to suffer such anguish for our love? I'd better have run away then!

Katerína : It was an evil day for me when I saw you. Joy I have known little of, but of sorrow, of sorrow, how much! And how much is still before me! But why think of what is to be! I am seeing you now, that much they cannot take away from me; and I care for nothing more. All I wanted was to see you. Now my heart is much easier; as though a load had been taken off me. I kept thinking you were angry with me, that you were cursing me. . . .

Borís : How can you! How can you!

Katerína : No, that is not what I mean; that is not what I wanted to say! I was sick with longing for you, that's it; and now, I have seen you. . . .

Borís : They must not come upon us here!

Katerína : Stay a minute! Stay a minute! Something I meant to say to you! I've forgotten! Something I had to say! Everything is in confusion in my head, I can remember nothing.

Borís : It's time I went, Kátya!

Katerína : Wait a minute, a minute!

Borís : Come, what did you want to say?

Katerína: I will tell you directly. (*Thinking a moment.*) Yes! As you travel along the highroads, do not pass by one beggar, give to every one, and bid them pray for my sinful soul.

Borís: Ah, if these people knew what it is to me to part from you! My God! God grant they may one day know such bitterness as I know now. Farewell, Kátya! (*Embraces her and tries to go away.*) Miscreants! monsters! Ah, if I were strong!

Katerína: Stay, stay! Let me look at you for the last time (*gazes into his face*). Now all is over with me. The end is come for me. Now, God be with thee. Go, go quickly!

Borís: (*Moves away a few steps and stands still.*) Kátya, I feel a dread of something! You have something fearful in your mind? I shall be in torture as I go, thinking of you.

Katerína: No, no! Go in God's name! (*Borís is about to go up to her.*) No, no, enough.

Borís: (*Sobbing.*) God be with thee!—There's only one thing to pray God for, that she may soon be dead, that she may not be tortured long!—Farewell!

Katerína: Farewell!

(*Borís goes out. Katerína follows him with her eyes and stands for some time, lost in thought.*)

SCENE IV

KATERÍNA (*alone*)

Where am I going now? Home? No, home or the grave— it is the same. Yes, home or the grave! . . . the grave! Better the grave. . . . A little grave under a tree . . . how sweet. . . . The sunshine warms it, the sweet rain falls on it . . . in the spring the grass grows on it, soft and sweet grass . . . the birds will fly in the tree and sing, and bring up their little ones, and flowers will bloom; golden, red, and blue . . . all sorts of flowers (*dreamingly*), all sorts of flowers . . . how still! how sweet! My heart is as it were lighter! But of life I don't want to think! Live again! No, no, no use . . . life is not good! . . . And people are hateful to me, and the house is hateful, and the walls are hateful! I will not go there! No, no, I will not go! If I go to them, they'll come and talk, and what do I want with that? Ah, it has grown dark! And there is singing again somewhere! What are they singing? I can't make out. . . . To die now. . . . What are they singing? It

is just the same whether death comes, or of myself . . . but
live I cannot! A sin to die so! . . . they won't pray for me!
If any one loves me, he will pray . . . they will fold my arms
crossed in the grave! Oh yes . . . I remember. But when
they catch me, and take me home by force. . . . Ah, quickly,
quickly! (*Goes to the river bank. Aloud.*) My dear one! My
sweet! Farewell! (*Exit.*)
(*Enter Mme. Kabanóva, Kabanóv, Kulíghin, and workmen
with torches.*)

The Thunderstorm is one of the best dramas in the
modern *répertoire* of the Russian stage. From the
stage point of view it is simply admirable. Every
scene is impressive, the drama develops rapidly, and
every one of the twelve characters introduced in it is a
joy to the dramatic artist. The parts of Dikóy, Varvára
(the frivolous sister), Kabanóff, Kudryásh (the sweet-
heart of Varvára), an old artisan-engineer, nay even
the old lady with two male servants, who appears only
for a couple of minutes—each one will be found a
source of deep artistic pleasure by the actor or actress
who takes it; while the parts of Katerína and Mme.
Kabanóva are such that no great actress would neglect
them.

Concerning the main idea of the drama, I shall have
to repeat here what I have already said once or twice
in the course of these sketches. At first sight it may
seem that Mme. Kabanóva and her son are exclusively
Russian types—types which exist no more in Western
Europe. But such an assertion seems to be hardly
correct. The submissive Kabanóffs may be rare in
England, or at least their sly submissiveness does not
go to the same lengths as it does in *The Thunderstorm.*
But even for Russian society Kabanóff is not very
typical. As to his mother, Mme. Kabanóva, every one
of us must have met her more than once in English
surroundings. Who does not know, indeed, the old
lady who for the mere pleasure of exercising her power
will keep her daughters at her side, prevent their

marrying, and tyrannise over them till they have grown grey-haired? or in thousands of other ways exercise her tyranny over her household? Dickens knew Mme. Kabanóva well, and she is still alive in these islands, as everywhere else.

OSTRÓVSKIY'S LATER DRAMAS

As Ostróvskiy advanced in years and widened the scope of his observations of Russian life, he drew his characters from other circles besides that of the merchants, and in his later dramas he gave such highly attractive, progressive types as *The Poor Bride*, Parásha (in a beautiful comedy, *An Impetuous Heart*), Agniya in *Carnival has its End*, the actor Neschastlívtseff (Mr. Unfortunate) in a charming idyll, *The Forest*, and so on. And as regards his 'negative' (undesirable) types, taken from the life of the St. Petersburg bureaucracy or from the millionaire and 'company-promoters' circles, Ostróvskiy deeply understood them and attained the artistic realisation of wonderfully true, coldly harsh, though apparently 'respectable' types, such as no other dramatic writer has ever succeeded in producing.

Altogether Ostróvskiy wrote about fifty dramas and comedies, and every one of them is excellent for the stage. There are no insignificant parts in them. A great actor or actress may take one of the smallest parts, consisting of perhaps but a few words pronounced during a few minutes' appearance on the stage, and yet feel that there is material enough in it to create a character. As for the main personages, Ostróvskiy fully understood that a considerable part in the creation of a character must be left to the actor. There are consequently parts which without such a collaboration would be pale and unfinished, while in the hands of a true actor they yield material for a deeply psychological and profoundly dramatic personification. This is why a lover of dramatic art finds such a deep æsthetic pleasure both in playing in Ostróvskiy's dramas and in reading them aloud.

Realism, in the sense which already has been indicated several times in these pages—that is, a realistic description of characters and events, subservient to ideal aims—is the distinctive feature of all Ostróvskiy's dramas.   As in the novels of Turguéneff, the simplicity of his plots is striking.   But you see life—true life with all its pettinesses—developing before you, and out of these petty details grows insensibly the plot.

'One scene follows another, and all of them are so commonplace, such an everyday matter!—and yet, out of them, a terrible drama has quite imperceptibly grown into being.   You could affirm that it is not a comedy being played before you, but life itself unrolled before your eyes—as if the author had simply opened a wall and shown you what is going on inside this or that house.'   In these words one of our critics, Skabit-chévskiy, has described Ostróvskiy's work.

In his dramas Ostróvskiy introduced an immense variety of characters taken from all classes of Russian life ; but he once for all abandoned the old romantic division of human types into 'good' and 'bad' ones. In real life these two divisions are blended together and merge into one another ; and while even now an English dramatic author cannot conceive a drama without 'the villain,' Ostróvskiy never felt the need of introducing that conventional personage.   Nor did he feel the need of resorting to the conventional rules of 'dramatic conflict.'   To quote once more from the same critic :

'There is no possibility of bringing his comedies under some general principle, such as a struggle of duty against inclination, or a collision of passions which calls forth a fatal result, or an antagonism between good and evil, or between progress and ignorance.   His comedies represent the most varied human relations.   Just as we find it in life, men stand in these comedies in different obligatory relations towards each other, which relations have, of course, their origin in the past; and when these men have been brought together, conflicts necessarily arise between them, out of these very relations. As to the outcome of the conflict, it is, as a rule, quite unforeseen, and often depends, as usually happens in real life, upon mere accidents.'

Like Ibsen, Ostróvskiy sometimes will not even undertake to say how the drama will end.

And finally, Ostróvskiy, notwithstanding the pessimism of all his contemporaries—the writers of the fifties—was not a pessimist. Even amidst the most terrible conflicts depicted in his dramas he retained the sense of the joy of life and of the unavoidable fatality of many of the miseries of life. He never recoiled before painting the darker aspects of the human turmoil, and he has given a most repulsive collection of family despots from the old merchant class, followed by a collection of still more repulsive types from the class of industrial 'promoters.' But in one way or another he managed either to show that there are better influences at work, or, at least, to suggest the possible triumph of some better element. He thus avoided falling into the pessimism which characterised his contemporaries, and he had nothing of the hysterical turn of mind which we find in some of his modern followers. Even at moments when, in some one of his dramas, life all round wears the gloomiest aspect (as, for instance, in *Sin and Misfortune may visit Every One*, which is a page from peasant life as realistically dark as Tolstóy's *Power of Darkness*, though better suited for the stage), even then a gleam of hope appears, at least, in the contemplation of nature, if nothing else remains to redeem the gloominess of human folly.

And yet there is one thing—and a very important one—which stands in the way of Ostróvskiy's occupying in international dramatic literature the high position to which his powerful dramatic talent entitled him, and being recognised as one of the great dramatists of our century. The dramatic conflicts which we find in his dramas are all of the simpler sort. There are none of the more tragical problems and entanglements which the complicated nature of the educated man of our own times and the different aspects of the great social questions are giving birth to in the conflicts arising now in every stratum and class of society. But it must also be said that the dramatist who can treat these modern problems of life in the same masterly way in which the Moscow writer has treated the simpler problems which he saw in his own surroundings is yet to come.

HISTORICAL DRAMAS—A. K. TOLSTÓY

At the time of a full development of his talent Ostróvskiy turned to historical drama, which he wrote in excellent blank verse, and published in succession, in 1862-1867, the dramas *Kozmá Mínin*, *The Voyevóda*, *Dmítri the Impostor*, and *Túshino* (the camp of the second Dmítri). But, like Shakespeare's plays from English history, and Púshkin's *Borís Godunóff*, they have more the character of dramatised chronicles than of dramas properly speaking. They belong too much to the domain of the epic, and the dramatic interest is too often sacrificed to the desire of introducing historical colouring.

The same is true, though in a lesser degree, of the historical dramas of Count ALEXÉI KONSTANTÍNOVITCH TOLSTÓY (1817-1875). A. K. Tolstóy was above all a poet; but he also wrote a historical novel from the times of John the Terrible, *Prince Serébryanyi*, which had a very great success, partly because in it for the first time censorship had permitted fiction to deal with the half-mad Tsar who played the part of the Louis XI. of the Russian Monarchy, but especially on account of its qualities as a historical novel. He also tried his talent in a dramatic poem, *Don Juan*, much inferior, however, to Púshkin's drama dealing with the same subject ; but his main work was a trilogy of three tragedies from the times of John the Terrible and the impostor Demetrius : *The Death of John the Terrible*, *The Tsar Theódor Ivánovitch*, and *Borís Godunóff.*

These three tragedies have a considerable value ; in each the situation of the hero is highly dramatic, and treated in an impressive way, while the settings in the palaces of the old Moscow Tsars are extremely decorative and impressive in their sumptuous originality. But in all three tragedies the development of the dramatic situation suffers from the intrusion of the epical descriptive element, and the characters are either not quite correct historically (Borís Godunóff is deprived of his rougher traits in favour of a certain quiet idealism which was a personal feature of the author), or they do not represent that entireness of character which we are accustomed to find in Shakespeare's dramas.   Of course, the tragedies of Tolstóy are extremely far from the romanticism of the dramas of Victor Hugo ; they are, all things considered, realistic dramas ; but in the framing of the human characters some romanticism is felt still, and this is especially evident in the construction of the character of John the Terrible.

An exception must, however, be made in favour of *The Tsar Theódor Ivánovitch.*   A. K. Tolstóy was a devoted personal friend of Alexander II. and, refusing all administrative posts of honour which were offered him, he preferred the modest position of a Head of the Imperial Hunt, which permitted him to retain his independence, while remaining in close contact with the Emperor.   Owing to this intimacy he must have had the best opportunities for observing, especially in the later years of Alexander II.'s reign, the struggles to which a good-hearted man of weak character is exposed when he is a Tsar of Russia.   Of course the Tsar Theódor is not in the least an attempt at portraying Alexander II.—this would have been beneath an artist

—but the weakness of Alexander's character must have suggested those features of reality in the character of Theódor which make it so much better painted than either John the Terrible or Borís Godunóff. The Tsar Theódor is a living creation.

OTHER DRAMATIC WRITERS

Of other writers for the stage we can only briefly mention the most interesting ones.

TURGUÉNEFF wrote, in 1848-1851, five comedies, which offer all the elements for refined acting, are very lively and, being written in a beautiful style (Turguéneff's prose !), are still the source of æsthetic pleasure for the more refined playgoers.

SUKHOVÓ-KOBÝLIN has already been mentioned. He wrote one comedy, *The Marriage of Kretchínskiy*, which made its mark and is still played with success. It was the first of a trilogy, of which the two other comedies, *The Affair* and *The Death of Tarélkin*, are also powerful satires against bureaucracy, but less effective on the stage than the former.

A. PÍSEMSKIY, the novelist (1820-1881), wrote, besides a few good novels and several insignificant comedies, one remarkably good drama, *A Bitter Fate*, from peasant life, which he knew well. It must be said that Leo Tolstóy's well-known *Power of Darkness*— also a peasant tragedy—notwithstanding all its merits, has not eclipsed the drama of Písemskiy.

The novelist A. A. POTYÉKHIN (1829-1902) also wrote for the stage, and must not be omitted even in such a rapid sketch of the Russian drama as this. His comedies, *Tinsel, A Slice Cut-off, A Vacant Situation, In Muddy Waters*, met with the greatest difficulties as regards censorship, and the third was never put on the stage ; but those which were played were always a success, while the themes that he treated always attracted the attention of our critics. The first of them, *Tinsel,* can be taken as a fair representative of the talent of Potyékhin.

This comedy answered a 'question of the day.' For several years Russian literature, following especially in the steps of SCHEDRÍN (see chapter viii.), delighted in the description of those functionaries of the Government boards and tribunals who lived (before the reforms of the sixties) almost entirely upon bribes. However, after the reforms had been carried through, a new race of functionaries had grown up, 'those who took no bribes,' but at the same time, owing to their strait-laced official rigorism, and their despotic and unbridled egotism, were even worse specimens of mankind than any of the 'bribe-takers' of old. The hero of *Tinsel* is precisely such a man. His character, with all its secondary features—his ingratitude and especially his love (or what passes for love in him)—is perhaps too much blackened for the purposes of the drama : men so consistently egotistical and formalistic are seldom, if ever, met with in real life. But one is almost convinced by the author of the reality of the type—with so masterly a hand does he unroll in a variety of incidents the 'correct' and deeply egotistic nature of his hero.

In this respect the comedy is very clever, and offers full opportunity for excellent acting.

A dramatic writer who enjoyed a long-standing success was A. I. PALM (1823-1885). In 1849 he was arrested for having been intimate with the circle of Petrashévskiy's friends (see DOSTOYÉVSKIY), and from that time his life was a series of misfortunes, so that he returned to literary activity only at the age of fifty. He belonged to the generation of Turguéneff, and, knowing well those types of noblemen whom the great novelist has depicted so well in his *Hamlets,* he wrote several comedies from the life of their circles. *The Old Nobleman* and *Our Friend Neklúzheff* were till lately favourite plays on the stage.

The actor, I. E. TCHERNYSHÓFF, who wrote several

comedies and one serious drama, *A Spoiled Life*, which produced a certain impression in 1861; N. SOLOVIÓFF, and a very prolific writer, V. A. KRYLÓFF (ALEXÁN-DROFF), must also be mentioned in this brief sketch.

And finally, two novelists who have produced remarkable dramas, ANTON TCHÉHOFF and MAXÍM GÓRKIY, must be mentioned; but I shall speak of them at more length in the next two chapters.

CHAPTER VII

FOLK-NOVELISTS

Their position in Russian literature—The early folk-novelists :
Grigoróvitch — Márko Vovtchók — Danilévskiy — Intermediate period : Kókoreff — Písemskiy — Potyékhin — Ethnographical research—The realistic school : Pomyalóvskiy—
Ryeshétnikoff — Levítoff — Gleb Uspénskiy — Zlatovrátskiy
and other folk-novelists : Naúmoff—Zasódimskiy—Sáloff—
Nefédoff—Modern realism : Maxím Górkiy.

AN important division of Russian novelists, almost
totally unknown in Western Europe, and yet representing
perhaps the most typical portion of Russian literature,
are the ' Folk-Novelists.'   It is under this name that we
know them chiefly in Russia, and under this name the
critic Skabitchévskiy has analysed them—first, in a
book bearing this title, and then in his *History of
Modern Russian Literature* (4th ed. 1900).   By ' Folk-
Novelists ' we mean, of course, not those who write *for*
the people, but those who write *about* the people : the
peasants, the miners, the factory workers, the lowest
strata of population in towns, the tramps.   Bret Harte
in his sketches of the mining camps, Zola in *L'Assom-
moir* and *Germinal*, Mr. W. S. Maugham in *Liza of
Lambeth*, Mr. Whiting in *No. 5 John Street*, belong to
this category ; but what is exceptional and accidental
in Western Europe is organic in Russia.

Quite a number of talented writers have devoted themselves during the last sixty years, some of them entirely,
to the description of this or that division of the Russian
people.   Every class of the toiling masses, which in other
literatures would have appeared in novels as the back-

ground for events going on amidst educated people (as in Hardy's *Woodlanders*), has had in the Russian novel its own painter.   All great questions concerning popular life which are debated in political and social books and reviews have been treated in the novel as well.   The evils of serfdom and, later on, the struggle between the tiller of the soil and growing commercialism ; the effects of factories upon village life, the great co-operative fisheries, peasant life in certain monasteries, life in the depths of the Siberian forests, slum life and tramp life—all these have been depicted by the folk-novelists, and their novels have been as eagerly read as the works of the greatest authors.   And while such questions as, for instance, the future of the village community, or of the peasants' Common Law Courts, are debated in the daily papers, in the scientific reviews, and the journals of statistical research, they are also dealt with by means of artistic images and types taken from life in the folk-novel.

Moreover, the folk-novelists, taken as a whole, represent a great school of realism in art, and in true realism they have surpassed all those writers who have been mentioned in the preceding chapters.   Of course, Russian 'realism,' as the reader of this book is already well aware, is something quite different from what was represented as 'naturalism' and 'realism' in France by Zola.   As already remarked, Zola, notwithstanding his propaganda of realism, always remained an inveterate romantic in the conception of his leading characters, both of the 'saint' and of the 'villain' type; and no doubt because of this—perhaps feeling it himself—he gave, as a compensation, an exaggerated importance to speculations about physiological heredity and to the accumulation of minor descriptive details, many of which, especially amongst his repulsive types, might have been omitted without depriving the characters of any significant feature. In Russia the 'realism' of Zola has always been considered too superficial, too outward, and while our folk-novelists also have often indulged in an unnecessary profusion of detail—sometimes decidedly ethnographical—they have aimed nevertheless at that *inner* realism which appears in the construction of such characters as are truly representative of life taken as a whole. Their aim has been to represent life without distortion—whether that distortion consists in introducing petty details, which may be true, but are accidental, or in endowing heroes with virtues or vices which are indeed met with here and there, but ought not to be generalised. Several novelists, as will be seen presently, have objected even to the usual ways of describing *types* and relating in novels the individual dramas of a few typical heroes. They have made the extremely bold attempt of describing *life itself*, in its succession of petty actions, moving on amidst its grey and dull surroundings, introducing only that dramatic element which results from the endless succession of petty and depressing details and wonted circumstances ; and it must be owned that they have not been quite unsuccessful in striking out this new line of art—perhaps the most tragical of all. Others, again, have introduced a new type of artistic representation of life, which occupies an intermediate position between the novel, properly so called, and a demographic description of a given population. Thus Gleb Uspénskiy knew how to intermingle artistic descriptions of typical village people with discussions belonging to the domain of folk-psychology in so interesting a manner that the reader willingly pardoned him these digressions ; while others, like Maxímoff, succeeded in making out of their ethnographical descriptions works of art, without in the least diminishing their scientific value.

THE EARLY FOLK-NOVELISTS

One of the earliest folk-novelists was GRIGORÓVITCH (1822-1899), a man of great talent, who sometimes is placed by the side of Tolstóy, Turguéneff, Gontcharóff,

Q

and Ostróvskiy. His literary career was very interesting. He was born of a Russian father and a French mother, and at the age of ten hardly knew Russian at all. His education was entirely foreign—chiefly French—and he did not grow up amidst the village life as Turgué-neff and Tolstóy did. Moreover, he never gave him-self exclusively to literature : he was a painter as well as a novelist, and at the same time a fine connoisseur of art, and for the last thirty years of his life he wrote almost nothing, but gave all his time to the Russian Society of Painters. And yet this half-Russian was one of those who rendered the same service to Russia before the abolition of serfdom that Harriet Beecher Stowe rendered to the United States by her description of the sufferings of the negro slaves.

Grigoróvitch was educated in the same military school of engineers as Dostoyévskiy, and after having finished his education there, he took a tiny room from the warder of the Academy of Arts, with the intention of giving himself entirely to art. However, in the studios he made the acquaintance of the Little Russian poet Shevtchénko, and next of Nekrásoff and Valerián Máykoff (a critic of great power, who died very young), and through them he found his vocation in literature.

In the early forties he was known only by a charming sketch, *The Organ Grinders,* in which he spoke with great warmth of feeling of the miserable life of this class of the St. Petersburg population. Russian society, in those years, felt the impression of the Socialist revival of France, and its best representatives were growing impatient with serfdom and absolutism. Fourier and Pierre Leroux were favourite writers in advanced intellectual circles, and Grigoróvitch was carried on by the growing current. He left St. Petersburg, went to stay for a year or two in the country, and in 1846 he published his first novel dealing with country life, *The Village.* He depicted in it, without any exaggeration, the dark sides of village life and the horrors of serfdom, and he did it so vividly that Byelínskiy, the critic, at once recognised in him a new writer of great power, and greeted him as such. His next novel, *Antón the Unfortunate*, also drawn from village life, was a tremendous success, and its influence was almost equal to that of *Uncle Tom's Cabin*. No educated man or woman of that generation, or of ours, could have read the book without weeping over the misfortunes of Antón, and finding better feelings grown in his heart towards the serfs. Several novels of the same character followed in the next eight years (1847-1855)—*The Fishermen, The Immigrants, The Tiller, The Tramp, The Country Roads*—and then Grigoróvitch came to a stop. In 1865 he took part with some of our best writers—Gontcharóff, Ostróvskiy, Maxímoff (the ethnographer), and several others—in a literary expedition organised by the Grand Duke Constantine for the exploration of Russia and voyages round the world on board ships of the Navy. Grigoróvitch made a very interesting sea-voyage; but his sketches of travel—*The Ship Retvizan*—cannot be compared with Gontcharóff's *Frigate Pallas*. On returning from the expedition he abandoned literature to devote himself entirely to art, and he subsequently brought out only a couple of novels and his *Reminiscences*. He died in 1899.

Grigoróvitch thus published all his chief novels between the years 1846 and 1855. Opinion about his work is divided. Some of our critics speak of it very highly, but others—and they are the greater number—say that his peasants are not real. Turguéneff made also the observation that his descriptions are too cold: the heart is not felt in them. This last remark may be true, although the average reader who did not know Grigoróvitch personally hardly would have made it; at any rate, at the time of the appearance of *Antón, The Fishermen*, etc., the great public judged the author of these works differently. As to his peasants, I will permit myself to make one suggestion. Undoubtedly they are slightly idealised; but it must also be said that the Russian peasantry does not present a compact, uniform mass. Several races have settled upon the territory of European Russia, and different portions of the population have followed different lines of development. The peasant from South Russia is quite different from the Northerner, and the Western peasants differ in every respect from the Eastern ones. Grigoróvitch described chiefly those living directly south of Moscow, in the provinces of Túla and Kalúga, and they are exactly that mild and slightly poetical, down-trodden and yet inoffensive, good-hearted race of peasants that Grigoróvitch described in his novels—a sort of combination of the Lithuanian and the Little Russian poetical mind, with Great Russian communal spirit. Ethnographers themselves see in the populations of this part of Russia a special ethnographical division.

Of course, Turguéneff's peasants (Túla and Oryól) are more real, his types are more definite, and every one of the modern folk-novelists, even of the less talented, has gone much further than Grigoróvitch did into the depths of peasant character and life. But such as they were, the novels of Grigoróvitch exercised a profound influence on a whole generation. They made us love the peasants and feel how heavy was the indebtedness towards them which weighed upon us—the educated part of society. They powerfully contributed towards creating a general feeling in favour of the serfs, without which the abolition of serfdom would have certainly been delayed for many years to come, and assuredly would not have been so sweeping as it was. And at a later epoch his work undoubtedly contributed to the creation of that movement 'towards the people' (*v naród*) which took place in the seventies.

Another writer of the same school, who also produced a deep impression on the very eve of the liberation of the serfs, was Mme. MARIE MÁRKOVITCH, who wrote under the pseudonym of MÁRKO VOVTCHÓK. She was a Great Russian—her parents belonged to the nobility of Central Russia—but she married the Little Russian writer MÁRKOVITCH, and her first book of stories from peasant life (1857-58) was written in excellent Little Russian. (Turguéneff translated them into Great Russian.) She soon returned, however, to her native tongue, and her second book of peasant stories, as well as her subsequent novels from the life of the educated classes, were written in Great Russian.

At the present time the novels of Márko Vovtchók may seem to be too sentimental—the world-famed novel of Harriet Beecher Stowe produces the same impression nowadays—but in those years, when the great question for Russia was whether the serfs should be freed or not, and when all the best forces of the country were needed for the struggle in favour of their liberation—in those years all educated Russia read the novels of Márko Vovtchók with delight, and wept over the fate of her peasant heroines. However, apart from this need of the moment—and art is bound to be at the service of society in such crises—the sketches of Márko Vovtchók had serious qualities. Their 'sentimentalism' was not the sentimentalism of the beginning of the nineteenth century, behind which was concealed an absence of real feeling. A loving heart throbbed in them; and there is in them real poetry, inspired by the poetry of the Ukraïnian folk-lore and its popular songs. With these Mme. Márkovitch was so familiar that, as has been remarked by Russian critics, she supplemented her imperfect knowledge of real popular life by introducing in a masterly manner many features inspired by the folk-lore and the popular songs of Little Russia. Her heroes were invented, but the atmosphere of a Little Russian village, the colours of local life, are in these sketches; and the soft poetical sadness of the Little Russian peasantry is rendered with the tender touch of a woman's hand.

Among the novelists of that period DANILÉVSKIY (1829-1890) must also be mentioned. Although he is better known as a writer of historical romances, his three long novels, *The Runaways in Novoróssiya* (1862), *Freedom, or the Runaways Returned* (1863), and *New Territories* (1867)—all dealing with the free settlers in Bessarabia—were widely read. They contain lively and very sympathetic scenes from the life of these settlers—mostly runaway serfs—who occupied, without the consent of the central government, the free lands in the newly annexed territories of South-western Russia, and became the prey of enterprising speculators.

INTERMEDIATE PERIOD

Notwithstanding all the qualities of their work, Grigoróvitch and Márko Vovtchók failed to realise that the very fact of taking the life of the poorer classes as the subject of novels ought to imply the working out of a special literary manner. The usual literary technique, evolved for the novel which deals with the leisured classes—with its mannerism, its ' heroes,' poetised now, as the knights used to be poetised in the tales of chivalry—is certainly not the most appropriate form for novels treating of the life of American squatters or Russian peasants. New methods and a different style had to be worked out ; but this was done step by step only, and it would be extremely interesting to show this gradual evolution, from Grigoróvitch to the ultra-realism of Ryeshétnikoff, and finally to the perfection of form attained by the realist-idealist Górkiy in his shorter sketches. Only a few intermediate steps can, however, be indicated in these pages.

I. T. KÓKOREFF (1826-1853), who died very young, after having written a few tales from the life of the petty artisans in towns, had not freed himself from the sentimentalism of a benevolent outsider ; but he knew this life from the inside : he was born and brought up in great poverty among these very people ; consequently, the artisans in his novels are real beings, described, as

Dobrolúboff said, 'with warmth and yet with tender restraint, as if they were his nearest kin.' However, 'No shriek of despair, no mighty wrath, no mordant irony came out of this tender, patiently suffering heart.' There is even a note of reconciliation with the social injustice.

A considerable step in advance was made by the folk-novel in A. TH. PÍSEMSKIY (1820-1881) and A. A. POTYÉKHIN (born 1829), although neither of them was exclusively a folk-novelist. Písemskiy was a contemporary of Turguéneff, and at a certain time of his career it seemed as if he were going to take a place by the side of Turguéneff, Tolstóy, and Gontcharóff. He undoubtedly possessed a great talent. There was power and true life in whatever he wrote, and his novel, *A Thousand Souls*, appearing on the eve of the emancipation of the serfs (1858), produced a deep impression. It was fully appreciated in Germany as well, where it was translated the next year. But Písemskiy was not a man of principle, and this novel was his last serious and really good production. When the great Radical and Nihilist movement took place (1858-1864), and it became necessary to take a definite position amidst the sharp conflict of opinions, Písemskiy, who was deeply pessimistic in his judgment of men and ideas, and considered 'opinions' as a mere cover for narrow egotism of the lowest sensual sort, took a hostile position towards this movement, and wrote such novels as *The Unruly Sea*, which were mere libels upon the young generation. This was, of course, the death of his by no means ordinary talent.

Písemskiy wrote also, during the early part of his literary career, a few tales from the life of the peasants (*The Carpenters' Artel*, *The St. Petersburg Man*, etc.), and a drama, from village life, *A Bitter Fate*, all of which have a real literary value. He displayed in them a knowledge of peasant life and a mastery of the spoken, popular Russian language, together with a perfectly realistic perception of peasant character. There was no trace of the idealisation which is so strongly felt in the later productions of Grigoróvitch, written under the influence of George Sand. The steady, common‑sense peasant characters that Písemskiy pictured are taken from a sound observation of life, and rival the best peasant characters of Turguéneff. As to the drama of Písemskiy (he was, by the way, a very good actor), it loses nothing from comparison with the best dramas of Ostróvskiy, and is more tragic than any of them, while in powerful realism it is by no means inferior to Tolstóy's *Power of Darkness*, with which it has much in common, and which it perhaps surpasses in its stage qualities.

The chief work of Potyékhin was his comedies, mentioned in the preceding chapter. All of them are from the life of the educated classes, but he wrote also a few less known dramas from peasant life, and twice —in his early career in the fifties, and later on in the seventies—he turned to the writing of short stories and novels from popular life.

These stories and novels are most characteristic of the evolution of the folk-novel during those years. In his earlier tales Potyékhin was entirely under the spell of the then prevailing manner of idealising the peasants; but in his second period, after having lived through the years of realism in the sixties, and taken part in the above-mentioned ethnographic expedition, he changed his manner. He entirely got rid of benevolent idealisation, and represented the peasants as they were. In the creation of individual characters he was undoubtedly successful, but the life of the village—the *mir*—without which Russian village life cannot be represented, and which so well appears in the works of the later folk-novelists, is yet missing. Altogether one feels that Potyékhin knew well the outer symptoms of the life of the Russian peasants, including their way of talking, but that he had not yet grasped the real soul of the peasant. This came only later on.

ETHNOGRAPHICAL RESEARCH

Serfdom was abolished in 1861, and the time for mere lamentation over its evils was gone. Proof that the peasants were human beings, accessible to all human feelings, was no longer needed. New and far deeper problems concerning the life and ideals of the Russian people rose before every thinking Russian. Here was a mass of nearly fifty million people, whose manners of life, whose creed, ways of thinking, and ideals were totally different from those of the educated classes, and who at the same time were as unknown to the would-be leaders of progress as if these millions spoke a quite different language and belonged to a quite different race.

Our best men felt that all the future development of Russia would be hampered by that ignorance, if it continued—and literature did its best to answer the great questions which besieged the thinking man at every step of his social and political activity.

The years 1858-1878 were years of the ethnographical exploration of Russia on such a scale that nowhere in Europe or America do we find anything similar. The monuments of old folk-lore and poetry; the common law of different parts and nationalities of the Empire; the religious beliefs and the forms of worship, and still more the social aspirations characteristic of the many sections of dissenters; the extremely interesting habits and customs which prevail in the different provinces; the economical conditions of the peasants; their domestic trades; the immense communal fisheries in South-eastern Russia; the thousands of forms taken by the popular co-operative organisations (the *Artels*); the 'inner colonisation' of Russia, which can only be compared with that of the United States; the evolution of ideas of landed property, and so on—all these became the subjects of extensive research.

The great ethnographical expedition organised by the Grand Duke Constantine, in which a number of our best writers took part, was only the forerunner of many expeditions, great and small, which were organised by the numerous Russian scientific societies for the detailed study of Russia's ethnography, folk-lore, and economics. There were men like YAKÚSHKIN (1820-1872), who devoted all his life to wandering on foot from village to village, dressed like the poorest peasant, and without any sort of thought of to-morrow ; drying his wet peasant cloth on his shoulders after a day's march under the rain, living with the peasants in their poor huts, and collecting folk-songs and ethnographic material of the highest value.

A special type of the Russian 'intellectuals' developed in the so-called 'Song-Collectors,' and 'Zemstvo Statisticians,' a group of people, old and young, who during the last twenty-five years have, as volunteers, devoted their lives to a house-to-house inquiry in behalf of the County Councils. (A. Oertel has admirably described these 'Statisticians' in one of his novels.)

Suffice it to say that, according to A. N. PÝPIN, the author of an exhaustive *History of Russian Ethnography* (4 vols.), not less than 4000 large works and bulky review articles were published during the twenty years 1858-1878, half of them dealing with the economical conditions of the peasants, and the other half with ethnography in its wider sense ; and research still continues on the same scale. The best of all this movement has been that it has not ended in dead material in official publications. Some of the reports, like MAXÍMOFF'S *A Year in the North, Siberia and Hard Labour*, and *Tramping Russia*, AFANÁSIEFF'S *Legends of the Russian People*, ZHELEZNÓFF'S *Urál Cossacks*, MÉLNIKÓFF'S (PETCHÉRSKIY) *In the Woods* and *On the Mountains*, or MORDÓVTSEFF'S many sketches, were so well written that they were as widely read as the best novels ; while the dry statistical reports were summed up in lively review articles (in Russia the reviews are much more bulky and the articles much longer than in England), which were widely read and discussed all over the country. Besides, admirable researches dealing with special classes of people, regions, and institutions were made by men like PRUGÁVIN (Nonconformism), ZASÓDIMSKIY, and PRYZHÓFF (*History of the Public Houses*, which is in fact a popular history of Russia; reprinted lately).

Russian educated society, which formerly hardly knew the peasants otherwise than from the balconies of their country houses, was thus brought in a few years into a close intercourse with all divisions of the toiling masses; and it is easy to understand the influence which this intercourse exercised, both upon the development of political ideas and the whole character of Russian literature.

The idealised novel of the past was now outgrown. The representation of 'the dear peasants' as a background for opposing their idyllic virtues to the defects of the educated classes was possible no more. The taking of the people as a mere material for burlesque tales, as NICHOLAS USPÉNSKIY and V. A. SLYEPTSÓFF tried to do, enjoyed but a momentary success. A new, eminently realistic school of folk-novelists was wanted. And the result was the appearance of quite a number of writers who broke new ground and, by cultivating a very high conception concerning the duties of art in the representation of the poorer, uneducated classes, opened, I am inclined to think, a new page in the evolution of the novel for the literature of all nations.

POMYALÓVSKIY

The clergy in Russia—that is, the priests, the deacons, the cantors, the bell-ringers—represent a separate class which stands between 'the classes' and 'the masses'—much nearer to the latter than to the former. This is especially true as regards the clergy in the villages, and it was still more so some fifty years ago. Receiving no salary, the village priest, with his deacon and cantors, lived chiefly by the cultivation of the land that was attached to the village church; and in my youth, in our Central Russia neighbourhood, during the hot summer months when they were hay-making or taking in the crops, the priest would always hurry through the mass in order to return to his field-work. The priest's house was in those years a log-house, only a little better built than the houses of the peasants, alongside which it stood, sometimes thatched, instead of being simply covered with straw which was held in position by means of straw ropes. His dress differed from that of the peasants more by its cut than by the materials it was made of, and between the church services and the fulfilment of his parish duties the priest might always be seen in the fields, following the plough or working in the meadows with the scythe.

All the children of the Russian clergy receive free education in special clerical schools, and later on, some of them, in seminaries; and it was by the description of the abominable educational methods which prevailed in these schools in the forties and fifties that POMYA-LÓVSKIY (1835-1863) acquired his notoriety. He was the son of a poor deacon in a village near St. Peters-burg, and had himself passed through one of these schools and a seminary. Both the lower and the higher schools were then in the hands of quite uneducated priests—chiefly monks—and the most absurd learning by rote of the most abstract theology was the rule. The general moral tone of the schools was extremely low, drinking went on to excess, and flogging for every lesson not recited by heart, sometimes two or three times a day, with all sorts of refinements of cruelty, was the chief instrument of education. Pomyalóvskiy passionately loved his younger brother and wanted at all hazards to save him from such an experience as his own; so he began to write for a pedagogical review, on the education given in the clerical schools, in order to get the means to educate his brother in a gymnasium. A most powerful novel, evidently taken from real life in these schools, followed, and numbers of priests, who had themselves been the victims of a like 'education,' wrote to the papers to confirm what Pomyalóvskiy had said. Truth, without any decoration, naked truth, with an absolute negation of art for art's sake, was the distinctive feature of Pomyalóvskiy, who went so far in this direction as even to part with the so-called heroes. The men whom he described were not sharply outlined types, but, if I may be permitted to express myself in this way, the 'neutral-tint' types of real life : those indefinite, not too good and not too bad characters of whom mankind is mostly composed, and whose inertia is everywhere the great obstacle to progress.

Besides his sketches from the life of the clerical schools, Pomyalóvskiy wrote also two novels from the life of the poorer middle classes : *Philistine Happiness* and *Mólotoff*—which is autobiographic to a great extent —and an unfinished larger novel, *Brother and Sister*. He displayed in these works the same broad humanitarian spirit as Dostoyévskiy had for noticing humane redeeming features in the most degraded men and women, but with the sound realistic tendency which was the distinctive feature of the young literary school of which he was one of the founders. And he depicted also, in an extraordinarily powerful and tragic manner, the hero from the poorer classes—who is imbued with hatred towards the upper classes and towards all forms of social life which exist for their advantage, and yet has not the faith in his own possibilities, which knowledge gives, and which a real force always has. Therefore this hero ends, either in a philistine family idyll, or, this failing, in a propaganda of reckless cruelty and of contempt towards all mankind, as the only possible foundation for personal happiness.

These novels were full of promise, and Pomyalóvskiy

was looked upon as the future leader of a new school of literature ; but he died, even before he had reached the age of thirty.

RYESHÉTNIKOFF

RYESHÉTNIKOFF (1841-1871) went still further in the same direction, and, with Pomyalóvskiy, he may be considered as the founder of the ultra-realistic school of Russian folk-novelists. He was born in the Uráls and was the son of a poor church cantor who became a postman. The family was in extreme poverty. An uncle took him to the town of Perm, and there he was beaten and thrashed all through his childhood. When he was ten years old they sent him to a miserable clerical school, where he was treated even worse than at his uncle's. He ran away, but was caught, and they flogged the poor child so awfully that he had to lie in a hospital for two months. As soon as he was taken back to school he ran away a second time, joining a band of tramping beggars. He suffered terribly during his peregrinations with them, and was caught once more, and again flogged in the most barbarous way. His uncle also was a postman, and Ryeshétnikoff, having nothing to read, used to steal newspapers from the post-office, and destroy them after having read them. This was soon discovered, the boy having destroyed some important Imperial manifesto addressed to the local authorities. He was brought before a court and condemned to be sent to a monastery for a few months (there were no reformatories then). The monks were kind to him, but they led a most dissolute life, drinking excessively, over-eating, and stealing away from the monastery at night, and they taught the boy to drink. In spite of all this, after his release from the monastery Ryeshétnikoff passed brilliantly the examinations in the district school, and was received as a clerk in the Civil Service, at a salary of six shillings, and later on half a guinea, per month. This meant, of course, the

most wretched poverty, because the young man took
no bribes, as all clerks in those times were accustomed
to do. The arrival of an inspector-general at Perm
saved him. This gentleman employed Ryeshétnikoff
as a copyist, and, having come to like him, gave him
the means to move to St. Petersburg, where he found
him a position as clerk in the Ministry of Finance at
almost double his former salary. Ryeshétnikoff had
begun to write already, at Perm, and he continued to
do so in the capital, sending contributions to some
of the lesser newspapers, until he made the acquaintance
of Nekrásoff. Then he published his novel, *Podlípovtsy*,
in *The Contemporary* (*Ceux de Podlipnaïa*, in a French
translation).

Ryeshétnikoff's position in literature is quite unique.
'The sound truth of Ryeshétnikoff'—in these words
Turguéneff characterised his writings. It is truth,
indeed, nothing but truth, without any attempt at
decoration or lyric effects—a sort of diary in which the
men with whom the author lived in the mining works
of the Uráls, in his Permian village, or in the slums of
St. Petersburg, are described. 'Podlípovtsy' means
the inhabitants of a small village Podlípnaya, lost
somewhere in the mountains of the Uráls. They are
Permians, not yet quite Russified, and are still in the
stage which so many populations of the Russian Empire
are living through nowadays—namely, the early agricultural. To live by hunting, as they formerly did, is
no more possible, and they begin to cultivate the land;
but few of them have for more than two months a year
pure rye-bread to eat : the remaining ten months they
are compelled to add the bark of trees to their flour in
order to have 'bread' at all. They have not the
slightest idea of what Russia is, or of the State, and
very seldom do they see a priest. They hardly know
how to cultivate the land. They do not know how to
make a stove, and periodical starvation during the
months from January to July has taken the very soul

and heart out of them. They stand on a lower level than real savages.

One of their best men, Pilá, knows how to count up to five, but the others are unable to do so. Pilá's conceptions of space and time are of the most primitive description, and yet this Pilá is a born leader of his semi-savage village people, and is continually making something for them. He tells them when it is time to plough ; he tries to find a sale for their small domestic industries ; he knows how to go to the next town, and when there is anything to be done there, he does it. His relations with his family, which consists of an only daughter, Apróska, are at a stage belonging to pre-historical anthropology, and yet he and his friend Sysóy love that girl Apróska so deeply, that after her death they are ready to kill themselves. They abandon their village to lead the hard life of boatmen on the river, dragging the heavy boats up the current. But these semi-savages are deeply human, and one feels that they are so, not merely because the author wants it, but in reality ; and one cannot read the story of their lives, and the sufferings which they endure with the resignation of a patient beast, without being moved at times even more deeply than by a good novel from our own life.

Another novel of Ryeshétnikoff, *The Glúmoffs*, is perhaps one of the most depressing novels in this branch of literature. There is nothing striking in it— no misfortunes, no calamities, no dramatic effects ; but the whole life of the ironworkers of the Uráls, who are described in this novel, is so gloomy, there is so little possibility of an escape from this gloominess, that sheer despair seizes you, as you gradually realise the immobility of the life which this novel represents. In *Among Men* Ryeshétnikoff tells the story of his own terrible childhood. As to his larger two-volume novel —*Where is it Better?*—it is an interminable string of misfortunes which befell a woman of the poorer classes, who came to St. Petersburg in search of work. We have here (as well as in another long novel, *One's Own Bread*) the same shapelessness and the same absence of strongly depicted individual characters as in *The Glümoffs*, but we have the collective character coming out in its full impressiveness, and we receive from it the same gloomy impression.

The literary defects of Ryeshétnikoff's work are only too evident. Yet, in spite of them, he may claim to be considered as the initiator of a new style of novel, which has its artistic value, notwithstanding its want of form and the ultra-realism of both its conception and structure. Ryeshétnikoff certainly could not inspire a school of imitators; but he has given hints to those who came after him as to what must be done to create the true folk-novel, and what must be avoided. There is not the slightest trace of romanticism in his work; no heroes; nothing but that great, indifferent, hardly individualised crowd, among which there are no striking colours, no giants; all is small; all interests are limited to a microscopically narrow neighbourhood. In fact, they all centre round the all-dominating question, Where to get food and shelter, even at the price of unbearable toil? Every person described has, of course, his individuality; but all these individualities are merged into one single desire—that of finding a living which shall not be sheer misery, shall not consist of days of well-being alternating with days of starvation. How lessen the hardships of work which is beyond a man's forces? how find a place in the world where work shall not be done amid such degrading conditions? these questions make the unanimity of purpose among all these men and women.

There are, I have just said, no heroes in Ryeshétnikoff's novels: that means, no 'heroes' in our usual literary sense; but you see real Titans—real heroes in the primitive sense of the word—heroes of endurance—such as the species must produce, when, a shapeless crowd, it bitterly struggles against frost and

R

hunger. The way in which these heroes support the
most incredible physical privations as they tramp from
one part of Russia to another, or have to face the most
cruel deceptions in their search for work—the way they
struggle for existence—is already striking enough ; but
the way in which they die is perhaps even more striking.
Many readers remember, of course, Tolstóy's *Three
Deaths* : the lady dying from consumption, and cursing
her illness ; the peasant who in his last hours thinks of
his boots, and directs to whom they shall be given, so
that they may go to the toiler most in need of them ;
and the third—the death of the birch-tree. For Ryeshétnikoff's heroes, who live all their lives without being
sure of bread for the morrow, death is not a catastrophe :
it simply means less and less force to get one's food, less
and less energy to chew one's dry piece of bread, less
and less bread, less oil in the lamp—and the lamp is
blown out.

Another most terrible thing in Ryeshétnikoff's novels
is his picture of how the habit of drunkenness takes
possession of men. You see it coming—see how it must
come, organically, necessarily, fatally—how it takes
possession of the man, and how it holds him till his death.
This Shakespearian fatalism applied to drink—whose
workings are only too well known to those who know
popular life—is perhaps the most terrible feature of
Ryeshétnikoff's novels. Especially is it apparent in
The Glúmoffs, where you see how the teacher in a mining
town, because he refuses to join the administration in
the exploitation of children, is deprived of all means of
living and, although he marries in the long run a splendid
woman, sinks at last into the clutches of the demon of
habitual drunkenness. Only the women do not drink,
and that saves the race from utter destruction ; in fact,
nearly every one of Ryeshétnikoff's women is a heroine
of persevering labour, of struggle for the necessities of
life, as the female is in the animal world ; and such the
women are in the rural masses of Russia.

If it is difficult to avoid romantic sentimentalism, when the author who describes the monotony of the everyday life of a middle-class crowd tries to induce his reader to sympathise nevertheless with this crowd, the difficulties are still greater when he descends a step lower in the social scale and deals with peasants, or, still worse, with those who belong to the lowest strata of city life. The most realistic writers have fallen into sentimentalism and romanticism when they attempted to do this. Even Zola in his novel, *Work*, falls into the trap. But that is precisely what Ryeshétnikoff never did. His writings are a violent protest against æsthetics, and even against all sorts of conventional art. He was a true child of the epoch characterised by Turguéneff in Bazároff. ' I do not care for the form of my writings : truth will speak for itself,' he seems to say to his readers. He would have felt ashamed if, even unconsciously, he had resorted anywhere to dramatic effects in order to touch his readers—just as the public speaker who entirely relies upon the beauty of the thought he develops would feel ashamed if some merely oratorical expression escaped his lips.

For myself, I think that a great creative genius was required in order to pick, as Ryeshétnikoff did, out of the monotonous life of the crowd those trifling expressions, those exclamations, those movements expressive of some feelings or some idea, without which his novels would have been quite unreadable. It has been remarked by one of our critics that when you begin to read a novel of Ryeshétnikoff you seem to have plunged into a chaos. You have the description of a commonplace landscape, which, in fact, is no ' landscape' at all ; then the future hero or heroine of the novel appears, and he or she is a person whom you may see in every crowd —with no claims to rise above the crowd, with hardly anything even to distinguish him or her from the crowd. This hero speaks, eats, drinks, works, swears, as every one else in the crowd does. He is not a chosen creature—

he is not a demoniacal character—a Richard III. in a fustian jacket ; nor is she a Cordelia or even a Dickens's ' Nell.' Ryeshétnikoff's men and women are exactly like thousands of men and women around them ; but gradually, owing to those very scraps of thought, to an exclamation, to a word dropped here and there, or even to a slight movement that is mentioned, you begin to feel interested in them. After thirty pages you feel that you are decidedly in sympathy with them, and you are so captured that you read pages and pages of these chaotic details with the sole purpose of solving the question which begins passionately to interest you : Will Peter or Anna find to-day the piece of bread which they long to have ? Will Mary get the work which might procure her a pinch of tea for her sick and half-crazy mother ? Will the woman Praskóvia freeze during that bitterly cold night when she is lost in the streets of St. Petersburg, or will she be taken at last to a hospital where she may have a warm blanket and a cup of tea ? Will the postman abstain from the ' fire-water,' and will he get a situation, or not ?

Surely, to obtain this result with such unconventional means reveals a great talent ; it means, to possess that power of moving one's readers—of making them love and hate—which makes the very essence of literary talent ; and this is why those shapeless, and much too long, and much too dreary novels of Ryeshétnikoff make a landmark in Russian literature. The sound truth of Ryeshétnikoff, free from the ' literary ' embellishments of the old romances, will not pass without leaving its traces.

LEVÍTOFF

Another folk-novelist of the same generation was LEVÍTOFF (1835 or 1842-1877). He described chiefly those portions of southern Middle Russia which are in the borderland between the wooded parts of the country and the treeless prairies. His life was extremely sad. He was born in the family of a poor country priest in a village of the province of Tambóf, and was educated in a clerical school of the type described by Pomyalóvskiy. When he was only sixteen he went on foot to Moscow, in order to enter the University, and then moved to St. Petersburg. There he was soon involved in some 'students' affair,' and was exiled in 1858 to Shenkúrsk, in the far north, and next removed to Vólogda. Here he lived in complete isolation from everything intellectual, and in awful poverty verging on starvation. Not until three years later was he allowed to return to Moscow, and, being absolutely penniless, he made all the journey from Vólogda to Moscow on foot, earning occasionally a few shillings by clerical work done for the cantonal board of some village. These years of exile left a deep trace upon all his subsequent life, which he passed in extreme poverty, never finding a place where he could settle, and drowning in drink the sufferings of a loving, restless soul.

During his early childhood he was deeply impressed by the charm and quiet of village life in the prairies, and he wrote later on : ' This quietness of village life passes before me, or rather flies, as something really living, as a well-defined image. Yes, I distinctly see above our daily life in the village somebody gliding—a little above the cross of our church, together with the light clouds —somebody light and soft of outline, having the mild and modest face of our prairie girls.' '. . . Thus, after many years spent amidst the untold sufferings of my present existence, do I represent to myself the genius of country life.'

The charm of the boundless prairies of South Russia— the Steppes—is so admirably rendered by Levítoff that no Russian author has surpassed him in the poetical description of their nature, excepting Koltsóff in his poetry. Levítoff was a pure flower of the Steppes, full of the most poetical love of his birthplace, and he certainly must have suffered deeply when he was thrown amidst the intellectual proletarians in the great, cold, and egotistic capital of the Nevá. Whenever he stayed at St. Petersburg or at Moscow he always lived in the poorest quarters, somewhere on the outskirts of the town : they reminded him of his native village ; and when he thus settled amongst the lowest strata of the population, he did so, as he wrote himself, ' to run away from the moral contradictions, the artificiality of life, the would-be humanitarianism, and the cut-and-dry imaginary superiority of the educated classes.' He could not live, for even a couple of months in succession, in relative well-being : he began to feel the gnawings of conscience, and it ended in his leaving behind his extremely poor belongings and going somewhere—anywhere where he would be poorer still, amidst other poor who live from hand to mouth.

I do not even know if I am right in describing Levítoff's works as novels. They are more like shapeless, lyrical-epical improvisations in prose. Only in these improvisations we have not the usual hackneyed presentment of the writer's compassion for other people's sufferings. It is an epical description of what the author has lived through in his close contact with all classes of people of the poorest sort, and its lyric element is the sorrow that he himself knew—not in imagination—as he lived that same life : the sorrow of want, of family troubles, of hopes unsatisfied, of isolation, of all sorts of oppression, and of all sorts of human weakness. The pages which he has given to the feelings of the drunken man, and to the ways in which this disease—drunkenness—takes possession of men, are something really terrible. Of course, he died young—from an inflammation of the lungs caught one day in January, as he went in an old summer coat to get ten shillings from some petty editor at the other end of Moscow.

The best known work of Levítoff is a volume of *Sketches from the Steppes* ; but he has also written scenes from the life of the towns, under the title of *Moscow Dens and Slums, Street Sketches,* etc., and a volume to which one of his friends must have given the title of *Sorrows of the Villages, the High Roads, and the Towns.* In the second of these works we find a simply terrifying collection of tramps and outcasts of the large cities—of men sunk to the lowest level of city slum-life, represented without the slightest attempt at idealising them—and yet deeply human. *Sketches from the Steppes* remains his best work. It is a collection of short poems, written in prose, full of admirable descriptions of prairie nature and of tiny details from the life of the peasants, with all their petty troubles, their habits, customs, and superstitions. Plenty of personal reminiscences are scattered through these sketches, and one often finds in them a scene of children playing in the meadows of the prairies and living in accordance with the life of nature, in which every little trait is pictured with a warm, tender love ; and almost everywhere one feels the unseen tears of sorrow shed by the author.

Amongst the several sketches of the life and work of Levítoff there is one—written with deep feeling and containing charming idyllic scenes from his childhood, as well as a terrible account of his later years—by A. Skabitchévskiy, in his *Folk-Novelists.*

GLEB USPÉNSKIY

GLEB USPÉNSKIY (1840-1902) widely differs from all the preceding writers. He represents a school in himself, and I know of no writer in any literature with whom he might be compared. Properly speaking, he is not a novelist ; but his work is not ethnography or demography either, because it contains, besides descriptions belonging to the domain of folk-psychology, all the elements of a novel. His first productions were novels with a leaning towards ethnography. Thus, *Ruin* is a

novel in which Uspénskiy admirably described how all the
life of a small provincial town, which had flourished
under the habits and manners of serfdom, went to ruin
after the abolition of that institution : but his later productions, entirely given to village life, and representing
the full maturity of his talent, had more the character
of ethnographic sketches, written by a gifted novelist,
than of novels proper.   They begin like novels.
Different persons appear before you in the usual way,
and gradually you grow interested in their doings and
their life.   Moreover, they are not offered you haphazard, as they would be in the diary of an ethnographer ; they have been chosen by the author because
he considers them typical of those aspects of village
life which he intends to deal with.   However, the
author is not satisfied with merely acquainting the
reader with these types : he soon begins to discuss
them and to talk about their position in village life and
the influence they must exercise upon the future of the
village ; and being already interested in the people, you
read the discussions with interest.   Then some admirable scene, which would not be out of place in a novel
of Tolstóy or Turguéneff, is introduced ; but after a
few pages of such artistic creation Uspénskiy becomes
again an ethnographer who discusses the future of the
village community.   He was too much of a political
writer to think always in images and to be a pure
novelist, but he was also too passionately impressed by
the individual facts which came under his observation
to discuss them calmly, as the merely political writer
would do.   In spite of all this, notwithstanding this
mixture of political literature with art, because of his
artistic gifts you read Uspénskiy just as you read a
good novelist.

Every movement among the educated classes in
favour of the poorer classes begins by an idealisation of
the latter.   It being necessary to clear away, first of
all, a number of prejudices which exist among the rich

as regards the poor, some idealisation is unavoidable. Therefore the earlier folk-novelist takes only the most striking types—those whom the wealthier people can better understand and sympathise with ; and he lightly passes over the less sympathetic features of the life of the poor. This was done in the forties in France and England, and in Russia by Grigoróvitch, Márko Vovtchók, and several others. Then came Ryeshétnikoff with his artistic Nihilism : with his negation of all the usual tricks of art, and his objectivism ; his blunt refusal to create 'types' and his preference for the quite ordinary man ; his manner of transmitting to you his love of his people, merely through the suppressed intensity of his own emotion. Later on, new problems arose for Russian literature. The readers were now quite ready to sympathise with the individual peasant or factory worker ; but they wanted to know something more, namely, what were the very foundations, the ideals, the springs of village life ? what were they worth in the further development of the nation ? what, and in what form, could the immense agricultural population of Russia contribute to the further development of the country and the civilised world altogether ? All such questions could not be answered by the statistician alone ; they required the genius of the artist, who must decipher the reply out of the thousands of small indications and facts ; and our folk-novelists understood this new demand of the reader. A rich collection of individual peasant types having already been given, it was now the life of the village—the *mir*, with its advantages and drawbacks, and its promises for the future—that the readers were anxious to find in the folk-novel. These were the questions which the new generation of folk-novelists undertook to discuss.

In this venture they were certainly right. It must not be forgotten that in the last analysis every economical and social question is a question of psychology of both the individual and the social aggregation. It cannot be solved by arithmetic alone. Therefore, in social science, as in human psychology, the poet often sees his way better than the physiologist. At any rate, he too has his voice in the matter.

When Uspénskiy began writing his first sketches of village life—it was in the early seventies—Young Russia was in the grip of the great movement 'towards the people,' and it must be owned that in this movement, as in every other, there was some idealisation. Those who did not know village life at all used to cherish idyllic illusions about the village community. In all probability Uspénskiy, who was born in a large industrial town, Túla, in the family of a small functionary, and hardly knew country life at all, shared these illusions, very probably in their most extreme aspect ; and while he still preserved them he went to a province of South-eastern Russia, Samára, which had lately become the prey of modern commercialism, and where, owing to a number of peculiar circumstances, the abolition of serfdom had been accomplished under conditions specially ruinous to the peasants and to village life altogether. Here he must have suffered intensely from seeing his youthful dreams vanishing ; and, as artists often do, he hastened to generalise ; but he had not the education of the thorough ethnographer, which might have prevented him from making too hasty ethnological generalisations from his limited materials, and he began to write a series of scenes from village life, imbued with pessimism. It was only much later on, while staying in a village of Northern Russia, in the province of Nóvgorod, that he came to understand the influences which the culture of the land and life in an agricultural village may exercise upon the tiller of the soil ; then only had he some glimpses of what are the social and moral forces of land cultivation and communal life, and of what free labour on a free soil might be. These observations inspired Uspénskiy with perhaps the best thing he wrote, *The Power of the Soil* (1882). It will remain, at any rate, his most important contribution in this domain—the artist appearing here in all the force of his talent and in his true function of explaining the inner springs of a certain mode of life.

ZLATOVRÁTSKIY AND OTHER FOLK-NOVELISTS

One of the great questions of the day for Russia is, whether we shall abolish the communal ownership of the land, as it has been abolished in Western Europe, and introduce instead of it individual peasant proprietorship ; or whether we shall endeavour to retain the village community, and do our best to develop it further in the direction of co-operative associations, both agricultural and industrial. A great struggle goes on accordingly among the educated classes of Russia upon this question, and in his first Samára sketches, entitled *From a Village Diary*, Uspénskiy paid a great deal of attention to this subject. He tried to prove that the village community, such as it is, results in a formidable oppression of the individual, in a hampering of individual initiative, in all sorts of oppression of the poorer peasants by the richer ones, and, consequently, in general poverty. He omitted, however, all the arguments which these same poorer peasants, if they should be questioned, would bring forward in favour of the present communal ownership of the land ; and he attributed to this institution what is the result of other general causes, as may be seen from the fact that exactly the same poverty, the same inertia, and the same oppression of the individual, are found in an even greater degree in Little Russia, where the village community has ceased to exist long since. Uspénskiy thus expressed—at least in those sketches which dealt with the villages of Samára—the views which prevail among the middle classes of Western Europe, and are current in Russia among the growing village *bourgeoisie*.

This attitude called forth a series of replies from another folk-novelist of an equally great talent, ZLATOV-RÁTSKIY (born 1845), who answered each sketch of

Uspénskiy's by a novel in which he took the opposite
view.   He had known peasant life in Middle Russia
from his childhood ; and the less illusions he had about
it the better was he able, when he began a serious
study of the peasants, to see the good features of
their lives, and to understand those types of them
who take to heart the interests of the village as a whole
—types that I also well knew in my youth in the same
provinces.

Zlatovrátskiy was accused, of course, of idealising the
peasants ; but the reality is, that Uspénskiy and Zlatovrátskiy complement each other.   Just as they complement each other geographically—the latter speaking for
the truly agricultural region of Middle Russia, while
Uspénskiy spoke for the periphery of this region—so also
they complement each other psychologically. Uspénskiy
was right in showing the drawbacks of the village community institution—deprived of its vitality by an omnipotent bureaucracy ; and Zlatovrátskiy was quite right,
too, in showing what sort of men are nevertheless bred
by the village-communal institutions and by attachment
to the land, and what services they could render to the
rural masses under different conditions of liberty and
independence.

Zlatovrátskiy's novels are thus an important ethnographical contribution, and they have at the same time
an artistic value.   His *Everyday Life in the Village*, and
perhaps even more his *Peasant Jurymen* (since 1864 the
peasant heads of households have acted in turn as jurors
in the law-courts), are full of the most charming scenes
of village life ; while his *Foundations* represents a serious
attempt at grasping in a work of art the fundamental
conceptions of Russian rural life.   In this last work we
also find types of men, who personify the revolt of the
peasant against both external oppression and the submissiveness of the mass to that oppression—men who,
under favourable conditions, might become the initiators
of movements of a deep purport.   That such types have

not been invented will be agreed to by every one who knows Russian village life from the inside.

The writers who have been named in the preceding pages are far from representing the whole school of folk-novelists. Not only has every Russian novelist of the past, from Turguéneff down, been inspired in some of his work by folk-life, but some of the best productions of the most prominent contemporary writers, such as Korolénko, Tchéhoff, Oertel, and many others (see next chapter), belong to the same category. There are besides quite a number of novelists distinctively of this class, who would be spoken of at some length in any course of Russian literature, but whom, unfortunately, I am compelled to mention in but a few lines.

NAÚMOFF was born at Tobólsk (in 1838), and, settling in Western Siberia after he had received a University education at St. Petersburg, he wrote a series of short novels and sketches in which he described life in West Siberian villages and mining towns. These stories were widely read, owing to their expressive, truly popular language, the energy with which they were imbued, and the striking pictures they contained of the advantage taken of the poverty of the mass by the richer peasants, known in Russia as 'mir-eaters' (miroyéd). In our movement 'towards the people' we used to reprint each novel in pamphlet form and distribute them in the villages.

ZASÓDIMSKIY (born 1843) belongs to the same period. Like many of his contemporaries he spent years of his youth in exile, but he remained still the same 'populist' that he was in his youth, imbued with the same love of the people and the same faith in the peasants. His *Chronicle of the Village Smúrino* (1874) and *Mysteries of the Steppes* (1882) are especially interesting, because Zasódimskiy made in these novels attempts at representing types of intellectual and protesting peasants, true to life, but usually neglected by our folk-novelists. Some of them are rebels who revolt against the conditions of village life, chiefly in their own personal interest, while others are peaceful religious propagandists, and still others are men who have developed under the influence of educated propagandists.

Another writer who excelled in the representation of the type of '*mir*-eaters' exploiters of the peasants in the villages of Russia was SÁLOFF (1843-1902).

PETROPÁVLOVSKIY (1857-1892), who wrote under the pseudonym of KARÓNIN, was, on the other hand, a poet of village life and of the cultivation of the fields. He was born in South-eastern Russia, in the province of Samára, but was early exiled to the government of Tobólsk, in Siberia, where he was kept many years, and from which he was released only to die soon after from consumption. He gave in his novels and stories several very dramatic types of village 'ne'er-do-wells,' but the novel which is most typical of his talent is *My World*. In it he tells how an 'intellectual,' 'rent in twain' and nearly losing his reason in consequence of this dualism, finds inner peace and reconciliation with life when he settles in a village and works in the same almost superhuman way that the peasants do, when hay has to be mown and the crops to be carried in. Thus living the life they lived, he is loved by them, and finds a healthy and intelligent girl to love him. This is, of course, to some extent an idyll of village life ; but so slight is the idealisation, as we know from the experience of those 'intellectuals' who went to the villages as equals coming among equals, that the idyll reads almost as a reality.

Several more folk-novelists ought to be mentioned. Such are L. MÉLSHIN (born 1860), the pseudonym of an exile 'P. YAROSHÉVITCH,' who is also a poet, and who, having been kept for twelve years at hard labour in Siberia as a political convict, has published two volumes of hard-labour sketches, *In the World of the Outcasts* (a work to be put by the side of Dostoyévskiy's *Dead-House*) ; S. ELPÁTIEVSKIY (born 1854), also an exile, who has given good sketches of Siberian tramps ; NEFÉDOFF (1847-1902), an ethnographer who has made valuable scientific researches and at the same time has published excellent sketches of factory and village life, and whose writings are thoroughly imbued with a deep faith in the store of energy and plastic creative power of the masses of the country people ; and several others. Every one of these writers deserves, however, more than a short notice, because each has contributed something, either to the comprehension of this or that class of the people, or to the working out of those forms of 'idealistic realism' which are best suited for dealing with types taken from the toiling masses, and which has lately made the literary success of Maxím Górkiy.

MAXÍM GÓRKIY

Few writers have established their reputation so rapidly as MAXÍM GÓRKIY. His first sketches (1892-1895) were published in an obscure provincial paper of the Caucasus, and were totally unknown to the literary world, but when a short tale of his appeared in a widely read review, edited by Korolénko, it at once attracted general attention. The beauty of its form, its artistic finish, and the new note of strength and courage which rang through it, brought the young writer immediately into prominence. It became known that 'Maxím Górkiy' was the pseudonym of a quite young man, A. PYÉSHKOFF, who was born in 1868 in Níjniy Nóvgorod, a large town on the Vólga ; that his father was a merchant or an artisan, his mother a remarkable peasant woman, who died soon after the birth of her son ; and that the boy, orphaned when only nine, was brought up in a family of his father's relatives. The childhood of 'Górkiy' must have been anything but happy, for one day he ran away and entered into service on a Vólga river steamer. This took place when he was only twelve. Later on he worked as a baker, became a street porter, sold apples in the streets, till at last he obtained the position of clerk at a lawyer's. In 1891 he lived and wandered on foot with the tramps in South Russia, and during these wanderings he wrote a number of short stories, of which the first was published in 1892, in a newspaper of Northern Caucasia. The stories proved to be remarkably fine, and when a collection of all that he had hitherto written was published in 1900, in four small volumes, the whole of a large edition was sold in a very short time, and the name of Górkiy took its place—to speak of the then living novelists only— by the side of those of Korolénko and Tchéhoff, immediately after the name of Leo Tolstóy. In Western Europe and America his reputation was made with the same rapidity, as soon as a couple of his sketches were translated into French and German, and from French or German into English.

It is sufficient to read a few of Górkiy's short stories —for instance, *Málva*, or *Tchelkásh*, or *The Ex-Men*, or *Twenty-Six Men and One Girl*—to realise at once the causes of his rapidly won popularity. The men and women he described were not heroes : they were the most ordinary tramps or slum-dwellers ; and what he wrote were not novels in the proper sense of the word, but merely sketches from life. And yet, in the literature of all nations, including the short stories of Guy de Maupassant and Bret Harte, there were few works in which such a fine analysis of complicated and struggling human feelings was given, such interesting, original, and new characters were so well depicted, and human psychology was so admirably interwoven with a back-ground of nature—a calm sea, menacing waves, or end-less, sunburnt prairies. In the first-named story you really *see* the promontory that juts out into 'the laugh-ing waters,' that promontory upon which the fisherman has pitched his hut ; and you understand why Málva, the woman who loves the fisherman and comes to see him every Sunday, loves that spot as much as she does the man himself. And then at every page you are struck by the quite unexpected variety of fine touches with which the love of that strange and complicated nature, Málva, is depicted, or by the unforeseen aspects under which both the ex-peasant fisherman and his peasant son appear in the short space of a few days. The variety of strokes, refined and brutal, tender and terribly harsh, with which Górkiy pictures human feelings is such that in comparison with his heroes the heroes and heroines of our best novelists seem so simple—so simplified—just like a flower in European decorative art in comparison with a real flower.

Górkiy is a great artist; he is a poet; but he is also a child of all that long series of folk-novelists whom Russia has had for the last half-century, and he has utilised their experience: he has found at last that happy combination of realism with idealism for which the Russian folk-novelists have been striving for so many years. Ryeshétnikoff and his school had tried to write novels of an ultra-realistic character without any trace of idealisation. They restrained themselves whenever they felt inclined to generalise, to create, to idealise. They tried to write mere diaries, in which events, great and small, important and insignificant, were related with an equal exactitude, without even changing the tone of the narrative. We have seen that in this way, by dint of their talent, they were able to obtain most poignant effects; but like the historian who vainly tries to be 'impartial,' yet always remains a party man, they had not avoided the idealisation which they so much dreaded. They could not above it. A work of art is always personal; do what he may, the author's sympathies will necessarily appear in his creation and he will always idealise those who answer to them. Grigoróvitch and Márko Vovtchók had idealised the all-pardoning patience and the all-enduring submissiveness of the Russian peasant; and Ryeshétnikoff had quite unconsciously, and maybe against his will, idealised

S

the almost supernatural powers of endurance which he had seen in the Uráls and in the slums of St. Petersburg. Both had idealised something : the ultra-realist as well as the romantic. Górkiy must have understood the significance of this ; at all events, he does not object in the least to a certain idealisation. In his adherence to truth he is as much of a realist as Ryeshétnikoff ; but he idealises in the same sense as Turguéneff did when he pictured Rúdin, Helen, or Bazároff. He even says that we *must* idealise, and he chooses for idealisation the type he admired most among those tramps whom he knew—the rebel. This made his success ; it appeared to be exactly what the readers of all nations were unconsciously calling for as a relief from the dull mediocrity and absence of strong individualities about them.

The stratum of society from which Górkiy took the heroes of his first short stories—and in short stories he appears at his best—is that of the tramps of Southern Russia : men who have broken with regular society, who never accept the yoke of permanent work, labouring only as long as they want to, as 'casuals' in the seaports on the Black Sea ; who sleep in doss-houses or in ravines on the outskirts of the cities, and tramp in the summer from Odessa to the Crimea, and from the Crimea to the prairies of Northern Caucasia, where they are welcome at harvest time.

That eternal complaint about poverty and bad luck, that helplessness and hopelessness which were the dominant notes with the early folk-novelists, are totally absent from Górkiy's stories. His tramps do not complain. 'Everything is all right,' one of them says ; 'no use to whine and complain—that would do no good. Live and endure till you are broken down, or if you are so already—wait for death. This is all the wisdom in the world—do you understand ?' (*Works*, i. p. 311).

Far from his whining and complaining about the

hard lot of his tramps, a refreshing note of energy and courage, which is quite unique in Russian literature, sounds through the stories of Górkiy. His tramps are miserably poor, but they 'don't care.' They drink, but there is nothing among them nearly approaching the drunkenness of despair which we saw in Levítoff. Even the most 'downtrodden' one of them—far from making a virtue of his helplessness, as Dostoyévskiy's heroes always did—dreams of reforming the world and making it rich. He dreams of the moment when 'we, once "the poor," shall vanish, after having enriched the Crœsuses with the richness of the spirit and the power of life' (*A Mistake*, i. p. 170).

Górkiy cannot stand whining; he cannot bear that self-castigation in which other Russian writers so much delight—which Turguéneff's sub-Hamlets used to express so poetically, of which Dostoyévskiy has made a virtue, and of which Russia offers such an infinite variety of examples. Górkiy knows the type, but he has no pity for such men. Better anything than one of those egotistic weaklings who gnaw all the time at their own hearts, compel others to drink with them in order to perorate before them about their 'burning souls'; those beings 'full of compassion,' which, however, never goes beyond self-commiseration, and 'full of love' which is never anything but self-love. Górkiy knows only too well these men who never fail to ruin wantonly the lives of those women who trust them; who do not even stop at murder, like Raskólnikoff, or the brothers Karamázoff, and yet whine about the circumstances which have brought them to it. 'What's all this talk about circumstances!' he makes Old Izerghil say. 'Every one makes his own circumstances! I see all sorts of men— but the strong ones—where are they? There are fewer and fewer noble men!'

Knowing how much the Russian 'intellectuals' suffer from this disease of whining, knowing how rare among them are the aggressive idealists, the real *rebels*, and how numerous, on the other hand, are the Nezhdánoffs (Turguéneff's *Virgin Soil*), even among those 'politicals' who march with resignation to Siberia, Górkiy does not take his types from among the 'intellectuals,' for he thinks that they too easily become 'the prisoners of life.'

In *Váreñka Olésova* Górkiy expresses all his contempt for the average 'intellectual' of our own days. He introduces to us the interesting type of a girl full of vitality ; a most primitive creature, absolutely untouched by any ideals of liberty and equality, but so full of an intense life, so independent, so much herself, that one cannot but feel greatly interested in her. She meets with one of those 'intellectuals' who know and admire higher ideals, but are weaklings, utterly devoid of the nerve of life. Of course, Váreñka laughs at the very idea of such a man's falling in love with her ; and these are the expressions in which Górkiy makes her define the usual hero of Russian novels :

'The Russian hero is always silly and stupid,' she says ; 'he is always sick of something ; always thinking about something that cannot be understood, and is himself so miserable, so mi-i-serable ! He will think, think, then talk, then he will go and make a declaration of love, and after that he thinks, and thinks again, till he marries. . . . And when he is married he talks all sorts of nonsense to his wife, and then abandons her' (*Váreñka Olésova*, ii. p. 281).

Górkiy's favourite type is the 'rebel'—the man in full revolt against society, but at the same time a strong man, a power ; and as he has found among the tramps with whom he has lived at least the embryo of this type, it is from this stratum of society that he takes his most interesting heroes.

In *Konováloff* Górkiy himself gives the psychology, or, rather, a partial psychology, of his tramp hero : 'An "intellectual" amongst those whom fate has ill-used—amongst the ragged, the hungry, and embittered half-men and half-beasts with whom the city slums teem.' 'Usually a being that can be included in no order,' the man who has 'been torn from all his moorings, who is hostile to everything and ready to turn upon anything the force of his angry, embittered scepticism' (ii. p. 23). His tramp feels that he has been defeated in life, but he does not seek excuse in circumstances. Konováloff, for instance, will not admit the theory which is in such vogue among the educated ne'er-do-well, namely, that he is the sad product of adverse conditions. 'One must be faint-hearted indeed,' he says, 'to become such a man.' 'I live, and something goads me on' . . . but 'I have no inner line to follow . . . do you understand me? I don't know how to say it. I have not that spark in my soul, . . . force, perhaps? Something is missing; that's all!' And when his young friend who has read in books all sorts of excuses for weakness of character mentions 'the dark hostile forces round you,' Konováloff retorts: 'Then make a stand! take a stronger footing! find your ground, and make a stand!'

Some of Górkiy's tramps are, of course, philosophers. They think about human life, and have had opportunities to know what it is. 'Every one,' he remarks somewhere, 'who has had a struggle to sustain in his life, and has been defeated by life, and now feels cruelly imprisoned amidst its squalor, is more of a philosopher than Schopenhauer himself; for abstract thought can never be cast into such a correct and vivid plastic form as that in which is expressed the thought born directly out of suffering' (ii. p. 31). 'The knowledge of life among such men is striking,' he says again.

Love of nature is, of course, another characteristic feature of the tramp—'Konováloff loved nature with a deep, inarticulate love, which was betrayed only by a glitter in his eyes. Every time he was in the fields, or on the river bank, he became permeated with a sort of peace and love which made him still more like a child.

Sometimes he would exclaim looking at the sky:
" Good ! " and in this exclamation there was more sense
and feeling than in the rhetoric of many poets. . . .
Like all the rest, poetry loses its holy simplicity and
spontaneity when it becomes a profession ' (ii. pp. 33-34).

However, Górkiy's rebel-tramp is not a Nietzsche
who ignores everything beyond his narrow egotism, or
imagines himself a 'super-man'; the 'diseased ambition' of an 'intellectual' is required to create the true
Nietzsche type.   In Górkiy's tramps, as in his women
of the lowest class, there are flashes of greatness of
character and a simplicity which is incompatible with
the super-man's self-conceit.   He does not idealise them
so as to make of them real heroes ; that would be too
untrue to life : the tramp is still a defeated being.   But
he shows how among these men, owing to an inner
consciousness of strength, there are moments of greatness, even though that inner force be not strong enough
to make out of Orlóff (in *The Orlóffs*) or Iliyá (in *The
Three*) a real power, a real hero—the man who fights
against those much stronger than himself.   He seems
to say : Why are not you, intellectuals, as truly 'individual,' as frankly rebellious against the society you
criticise, and as strong as some of these submerged
ones are ?

In his short stories Górkiy is great ; but like his two
contemporaries, Korolénko and Tchéhoff, whenever he
has tried to write a longer novel, with a full development
of characters, he has not succeeded.   Taken as a whole
Fomá Gordéeff, notwithstanding several beautiful and
impressive scenes, is weaker than most of Górkiy's
short stories ; and while the first portion of *The Three*—
the idyllic life of the three young people, and the
tragical issues foreshadowed in it—makes us expect
to find in this novel one of the finest productions
in Russian literature, its end is disappointing.   The
French translator of *The Three* has even preferred to
terminate it abruptly, at the point where Iliyá stands

on the grave of the man whom he has killed, rather than to give Górkiy's end of the novel.

Why Górkiy should fail in this direction is, of course, too delicate and too difficult a question to answer. One cause, however, may be suggested. Górkiy, like Tolstóy, is too honest an artist to 'invent' an end which the real lives of his heroes do not suggest to him, although that end might have been very picturesque; and the class of men whom he so admirably depicts is not possessed of that consistency and that 'oneness' which are necessary to render a work of art perfect and to give it that final accord without which it is never complete.

Take, for instance, Orlóff in *The Orlóffs*. 'My soul burns within me,' he says. 'I want space, to give full swing to my strength. I feel within me an indomitable force! If the cholera, let us say, could become a man, a giant—were it Iliyá Múromets himself—I would meet it! "Let it be a struggle to the death," I would say; "you are a force, and I, Gríshka Orlóff, am a force too: let us see which is the better!"'

But that power, that force does not last. Orlóff says somewhere that 'he is torn in all directions at once,' and that his fate is to be—not a fighter of giants, but merely a tramp. And so he ends. Górkiy is too great an artist to make of him a giant-killer. It is the same with Iliyá in *The Three*. This is a powerful type, and one feels inclined to ask, Why did not Górkiy make him begin a new life under the influence of those young propagandists of Socialism whom he meets? Why should he not die, let us say, in one of those encounters between working-men on strike and soldiers which took place in Russia precisely at the time Górkiy was finishing this novel? But here, too, Górkiy's reply probably would be that such things do not happen in real life. Men like Iliyá, who dream only of the 'clean life of a merchant,' do not join in labour movements. And he preferred to give a very disappointing end to his hero—

to make him appear miserable and small in his attack upon the wife of the police-officer, so as to turn the reader's sympathies towards even this woman—rather than to make of Iliyá a prominent figure in a strike-conflict. If it had been possible to idealise Iliyá so much, without overstraining the permissible limits of idealisation, Górkiy probably would have done it, because he is entirely in favour of idealisation in realistic art ; but this would have been pure romanticism.

Over and over again he returns to the idea of the necessity of an ideal in the work of the novel-writer. 'The cause of the present unsteadiness of opinion (in Russian society) is,' he says, 'the neglect of idealism. Those who have exiled from life all romanticism have stripped us so as to leave us quite naked : this is why we are so uninteresting to one another, and so disgusted with one another' (*A Mistake*, i. p. 151). And in *The Reader* (1898) he develops his æsthetic canons in full. He tells how one of his earliest productions, on its appearance in print, is read one night before a circle of friends. He receives many compliments for it, and after leaving the house is tramping along a deserted street, feeling for the first time in his existence the happiness of life, when a person unknown to him, and whom he had not noticed among those present at the reading, overtakes him, and begins to talk about the duties of the author.

'You will agree with me,' the stranger says, 'that the duty of literature is to aid man in understanding himself, to raise his faith in himself, to develop his longing for truth ; to combat what is bad in men ; to find what is good in them, and to wake up in their souls shame, anger, courage ; to do everything, in short, to render men strong in a noble sense of the word, and capable of inspiring their lives with the holy spirit of beauty' (iii. p. 241). 'It seems to me, we need once more to have dreams, pretty creations of our fancy and visions, because the life we have built up is poor in colour, is dim and dull. . . . Well, let us try ; maybe imagination will help man to rise for a moment above the earth and find on it his true place, which he has lost' (p. 245).

But further on Górkiy makes a confession which explains perhaps why he has not yet succeeded in creating a longer character-novel. 'I discovered in myself,' he says, 'many good feelings and desires—a fair proportion of what is usually called good ; but *a feeling which could unify all this*—a well-founded, clear thought, embracing all the phenomena of life—I did not find in myself.' And on reading this, one at once thinks of Turguéneff, who saw in such a 'freedom,' in such a unified comprehension of the universe and its life, the first step towards becoming a great artist.

'Can you,' the *Reader* goes on to ask, 'create for men ever so small an illusion that has the power to raise them? No!' 'All of you teachers of the day take more than you give, because you speak only about faults—you see only those. But there must also be good qualities in men : you possess some, don't you? . . . Don't you notice that owing to your continual efforts to define and to classify them, the virtues and the vices have been entangled like two balls of black and white thread which have become grey by taking colour from each other?' . . . 'I doubt whether God has sent you on earth. If He had sent messengers, He would have chosen stronger men than you are. He would have lighted in them the fire of a passionate love of life, of truth, of men.'

'Nothing but everyday life, everyday life, only everyday people, everyday thoughts and events!' the same pitiless *Reader* continues. 'When will you, then, speak of "the rebel spirit," of the necessity of a new birth of the spirit? Where is, then, the calling to the creation of a new life? where the lessons of courage? where the words which would give wings to the soul?'

'Confess, you don't know how to represent life, so that your pictures of it shall provoke in a man a redemptive spirit of shame and a burning desire of creating new forms of life. . . . Can you accelerate the pulsation of life? Can you inspire it with energy, as others have done?'

'I see many intelligent men round about me, but few noble ones among them, and these few are broken and suffering souls. I don't know why it should be so, but so it is : the better the man, the cleaner and the more honest his soul, the less energy he has; the more he suffers and the harder is his life. . . . But although they suffer so much from feeling the want of something better, they have not the force to create it.'

'One thing more'—said after an interval my strange interlocutor. 'Can you awake in man a laughter full of the joy of life and at the same time elevating to the soul? Look, men have quite forgotten good wholesome laughter!'

'The sense of life is not in self-satisfaction; after all, man is better than that. The sense of life is in the beauty and the force of striving towards some aim; every moment of one's being ought to have its higher aim.' 'Wrath, hatred, shame, loathing, and finally a grim despair—these are the levers by means of which you may destroy everything on earth.' 'What can you do to awake a thirst for life when you only whine, sigh, moan, or coolly point out to man that he is nothing but dust?'

'Oh, for a man, firm and loving, with a burning heart and a powerful all-embracing mind. In the stuffy atmosphere of shameful silence his prophetic words would resound like an alarm-bell, and perhaps the mean souls of the living dead would shiver!' (p. 253).

These ideas of Górkiy about the necessity of something better than everyday life—something that shall elevate the soul—fully explain also his drama, *At the Bottom* (or *The Lower Depths*), which has had such a success at Moscow, but played by the very same artists at St. Petersburg evoked but little enthusiasm. The idea is the same as that of Ibsen's *Wild Duck*. The inhabitants of a doss-house, all of them, maintain their life-power only as long as they cherish some illusion: the drunkard actor dreams of recovery in some special retreat; a fallen girl takes refuge in her illusion of real love, and so on. And the dramatic situation of these beings, with already so little to retain them in life, is only the more poignant when the illusions are destroyed. The drama is powerful. It must lose, though, on the stage on account of some technical mistakes (a useless fourth act, the unnecessary person of a woman introduced in the first scene and then disappearing); but apart from these mistakes it is eminently dramatic. The positions are really tragical, the action is rapid, and as to the conversations of the inhabitants of the doss-house and their philosophy of life, both are above all praise. Altogether one feels that Górkiy is very far yet from having said his last word. The question is only whether in the classes of society he now frequents he will be able to discover the further developments—undoubtedly existing—of the types which he understands best. Will he find among them further materials responding to the æsthetic canons whose following has hitherto been the source of his power?

These were the questions I asked myself in 1904. Next year there began in Russia the revolutionary movements of 1905, and Górkiy took part in them. He had to emigrate, and for a number of years his work lost the freshness and the inspirations of his earlier short stories. Only in his *Childhood*, published since his return to Russia, did he once more show those high qualities of creation that are mentioned in the preceding pages.

CHAPTER VIII

POLITICAL LITERATURE—SATIRE—ART CRITICISM— LATER PERIOD NOVELISTS

POLITICAL LITERATURE—Difficulties due to censorship—The 'circles'—Westerners and Slavophiles—Political literature abroad: Hérzen—Ogaryóff—Bakúnin—Lavróff—Stepniák— Tchertkóff — *The Contemporary* and Tchernyshévskiy — SATIRE: Schedrín (Saltykóff)—ART CRITICISM: Its importance in Russia—Byelínskiy—Dobrolúboff—Písareff—Mihailóvskiy—Tolstóy's *What is Art?*—LATER PERIOD NOVELISTS: Oertel—Korolénko—Present drift of literature: Merezhkóvskiy—Boborýkin—Potápenko—Tchéhoff.

POLITICAL LITERATURE

TO speak of political literature in a country which has no political liberty, and where nothing can be printed without having been approved by a rigorous censorship, sounds almost like irony. And yet, notwithstanding all the efforts of the Government to prevent the discussion of political matters in the press, or even in private circles, that discussion goes on, under all possible aspects and under all imaginable pretexts. As a result it would be no exaggeration to say that in the necessarily narrow circle of educated Russian 'intellectuals' there is as much interest, all round, in matters political as there is in the educated circles of any other European country, and that a certain knowledge of the political life of other nations is widespread among the reading portion of Russians. Only the knowledge of the political history of modern Europe was limited, owing to the impossibility of discussing this subject in the press and the universities.

It is well known that everything that was printed in Russia, up to the end of the year 1905, had to be submitted to censorship, either before it went to print, or afterwards. Besides, to found a review or a paper the editor must offer satisfactory guarantees of not being 'too advanced' in his political opinions, otherwise he will not be authorised by the Ministry of the Interior to start the paper or the review and to act in the capacity of its editor. In certain cases a paper or a review, published in one of the two capitals, but never in the provinces, may be allowed to appear without passing through the censor's hands before going to print; but a copy of it must be sent to the censor as soon as the printing begins, and every number may be stopped and prevented from being put into circulation before it has left the printing-office, to say nothing of subsequent prosecution. The same condition of things exists for books. Even after the paper or the book had been authorised by the censor it was often subject to a prosecution. The law of 1864 was very definite in stating the conditions under which such prosecution could take place; namely, it had to be made before a regular court, within one month after publication; but this law was never respected by the Government. Books were seized and destroyed—reduced to pulp— without the affair ever being brought before a court, and I know editors who have been plainly warned that if they insisted upon this being done, they would simply be exiled, by order of the administration, to some remote province. This is not all. A paper or a review could receive a first, a second, and a third warning, and after the third warning it was suspended, by virtue of that warning. Besides, the Ministry of the Interior, the governors of the provinces, and even the heads of the police in the capitals may at any time prohibit the sale of the paper in the streets and the shops, deprive the paper of the right of inserting advertisements, and condemn the editor to a heavy fine and imprisonment.

The arsenal of punishments is thus pretty large ; but there is still something else. It is the system of ministerial circulars. Suppose a strike takes place, or some scandalous bribery has been discovered in some branch of the administration. Immediately all papers and reviews receive a circular from the Ministry of the Interior prohibiting them to speak of that strike or that scandal. Even less important matters will be tabooed in this way. Thus a few years ago an anti-Semitic comedy was put on the stage at St. Petersburg. It was imbued with the worst spirit of national hatred towards the Jews, and the actress who was given the main part in it refused to play. She preferred to break her agreement with the manager rather than to play in that comedy. Another actress was engaged. This became known to the public, and at the first representation a formidable demonstration was made against the actors who had accepted parts in the play, as also against the author. Some eighty arrests—chiefly of students and littérateurs—were made from among the audience, and for two days the St. Petersburg papers were full of discussions of the incident ; but then came the ministerial circular prohibiting any further reference to the subject, and on the third day there was not a word said about the matter in all the press of Russia.

Socialism, the social question altogether, and the labour movement are continually tabooed by ministerial circulars—to say nothing of society and Court scandals, or of the thefts which may be discovered from time to time in the higher administration. At the end of the reign of Alexander II. the theories of Darwin, Spencer, and Buckle were tabooed in the same way, and their works were prevented from being kept by the circulating libraries.

This is what censorship means nowadays. As to what it was formerly, a very amusing book could be made of the antics of the different censors, simply by utilising Skabitchévskiy's *History of Censorship*. Suffice it to say that when Púshkin, speaking of a lady, wrote, 'Your divine features,' or mentioned 'her celestial beauty,' the censorship would cross out these verses and write, in red ink on the MS., that such expressions were offensive to divinity and could not be allowed. Verses were mutilated without any regard to the rules of versification; and sometimes the censor introduced, in a novel, scenes of his own.

Under such conditions political thought had continually to find new channels for its expression. Quite a special language was developed, therefore, in the reviews and papers for the treatment of forbidden subjects and for expressing ideas which censorship would have found objectionable; and this way of writing was resorted to even in works of art. A few words dropped by a Rúdin, or by a Bazároff in a Turguéneff novel, conveyed quite a world of ideas. However, other channels besides mere allusion were necessary, and therefore political thought found its expression in various other ways: first of all, in literary and philosophical circles which impressed their stamp on the entire literature of a given epoch; then, in art criticism, in satire, and in literature published abroad: in Switzerland or in England.

THE 'CIRCLES'—WESTERNERS AND SLAVOPHILES

It was especially in the forties and fifties of the nineteenth century that the 'circles' played an important part in the intellectual development of Russia. No sort of expression of political thought in print was possible at that time. The two or three semi-official newspapers which were allowed to appear were absolutely worthless; the novel, the drama, the poem, had to deal with the most superficial matters only, and the heaviest books of science and philosophy were as liable to be prohibited as the lighter sort of literature. Private intercourse was the only possible means of exchanging ideas, and therefore all the best men of the time joined some 'circle,' in which more or less advanced ideas were expressed in friendly conversation. There are even men like STANKÉVITCH (1817-1840) who are mentioned in every course of Russian literature, although they have never written anything, simply for the moral influence they exercised within their circle. (Turguéneff's *Yákov Pásynkoff* was inspired by such a personality.)

It is quite evident that under such conditions there was no room for the development of political parties properly speaking. However, from the middle of the nineteenth century two main currents of philosophical and social thought, which took the name of 'Western' and 'Slavophile,' were always apparent. The Westerners were, broadly speaking, for Western civilisation. Russia, they maintained, is no exception in the great family of European nations. She will necessarily pass through the same phases of development that Western Europe has passed through, and consequently her next step will be the abolition of serfdom and, after that, the evolution of the same political institutions as have been evolved in Western Europe. Upon this foundation Russia will be able to develop whatever original features she may possess. The Slavophiles, on the other side, maintained that Russia had a mission of her own. She had not known foreign conquest like that of the Normans; she had retained still the structure of the old clan period, and therefore she must follow her own quite original lines of development, in accordance with what the Slavophiles described as the three fundamental principles of Russian life: the Greek Orthodox Church, the absolute power of the Tsar, and the people.

These were, of course, very wide programmes, which admitted of many shades of opinion and gradations, and both parties developed, each in its own direction. Thus, in the sixties of the nineteenth century, for the great bulk of the 'Westerners,' Western liberalism of the Whig or the Guizot type was the highest ideal that

Russia had to strive for.   They maintained, moreover, that everything which has happened in Western Europe in the course of her evolution—such as the depopulation of the villages, the horrors of freshly developing capitalism (revealed in England by the Parliamentary Commissions of the forties), the powers of bureaucracy which had developed in France, and so on—must necessarily be repeated in Russia as well : they were unavoidable *laws* of evolution.   This was the opinion of the rank-and-file ‘ Westerner.’

As to the more intelligent and the better educated representatives of this same party, like Hérzen, Tcherny-shévskiy, and many others, they were under the influence of advanced European thought, and held different views. In their opinion the hardships suffered by working-men and agricultural labourers in Western Europe from the unbridled power won by the landlords and the middle classes in the representative institutions, and the limitations of political liberties introduced in the continental States of Europe by their bureaucratic centralisation, were by no means ‘ historical necessities.’   Russia, they maintained, need not necessarily repeat these mistakes ; she must, on the contrary, profit by the experience of her elder sisters, and if she succeeds in attaining the era of industrialism without having lost her communal land-ownership, or the autonomy of certain parts of the Empire, or the self-government of the *mir* in her villages, this will be an immense advantage.   It would be therefore the greatest political mistake to go on destroying her village community, to favour the concentration of the land in the hands of a landed aristocracy, and to let the political life of so immense and varied a territory be concentrated in the hands of a central governing body, in accordance with the Prussian or the Napoleonic ideals of political centralisation—especially now that the powers of capitalism are so great.

Similar gradations of opinion prevailed among the Slavophiles.   Their best representatives — the two

T

brothers AKSÁKOFF, the two brothers KIRÉYEVSKIY, HOMYAKÓFF, etc., were much in advance of the rank and file of their party, who reached by insensible degrees the reactionaries pure and simple. The latter were simply fanatics of the absolute rule and the Orthodox Church, to which feelings they usually added a sort of sentimental attachment to the ' good old times,' understanding under this name all sorts of things : patriarchal habits of the times of serfdom, manners of country life, folk-songs, traditions, and folk-dress. At a time when the real history of Russia had hardly begun to be deciphered, they did not even suspect that the federalist principle had prevailed in Russia down to the Mongol invasion ; that the authority of the Moscow Tsars was of a relatively late creation (fifteenth, sixteenth, and seventeenth centuries) ; and that autocracy was not at all an inheritance of *old* Russia, but was chiefly the work of that same Peter whom they execrated for having violently introduced Western habits of life. Few of them realised also that the religion of the great mass of the Russian people was *not* the religion which is professed by the official ' Orthodox ' Church, but a thousand varieties of 'Dissent.' They thus imagined that they represented the ideals of the Russian *people*, while in reality they represented the ideals of the Russian *State* and the Moscow *Church*, which are of a mixed Byzantine, Latin, and Mongolian origin. With the aid of the fogs of German metaphysics—especially of Hegel—which were in great vogue at that time, and with that love of abstract terminology which prevailed in the first half of the nineteenth century, discussion upon such themes could evidently last for years without coming to a definite conclusion.

However, with all that, it must be owned that through their best representatives the Slavophiles powerfully contributed towards the creation of a school of history and law which put historical studies in Russia on a true foundation, by making a sharp distinction between the history and the law of the Russian *State* and the history and the law of the Russian *people*. BYELYÁEFF (1810-1873), ZABYÉLIN (born 1820), and KOSTOMÁROFF (1818-1885) were the first to write the real history of the Russian *people*; and of these three the two first were Slavophiles; while Kostomároff, an Ukraïnian nationalist, was under the influence of the scientific ideas of the Slavophiles.[1] They brought into evidence the federalistic character of early Russian history. They destroyed the legend, propagated by Karamzín, of an uninterrupted transmission of royal power, that was supposed to have taken place for a thousand years, from the times of the Norman Rurik till to-day. They brought into evidence the violent means by which the princes of Moscow crushed the independent city-republics of the pre-Mongolian period, and gradually, with the aid of the Mongol Khans, became the Tsars of Russia; and they told (especially Byelyáeff, in his *History of the Peasants in Russia*) the gruesome tale of the growth of serfdom from the seventeenth century, under the Moscow Tsars. Besides, it is mainly to the Slavophiles that we owe the recognition of the fact that two different codes exist in Russia—the Code of the Empire, which is the code of the educated classes, and the Common Law, which is (like the Norman law in Jersey) widely different from the former, and very often preferable, in its conceptions of land-ownership, inheritance, etc. It is the law which prevails among the peasants, its details varying in different provinces.

In the absence of political life the philosophical and literary struggles between the Slavophiles and the Westerners absorbed the minds of the best men of the literary circles of St. Petersburg and Moscow in the years 1840-1860. The question whether or not each nationality is the bearer of some pre-determined mission in history, and whether Russia has some such special mission, was eagerly discussed in the circles to which, in the forties, belonged Bakúnin, the critic Byelínskiy,

---

[1] Byelyáeff was a pioneer of these ideas in the historical periodical *Vremennik*, which he founded as early as 1848.

Hérzen, Turguéneff, the Aksákoffs and the Kiréyevskiys, Kavélin, Bótkin, and, in fact, all the best men of the time. But when later on serfdom was being abolished (in 1857-1863) the very realities of the moment established upon certain important questions a temporary agreement between some Slavophiles and Westerners—the most advanced socialistic Westerners, like Tchernyshévskiy, joining hands with the advanced Slavophiles in their desire to maintain the really fundamental institutions of the Russian peasants : the village community, the common law, and the federalistic principles ; while the more advanced Slavophiles made substantial concessions as regards the ' Western ' ideals embodied in the Declaration of Independence and the Declaration of the Rights of Man. It was to these years (1861) that Turguéneff alluded when he said in *A Nobleman's Retreat*, that in the discussion between Lavrétskiy and Pánshin, he—' an inveterate Westerner '—had given the superiority in argument to the defender of Slavophile ideas because they had prevailed then in real life.

At present the struggle between the Westerners and the Slavophiles has come to an end. The much-regretted philosopher, VLADÍMIR SOLOVIÓFF (1853-1900), who was sometimes described as a representative of the Slavophile school, collaborated with Aksákoff in his paper *Rus* only during the first years of his literary career. He was well versed in history and philosophy, and had a broad mind, so that he soon broke with Slavophile ' nationalism,' and in 1884 he began a remarkable discussion with Aksákoff and combated all the fundamental canons of the Slavophile nationalists. As to the present representatives of this school, having none of the inspiration which characterised its founders, they have sunk to the level of mere Imperialistic dreamers and warlike Nationalists, or of Orthodox Ultramontanes, whose intellectual influence is *nil*. At the present moment the main struggle goes on between the defenders of autocracy and those of freedom ; the defenders of capital and those of labour ; the defenders of centralisation and bureaucracy and those of the republican federalistic principle, municipal independence, and the independence of the village community.

POLITICAL LITERATURE ABROAD

One great drawback in Russia has been that no portion of the Slavonian countries has ever obtained political freedom, as did Switzerland or Belgium, so as to offer to Russian political refugees an asylum where they would not feel quite separated from their mother country. Russians, when they were compelled to leave Russia, had therefore to go to Switzerland or to England, where they remained, until quite lately, absolute strangers. Even France, with which they had more points of contact, was only occasionally open to them ; while the two countries nearest to Russia—Germany and Austria—not being themselves free, remained closed to all political refugees. In consequence, till quite lately, political and religious emigration from Russia has been insignificant, and only for a few years in the nineteenth century has political literature published abroad exercised a real influence in Russia. This was during the times of Hérzen and his paper *The Bell.*

HÉRZEN (1812-1870) was born in a rich family at Moscow—his mother, however, being a German—and he was educated in the old-nobility quarter of the ' Old Equerries.' A French emigrant, a German tutor, a Russian teacher who was a great lover of freedom, and the rich library of his father, composed of French and German eighteenth-century philosophers—these were his teachers. The reading of the French encyclopædists left a deep impression on his mind, so that even later on, when he paid, like all his young friends, a tribute to the study of German metaphysics, he never abandoned the concrete ways of thought and the naturalistic turn of mind which he had borrowed from the French eighteenth-century philosophers.

He entered the physical and mathematical faculty of the Moscow University. The French Revolution of 1830, breaking through the dark reaction which had prevailed in Europe since the beginning of the century, produced a deep impression on thinking minds all over Europe ; and a circle of young men, which included Hérzen, his intimate friend, the poet Ogaryóff, Pássek, the future explorer of folk-lore, and several others, came to spend whole nights in reading and discussing political and social matters, especially Saint-Simonism. Under the impression of what they knew about the Decembrists, Hérzen and Ogaryóff, when they were mere boys, had already taken 'the Hannibal oath' of avenging the memory of these forerunners of liberty. The result of these youthful gatherings was that at one of them some song was sung in which there was disrespectful allusion to Nicholas I. This reached the ears of the State police. Night searchings were made at the lodgings of the young men, and all were arrested. Some were sent to Siberia, and the others would have been marched as soldiers to a battalion, like Polezháyeff and Shevtchénko, had it not been for the interference of certain persons in high places. Hérzen was sent to a small town on the slopes of the Uráls, Vyátka, and remained full six years in exile.

When he was allowed to return to Moscow in 1840, he found the literary circles entirely under the influence of German philosophy, losing themselves in metaphysical abstractions. 'The absolute' of Hegel, his triad-scheme of human progress, and his assertion to the effect that 'all that exists is reasonable' were eagerly discussed. This last had brought the Moscow Hegelians, at the head of whom stood N. V. STANKÉ-VITCH (1813-1840) and MIKHAÍL BAKÚNIN (1814-1876), to the conclusion that even despotism is 'reasonable.' Byelínskiy, coming then to recognise that even

the despotism of Nicholas I. was 'historically necessary,' expressed these views with his habitual energy
in an article on Púshkin's *Borodinó Anniversary*, which
produced a great impression. Hérzen saw himself
compelled also to study the philosophy of Hegel; but
this study did not alter his views; he remained a
follower of the encyclopædists and an admirer of the
principles of the great French Revolution. Later on,
when Bakúnin also went abroad, in 1842, and after a
stay at Berlin broke at last with the fogs of German
metaphysics, and, leaving Berlin for Dresden and afterwards for Paris, began to familiarise his Russian friends
with the teachings of Socialism, developed then in
France, the Russian circles began to change their views,
and Byelínskiy began, with the others, to study the
French Socialists, especially Fourier and Pierre Leroux.
They then constituted the left wing of the 'Westerners,'
to which Turguéneff, Kavélin, and so many of our
writers belonged, and broke entirely with the Slavophiles.

By the end of 1840 Hérzen was exiled once more—
this time to Nóvgorod, and only with great difficulty
could he obtain, in 1842, the permission to return to
Moscow, and then to go abroad. He left Russia in
1847, never more to return. Bakúnin and Ogaryóff
were already abroad, and after a journey to Italy, which
was then making heroic efforts to free itself from the
Austrian yoke, he soon joined his friends in Paris, which
was then on the eve of the Revolution of 1848.

He lived through the youthful enthusiasm of the
movement which embraced all Europe in the spring of
1848, and he also lived through all the subsequent dis-
appointments and the massacre of the Paris proletarians
during the terrible days of June. The quarter where
he and Turguéneff stayed at that time was surrounded
by a chain of police-agents who knew them both personally, and they could only rage in their rooms as
they heard the volleys of rifle-shots, announcing that

the vanquished working-men who had been taken prisoners were being shot in batches by the triumphing *bourgeoisie*. Both have left most striking descriptions of those days—Hérzen's *June Days* being one of the best pieces of Russian literature.

Deep despair took hold of Hérzen when all the hopes raised by the revolution had so rapidly come to nought and a fearful reaction had spread all over Europe, re-establishing Austrian rule over Italy and Hungary, paving the way for Napoleon III. at Paris, and sweeping away everywhere the very traces of a widespread socialistic movement. Hérzen then felt a deep despair as regards Western civilisation altogether, and expressed it in most moving pages in his book *From the Other Shore*. It is a cry of despair—the cry of a prophetic politician in the voice of a great poet.

Later on Hérzen founded, at Paris, with Proudhon, a paper, *La Voix du Peuple*, of which almost every number was confiscated by the police of Napoleon III. The paper could not live, and Hérzen himself was soon expelled from France. He was naturalised in Switzerland, and finally, after the tragic loss of his mother and his son in a shipwreck, he definitely settled at London in 1852. Here the first leaf of a free Russian press was printed that same year, and very soon Hérzen became one of the strongest influences in Russia. He started first a review, the name of which, *The Polar Star*, was a remembrance of the almanac published under this name by Ryléeff (see chapter i.) ; and in this review, which at once produced a great impression in Russia, he published, besides political articles and most valuable material concerning the recent history of Russia, his admirable memoirs — *Past Facts and Thoughts.*

Apart from the historical value of these memoirs—Hérzen knew all the historical personages of his time—they certainly are one of the best pieces of poetical literature in any language. The descriptions of men

and events which they contain, beginning with Russia
in the forties and ending with the years of exile, reveal
at every step an extraordinary philosophical intelligence; a profoundly sarcastic mind, combined with a
great deal of good-natured humour; a deep hatred of
oppressors and a deep personal love for the simple-
hearted heroes of human emancipation. At the same
time these memoirs contain such fine, poetical scenes from
the author's personal life, as his love of Nathalie—later
his wife—or such deeply impressive chapters as *Oceano
Nox*, where he tells about the loss of his son and mother.
One chapter of these memoirs has not yet been published in full, and from what Turguéneff told me about
it, it must be of the highest beauty. 'No one has ever
written like him,' Turguéneff said; 'it is written in
tears and blood.'

A paper, *The Bell*, soon followed *The Polar Star*, and
it was through this paper that the influence of Hérzen
became a real power in Russia. It appears now, from
the lately published correspondence between Turguéneff
and Hérzen, that the great novelist took a very lively
part in *The Bell*. It was he who supplied his friend
Hérzen with the most interesting material and gave him
hints as to what attitude he should take upon this or
that subject.

These were, of course, the years when Russia was on
the eve of the abolition of serfdom and of a thorough
reform of most of the antiquated institutions of
Nicholas I., and when every one took an interest in
public affairs. Numbers of memoirs upon the questions
of the day were addressed to the Tsar by private persons,
or simply circulated in private, in MS.; Turguéneff
would get hold of them, and they would be discussed
in *The Bell*. At the same time *The Bell* was revealing
such facts of maladministration as it was impossible to
bring to public knowledge in Russia itself, while the
leading articles were written by Hérzen with a force,
an inner warmth, and a beauty of form which are

seldom found in political literature. I know of no West European writer with whom I should be able to compare Hérzen. *The Bell* was smuggled into Russia in large quantities and could be found everywhere. Even Alexander II. and the Empress Marie were among its regular readers.

Two years after serfdom had been abolished, and while all sorts of urgently needed reforms were still under discussion—that is, in 1863—began, as is known, the uprising of Poland; and this uprising, crushed in blood and on the gallows, brought the liberation movement in Russia to a complete end. Reaction got the upper hand; and the popularity of Hérzen, who had supported the Poles, was necessarily gone. *The Bell* was read no more in Russia, and the efforts of Hérzen to continue it in French brought no results. A new generation came then to the front—the generation of Bazároff and of 'the populists,' whom Hérzen did not understand from the outset, although they were his own intellectual sons and daughters, dressed now in a new, more democratic and realistic garb. He died in isolation at Paris, in 1870.

The works of Hérzen, even now, are not allowed to be published in full in Russia, and they are not sufficiently known to the younger generation. It is certain, however, that when the time comes for them to be read again, Russians will discover in Hérzen a very profound thinker, whose sympathies were entirely with the working classes, who understood the forms of human development in all their complexity, and who wrote in a style of unequalled beauty—the best proof that his ideas had been thought out in detail and under a variety of aspects.

Before he had emigrated and founded a free press at London, Hérzen had written in Russian reviews under the name of ISKANDER, treating various subjects, such as Western politics, socialism, the philosophy of natural sciences, art, and so on. He also wrote a novel, *Whose*

Fault is it? which is often spoken of in the history of the development of intellectual types in Russia. The hero of this novel, Béltoff, is a direct descendant from Lérmontoff's Petchórin, and occupies an intermediate position between him and the heroes of Turguéneff.

The work of the poet OGARYÓFF (1813-1877) was not very large, and his intimate friend, Hérzen, who was a great master in personal characteristics, could say of him that his chief life-work was the working out of such an ideal personality as he was himself. His private life was most unhappy, but his influence upon his friends was very great. He was a thorough lover of freedom, who, before he left Russia, set free his ten thousand serfs, surrendering all the land to them, and who, throughout all his life abroad, remained true to the ideals of equality and freedom which he had cherished in his youth. Personally, he was the gentlest imaginable of men, and a note of resignation, in the sense of Schiller's, sounds throughout his poetry, amongst which fierce poems of revolt and of masculine energy are few.

As to MIKHAIL BAKÚNIN, the other great friend of Hérzen, his work belongs chiefly tò the International Working-Men's Association, and hardly can find a place in a sketch of Russian literature; but his personal influence on some of the prominent writers of Russia, including Byelínskiy, was great. He was the typical revolutionist, whom nobody could approach without being inspired by a revolutionary fire. Besides, if advanced thought in Russia has always remained true to the cause of the different nationalities—Polish, Finnish, Little Russian, Caucasian — oppressed by Russian tsardom, or by Austria, it owes this to a very great extent to Ogaryóff and Bakúnin. In the European labour movement Bakúnin became the soul of the left wing of the International Working-Men's Association, and he was the founder of modern

Anarchism, or anti-State Socialism, of which he laid down the foundations upon wide considerations of the philosophy of history.

Finally I must mention among the Russian political writers abroad, PETER LAVRÓFF (1823-1901). He was a mathematician and a philosopher who represented, under the name of 'anthropologism,' a reconciliation of modern natural science materialism with Kantianism. He was a colonel of artillery, a professor of mathematics, and a member of the St. Petersburg newly formed municipal government, when he was arrested and exiled to a small town in the Uráls. One of the young Socialist circles kidnapped him from there and shipped him abroad, where he began to publish in the year 1874, first at Zurich and then at London, the Socialist review *Forward*. Lavróff was an extremely learned encyclopædist, who made his reputation by his *Mechanical Theory of the Universe* and by the first chapters of a very exhaustive history of mathematical sciences. His later work, *History of Modern Thought*, of which unfortunately only the four or five introductory volumes have been published, would certainly have been an important contribution to evolutionist philosophy if it had been completed. In the Socialist movement he belonged to the social-democratic wing, but was too widely learned and too much of a philosopher to join the German social-democrats in their ideals of a centralised communistic State, or in their narrow interpretation of history. However, the work of Lavróff which gave him the greatest notoriety and best expressed his own personality was a small work, *Historical Letters*, which he published in Russia under the pseudonym of MÍRTOFF and which can now be read in a French translation. This little work appeared at the right moment—just when our youth, in the years 1870-1873, were endeavouring to find a new programme of action amongst the people. Lavróff stands out in it as a preacher of activity amongst the people, speaking to the educated youth of their indebtedness to the people, and of their duty to repay the debt which they had contracted towards the poorer classes during the years they had passed in the Universities—all this, developed with a profusion of historical hints, of philosophical deductions, and of practical advice. These letters had a deep influence upon our youth. The ideas which Lavróff preached in 1870 he confirmed by all his subsequent life. He lived to the age of eighty-two, and passed all his life in strict conformity with his ideal, occupying at Paris two small rooms, limiting his daily expenses for food to a ridiculously small amount, earning his living by his pen, and giving all his time to the spreading of the ideas which were so dear to him.

NICHOLAS TURGUÉNEFF (1789-1871) was a remarkable political writer, who belonged to two different epochs. In 1818 he published in Russia a *Theory of Taxation* — a book quite striking for its time and country, as it contained the development of the liberal economical ideas of Adam Smith; and he was already beginning to work for the abolition of serfdom. He made a practical attempt by partly freeing his own serfs, and wrote on this subject several memoirs for the use of Emperor Alexander I. He also worked for constitutional rule, and soon became one of the most influential members of the secret society of the Decembrists; but he was abroad in December 1825, and therefore escaped being executed with his friends. After that time N. Turguéneff remained in exile, chiefly at Paris, and in 1857, when an amnesty was granted to the Decembrists, and he was allowed to return to Russia, he did so for a few weeks only.

He took, however, a lively part in the emancipation of the serfs, which he had preached since 1818 and which he had discussed also in his large work, *La Russie et les Russes*, published in Paris in 1847. Now he devoted to this subject several papers in *The Bell* and several pamphlets. He continued at the same time to advocate the convocation of a General Representative Assembly, the development of provincial self-government, and other urgent reforms. He died at Paris in 1871, after having had the happiness which had come to few Decembrists—that of taking, towards the end of his days, a practical part in the realisation of one of the dreams of his youth, for which so many of our noblest men had given their lives.

I pass over in silence several other writers, like PRINCE DOLGORÚKIY, and especially a number of Polish writers, who emigrated from Russia and wrote mainly in French.

I omit also quite a number of socialistic and constitutional papers and reviews which have been published in Switzerland or in England during the last twenty years, and will only mention, and that only in a few words, Professor M. P. DRAGOMÁNOFF (1841-1895), a champion of Ukraïnian autonomy and federalism in Russia, and the founder of a Socialist literature in the Ukraïnian language, and my friend STEPNIÁK (1852-1897). Stepniák's writings were chiefly in English, but now that they are translated into Russian they will certainly win for him an honourable place in the history of Russian literature. His two novels, *The Career of a Nihilist* (*Andréi Kozhuhóff* in Russian) and *The Stundist Pável Rudénko*, as also his earlier sketches, *Underground Russia*, revealed his remarkable literary talent, but a stupid railway accident put an end to his young life, so rich in vigour and thought and so full of promise. It must also be mentioned that as the greatest Russian writer of our own time, LEO TOLSTÓY, could not have many of his works printed in Russia, his friend, V. TCHERTKÓFF, started therefore in England a regular publishing-office, both for publishing Tolstóy's works and for bringing to light the religious movements which were going on in Russia, and the prosecutions directed against them by the Government.

TCHERNYSHÉVSKIY AND *THE CONTEMPORARY*

The most prominent among political writers in Russia itself has undoubtedly been TCHERNYSHÉVSKIY (1828-1889), whose name is indissolubly connected with that of the review, *Sovreménnik* (*The Contemporary*). The influence which this review exercised on public opinion in the years of the abolition of serfdom (1857-1862) was equal to that of Hérzen's *Bell*, and this influence was mainly due to Tchernyshévskiy, and partly to the critic Dobrolúboff.

Tchernyshévskiy was born in South-eastern Russia, at Sarátoff—his father being a well-educated and respected priest of the cathedral—and he received his early education first at home and next in the Sarátoff seminary. He left the seminary, however, in 1844, and two years later entered the philological department of the St. Petersburg University.

The quantity of work which Tchernyshévskiy performed during his life, and the immensity of knowledge which he acquired in various branches, was simply stupendous. He began his literary career by works on philology and literary criticism ; and he wrote in this last branch three remarkable works, *The Æsthetical Relations between Art and Reality*, *Sketches of the Gógol Period*, and *Lessing and His Time*, in which he developed a whole theory of æsthetics and literary criticism. His main work, however, was accomplished during the four years, 1858-1862, when he wrote in *The Contemporary* exclusively on political and economical matters. These were the years of the abolition of serfdom, and opinion, both in the public at large and in the Government spheres, was quite unsettled even as to the leading principles which should be followed in accomplishing it. The two main questions were : should the liberated serfs receive the land which they were cultivating for themselves while they were serfs—and if so, on what conditions ? And next—should the village community institutions be maintained and the land held, as of old, in common—the village community becoming in this case the basis for the future self-government institutions? All the best men of Russia were in favour of an answer in the affirmative to both these questions, and even in the higher spheres opinion went the same way ; but all the reactionists and 'esclavagist' serf-owners of the old school bitterly opposed this view. They wrote memoirs upon memoirs and addressed them to the Emperor and the Emancipation Committees, and it was necessary, of course, to analyse their arguments and to produce weighty historical and economical proofs against them. In this struggle Tchernyshévskiy, who was, of course, as was Hérzen's *Bell*, with the advanced party and the defenders of the village community, supported it with all the powers of his great intelligence, his wide erudition, and his formidable capacity for work ; and if this party carried the day and finally converted Alexander II. and the official leaders of the Emancipation Committees to its views, it was certainly to a great extent owing to the energy of Tchernyshévskiy and his friends.

It must also be said that in this struggle *The Contemporary* and *The Bell* found a strong support in two advanced political writers from the Slavophile camp: KÓSHELEFF (1806-1883) and YÚRIY SAMÁRIN (1819-1876). The former had advocated, since 1847—both in writing and in practice—the liberation of the serfs 'with the land,' the maintenance of the village community, and peasant self-government, and now Kósheleff and Samárin, both influential landlords, energetically supported these ideas in the Emancipation Committees, while Tchernyshévskiy fought for them in *The Contemporary* and in his *Letters without an Address* (written apparently to Alexander II. and published only later on in Switzerland).

No less a service did Tchernyshévskiy render to Russian society by educating it in economical matters and in the history of modern times. In this respect he acted with a great pedagogical talent. He translated Mill's *Political Economy*, and wrote *Notes* to it, in a socialistic sense; moreover, in a series of articles, like *Capital and Labour, Economical Activity and the State*, he did his best to spread sound economic ideas. In the domain of history he did the same, both in a series of translations and in a number of original articles upon the struggle of parties in modern France.

In 1863 Tchernyshévskiy was arrested, and while he was kept in the fortress he wrote a remarkable novel, *What is to be Done?* From the artistic point of view this novel leaves much to be desired; but for the Russian youth of the times it was a revelation, and it became a programme. Questions of marriage, and separation after marriage in case such a separation becomes necessary, agitated Russian society in those years. To ignore such questions was absolutely impossible. And Tchernyshévskiy discussed them in his novel, in describing the relations between his heroine, Vyéra Pávlovna, her husband Lopukhóff, and the young doctor with whom she fell in love after her marriage—indicating the only solution which perfect honesty and straightforward common sense could approve in such a case. At the same time he preached—in veiled words, which were, however, perfectly well understood—Fourierism, and depicted in a most attractive form the communistic associations of producers. He also showed in his novel what true 'Nihilists' were, and in what they differed from Turguéneff's Bazároff. No novel of Turguéneff and no writings of Tolstóy or any other writer have ever had such a wide and deep influence upon Russian society as this novel had. It became the watchword of Young Russia, and the influence of the ideas it propagated has never ceased to be apparent since.

In 1864 Tchernyshévskiy was exiled to hard labour in Siberia, for the political and socialist propaganda which he had been making; and for fear that he might

U

escape from Transbaikália he was soon transported to a very secluded spot in the far north of Eastern Siberia —Vilúisk—where he was kept till 1883. Then only was he allowed to return to Russia and to settle at Astrakhán. His health, however, was already quite broken. Nevertheless, he undertook the translation of the *Universal History* of Weber, to which he wrote long addenda, and he had translated twelve volumes of it when death overtook him in 1889. Storms of polemics have raged over his grave, although all his ideas, even yet, cannot be discussed in the Russian press. No other man has been so much hated by his political adversaries as Tchernyshévskiy. But even these are bound to recognise now the great services he rendered to Russia during the emancipation of the serfs, and his educational influence.

THE SATIRE : SALTYKÓFF

With all the restrictions imposed upon political literature in Russia, the satire necessarily became one of the favourite means of expressing political thought. It would take too much time to give even a short sketch of the earlier Russian satirists, as in order to do that one would have to go back as far as the eighteenth century. Of Gógol's satire I have already spoken ; consequently I shall limit my remarks under this head to only one representative of modern satire, SALTYKÓFF, who is better known under his *nom de plume* of SCHEDRÍN (1826-1889).

The influence of Saltykóff in Russia was very great, not only with the advanced section of Russian thought, but among the general readers as well. He was perhaps one of Russia's most popular writers. Here I must make, however, a personal remark. One may try as much as possible to keep to an objective stand-point in the appreciation of different writers, but a subjective element will necessarily interfere, and I personally must say that although I admire the great talent of Saltykóff, I never could become as enthusiastic over his writings as the very great majority of my friends did. Not that I dislike satire : on the contrary ; but I like it much more definite than it is in Saltykóff. I fully recognise that his remarks were sometimes extremely deep, and always correct, and that in many cases he foresaw coming events long before the common reader could guess their approach ; I fully admit that the satirical characterisations he gave of different classes of Russian society belong to the domain of good art, and that his types are really typical—and yet, with all this, I find that these excellent characterisations and these acute remarks are too much lost amidst a deluge of insignificant talk, which was certainly meant to conceal their point from the censorship, but which mitigates the sharpness of the satire and tends to deaden its effect.[1]

Saltykóff began his literary career very early and, like most of our best writers, he knew something of exile. In 1847 he frequented the circles of Petrashévskiy. Then, in 1848, he wrote a novel, *A Complicated Affair*, in which some socialistic tendencies were expressed in the shape of a dream of a certain poor functionary. It so happened that the novel appeared in print just a few weeks after the February revolution of 1848 had broken out, and when the Russian Government was especially on the alert. Saltykóff was thereupon exiled to Vyátka, a miserable provincial town in East Russia, and was ordered to enter the civil service. The exile lasted seven years, during which he became thoroughly acquainted with the world of functionaries grouped around the governor of the province. Then in 1857 better times came for Russian literature, and Saltykóff, who was allowed to return to the capitals, utilised his

---

[1] In his *Critical Studies of Russian Literature*, 2 vols., 1888, and in a sketch, *Saltykóff-Schedrín*, 1906, Prof. K. K. Arsénieff has given an excellent analysis of the work of Saltykóff.

knowledge of provincial life in writing a series of
Provincial Sketches.

The impression produced by these *Sketches* was
simply tremendous. All Russia talked of them. Saltykóff's talent appeared in them in its full force, and
with them was opened quite a new era in Russian
literature. A great number of imitators began in their
turn to dissect the Russian administration and the
failure of its functionaries. Of course, something of
the sort had already been done by Gógol, but Gógol,
who wrote twenty years before, was compelled to con-
fine himself to generalities, while Saltykóff was enabled
now to name things by their names and to describe
provincial society as it was — denouncing the venal
nature of the functionaries, the rottenness of the whole
administration, the absence of comprehension of what
was vital in the life of the country, and so on.

When Saltykóff was permitted to return to St.
Petersburg, after his exile, he did not abandon the
service of the State, which he had been compelled to
enter at Vyátka. With but a short interruption he
remained a functionary till the year 1868, and twice
during that time he was vice-governor, and even
governor of a province. It was only then that he
definitely left the service, to act, with Nekrásoff, as co-
editor of a monthly review, *Otéchestvennyia Zapíski*,
which became, after *The Contemporary* had been suppressed, the representative of advanced democratic
thought in Russia, and retained this position till 1884,
when it was suppressed in its turn. By that time the
health of Saltykóff was broken down, and after a very
painful illness, during which he nevertheless continued
to write, he died in 1889.

The *Provincial Sketches* determined once for all the
character of Saltykóff's work. His talent only deepened
as he advanced in life, and his satires went more and
more profoundly into the analysis of modern civilised
life, the many causes which stand in the way of progress,

and the infinity of forms which the struggle of reaction
against progress is taking nowadays. In his *Innocent
Tales* he touched upon some of the most tragic aspects
of serfdom. Then, in his representation of the modern
knights of industrialism and plutocracy, with their ap-
petites for money-making and enjoyments of the lower
sort, their heartlessness, and their hopeless meanness,
Saltykóff attained the heights of descriptive art ; but
he excelled perhaps even more in the representation of
that 'average man' who has no great passions, but
for the mere sake of not being disturbed in the process
of enjoyment of his philistine well-being will not recoil
before any crime against the best men of his time, and,
if need be, will lend a ready hand to the worst enemies
of progress. In flagellating that 'average man,' who,
owing to his unmitigated cowardice, has attained such
a luxurious development in Russia, Saltykóff produced
his greatest creations. But when he came to touch
those who are the real geniuses of reaction—those who
keep 'the average man' in fear, and inspire reaction, if
need be, with audacity and ferocity—then Saltykóff's
satire either recoiled before its task, or the attack was
veiled in so many funny and petty expressions and
words that all its venom was gone.

When reaction had obtained the upper hand in 1863,
and the carrying out of the reforms of 1861 and of
those still to be undertaken fell into the hands of the
very opponents of these reforms, and the former serf-
owners were doing all they could in order to recall serfdom once again to life, or, at least, so to bind the peasant
by over-taxation and high rents as to practically enslave
him once more, Saltykóff brought out a striking series
of satires which admirably represented this new class
of men. *The History of a City*, which is a comic history
of Russia, full of allusions to contemporary currents of
thought, *The Diary of a Provincial in St. Petersburg,*
Letters from the Provinces, and *The Pompadours* belong
to this series ; while in *Those Gentlemen of Tashkent* he

represented all that crowd which hastened now to make fortunes by railway-building, advocacy in reformed tribunals, and annexation of new territories. In these sketches, as well as in those which he devoted to the description of the sad and sometimes psychologically unsound products of the times of serfdom (*The Gentlemen Golovlóffs, Poshekhónsk Antiquity*), he created types, some of which, like Judushka, have been described by some critics as almost Shakespearian.

Finally, in the early, eighties, when the terrible struggle of the terrorists against autocracy was over, and with the advent of Alexander III. reaction was triumphant, the satires of Schedrín became a cry of despair. At times the satirist becomes great in his sad irony, and his *Letters to My Aunt* will live, not only as a historical but also as a deeply human document. It must, however, be said that even here the satire of Schedrín did not reach the stinging power which satire must have in order that men should feel the effects of its whip.

It is also worthy of note that Saltykóff had a real talent for writing tales. Some of them, especially those which deal with children under serfdom, are of great beauty.

LITERARY CRITICISM

The main channel through which political thought found its expression in Russia during the last fifty years was, however, literary criticism, which consequently reached with us a development and an importance that it has in no other country. The real soul of a Russian monthly review is its art critic. His article is a much greater event than the novel of a favourite writer which may appear in the same number. The critic of a leading review is the intellectual leader of a large portion of the younger generation; and it so happened that throughout the last half-century we have had in Russia a succession of art critics who have exercised upon the intellectual aspects of their own times a far greater, and especially a far more widespread, influence than any novelist or any writer in any other domain. It is so generally true that the intellectual aspect of a given epoch can be best characterised by naming the art critic of the time who exercised the main influence. It was Byelínskiy in the thirties or forties, Tchernyshévskiy and Dobrolúboff in the fifties and the early sixties, and Písareff in the later sixties and seventies, who were respectively the rulers of advanced thought in their generation of educated youth. It was only later on, when real political agitation began—taking at once two or three different directions, even in the advanced camp—that Mihailóvskiy, the leading critic from the eighties till the end of the century, represented one of its directions.

This means, of course, that literary criticism has in Russia certain special aspects. It is not limited to a criticism of works of art from the purely literary or æsthetic point of view. Whether a Rúdin or a Katerína are types of real, living beings, and whether the novel or the drama is well built, well developed, and well written—these are, of course, the first questions considered. But they are soon answered ; and there are infinitely more important questions, which are raised in the thoughtful mind by every good work of art : the questions concerning the position of a Rúdin or a Katerína in society ; the part, bad or good, which they play in it ; the ideas which inspire them, and the value of these ideas ; and then—the actions of the heroes, and the social causes of these actions.

In a good work of art the actions of the heroes are evidently what they would have been under similar conditions in reality ; otherwise it would *not* be good art. Therefore they can be discussed as facts of life. But these actions and their causes and consequences open the widest horizons to a thoughtful critic, for an appreciation of both the ideals and the prejudices of society, for the analysis of passions, for a discussion of the types of men and women which prevail at a given moment. In fact, a good work of art gives material for discussing nearly the whole of the mutual relations in a society of a given type. The author, if he is a thoughtful poet, has himself either consciously or often unconsciously considered all that. It is his life-experience which he gives in his work. Why, then, should not the critic bring before the reader all those thoughts which must have passed through the author's brain, or have affected him unconsciously when he produced these scenes, or pictured that corner of human life?

This is what Russian literary critics have been doing for the last fifty years; and as the field of fiction and poetry is unlimited, there is not one of the great social and human problems which they have not had to discuss in their critical reviews. This is also why the works of the four critics just named are as eagerly read and reread now at this moment as they were twenty or fifty years ago : they have lost nothing of their freshness and interest. If art is a school of life—the more so are such works.

It is extremely interesting to note that art criticism in Russia took from the very outset (in the twenties), and quite independently of all imitation of Western Europe, the character of *philosophical æsthetics*. The revolt against pseudo-classicism had only just begun under the banner of romanticism, and the appearance of Púshkin's *Ruslán and Ludmíla* had just given the first practical argument in favour of the romantic rebels, when the poet VENEVÍTINOFF (see chapter ii.), soon followed by NADÉZHDIN (1804-1856) and POLEVÓY (1796-1846)— the real founder of serious journalism in Russia—laid the foundations of new art criticism. Literary criticism, they maintained, must analyse, not only the æsthetic value of a work of art, but, above all, its leading idea— its 'philosophical'—its social meaning.

Venevítinoff, whose own poetry bore such a high

intellectual stamp, boldly attacked the absence of higher
ideas among the Russian romantics, and wrote that 'the
true poets of all nations have always been philosophers
who reached the highest summits of culture.' A poet
who is satisfied with his own self, and does not pursue
aims of general improvement, is of no use to his contemporaries.[1]

Nadézhdin followed on the same lines, and boldly
attacked Púshkin for his absence of higher inspiration
and for producing a poetry of which the only motives
were 'wine and women.' He reproached our romantics
with an absence of ethnographical and historic truth in
their work, and the meanness of the subjects they chose
in their poetry. As to Polevóy, he was so great an
admirer of the poetry of Byron and Victor Hugo that
he could not pardon Púshkin and Gógol the absence of
higher ideas in their work : having nothing in it that
might raise men to higher ideas and actions, their work
could stand no comparison whatever with the immortal
creations of Shakespeare, Hugo, and Goethe. This
absence of higher leading ideas in the work of Púshkin
and Gógol so much impressed the two just-named
critics that they did not even notice the immense service
which these founders of Russian literature had rendered
to us by introducing that sound naturalism and realism
which became since a distinctive feature of Russian art,
and the need of which both Nadézhdin and Polevóy
were the first to recognise. It was Byelínskiy who had
to take up their work, to complete it, and to show what
was the technique of really good art, and what its contents ought to be.

To say that BYELÍNSKIY (1810-1848) was a very
gifted art critic would thus mean nothing. He was in
reality, at a very significant moment of human evolution,
a teacher and an educator of Russian society, not only

---

[1] I borrow these remarks about the predecessors of Byelínskiy
from an article on Literary Criticism in Russia, by Professor Ivánoff,
in the *Russian Encyclopædic Dictionary*, vol. xxxii. p. 771.

in art—its value, its purport, its comprehension—but also in politics, in social questions, and in humanitarian aspirations.

He was the son of an obscure army surgeon, and spent his childhood in a remote province of Russia. Well prepared by his father, who knew the value of knowledge, he entered the University of St. Petersburg, but was excluded from it in 1832 for a tragedy which he wrote, in the style of Schiller's *Robbers*, and which was an energetic protest against serfdom. He soon joined the circle of Hérzen, Ogaryóff, Stankévitch, etc., and after having written since 1831 small notes of literary criticism, he began his literary career in 1834 by a critical review of literature, which at once attracted notice. From that time till his death he wrote critical articles and bibliographical notes for some of the leading reviews, and he worked so extremely hard that at the age of thirty-eight he died from consumption. He did not die too soon. The revolution had broken out in Western Europe, and when Byelínskiy was on his deathbed an agent of the State police would call from time to time to ascertain whether he was still alive. The order was given to arrest him if he should recover, and his fate certainly would have been the fortress and at the best —exile.

When Byelínskiy first began to write he was entirely under the influence of the idealistic German philosophy. He was inclined to maintain that art is something too great and too pure to have anything to do with the questions of the day. It was a reproduction of 'the general idea of the life of nature.' Its problems were those of the universe—not of poor men and their petty events. It was from this idealistic point of view of beauty and truth that he discussed the main principles of art, and explained the process of artistic creation. In a series of articles on Púshkin he wrote, in fact, a history of Russian literature down to Púshkin, from that point of view.

Holding such abstract views Byelínskiy even came, during his stay at Moscow, to consider, with Hegel, that 'all that which exists is reasonable,' and to preach 're-conciliation' with the despotism of Nicholas I. However, under the influence of Hérzen he soon shook off the fogs of German metaphysics, and soon after having removed to St. Petersburg he opened a new page of activity.

Under the impression produced upon him by the realism of Gógol, whose best works were just appearing, he came to understand that true poetry *is* real : that it must be a poetry of life and of reality. And under the influence of the political movement which was going on in France he arrived at advanced political ideas. He was a great master of style, and whatever he wrote was so full of energy, and at the same time bore so truly the stamp of his most sympathetic personality, that it always produced a deep impression upon his readers. And now all his aspirations towards what is grand and high, and all his boundless love of truth, which he formerly had given in the service of personal self-improvement and ideal art, were given to the service of man within the poor conditions of Russian reality. He pitilessly analysed that reality, and wherever he saw in the literary works which passed under his eyes, or only felt, insincerity, haughtiness, absence of general interest, attachment to old-age despotism, or slavery in any form— including the slavery of woman—he fought these evils with all his energy and passion. He thus became a political writer in the best sense of the word at the same time that he was an art critic ; he became a teacher of the higher humanitarian principles.

In his *Letter to Gógol* concerning the latter's *Correspondence with Friends* (see chapter iii.) he gave quite a programme of urgent social and political reforms ; but his days were numbered. His review of the literature for the year 1847, which was especially beautiful and deep, was his last work. Death spared him from seeing the dark cloud of reaction in which Russia was wrapped from 1848 to 1855.

VALERIÁN MÁYKOFF (1823-1847), who promised to become a critic of great power on the same lines as Byelínskiy, died unfortunately too young, and it was Tchernyshévskiy, soon followed by Dobrolúboff, who continued and further developed the work of Byelínskiy and his predecessors.

The leading idea of TCHERNYSHÉVSKIY was that art cannot be its own aim; that life is superior to art; and that the aim of art is *to explain life, to comment upon it*, and *to express an opinion about it*. He developed these ideas in a thoughtful and stimulating work, *The Æsthetic Relations of Art to Reality*, in which he demolished the current theories of æsthetics, and gave a realistic definition of the beautiful. The sensation, he wrote, which the beautiful awakens in us is a feeling of bright happiness, similar to that which is awakened by the presence of a beloved being. It must therefore contain something dear to us, and that dear something is *life*. 'To say that that which we name "Beauty" is life; that that being is beautiful in which we see life—life as it ought to be according to our conception—and that object is beautiful which speaks to us of life—this definition, we should think, satisfactorily explains all cases which awaken in us the feeling of the beautiful.' The conclusion to be drawn from such a definition was that the beautiful in art, far from being superior to the beautiful in life, can only represent that conception of the beautiful which the artist has borrowed from life. As to the aim of art, it is much the same as that of science, although its means of action are different. The true aim of art is to remind us of what is interesting in human life, and to teach us how men live and how they ought to live. This last part of Tchernyshévskiy teachings was especially developed by Dobrolúboff.

DOBROLÚBOFF (1836-1861) was born in Nízhniy-Nóvgorod, where his father was a parish priest, and he received his education first in a clerical school and after that in a theological high school. In 1853 he entered the Pedagogical Institute at St. Petersburg. His parents died the next year, and he had then to maintain all his brothers and sisters. Lessons, for which he was paid ridiculously low prices, and translations, almost equally badly paid—all that in addition to his student's duties—meant working terribly hard, and this broke down his health at an early age. In 1855 he made the acquaintance of Tchernyshévskiy, and, having finished in 1857 his studies at the Institute, he took in hand the critical department of *The Contemporary*, and again worked passionately. Four years later, in November 1861, he died, at the age of twenty-five, having literally killed himself by overwork, leaving four volumes of critical essays, each of which is a serious original work. Such essays as *The Kingdom of Darkness, A Ray of Light, What is Oblómovism? When comes the Real Day?* had especially a profound effect on the development of the youth of those times.

Not that Dobrolúboff had a very definite criterion of literary criticism, or that he had a very distinct programme as to what was to be done. But he was one of the purest and the most solid representatives of that type of new men—the realist-idealist—whom Turguéneff saw coming by the end of the fifties. Therefore, in whatever he wrote one felt the thoroughly moral and thoroughly reliable, slightly ascetic 'rigorist,' who judged all facts of life from the standard of—'What good will they bring to the toiling masses?' or, 'How will they favour the creation of men whose eyes are directed that way?' His attitude towards professional æsthetics was most contemptuous, but he felt deeply, and enjoyed the great works of art. He did not condemn Púshkin for his levity, or Gógol for his absence of ideals. He did not advise any one to write novels or poems with a set purpose : he knew the results

would be poor if the author did not thoroughly know
the life he described, and the author's purpose was not
coming from his own innermost ideals.　He admitted
that the great geniuses were right in creating unconsciously, because he understood that the real artist
creates only when he has been struck by this or that
aspect of reality.　He asked only from a work of art,
whether it truly and correctly reproduced life, or not?
If not, he passed it by; but if it did truly represent
life, then he wrote essays *about this life*; and his
articles were essays on moral, political, or economical
matters—the work of art yielding only the facts for
such a discussion.　This explains the influence Dobrolúboff exercised upon his contemporaries.　Such essays,
written by such a personality, were precisely what was
wanted in the turmoil of those years for preparing
better men for the coming struggles.　They were a
school of political and moral education.

PÍSAREFF (1841-1868), the critic who succeeded, so
to speak, Dobrolúboff, was a quite different man.　He
was born in a rich family of landlords and had received
an education during which he had never known what it
meant to want anything; but he soon realised the
drawbacks of such a life, and when he was at the St.
Petersburg University he abandoned the rich house of
his uncle and settled with a poor student comrade, or
lived in an apartment with a number of other students
—writing amidst their noisy discussions or songs.　Like
Dobrolúboff he worked excessively hard, and astonished
every one by his varied knowledge and the facility with
which he acquired it.　In 1862, when reaction was
beginning to reappear, he permitted a comrade to print
in a secret printing-office an article of his—the criticism
of some reactionary political pamphlet—which article
had not received the authorisation of the censorship.
The secret printing-office was seized, and Písareff was
locked for four years in the fortress of St. Peter and St.
Paul.　There he wrote all that made him widely known

in Russia.   When he came out of prison his health was already broken, and in the summer of 1868 he was drowned while bathing in one of the Baltic seaside resorts.

Upon the Russian youth of his own time, and consequently on whatever share, as men and women later on, they brought to the general progress of the country, Písareff exercised an influence which was as great as that of Byelínskiy, Tchernyshévskiy, and Dobrolúboff. Here again it is impossible to determine the character and the cause of this influence by merely referring to Písareff's canons in art criticism.   His leading ideas on this subject can be explained in a few words ; his ideal was 'the thoughtful realist'—the type which Turguéneff had just represented in Bazároff, and which Písareff further developed in his critical essays.   He shared Bazároff's low opinion of art, but, as a concession, demanded that Russian art should, at least, reach the heights which art had reached with Goethe, Heine, and Börne in elevating mankind—or else that those who are always talking of art, but can produce nothing approaching it, should rather give their forces to something more within their reach.   This is why he devoted most elaborate articles to depreciating the futile poetry of Púshkin.   In ethics he was entirely at one with the 'Nihilist' Bazároff, who bowed before no authority but that of his own reason.   And he thought (like Bazároff in a conversation with Pável Petróvitch) that the main point, *at that given moment*, was to develop the *thorough, scientifically educated realist*, who would break with all the traditions and mistakes of the olden time, and would work, looking upon human life with the sound common sense of a realist.   He even did something himself to spread the sound natural science knowledge that had suddenly developed in those years, and wrote a most remarkable exposition of Darwinism in a series of articles entitled *Progress in the World of Plants and Animals.*

But all this does not yet explain the influence which Písareff exercised in those years upon the development of Russian youth.   The real cause of Písareff's influence was elsewhere, and may be best explained by the following example.   There appeared a novel in which the author had told how a girl, good-hearted, honest, but quite uneducated, quite commonplace as to her conceptions of happiness and life, and full of the current society prejudices, fell in love, and was brought to all sorts of misfortunes.   This girl—Písareff at once understood — was not invented.   Thousands upon thousands of like girls exist, and their lives have the same run.   They are, he said, 'Muslin Girls.' Their conception of the universe does not go much beyond their muslin dresses.   And he reasoned how with their 'muslin education' and their 'muslin-girl conceptions' they must unavoidably come to grief. And by this article, which every girl in every educated family in Russia read, he induced thousands upon thousands of Russian girls to say to themselves : 'No, never will I be like that poor muslin girl.   I will conquer knowledge ; I will think ; and I will make for myself a better future.'   Each of his articles had a similar effect.   It gave to a young mind the first shock. It opened the young man's and the young woman's eyes to those thousands of details of life which habit makes us cease to perceive, but the sum of which makes precisely that stifling atmosphere under which the heroines of 'Krestóvskiy-pseudonym' used to wither.   From that life, which could promise only deception, dullness, and vegetative existence, he called the youth of both sexes to a life full of the light of knowledge, a life of work, of broad views and sympathies, which was now opened for the 'thoughtful realist.'   And his voice was heard, his call for higher development and higher ideals was followed.

The time has not yet come to fully appreciate the work of MIHAILÓVSKIY (1842-1904), who in the seventies became the leading critic, and remained so till his death. Moreover, his proper position would not be understood without my entering into many details concerning the character of the intellectual movement in Russia for the last thirty years, and this movement has been extremely complex. Suffice it to say that with Mihailóvskiy literary criticism took a philosophical turn. Within this period Spencer's philosophy had produced a deep sensation in Russia, and Mihailóvskiy submitted it to a severe analysis from the anthropological standpoint, showing its weak points and working out his own *Theory of Progress*, which will certainly be spoken of with respect in Western Europe when it becomes known outside Russia. His very remarkable articles on *Individualism*, on *Heroes and the Crowd*, on *Happiness*, have the same philosophical value ; while even from the few quotations from his *Left and Right Hand of Count Tolstóy*, which were given in a preceding chapter, it was easy to see which way his sympathies went.

It must, however, be said that as a *literary* critic, Mihailóvskiy remained far behind Byelínskiy. He was not endowed with that artistic insight which was so well developed in his great predecessor.

Of the other critics of the same tendencies I shall only name SKABITCHÉVSKIY (born 1838), the author of a well-written and very useful history of modern Russian literature, already mentioned in these pages ; S. VENGUÉROFF, the already mentioned author of several capital works on modern Russian literature ; and K. ARSÉNIEFF (born 1837), whose *Critical Studies* (1888) are the more interesting as they deal at some length with some of the less known poets and the younger contemporary writers. Of authors who occasionally wrote critical essays let me mention P. POLEVÓY (1839-1903), the author of historical novels, who wrote also a popular and quite valuable *History of the Russian Literature*. To my regret I must pass over in silence the valuable critical work done by DRUZHÍNIN (1824-

X

1864) after the death of Byelínskiy, P. V. ANNENKOFF, (1812-1887), as also A. GRIGÓRIEFF (1822-1864), a brilliant and original critic from the Slavophile camp. He took the 'æsthetical' point of view and combated the utilitarian views upon art, but had no great success.

TOLSTÓY'S *WHAT IS ART?*

It is thus seen that for the last eighty years, beginning with Venevítinoff and Nadézhdin, Russian art critics have worked to establish the idea that art has a *raison d'être* only when it is 'in the service of society' and contributes towards raising society to higher humanitarian conceptions—*by those means which are proper to art, and distinguish it both from science and political literature.* This idea which so much shocked Western readers when Proudhon developed it has been advocated in Russia by all those who have exercised a real influence upon critical judgment in art matters. And they were supported *de facto* by some of our greatest poets, such as Lérmontoff and Turguéneff. As to the critics of the other camp, like Druzhínin, Annenkoff, and A. Grigórieff, who took either the opposite view of 'art for art's sake,' or some intermediate view—who preached that the true domain of art is 'The Beautiful' and clung to the theories of the German æsthetical writers : if they were of some help to our best authors in indicating to them the minor faults or the beauties of their works, they got no hold upon Russian thought.

The metaphysics of the German æsthetical writers was more than once demolished, in the opinion of Russian readers—especially by Byelínskiy, in his *Review of Literature for 1847,* and by Tchernyshévskiy in his *Æsthetic Relations of Art to Reality.* In this *Review* Byelínskiy fully developed his ideas concerning art in the service of mankind, and proved that although art is not identical with science, and differs from it by the way it treats the facts of life, it nevertheless has

with it a *common aim*. The man of science *demonstrates*
—the poet *shows*; but both *convince*; the one by his
arguments, the other—by his scenes from life. The
same was done by Tchernyshévskiy when he maintained
that the aim of art is not unlike that of history : that
it *explains to us life*, and that consequently art which
should merely reproduce facts of life without adding
to our comprehension of it would not be art at all.

These few remarks will explain why Tolstóy's *What
is Art?* produced much less impression in Russia than
abroad. What struck us in it was not its leading idea,
which was quite familiar to us, but the fact that the
great artist also made it his own, and was supporting it
by all the weight of his artistic experience; we admired
also the literary form he gave the idea. Moreover,
we read with the greatest interest his witty criticisms
of both the 'decadent' would-be poets and the librettos
of Wagner's operas ; to which latter, let me add by the
way, Wagner wrote, in places, wonderfully beautiful
music, as soon as he came to deal with the universal
human passions—love, compassion, envy, the joy of life,
and so on, and forgot all about his fairy-tale background.

What is Art? offered the more interest in Russia
because the defenders of pure art and the haters of the
'nihilists in art' used to quote Tolstóy as of their camp.
In his youth indeed he seems not to have had very
definite ideas about this subject. At any rate, when,
in 1859, he was received as a member of the Society
of Friends of Russian Literature, he pronounced a
speech on the necessity of *not* dragging art into the
smaller disputes of the day, to which the Slavophile
Homyakóff replied in a fiery speech, contesting his
ideas with great energy.

'There are moments—great historic moments'—Homyakóff
said—'when self-denunciation [he meant on the part of
society] has especial, incontestable rights. . . . The "accidental" and the "temporary" in the historical development of
a nation's life acquire then the meaning of the universal and

the broadly human, because all generations and all nations can understand, and do understand, the painful moans and the painful confessions of a given generation or a given nation.'
. . . 'An artist'—he continued—'is not a theory; he is not a mere domain of thought and cerebral activity. He is a man —always a man of his own time—usually one of its best representatives. . . . Owing to the very impressionability of his organism, without which he would not have been an artist, he, more than the others, receives both the painful and the pleasant impressions of the society in the midst of which he was born.'

Showing that Tolstóy had already taken just this standpoint in some of his works; for example, in describing the death of the horse-driver in *Three Deaths*; Homyakóff concluded by saying: 'Yes, you have been, and you will be one of those who denounce the evils of society. Continue to follow the excellent way you have chosen.'[1]

At any rate, in *What is Art?* Tolstóy entirely breaks with the theories of 'art for art's sake,' and makes an open stand by the side of those whose ideas have been expounded in the preceding pages. He only defines still more correctly the domain of art when he says that the artist always aims at communicating to others the same feelings which he experiences at the sight of nature or of human life. Not to *convince*, as Tchernyshévskiy said, but to *infect* the others with his own *feelings*, which is certainly more correct. However, 'feeling' and 'thought' are inseparable. A feeling seeks words to express itself, and a feeling expressed in words is a thought. And when Tolstóy says that the aim of artistic activity is to transmit 'the highest feelings which humanity has attained' and that art must be 'religious'—that is, wake up the highest and the best aspirations—he only expresses in other words what all our best critics since Venevítinoff, Nadézhdin,

---

[1] The speech of Homyakóff is reproduced in Skabitchévskiy's *History* (l.c.). I was very anxious to get Tolstóy's speech, but it had not been printed, and the manuscript of it could not be found.

and Polevóy have said. In fact, when he complains that nobody teaches men *how to live*, he overlooks that that is precisely what good art is always doing, and what our art critics have done. Byelínskiy, Dobrolúboff, Písareff, and their continuators have done nothing but *to teach men how to live.* They studied and analysed life, as it had been understood by the greatest artists of each century, and they drew from their works conclusions as to 'how to live.'

More than this. When Tolstóy, armed with his powerful criticism, castigates what he so well describes as 'counterfeits of art,' he continues the work that Tchernyshévskiy, Dobrolúboff, and especially Písareff had done. He sides with Bazároff. Only, this intervention of the great artist gives a heavier blow to the ' art for art's sake ' theory, still in vogue in Western Europe, than anything that Proudhon or our Russian critics, unknown in the West, could possibly have done.

As to Tolstóy's idea concerning the value of a work of art being measured by its accessibility to the great number, which has been so fiercely attacked on all sides, and even ridiculed—this assertion, although it has perhaps not been well expressed, contains nevertheless, I believe, the germs of a great idea which sooner or later is certain to make its way. It is evident that every form of art has a certain conventional way of expressing itself—its own way of ' infecting others with the artist's feelings '—and therefore requires a certain training to understand it. Tolstóy is hardly right in overlooking the fact that some training is required for rightly comprehending, and being influenced by, even the simplest forms of art, and his criterion of ' universal understanding ' seems therefore far-fetched.

However, there lies in what he says a deep idea. Tolstóy is certainly right in asking why the Bible has not yet been superseded, as a work of art accessible to every one. Michelet had already made a similar remark, and had said that what was wanted by our century was

Le Livre, The Book, which shall contain, in a great poetical form accessible to all, the embodiment of nature with all her glories and of the history of all mankind in its deepest human features. Humboldt had aimed at this in his *Cosmos*; but grand though his work is, it is accessible to only the very few. It was not he who should transfigure science into poetry. And we have no work of art which even approaches this need of modern mankind.

The reason is self-evident: *Because art has become too artificial*; because, being chiefly for the rich, it has too much specialised its ways of expression, so as to be understood by the few only. In this respect Tolstóy is absolutely right. Take the mass of excellent works that have been mentioned in this book. How very few of them will ever become accessible to a large public! The fact is, that a new art is indeed required. And it will come when the artist, having understood this idea of Tolstóy's, shall say to himself: ' I may write highly philosophical works of art in which I depict the inner drama of the highly educated and refined man of our own times; I may write works which contain the highest poetry of nature, involving a deep knowledge and comprehension of the life of nature; but, if I can write such things, I must also be able, if I am a true artist, to speak to all: to write other things which will be as wide in conception as these, but which every one, including the humblest miner or peasant, will be able to understand and enjoy!' To say that a folk-song is *greater* art than a Beethoven sonata is not correct: we cannot compare a storm in the Alps, and the struggle against it, counterparts of which we find in Beethoven's music, with a fine, quiet midsummer day and hay-making, to which corresponds a given folk-song. But truly great art, which, notwithstanding its depth and its lofty flight, will penetrate into every peasant's hut and inspire every one with higher conceptions of thought and life— such an art is really wanted. I think it is possible.

SOME LATER PERIOD NOVELISTS

It did not enter into the plan of this book to analyse present-day Russian writers. Another volume would have been required to do them justice, not only on account of the literary importance of some of them, and the interest of the various. directions in art which they represent, but especially because, in order to explain properly the character of the present literature and the different currents in Russian art, it would have been necessary to enter into many details concerning the unsettled conditions under which the country had been living during the last forty years. Moreover, most of the contemporary writers have not yet said their last word, and we can expect from them works of even greater value than any they have hitherto produced. I was compelled, therefore, to limit myself to brief remarks concerning those of the younger novelists whose literary character was already quite determined. Two of them, Tchéhoff and Oertel, are unfortunately no more.

OERTEL (1855-1908) was a very sympathetic writer who abandoned literature just at a time when his last novel, *Smyéna* (*Changing Guards*), had given proofs of a further development of his talent. He was born in the borderland of the Russian Steppes, and was brought up on one of the large estates of this region. Later on he went to the University of St. Petersburg, but he soon was compelled to leave it after some ' students' disorders,' and was interned in the town of Tver. He soon returned, however, to his native Steppe region, which he cherished with the same love as Nikítin, Koltsóff, and Levítoff.

Oertel began his literary career by short sketches which are now collected in two volumes under the name of *Notebook of a Prairie-Man*, and whose manner suggests Turguéneff's *Sportsman's Notebook*. The nature of the prairies is described in these little stories with great warmth and poetry, and the types of peasants who appear in the stories are perfectly true to nature, without any attempts at idealisation. One feels only that the author is no great admirer of the 'intellectuals' and fully appreciates the general ethics of rural life. Some of these sketches, especially those which deal with the growing *bourgeoisie du village*, are highly artistic. *Two Couples* (1887), in which the parallel stories of two young couples in love—one of educated people and the other of peasants—are given, is a story evidently written under the influence of the ideas of Tolstóy, and bearing traces of a preconceived idea, which spoils in places the artistic value of the novel. There are nevertheless admirable scenes, testifying to very fine powers of observation.

However, the real force of Oertel is not in discussing psychological problems. His true domain is the description of whole regions, with all the variety of types of men which one finds amidst the mixed populations of South Russia, and this force appears at its best in *The Gardénins, their Retainers, their Followers, and their Enemies*, and in *Changing Guards*. Russian critics have, of course, very seriously and very minutely discussed the young heroes, Efrem and Nicholas, who appear in *The Gardénins*, and they have made a rigorous inquiry into the ways of thinking of these young men. But this is of a quite secondary importance, and one almost regrets that the author, paying a tribute to his times, has given the two young men more attention than they deserve, being only two more individuals in the great picture of country life which he has drawn for us. The fact is, that just as we have in Gogól's tales quite a world opening before us—a Little Russian village, or provincial life—so also here we see, as the very title of the novel suggests, the whole life of a large estate at the times of serfdom, with its mass of retainers, followers, and foes, all grouped round the horse-breeding establishment which makes the fame of

the estate and the pride of all connected with it.   It is
the life of that crowd of people, the life at the horse-
fairs and the races, not the discussions or the loves of a
couple of young men, which makes the main interest of
the picture; and that life is really reproduced in as
masterly a manner as it is in a good Dutch picture
representing some village fair.   No writer in Russia
since Serghéi Aksákoff and Gógol has so well succeeded
in painting a whole corner of Russia with its scores of
figures, all living and all placed in those positions of
relative importance which they occupy in real life.

The same power is felt in *Changing Guards*.   The
subject of this novel is very interesting.   It shows how
the old noble families disintegrate, like their estates,
and how another class of men—merchants and un-
scrupulous adventurers—get possession of these estates,
while a new class made up of the younger merchants
and clerks, who are beginning to be inspired with some
ideas of freedom and higher culture, constitutes already
the germ of a new stratum of the educated classes.   In
this novel, too, some critics fastened their attention
chiefly on the undoubtedly interesting types of the
aristocratic girl, the Nonconformist peasant whom she
begins to love, the practical Radical young merchant—
all painted quite true to life; but they overlooked what
makes the real importance of the novel.   Here again
we have quite a region of South Russia (as typical as
the Far West is in the United States), throbbing with
life and full of living men and women, as it was some
twenty years after the liberation of the serfs, when a new
life, not devoid of some American features, was beginning
to appear.   The contrast between this young life and the
decaying mansion is very well reproduced, too, in the
romances of the young people—the whole bearing the
stamp of the most sympathetic individuality of the author.

KOROLÉNKO was born (in 1853) in a small town of
Western Russia, and there he received his first educa-

tion. In 1872 he was at the Agricultural Academy of Moscow, but was compelled to leave after having taken part in some students' movement. Later on he was arrested as a 'political,' and exiled, first to a small town of the Uráls, and then to Western Siberia, and from there, after his refusal to take the oath of allegiance to Alexander III., he was transported to a Yakút encampment several hundred miles beyond Yakútsk. There he spent several years, and when he returned to Russia in 1886, not being allowed to stay in University towns, he settled at Nízhniy-Nóvgorod.

Life in the far north, in the wildernesses of Yakútsk, in a small encampment buried for half the year in the snow, produced upon Korolénko an extremely deep impression, and the little stories which he wrote about Siberian subjects (*The Dream of Makár, The Man from Sakhalín,* etc.) were so beautiful that he was unanimously recognised as a true heir to Turguéneff. There was in the little stories of Korolénko a force, a sense of proportion, a mastery in depicting the characters, and an artistic finish, which not only distinguished him from most of his young contemporaries, but revealed in him a true artist. *What the Forest Says*, in which he related a dramatic episode from serfdom times in Lithuania, only further confirmed the high reputation which Korolénko had already won. It is not an imitation of Turguéneff, and yet it at once recalled, by its comprehension of the life of the forest, the great novelist's beautiful sketch, *The Woodlands* (*Polyesie*). *In Bad Society* is evidently taken from the author's childhood, and this idyll among tramps and thieves who concealed themselves in the ruins of some tower is of such beauty, especially in the scenes with children, that every one found in it a truly 'Turguéneff charm.' But then Korolénko came to a halt. His *Blind Musician* was read in all languages, and admired—again for its charm ; but it was felt that the over-refined psychology of this novel is hardly correct ; and no greater production worthy of the extremely sympathetic and rich talent of Korolénko has appeared since.   It must also be said that one great novel of his (*Prókhor and the Students*) was forbidden by censorship, and only one chapter from another novel, badly mutilated by the censor's red ink, was permitted to see the light.

This may seem strange, but the same would have to be said of all the contemporaries of Korolénko, among whom there are writers of great talent.   To analyse the causes of this fact, especially with reference to so great an artist as Korolénko, would certainly be a tempting task.   But this would require speaking at some length of the change which took place in the Russian novel during the last twenty years or so, in connection with the political life of the country.   A few hints will perhaps explain what is meant.   In the seventies quite a special sort of novel had been created by a number of young novelists—mostly contributors of the reviews *Rússkoye Slóvo* and *Dyélo*.   The 'thoughtful realist'—such as he was understood by Písareff—was their hero, and however imperfect the technique of these novels might have been in some cases, their leading idea was most honest, and the influence they exercised upon Russian youth was in the right direction.   This was the time when Russian women were making their first steps towards higher education, and trying to conquer some sort of economical and intellectual independence.   To attain this, they had to sustain a bitter struggle against their elders. 'Madame Kabanóva' and 'Dikóy' (see chapter vi.) were alive then in a thousand guises, in all classes of society, and our women had to struggle hard against their parents and relatives, who did not understand their children ; against 'society' as a whole, which hated the 'emancipated woman'; and against the Government, which only too well foresaw the dangers that a new generation of educated women would re-present for an autocratic bureaucracy.   It was of the first necessity, then, that at least in the men of the same generation the young fighters for women's rights should find helpers, and not that sort of men about whom Turguéneff's heroine in *Correspondence* wrote (see chapter iv.). In this direction our men-novelists and one lady, SOPHIE SMIRNÓVA (*The Little Fire, The Salt of the Earth*, published in 1871-1872), have done good service, both in maintaining the energy of women in their hard struggle and in inspiring men with respect towards that struggle and those who fought in it.

Later on a new element became prominent in the Russian novel. It was the 'populist' idea—love to the masses of toilers and work among them—which became for the next twenty years a favourite theme in this category of novels. These novels contributed now to maintain the new movement and to inspire men and women in that sort of work, of which an instance has been given in a preceding page, in speaking of *The Great Bear*. The workers in both these fields were numerous, and I can only name in passing MOR-DÓVTSEFF (in *Signs of the Times*), SCHELLER, who wrote under the name of A. MIKHÁILOFF, STANYUKÓ-VITCH, NOVODVÓRSKIY, BARANTSÉVITCH, MATCH-TÉTT, MÁMIN, and the poet NÁDSON, who all, either directly or indirectly, worked through the novel and poetry in the same direction.

However, the struggle for liberty which was begun about 1857, after having reached its culminating point in 1881, came to a temporary end, and for the next ten years prostration seemed to spread amidst the Russian 'intellectuals.' Faith in the old ideals and the old in-spiring watchwords—even faith in men—was passing away, and new tendencies began to make their way in art—partly under the influence of this phase of the Russian movement, and partly also under the influence of Western Europe. A sense of fatigue became evident. Faith in knowledge was shaken. Social ideals were relegated to the background. 'Rigorism' was condemned, and 'popularism' began to be represented as ludicrous, or, when it reappeared, it was in some religious form, as Tolstóyism. Instead of the former enthusiasm for 'mankind,' the 'rights of the individual' were proclaimed, which 'rights' did not mean equal rights for all, but the rights of the few over all the others.

In these unsettled conditions of social ideas our younger novelists—always anxious to reflect in their art the questions of the day—have had to develop ; and this confusion necessarily stood in the way of their producing anything as definite and as complete as did their predecessors of the previous generation. There was a lack of definite individualities in society ; and a true artist is incapable of inventing what does not exist.

DMÍTRIY MEREZHKÓVSKIY (born 1866) may be taken to illustrate the difficulties which a writer, even though endowed with a by no means ordinary talent, found in reaching his full development under the social and political conditions which prevailed in Russia during the period just mentioned. Leaving aside his poetry—although it is also very characteristic—and taking only his novels and critical articles, we see how, after having started with a certain sympathy, or at least with a certain respect, for those Russian writers of the previous generation who wrote under the inspiration of higher social ideals, Merezhkóvskiy gradually began to suspect these ideals, and finally ended by treating them with contempt. He found that they were of no avail, and he began to speak more and more of 'the sovereign rights of the individual,' but not in the sense in which they were understood by Godwin and other eighteenth-century philosophers, nor in the sense which Písareff attributed to them when he spoke of the 'thoughtful realist' ; Merezhkóvskiy took them in the sense—desperately vague, and narrow when not vague—attributed to them by Nietzsche.   At the same time he began to speak more and more of ' Beauty ' and 'the worship of the Beautiful,' but again not in the sense which idealists attributed to such words, but in the limited, erotic sense in which ' Beauty ' was understood by the ' Æsthetics ' of the leisured class in the forties.

The main work which Merezhkóvskiy undertook offered great interest. He began a trilogy of novels in which he intended to represent the struggle of the antique pagan world against Christianity : on the one hand, the Hellenic love and poetic comprehension of nature, and its worship of sound, exuberant life ; and on the other, the life-depressing influences of Judaic Christianity, with its condemnation of the study of nature, of poetry, art, pleasure, and healthy life altogether.   The first novel of the trilogy was *Julian the Apostate*, and the second, *Leonardo da Vinci* (both have been translated into English).   They were the result of a careful study of the antique Greek world and the Renaissance, and, notwithstanding some defects (absence of real feeling, even in the glorification of the worship of Beauty, and a certain abuse of archæological details), both contained beautiful and impressive scenes ; while the fundamental idea—the necessity of a synthesis between the poetry of nature of the antique world and the higher humanising ideals of Christianity—was forcibly impressed upon the reader.

Unfortunately, Merezhkóvskiy's admiration of antique ' Naturism ' did not last.   He had not yet written the third novel of his trilogy when modern ' Symbolism ' and mysticism began to penetrate into his works.

It may seem strange to the West Europeans, and especially to English readers, to hear of such a rapid succession of different moods of thought in Russian society, sufficiently deep to exercise such an influence upon the novels as has just been mentioned.   And yet so it is, in consequence of the historical phase which

Russia is living through. There is even a very gifted novelist, BOBORÝKIN (born 1836), who has made it his peculiar work to describe in novels the prevailing moods of Russian educated society in their rapid succession for the last thirty years. The technique of his novels is always excellent; his observations are always correct; his personal point of view is that of an honest advanced progressive; and his novels can always be taken as true and good pictures of the tendencies which prevailed at a given moment amongst the Russian 'intellectuals.' For the history of thought in Russia they are simply invaluable; and they must have helped many a young reader to find his or her way amidst the various facts of life; but the variety of currents which have been chronicled by Boborýkin would appear simply puzzling to a Western reader.

Boborýkin has been reproached by some critics with not having sufficiently distinguished between what was important in the facts of life which he described and what was irrelevant or only ephemeral; but this reproach is hardly correct. The main defect of his work lies perhaps elsewhere; namely, in that the individuality of the author is hardly felt in it at all. He seems to record the kaleidoscope of life without living with his heroes, and without suffering or rejoicing with them. He has noticed and perfectly well observed those persons whom he describes; his judgment of them is that of an intelligent, experienced man; but none of them has impressed him enough to become part of himself. Therefore they do not strike the reader with any sufficient depth of impression.

One of our contemporary authors, also endowed with great talent, who is publishing a simply stupefying quantity of novels, is POTÁPENKO. He was born in 1856, in South Russia, and after having studied music, he began writing in 1881. He soon became a favourite writer, and remained a favourite, even though his later novels bore traces of hasty work. Amidst the dark colours which prevailed then amongst the Russian novelists, Potápenko was a happy exception. Some of his novels are full of highly comic scenes, and compel the reader to laugh heartily. But even when there are no such scenes, and the facts are, on the contrary, sad, or even tragical, the effect of the novel is not depressing—perhaps because the author never departs from his own point of view of a satisfied optimist. In this respect Potápenko is absolutely the opposite of most of his contemporaries, and especially of Tchéhoff.

A. P. TCHÉHOFF

Of all the later period Russian novelists A. P. Tchéhoff (1860-1904) was undoubtedly the most deeply original. It was not a mere originality of style. His style, like that of every great artist, bears of course the stamp of his personality ; but he never tried to strike his readers with some style effects of his own : he probably despised them, and he wrote with the same simplicity as Púshkin, Turguéneff, and Tolstóy have written. Nor did he choose some special contents for his tales and novels, or appropriate to himself some special class of men. Few authors, on the contrary, have dealt with so wide a range of men and women, taken from all the layers, divisions, and subdivisions of Russian society, as Tchéhoff did. And with all that, as Tolstóy has remarked, Tchéhoff represents something of his own in art ; he has struck a new vein, not only for Russian literature, but for literature altogether, and thus belongs to all nations. His nearest relative is Guy de Maupassant, but a certain family resemblance between the two writers exists only in a few of their short stories. The manner of Tchéhoff, and especially the mood in which all the sketches, the short novels, and the dramas of Tchéhoff are written, is entirely his own. And then there is all the difference between the two writers which exists between contemporary France and Russia at that special period of development through which our country has been passing lately.

The biography of Tchéhoff can be told in a few words.   He was born in 1860, in South Russia, at Taganróg.   His father was originally a serf, but he had apparently exceptional business capacities, and freed himself early in his life.   To his son he gave a good education—first in the local gymnasium (college) and later on at the University of Moscow.   'I did not know much about faculties at that time,' Tchéhoff wrote once in a short biographical note, 'and I don't well remember why I chose the medical faculty; but I never regretted that choice later on.'   He did not become a medical practitioner; but a year's work in a small village hospital near Moscow, and similar work later on, when he volunteered to stand at the head of a medical district during the cholera epidemics of 1892, brought him into close contact with a wide world of men and women of all sorts and characters; and, as he himself has noticed, his acquaintance with natural sciences and with the scientific method of thought helped him a great deal in his subsequent literary work.

Tchéhoff began his literary career very early. Already during the first years of his University studies —that is, in 1879—he began to write short humorous sketches (under the pseudonym of Tchehónte) for some weeklies.   His talent developed rapidly; and the sympathy with which his first little volumes of short sketches was met in the press, and the interest which the best Russian critics (especially Mikhailóvskiy) took in the young novelist, must have helped him to give a more serious turn to his creative genius.   With every year the problems of life which he treated were deeper and more complicated, while the form he attained bore traces of an increasingly fine artistic finish.   When Tchéhoff died, at the age of only forty-four, his talent had already reached its full maturity.   His last production—a drama—contained such fine poetical touches,

Y

and such a mixture of poetical melancholy with strivings towards the joy of a well-filled life, that it might have seemed to open a new page in his creation if it were not known that consumption was rapidly undermining his life.

No one has ever succeeded, as Tchéhoff has, in representing the failures of human nature in our present civilisation, and especially the failure, the bankruptcy of the educated man in the face of the all-invading meanness of everyday life. This defeat of the 'intellectual' he has rendered with a wonderful force, variety, and impressiveness. And there lies the distinctive feature of his talent.

When you read the sketches and the stories of Tchéhoff in chronological succession, you see first an author full of the most exuberant vitality and youthful fun. The stories are, as a rule, very short; many of them cover only three or four pages; but they are full of the most infecting merriment. Some of them are mere farces: but you cannot help laughing in the heartiest way, because even the most ludicrous and impossible ones are written with an inimitable charm. And then, gradually, amidst that same fun, comes a touch of heartless vulgarity on the part of some of the actors in the story, and you feel how the author's heart throbs with pain. Slowly, gradually, this note becomes more frequent; it claims more and more attention; it ceases to be accidental; it becomes organic—till at last, in every story, in every novel, it stifles everything else. It may be the wreckless heartlessness of a young man who, 'for fun,' will make a girl believe that she is loved, or the absence of the most ordinary humanitarian feeling in the family of an old professor—it is always the same note of heartlessness and meanness which resounds, the same absence of the more refined human feelings, or, still worse, the moral bankruptcy of 'the intellectual.'

Tchéhoff's heroes are not people who have never

heard better words, or never conceived better ideas, than those which circulate in the lowest circles of the philistines. No, they have heard such words, and their hearts have beaten once upon a time at the sound of such words. But the commonplace everyday life has stifled all such aspirations, apathy has taken its place, and now there remains only a haphazard existence amidst a hopeless meanness. The meanness which Tchéhoff represents is the one which begins with the loss of faith in one's forces and the gradual loss of all those brighter hopes and illusions which make the charm of all activity, and then, step by step, this meanness destroys the very springs of life : broken hopes, broken hearts, broken energies. Man reaches a stage when he can only mechanically repeat certain actions from day to day, and goes to bed, happy if he has 'killed' his time in any way, gradually falling into a complete intellectual apathy and a moral indifference. The worst is that the very multiplicity of samples which Tchéhoff gives, without repeating himself, from so many different layers of society, seems to tell the reader that it is the rottenness of a whole civilisation, of an epoch, which the author divulges to us.

Speaking of Tchéhoff, Tolstóy made the deep remark that he was one of those few whose novels are willingly reread more than once. This is quite true. Every one of Tchéhoff's stories—it may be the smallest bagatelle or a small novel, or it may be a drama—produces an impression which cannot easily be forgotten. At the same time they contain such a profusion of minute detail, admirably chosen so as to increase the impression, that in rereading them one always finds a new pleasure. Tchéhoff was certainly a great artist. Besides, the variety of the men and women of all classes which appear in his stories, and the variety of psychological subjects dealt in them, is simply astounding. And yet every story bears so much the stamp of the author that in the most insignificant of them you recognise Tchéhoff, with his proper individuality and manner, with his conception of men and things.

Tchéhoff has never tried to write long novels or romances. His domain is the short story, in which he excels. He certainly never tries to give in it the whole history of his heroes from their birth to the grave: this would not be the proper way in a short story. He takes one moment only from that life, only one episode. And he tells it in such a way that the reader for ever retains in memory the type of men or women represented; so that, when later on he meets a living specimen of that type, he exclaims: 'But this is Tchéhoff's Ivánoff, or Tchéhoff's "Darling"!' In the space of some twenty pages, and within the limitations of a single episode, there is revealed a complicated psychological drama—a world of mutual relations. Take, for instance, the very short and impressive sketch, *From a Doctor's Practice*. It is a story in which there is no story after all. A doctor is invited to see a girl, whose mother is the owner of a large cotton mill. They live there, in a mansion close to, and within the enclosure of, the immense buildings. The girl is the only child, and is worshipped by her mother. But she is not happy. Indefinite thoughts worry her: she is stifled in that atmosphere. Her mother is also unhappy on account of her darling's unhappiness, and the only happy creature in the household is the ex-governess of the girl, now a sort of lady-companion, who really enjoys the luxurious surroundings of the mansion and its rich table. The doctor is asked to stay over the night, and tells to his sleepless patient that she is not bound to stay there: that a really well-intentioned person can find many places in the world where she would find an activity to suit her. And when the doctor leaves next morning the girl has put on a white dress and has a flower in her hair. She looks very earnest, and you guess that she meditates already a new start in her life. Within the limits of these few traits quite a world of aimless philistine life has thus been unveiled before your eyes, a world of factory life, and a world of new longings making an irruption into it, and finding support from the outside. You read all this in the little episode. You see with a striking distinctness the four main personages upon whom light has been focussed for a short moment. And in the hazy outlines which you rather guess than see on the picture round the brightly lighted spot, you discover quite a world of complicated human relations, at the present moment and in times to come. Take away anything of the distinctness of the figures in the lighted spot, or anything of the haziness of the remainder—and the picture will be spoiled.

Such are nearly all the stories of Tchéhoff. Even when they cover some fifty pages they have the same character.

Tchéhoff wrote a couple of stories from peasant life. But peasants and village life are not his proper sphere. His true domain is the world of the 'intellectuals'— the educated and the half-educated portion of Russian society—and these he knows in perfection. He shows their bankruptcy, their inaptitude to solve the great historical problem of renovation which fell upon them, and the meanness and vulgarity of everyday life under which an immense number of them succumb. Since the times of Gógol no writer in Russia has so wonderfully represented human meanness under its varied aspects. And yet, what a difference between the two ! Gógol took mainly the outer meanness, which strikes the eye and often degenerates into farce, and therefore in most cases brings a smile on your lips or makes you laugh. But laughter is always a step towards reconciliation. Tchéhoff also makes you laugh in his earlier productions, but in proportion as he advances in age, and looks more seriously upon life, the laughter disappears, and although a fine humour remains, you feel that he now deals with a kind of meanness and philistinism which provokes not smiles but suffering in the

author.   A 'Tchéhoff sorrow' is as much characteristic
of his writings as the deep furrow between the brows of
his lively eyes is characteristic of his good-natured face.
Moreover, the meanness which Tchéhoff depicts is much
deeper than the one which Gógol knew.   Deeper conflicts are now going on in the depths of the modern
educated men, of which Gógol knew nothing seventy
years ago.   The 'sorrow' of Tchéhoff is also that of a
much more sensitive and a more refined nature than the
'unseen tears' of Gógol's satire.

Better than any Russian novelist Tchéhoff understands the fundamental vice of that mass of Russian
'intellectuals,' who very well *see* the dark sides of
Russian life but have no force to join that small minority
of younger people who dare to rebel against the evil.   In
this respect only one more writer—and this one was
a woman, Hvóschinskaya ('Krestóvskiy-pseudonym')
—can be placed by the side of Tchéhoff.   He knew,
and more than knew—he felt with every nerve of his
poetical mind—that, apart from a handful of stronger
men and women, the true curse of the Russian 'intellectual' is the weakness of his will, the insufficient
strength of his desires.   Perhaps he felt it in himself.
And when he was asked once (in 1894) in a letter—
'What should a Russian desire at the present time?' he
wrote in return: 'Here is my reply: desire!   He needs
most of all desire—force of character.   We have enough
of that whining shapelessness.'

This absence of strong desire, and weakness of will, he
continually, over and over again, represented in his heroes.
But this predilection was not a mere accident of tempera-
ment and character.   It was a direct product of the times
he lived in.

Tchéhoff, we saw, was nineteen years old when he
began to write in 1879.   He thus belongs to the generation which had to live through, during their best years,
the worst years which Russia has passed through in the
second half of the nineteenth century.   With the tragic

death of Alexander II. and the advent to the throne of
his son, Alexander III., a whole epoch—the epoch of
progressive work and bright hopes—had come to a final
close.   All the sublime efforts of that younger generation
which had entered the political arena in the seventies,
and had taken for its watchword the symbol, 'Be with
the people!' had ended in a crushing defeat—the victims
moaning now in fortresses and in the snows of Siberia.
More than that, all the great reforms, including the
abolition of serfdom, which had been realised in the
sixties by the Hérzen, Turguéneff, and Tchernyshévskiy
generation, began now to be treated as so many mistakes
by the reactionary elements which had now rallied round
Alexander III.   Never will a Westerner understand the
depth of despair and the hopeless sadness which took
hold of the intellectual portion of Russian society for the
next ten or twelve years after that double defeat, when
it came to the conclusion that it was incapable to break
the inertia of the masses, or to move history so as to fill
up the gap between its high ideals and the heart-rending
reality.   In this respect the eighties were perhaps the
gloomiest period that Russia lived through for the last
hundred years.   In the fifties the 'intellectuals' had at
least full hope in their forces ; now—they had lost even
these hopes.   It was during those very years that
Tchéhoff began to write ; and, being a true poet, who
feels and responds to the moods of the moment, he
became the painter of that breakdown—of that failure
of the 'intellectuals' which hung as a nightmare above
the civilised portion of Russian society.   And again,
being a great poet, he depicted that all-invading philistine meanness in such features that his picture will live.
How superficial, in comparison, is the philistinism described by Zola.   Perhaps France even does not know
that disease which was gnawing then at the very marrow
of the bones of the Russian 'intellectual.'

   With all that Tchéhoff is by no means a pessimist in
the proper sense of the word ; if he had come to despair,

he would have taken the bankruptcy of the 'intellectuals' as a necessary fatality. A word such as, for instance, *fin de siècle*, would have been his solace. But Tchéhoff could not find satisfaction in such words because he firmly believed that a better existence was possible— and would come. 'From my childhood,' he wrote in an intimate letter, ' I have believed in progress, because the difference between the time when they used to flog me and when they stopped to do so [in the sixties] was tremendous.'

There are three dramas of Tchéhoff—*Ivánoff, Uncle Ványa (Uncle John)*, and *The Cherry-Tree Garden*, which fully illustrate how his faith in a better future grew in him as he advanced in age. Ivánoff, the hero of the first drama, is the personification of that failure of the 'intellectual' of which I just spoke. Once upon a time he had had his high ideals and he still speaks of them, and this is why Sásha, a girl full of the better inspirations—one of those fine intellectual types in the representation of which Tchéhoff appears as a true heir of Turguéneff—falls in love with him. But Ivánoff knows himself that he is played out ; that the girl loves in him what he is no more ; that the sacred fire is with him a mere reminiscence of the better years, irretrievably past ; and while the drama attains its culminating point, just when his marriage with Sásha is going to be celebrated, Ivánoff shoots himself. Pessimism is triumphant.

Uncle Ványa ends also in the most depressing way ; but there is some faint hope in it. The drama reveals an even still more complete breakdown of the educated 'intellectual,' and especially of the main representative of that class—the professor, the little god of the family, for whom all others have been sacrificing themselves, but who all his life has only written beautiful words about the sacred problems of art, while all his life he remained the most perfect egotist. But the end of this drama is different. The girl, Sónya, who is the counterpart of Sásha, and has been one of those who sacrificed themselves for the professor, remains more or less in the background of the drama, until, at its very end, she comes forward in a halo of endless love. She is neglected by the man whom she loves. This man—an enthusiast—prefers, however, a beautiful woman (the second wife of the professor) to Sónya, who is only one of those workers who bring life into the darkness of Russian village life, by helping the dark mass to pull through the hardships of their lives.

The drama ends in a heart-rending musical accord of devotion and self-sacrifice on behalf of Sónya and her uncle. 'It cannot be helped,' Sónya says, 'we must live! Uncle John, we shall live. We shall live through a long succession of days, and of long nights ; we shall patiently bear the sufferings which fate will send upon us ; we shall work for the others—now, and later on, in old age, knowing no rest ; and when our hour shall have come, we shall die without murmur, and there, beyond the grave . . . we shall rest !'

There is, after all, a redeeming feature in that despair. There remains the faith of Sónya in her capacity to work, her readiness to face the work, even without personal happiness.

But in proportion as Russian life becomes less gloomy ; in proportion as hopes of a better future for our country begin to bud once more in the youthful beginnings of a movement amongst the working classes in the industrial centres, to the call of which the educated youth answer immediately ; in proportion as the 'intellectuals' revive again, ready to sacrifice themselves in order to conquer freedom for the grand whole—the Russian people—Tchéhoff also begins to look into the future with hope and optimism. The *Cherry-Tree Garden* was his last swan-song, and the last words of this drama sound a note full of hope in a better future. The cherry-tree garden of a noble landlord, which used to be a true fairy garden when the trees were in full bloom, and nightingales sang in their thickets, has been pitilessly cut down by the money-making middle-class man. No blossom, no nightingales—only dollars instead. But Tchéhoff looks further into the future: he sees the place again in new hands, and a new garden is going to grow instead of the old one—a garden where all will find a new happiness in new surroundings. Those whose whole life was for themselves alone could never grow such a garden; but some day soon this will be done by beings like Anya, the heroine, and her friend, 'the perpetual student.' . . .

The influence of Tchéhoff, as Tolstóy has remarked, will last, and will not be limited to Russia only. He has given such a prominence to the short story and its ways of dealing with human life that he has thus become a reformer of our literary forms. In Russia he has already a number of imitators who look upon him as upon the head of a school; but—will they have also the same inimitable poetical feeling, the same charming intimacy in the way of telling the stories, that special form of love of nature, and above all, the beauty of Tchéhoff's smile amidst his tears?—all qualities inseparable from his personality.

As to his dramas, they are favourites on the Russian stage, both in the capitals and in the provinces. They are admirable for the stage and produce a deep effect; and when they are played by such a superior cast as that of the Artistic Theatre at Moscow—as the *Cherry-Tree Garden* was played lately—they become dramatic events.

In Russia Tchéhoff was perhaps the most popular of the younger writers. His popularity does not decrease; he is placed now immediately after Tolstóy, and his works are read immensely. Separate volumes of his stories, published under different titles—*In Twilight, Sad People*, and so on—ran each through ten to fourteen editions, while full editions of Tchéhoff's *Works*, in ten and fourteen volumes, sold in fabulous numbers: of the *Works*, which were given as a supplement to a weekly

illustrated paper, more than 200,000 copies were circulated in one single year.

In Germany Tchéhoff has produced a deep impression ; his best stories have been translated more than
once, so that one of the leading Berlin critics exclaimed
lately : ' Tschéchoff, Tschéchoff, und kein Ende!' (Tchéhoff, Tchéhoff, and no end).   In Italy he begins to be
widely read.   And yet it is only his stories which are
known beyond Russia.   To audiences outside the
borders of Russia his dramas seem to be ' too Russian,'
the characters too full of inner contradictions.

If there is any logic in the evolution of societies, such
a writer as Tchéhoff had to appear before literature could
take a new direction and produce the new types which
already are budding in life.   At any rate, an impressive
parting word had to be pronounced, and this is what
Tchéhoff has done.

BIBLIOGRAPHICAL NOTES

While this book was being prepared for print a work
of great value for all the English-speaking lovers of
Russian literature appeared in America.   I mean the
*Anthology of Russian Literature from the Earliest Period
to the Present Time*, by Leo Wiener, assistant professor
of Slavic languages at Harvard University, published in
two stately volumes by H. G. P. Putnam's Sons at New
York.   The first volume (400 pages) contains a rich
selection from the earliest documents of Russian literature—the annals, the epic songs, the lyric folk-songs,
etc.—as also from the writers of the seventeenth and the
eighteenth centuries.   It contains, moreover, a general
short sketch of the literature of the period and a mention
is made of all the English translations from the early
Russian literature.   The second volume (500 pages)
contains abstracts, with short introductory notes and a

full bibliography, from all the chief authors of the nineteenth century, beginning with Karamzín and ending
with Tchéhoff, Górkiy, and Merezhkóvskiy. All this
has been done with full knowledge of Russian literature
and of every author; the choice of characteristic abstracts hardly could be better, and the many translations
which Mr. Wiener himself has made are very good. In
this volume, too, all the English translations of Russian
authors were mentioned, their number having considerably increased within the last few years.[1] Many of the
Russian authors have hardly been translated at all, and
in such cases there is nothing else left but to advise the
reader to peruse French or German translations. Both
are more numerous than the English, a considerable
number of the German translations being embodied in
the cheap editions of Reklam.

A work concerning Malo-Russian (Little Russian)
literature, on lines similar to those followed by Mr.
Wiener, has appeared lately under the title, *Vik; the
Century, a Collection of Malo-Russian Poetry and Prose
published from 1708 to 1898*, 3 vols. (Kiev, Peter Barski);
(analysed in *Athenæum*, January 10, 1903).

Of general works which may be helpful to the student
of Russian literature I shall name Ralston's *Early Russian
History, Songs of the Russian People*, and *Russian Folk-
Tales* (1872-1874), as also his translation of Afanásieff's
Legends; Rambaud's *La Russie épique* (1876) and his
excellent *History of Russia* (Engl. trans.); *Le roman
russe*, by Vogüe; *Impressions of Russia*, by George
Brandes (translated by Eastman; Boston, 1889), and
his *Moderne Geister*, which contains an admirable chapter
on Turguéneff.

Of general works in Russian the following may be
named: *History of Russian Literature in Biographies
and Sketches*, by P. Polevóy, 2 vols., illustrated (1883;
new edition, enlarged, in 1903); and *History of the*

---

[1] Thus, the chief works of Dostoyévskiy have been translated by
Mrs. Constance Garnett—the translator of Turguéneff.

New Russian Literature from 1848 to 1898, by A. Ska-bitchévskiy, 4th ed., 1900, with 52 portraits. Both are reliable, well written, and not bulky works—the former being rather popular in character, while the latter is a critical work which goes into the analysis of every writer. The recently published *Gallery of Russian Writers*, edited by I. Ignátoff (Moscow, 1901), contains over 250 good portraits of Russian authors, accompanied by one-page notices, quite well written, of their work. A very exhaustive work is the *History of Russian Literature* by A. Pýpin, in 4 vols., 1889, beginning with the earliest times and ending with Púshkin, Lérmontoff, Gógol, and Koltsóff. The same author has written a *History of Russian Ethnography*, also in 4 vols. Among works dealing with portions only of Russian literature the following may be mentioned : Tchernyshévskiy's *Critical Articles*, St. Petersburg, 1893 ; Annenkoff's *Púshkin and His Time* ; O. Miller's *Russian Writers after Gógol* ; Merezhkóvskiy's books on Púshkin and another on Tolstóy ; and Arsénieff's *Critical Studies of Russian Literature*, 2 vols., 1888 (mentioned in the text) ; and above all, of course, the collections of *Works* of our critics : Byelínskiy (12 vols.), Dobrolúboff (4 vols.), Písareff (6 vols.), and Mihailóvskiy (6 vols.), completed by his *Literary Reminiscences*.

A work of very great value, which is still in progress, is the *Biographic Dictionary of Russian Writers*, published and nearly entirely written by S. Venguéroff, who is also the editor of new, scientifically prepared editions of the complete works of several authors (Byelínskiy is now published). Excellent biographies and critical sketches of all Russian writers will be found in the *Russian Encyclopædic Dictionary* of Brockhaus-Efron. The first two volumes of this Dictionary (they are now completed in an Appendix) were brought out as a translation of the *Lexikon* of Brockhaus ; but the direction was taken over in good time by a group of Russian men of science, including Mendeléeff, Woyéikoff, V. Solovióff, etc., who have made of the eighty-two volumes of this *Dictionary*, completed in 1904, one of the best encyclopædias in Europe. Suffice it to say that all articles on chemistry and chemical technics have been either written or carefully revised by Mendeléeff. A second, revised, edition of this work is being published ; while a new *Encyclopædic Dictionary* on a smaller scale, profusely illustrated, is issued by the publishers Granat.

Another very valuable Russian publication of Prof. S. A. Vengueroff, *Russian Literature of the Twentieth Century, 1890-1910,* is now in progress. The first four parts already published contain introductory sketches of the Editor, autobiographic notes of Merezhkóvskiy, Sologúb, Bálmont, Bryrísoff, Mrs. Garévitch, and several others, and a number of critical articles of different authors dealing with the Russian ' Modernist,' ' Impressionist,' ' Symbolist,' and ' Decadent ' prose-writers and poets, whom Prof. Vengueroff describes under the genetic name of ' Neo-Romanticists.'

Complete editions of the works of most of the Russian writers have lately been published, some of them by the editor Marks, in connection with his weekly illustrated paper, at astoundingly low prices, which can only be explained by a circulation which exceeds 200,000 copies every year. The works of Gógol, Turguéneff, Gontcharóff, Ostróvskiy, Boborýkin, Tchéhoff, Alexéi Tolstóy, Schedrín, and most minor writers, are in this case.

APPENDIX A

From Púshkin's Lyrics

xxx

That glorious moment I remember,
Before my eyes appearedst thou,
As a swift-passing fairy vision,
An angel of the purest charm.

Amidst the pangs of hopeless sadness,
Amidst the din of noisy life,
I heard resound thy voice's music,
And saw thy dear face in my dreams.

Years went. The stormy days of passion
Destroyed the charms of olden days,
And I forgot thy voice so gentle,
And saw no more thy face divine.

And in my exile's gloomy darkness
I lingered on in loneliness,
Bereft of thee, my inspiration,
Bereft of tears, of life, of love.

But now my soul no longer slumbers:
Once more appearest thou to me,
As a swift-passing, fairy vision,
An angel of the purest charm.

In ecstasy my heart is beating,
It has recovered once again
Its goddess and its inspiration,
Its tears, its life, its love.

351

From PÚSHKIN'S 'EVGHÉNIY ONYÉGHIN'

XLIII

ONYÉGHIN, I was younger then,
And better looking, I suppose,
And I loved you.—But what,
What did I find then in your heart?
What answer?—None but cold reproof!
Of course, it was not new to you
The love of a young country girl . . .
E'en now my very blood congeals
When I remember your cold look,
And that hard sermon, colder still.

XLIV

Well, in our humble wilderness,
Far from the world of life called high
I did not please you. . . . Then, why now
Do you thus watch my ev'ry step?
Why such display of your attention?
Is it because I now appear
In new surroundings of high life?
That I am rich and widely known?
That, for my husband's wide renown
We are so well received at Court?
And that my fall, in these conditions,
Would be commented ev'rywhere,
And would in high society bring
To you an envied reputation?

XLV

You see me crying—if your Tánya
You still remember even now,
Then know,—your chiding's bitter sting,
The cold and stern words that you said—
If it were only in my power—
I should prefer them to your passion,
To these your letters and your tears!

XLVI

For me, Onyéghin, all that wealth,
That showy tinsel of Court life,
All my successes in the world,
My well-appointed house and balls, . . .
For me, are nought!—I gladly would
Give up these rags, this masquerade,
And all this brilliancy and din,
For a few books, a garden wild,
Our weather-beaten house, so poor—
Those very places where I met
With you, Onyéghin, that first time;
And for the churchyard of our village,
Where now a cross and shady trees
Stand on the grave of my poor nurse.

XLVII

And happiness was possible then!
It was so near! . . . But now it's over.
Maybe, I was too rash . . . alas!
But mother's tears appealed to me—
And for poor Tánya all was one! . . .
You must—I must entreat you—leave me!
I know that in your heart you have
Fierce pride and honour.   I love you—
Why should I hide the truth from you?
But I am given to another,
And true to him I shall remain.

APPENDIX B

From GRIBOYÉDOFF'S 'GÓRE OT UMÁ' (MISFORTUNE
FROM INTELLIGENCE)

SCENE AT A BALL GIVEN BY FÁMUSOFF

Tchátskiy is a young man, just returned from a journey to
Western Europe.   He is in love with *Sophie*, the daughter of
an important gentleman of the Moscow nobility, *Fámusoff*.
Tchátskiy and Sophie were playmates in their childhood.   But
on his return Tchátskiy finds Sophie in love with *Moltchálin*—

an insignificant clerk, her father's secretary. At a ball given by Fámusoff Tchátskiy makes to Sophie some stinging remarks about Moltchálin—with the following result. 'All Moscow,' which already disliked Tchátskiy for his usually sarcastic attitude, now declares that he is insane.

Sophie and *Mr. D.*

Sophie (*speaking of Tchátskiy who has just said to her something unpleasant about Moltchálin*):
  Oh, what a terrible man! Always enjoying
  To run the others down . . .
Mr. D. (*approaches her*):   You seem distrait?
Sophie: Of Tchátskiy I was thinking.
Mr. D.:   Well,
  How do you find him since his journey?
Sophie: He surely is not sound in mind.
Mr. D.: You mean insane?
Sophie: Not quite so bad as that.
Mr. D.: However, something wrong?
Sophie: It would seem so.
Mr. D.: He is so young! How is it possible?
Sophie: It can't be helped! (*To herself*) Ah, M. Tchátskiy,
  You are so fond of treating others
  As if they were a lot of fools,
  How will you like it now yourself?   (*Exit.*)

Mr. D. and *Mr. N.*

Mr. D.: Did you hear that?
Mr. N.:   Hear what?
Mr. D.: About that Tchátskiy . . .
Mr. N.:   What about him?
Mr. D.: Gone mad . . .
Mr. N.:   What nonsense!
Mr. D.: I don't say so—but others do.
Mr. N.: And you are ready to repeat it?
Mr. D.: You're right. I'd better make inquiries. (*Exit.*)

Mr. N. and *Zagorétskiy* (The Town Gazette).

Mr. N.: Perhaps you heard of Tchátskiy . . .
Zagor.:   Well?
Mr. N.: They say he has gone mad . . .

Zagor.:   Oh, yes!
  Of course I know!   His uncle
  Has had him sent to an asylum.
  The doctors carried him away,
  And chained him up, fast to the wall.
Mr. N.: What nonsense!   He was here just now,
  In this same hall . . .
Zagor.:   They've let him loose!
Mr. N.: You are as good, as a newspaper.
  But—do be cautious : keep it secret,
  I spoke to you in confidence.   (*Exit.*)

Zagorétskiy alone.   Then he is approached by a Lady.

Zagor.: What Tchátskiy can it be?   I think
  I knew some one who had that name.
  (*To the lady.*)   You must have heard the news?
A Lady: What news?
Zagor.:   Of Tchátskiy.   He was here just now,
  In this same hall.
A Lady: Oh, yes! Quite right,
  We had a little conversation . . .
Zagor.: Well, I can tell you : he's insane!
A Lady: What do you say?
Zagor.:   Insane, gone mad!
A Lady: How strange!—You hardly would believe it:
  To say the same I just was going!

Enters Old Countess.

A Lady: O countess, dear!   What news!
  What charming, what delightful news!
Countess: My dear, I don't hear well to-day.
  Repeat it louder . . .
A Lady: Have no time,
  But he will tell you all the story . . . (*Runs away.*)

Old Countess and *Zagorétskiy.*

Countess: A fire, she says, in this same story?
Zagor.: No.   Tchátskiy is the cause of this unrest.
Countess: What?   Tchátskiy put under arrest?
Zagor.: He got a bullet in his head,
  And now has lost his reason . . .

Countess : Convicted of high treason ?
Oh, these abominable freemasons !
Zagor. : No means to make her understand ! (*Slips away.*)

Countess and *Old Prince.*

Countess : Antón Antónytch, . . . All panic-stricken . . .
Prince, prince, come here, directly, please !
Poor man ! With one foot in the grave !
And still he cannot miss a ball . . .
Prince : Ah, hm !
Countess :   He hears nothing, quite deaf !
Perhaps you saw. . . . Did the police come here ?
Prince : Eh, hm !
Countess :   Who marched Tchátskiy to the jail ?
Prince : Oh, hm !
Countess :   How suddenly 'twas done ! . . .
They put him in a soldier's dress,
And took him straight to the battalion.—
Of course—convicted of high treason !
Prince : Uh, hm !
Countess : What ? Eh, old man ? Quite deaf ?
Oh, deafness is a great defect !

INDEX

ABLESÍMOFF, writer of comedies, 211

Abolition of Serfdom Committees, 125

Absolutism, justified by Hegelians, 295

Æsthetics, philosophical, 312; theories of, 316; of the leisured class, 334

Afanásieff, ethnographer, 250

Agricultural Academy of Moscow, 330

—— hardships of labourers in Western Europe, 289; population of Russia, 265

—— village, life in an, 266

'Akib, the Assyrian King,' 6

Aksákoff, Iván, Slavophile writer, 194, 290, 292

—— Konstantín, Slavophile writer, 194, 290, 292

—— Serghéi Timoféevitch, sketch of his works, 194, 195; his unique position in Russian literature, 194; mentioned, 329

Alexander the Great, legends of, 6

Alexander I., education of, 36; his readiness to grant Russia a constitution, 36; grants Poland and Finland a constitution, 36; falls under the influence of German mystics, 36; concludes the Holy Alliance with Germany and Austria, 37; sudden, mysterious death of, 37

Alexander II., warned by Tolstóy, 128; coronation amnesty of, 179

Alexéy the Priest's Son, 7

Alexéyeff, Vasiliy Ivánovitch, a 'populist,' 145; tutor to Tolstóy's children, 145

Alexis, Tsar, liking for the drama of, 208

America, features of a new life in, 329

American squatters, 125, 246

Anabaptists, early, popular Christian movement of the, 148

Anarchism, no - government principles of, 158; modern, founded by Mikhail Bakúnin, 299-300

Annals, richness of Russian, 13; composition of, 14; historical facts and mythical traditions of, 14; literary value of, 15; loss of animation in, 17

Annenkoff, P. V., critic, 117, 322

Antique Greek world, study of the, 334

Anti-Semitic comedy, reception of, 286

Antónovitch, Grand Duke Iván, imprisonment of, 31

Apocryphal Gospels, wide circulation of, in Russia, 17

Arakchéeff, General, rule of, in Russia, 36; cruelty of, 36

Archæological details, abuse of, 334

Arctic Exploration, Lomonósoff's memoir on, 26

Armenia, popular Christian movement in, 148

Armenian language, 2

Arsénieff, K. K., critic, 189, 197, 307 n, 321

Art for art's sake, 322, 324, 325 ; poets of, 202-205
—— its impulses, 174 ; counterfeits of, 325 ; criticism, canons in, 319 ; latest works of, 157-163 ; main principles in, 314 ; utilitarian views upon, 322 ; new tendencies in, 332 ; purpose of, 325, 326
Artels (co-operative organisations), 249
Aryan language, Russian branch of, 2
Asceticism, 17
Ashwell, Lena, 219
Audubon, John James, naturalist, 195
Auerbach, Berthold, 127, 207
Avvakúm, a Nonconformist, priest, memoirs of, 19-21, 33 ; exiled to Siberia, 20 ; taken to the Amúr, 20 ; quotations from memoirs, 20-21 ; recalled to Moscow, 21 ; burned at the stake, 21

BAGRYÁNSKIY, Dr., a freemason, 31
Bakúnin, Mikhaíl, a revolutionist, 294 ; founder of modern anarchism, 299-300 ; mentioned, 291, 295
Balakláva, Tolstóy in the battle of, 117 ; his songs on the disaster of, 118
Balkan Peninsula, Turkish invasion of the, 15
Balzac, Honoré de, mentioned, 61, 90
Barantsévitch, novelist, 332
Baratýnskiy, poet, friend of Púshkin, 66 ; his exile in Finland, 66
Barbier, Henri Auguste, mentioned, 41, 190, 205
Bárdina, the trial of, 144
Bards, Northern and Little Russian, 5 ; ancient instruments of, 6 ; disappearance of, 7

Baskáks, visits of, to Russia, 16
Bayán, a Russian bard, recitations and songs of, 12
Beautiful, realistic definition of the, 316 ; worship of the, 334
Beauty and truth, idealistic point of view of, 314
Beethoven, mentioned, 326
Bell, The, a famous revolutionary paper, 119 ; mentioned, 293, 301, 303, 304
Belles-lettres, Academy of, founded by Catherine II., 27
Béranger, Pierre Jean de, mentioned, 2, 205
Bestúzheff, Alexander (Marlínskiy), prose writer, 68
Bible, Russian translation of the, 3 ; first Russian, 19 ; why it has not yet been superseded, 325
Biblical, Old Slavonian, no more used in current language, 22
Bibliographical notes, 347-350
Birukóff, *Biography of Tolstóy*, 137 ; mentioned, 145, 157 *n*, 162
Bismarck, mentioned, 130
'Black People' and 'White People,' 14
Black Sea, Russia takes firm hold of, 28
Blood-revenge of Scandinavian heroes, 9
Boborýkin, novelist, sketch of, 197, 335
Bodenstedt, friend and German translator of Lérmontoff's poems, 55-56, 59
Bogdanóvitch, poet, 29
Bondaryóff, a Nonconformist peasant, 148
Books, censorship on, in Russia, 287
Borodín, music of, 12, 13
Bótkin, literary circles of, 292
Brandes, George, *Moderne Geister*, 94 ; extracts from, 94-95, 97-98, 122
Brehm, naturalist, 195

Browning, Robert, mentioned, 41, 190, 205

Buckle, Henry Thomas, mentioned, 286

Buhle, Professor, mentioned, 213

Bulgaria, falls under the rule of the Osmanlis, 15

Bulgarian language, 2

Bureaucratic centralisation, 289

Burial, peasant women's old songs at, 6

Burns, Robert, mentioned, 206

Byelínskiy, critic, sketch of his life and works, 313-316; ancestry of, 314; beginning of his career, 314; mentioned, 178, 196, 243, 291, 294, 295, 299, 319, 321, 322, 325

Byelyáeff, historian, 291 *n*

Bylíny, epic songs, 6; early Russian explorers of, 8

Byron, Lord, mentioned, 35, 41, 43, 46, 47, 49, 54, 65, 67, 68, 205, 206, 313

Byronism, mantle of, 50, 60

—— Púshkin's, 47, 56

Byronists, Don Juanesque features of the, 177

Byzantine Church, adherence to the, in Russia, 17; teachings of the, 17

—— gnosticism, 4; historians, 4; ideals of the Russian Church, 16; habits of Moscow, 70

CAPITALISM, powers of, 289

Cat-o'-nine-tails, punishment of the, 179

Catherine II., times of, 27-29; literature in the early part of her reign, 27; her progressive ideas, 27; her intercourse with French philosophers, 27; composes her remarkable *Instruction* (*Nakáz*) to the deputies, 27; her comedies, 27; edits a monthly review, 27;

her *coup d'état* against Peter III., 27; first to introduce Russian peasants on the stage, 211

Caucasians, the most beautiful people of Europe, 55

Caucasus 'Society,' descriptions of, 63

—— the, one of the most beautiful regions on earth, 55

Censorship, rigorous Russian, 284-285

Central Russia, invaded by Cossack bands, 18

Cervantes, Miguel de, laughter of, 2, 96

Chansonnettes, playful, 2

Charles XII. of Sweden, defeated by Peter I., 39

Christ, the teachings of, 150

Christian Brotherhoods, early, development of Christianity on lines of, 17

—— ethics, main points of the, 153-157

—— humility, 154

—— literature in Russia, 17

—— mysticism, 29

—— nationality, the Church endeavours to create it, 15

—— teaching, interpretation of, 148-157; moral aspects of, 150

Christianity, antagonism of church in Central Russia to reformation of, 17; development of, 17; rationalistic interpretation of, 149; dogmatic elements of, 150; spread of, in Russia, 30; understanding of, by the masses, 4

Christmas, pagan songs of, 6

Church, lower clergy of the, impositions on, 20

—— Russian, centralised state at Moscow, supported by the, 15

—— and State, attitude of negation towards, 157

Church Christianity, 150 *n*

Churches, hatred of, towards each other, 148

Cicero, powerful oratory of, 25

Circassians, expeditions against the, 60

'Circles,' the important part played by, in the intellectual development of Russia, 287

Civilisation, based on Capitalism and State, 139

Classicism, defeat of, in Russia, 45

Classics, Russian, circulation of, 5

Clergy, the, in Russia, 251-252

Codes of the Empire and the Common Law, 291

Colonisation, inner, of Russia, 249

Common Law Courts, peasants', 240

Communal land-ownership, 289 ; principles in Russian life, 34 ; spirit of Russian popular life, 9

Communism, teaching of free, 154

Constantine (Nikoláevitch), Grand Duke, organises ethnographical expeditions, 249

——— (Pávlovitch) proclaimed Emperor, 37 ; abdication of, 37

Constantinople, annalists and historians of, 14

Contemporary, The (Sovreménnik), Tolstóy contributes to, 115, 117 ; its fight for the liberation of the peasants, 119 ; mentioned, 188, 196, 223, 255, 303, 304, 308, 317

Contemporary novelists, 327-347

Coolidge, Professor, mentioned, 40

Co-operative organisations, 249

Copernicus, mentioned, 26

Coppe, mentioned, 206

Cornwall, Barry, mentioned, 206

Corps of pages, 31

Cossacks, invasion of Central Russia, by, 18

County Councils, 250

Crabbe, mentioned, 205

Criticism, literary, in Russia, 310-326

Cruikshank, mentioned, 219

Czech language, 2

Czechs, old literature of, 2

DAL, Dr. V. (KOZÁK LUGÁNSKIY), sketch of his life and works, 195-196 ; naturalist and ethnographer, 195 ; connoisseur of the Russian language and dialects, 195 ; his main work, *An Explanatory Dictionary of the Russian Language*, 196

Danilévskiy, folk-novelist, 245-246

Dante, Alighieri, mentioned, 65, 206

Dargomýzhskiy, successful operas of, 13, 49

Darwin, Charles Robert, mentioned, 286

'Darwinism,' 115, 319

'Decadent' would-be poets, 323

'Decembrists,' the, 36-39 ; humanitarian ideas of, 37 ; denounced to the State, 37 ; programme openly proclaimed, 38 ; Nicholas I. hangs five and exiles others to Siberia, 38 ; mentioned, 128, 193, 214, 215, 294, 301

Délwig, Russian poet, friend of Púshkin, 66

Demetrius, the pretender, takes possession of the throne at Moscow, 18 ; overthrown, 18, 49

Demon of habitual drunkenness, 258

Denck, Hans, early Anabaptist, 148

Derzhávin, poet-laureate to Catherine II., 28 ; his poetry

of nature, 28 ; mentioned, 33, 42

Dickens, Charles, humour of, 2 ; mentioned, 219, 261

Discussions, unnatural theoretical, 183

'Dissent,' varieties of, 290

'Disturbed Years,' traces of, in popular songs, 19 ; Richard James collects songs relating to the, 19

Dmítrieff, fable-writer, 64

Dobrolúboff, literary critic, sketch of, 316-318 ; birth and ancestry, 316 ; his work on *The Contemporary*, 317 ; death from overwork of, 317 ; mentioned, 119, 179, 188, 224, 247, 303, 311, 319, 325

Dobrýnya, the dragon-killer, 7 ; represents the sun, 8, 10

Dolgorúkiy, Prince, political writer, 302

Dolgúshin groups, trial of the, 144

Don, blue waters of the, 10

Dostoyévskiy, sketch of his life and works, 177-187 ; his first novel, *Poor People*, 177 ; congratulated by Grigoróvitch and Nekrásoff, 178 ; warm reception from Byelínskiy, 178 ; his extremely sad life, 178 ; condemned to death, 178 ; reprieved by Nicholas I., 178 ; transported to Siberia, 178 ; contracts epilepsy, 179 ; pardoned and returns to Russia, 179 ; death of, 179 ; a prolific writer, 179 ; his novels described, 179-187 ; mentioned, 90, 92, 188, 201, 237, 242, 253, 275

Dover, the cliffs of, 55

Dragománoff, M. P., political writer, 302

Drama in Russia, the, origin of 208 ; Peter I. opens a theatre in Moscow, 209 ; theatres become a permanent institution, 210

Dramatic art, development of, in Russia, 80

Drunkenness, Russian habits of, 258 ; the terrible disease of, 262

Druzhínin, critic, 117, 321

Duse, Leonora, actress, 219

EASTER, pagan songs of, 6

Eastern heroes, exploits of, 8

—— legends, Russian versions of, 6

—— Russia, spoken language of, 4

—— traditions, spread of, in Russia, 9

Edinburgh, Princess Vorontsóva-Dáshkova in, 27 *n.*

Educated man in Russia, despair of the, 98

—— women, new generation of, 331

Eighteenth - century philosophers, 2

Eliot, George, mentioned, 197

Elpátievskiy, S., folk-novelist, 270

Elsler, Fanny, mentioned, 218

English writers, terseness of, 2

Epic narrative, quiet recitative of, 6

Epic poetry, freshness and vigour of the early, 16

—— songs, collection of, 7 ; Russia's rich collection of, 7 ; heroes of, 7 ; important parts of witchcraft in, 7 ; proscribed by Russian Church, 12

Ergólskaya, T. A., a relative of Tolstóy, 116

Ethnographical research in Russia, 249-251

Euler, Leonhard, mathematician, 25

European society, conventional life of, 47

FAUST, Dr., 3

Feudal princes, power of, destroyed by Tsar John IV., 18

Finland, constitution of, 36

Folk-literature, of Russia, early, 5; of European nations, 5; first existence of, in seventeenth century, 19

Folk-lore, powerful influence of, on Russian literature, 12; sadness, melancholy and resignation of Russian, 16

Folk-novelists, 239-283; their position in Russian literature, 239; realistic school of, 240

Folk-songs, astonishing wealth of Russian lyric, 5; importance in Russian country life of, 12

Fonvízin, *see* Wízin, Von

Forward, a socialist review published by Peter Lavróff, 300

Fourier, François, mentioned, 178, 242, 295

Fourierism, 305

Fourierists, 178

Franklin, Benjamin, 32

Freemasons, widespread movement of, in Russia, 29; their effort for spreading moral education among the people, 30; tendency towards mysticism of, 31; their deep influence on Russia, 31; Alexander I. grants them more freedom, 31

Free thought stifled in Russia, 38

French Revolution of 1830, 294; of 1848, 295

—— Socialists, 295

Frey, a 'populist,' 145

Froebel, educational reformer, 127

From Whence and How came to be the Land of Russia, early attempts at writing history, 14

Fyódoroff, a 'populist,' 145

GARNETT, Mrs. Constance, translator of Turguéneff, 103

Georgian language, 2

Gérbel, N., poet and translator, 205-206

German metaphysics, fogs of 290, 295, 315, vagueness of, 2; mentioned, 322

Germany, mystical teachings of, 29, 36

Glínka, music of, 13; *Ruslán i Ludmíla* (opera), 44 *n*

Goethe, references to, 2, 3, 41, 42, 46, 66, 124, 189, 205, 206, 313

Godwin, philosopher, mentioned, 333

Gógol, Nicoláy Vasílievitch, sketch of his life and works, 69-91; birth and ancestry of, 69; his first tales, 69; his wit and humour, 71; the plot of his novel *Tarás Búlba*, 73-75; his prose-comedy, *The Inspector-General (Revizór)*, described, 76-82; extracts from, 79-81; hostile criticism on, 82; his comedies, 82; *Dead Souls* his main work, 82-87; extracts from, 83-84; he suffers from a nervous disease, 87; falls under influence of 'pietists,' 87; his death, 87; his influence on the minds of Russians, 88; forerunner of the literary movement against serfdom, 88; literary influence of, 89; a great artist, 89; introduces the social element into Russian literature, 89; references to, 4, 5, 29, 62, 68, 90, 91, 92, 100, 178, 194, 195, 213, 219, 220, 306, 308, 313, 315, 317, 328, 329, 341, 342

Gontcharóff, sketch of his life and works, 164-177; his novel *Oblómoff* described, 165-176; extracts from autobiography of, 167 ; extracts from *Oblómoff*, 168-173 ; his last novel, *The Precipice* described, 176-177 ; references to, 5, 126, 185, 223, 241, 243 247

Górkiy, Maxím (A. Pyéshkoff), sketch of his life and works, 271-283 ; his first sketches, 271 ; his unhappy childhood, 271 ; his reputation in Western Europe and America, 272 ; causes of his popularity, 272 ; his adherence to truth, 274 ; sketch of his characters, 274-280 ; extracts from *The Reader*, 280-282 ; his part in the revolutionary movements of 1905, 283 ; references to, 12 *n*, 238, 246

Gospels, the, rendering of, 3

Græco-Latin Theological Academy of Kíeff, 208 ; learned men from the, 19-20

Grammar, of the Russian language, 3

Greece, learned men of, 19-20

Greek Church, widespread separation of the people from the, 20

—— models, inspiration of, 14

Gregory, mentioned, 208

Griboyédoff, comedy writer, sketch of his life and works, 213-218 ; influence of Schlötzer and Professor Buhle on, 213 ; enters the military service, 214 ; becomes friendly with 'Decembrists,' 214 ; sent to Teheran, 214 ; arrested, 214 ; his habitual brightness, 215 ; set free, 215 ; takes part in the war against Persia, 215 ; marries, 215 ; killed at Teheran, 215 ; his *Misfortune from Intelligence* described, 216-218 ; extract from, 353-356 ; references to, 22, 81, 223

Grigórieff, A., critic, 117, 322

Grigoróvitch, a talented folk-novelist, sketch of his life and works, 241-244 ; references to, 90, 177, 178, 246, 248, 265, 273

Grimm, the brothers, collection of fairy tales, 6 ; influence of, 8

Gutzkow, mentioned, 206

HAMLETISM in Russian life, 101, 114

Hannibal oath, the, 294

Hardy, mentioned, 240

Harte, Bret, mentioned, 239, 272

Hatzfeld, Countess of, 97

Heath, Richard, xii, 148

Hegel, mentioned, 290, 294, 295, 315

Heine, mentioned, 2, 46, 205, 206

Helen, legends of, 6

Hellert, lectures of, 31

Hemnitzer, writer of fables, 29

Herder, Johann Gottfried, poems of, in Russia, 35

Hérzen, Alexander (Iskánder), sketch of his life and works, 293-299 ; birth and ancestry, 293 ; enters Moscow University, 294 ; exiled to Vyátka, 294 ; returns to Moscow, 294 ; exiled to Nóvgorod, 295 ; founds a paper at Paris, 296 ; expelled from France, 296 ; naturalised in Switzerland, 296 ; starts *The Polar Star* in London, 296 ; starts *The Bell* and becomes powerful in Russia, 297 ; destruction of his popularity, 298 ; death of, 298 ; references to, 61, 119, 188, 197, 289, 292, 314, 315, 343

Hiawatha, two Russian translations of, 2

Hilferding, A., 7

Hmelnítskiy, translations from Molière of, 213

Hoffmann, 185

Holberg, Danish comedy writer, 29

Holy Books, printing of, 19 ;

handwritten copies of, 19, revision of, by comparison with Greek texts, 19; revision of, by Kryzhánitch, 22

Homer, epics of, 10, 195

Homyakóff, 'Slavophile,' 290; extracts from speech of, on art, 323-324

Hood, Thomas, 206

Hugo, Victor, mentioned, 41, 190, 205, 235, 313

Humboldt, mentioned, 26, 326

Hundred - and - Ninety - Three, trial of the, 144

Huxley, Thomas Henry, 26

Huyghens, Constantijn, 26

Hvóschinskaya, Nathalie D., (later Zaionchkóvskaya), signed 'V. Krestóvskiy-pseudonym,' sketch of her works, 197-200; _The Great Bear_, described, 198-199; her 'subjective realism,' 200; mentioned, 342

Ibsen, Henrik, mentioned, 233, 282

Icelandic _sagas_, 6; interpretation of, by early explorers, 8

Igor, a prince of Kíeff, 10; the _Lay_ of his raid, 10-12; speech to warriors of, 10; defeat of, 11

Iliad, Russia's lack of an, 10

Iliyá of Múrom, 7; features of God of Thunders in, 8; historic personage of, 8; mentioned, 10

Indo-European language, 2

Intellectual unity of Russian nation, 5

'Intellectuals,' Russian, mentioned, 250, 275, 332, 335, 341, 342

International Working - Men's Association, 299

Italian language, melodiousness of, 56

Ivánoff, Professor, 313 _n_

James, Richard, collector of songs relating to the 'Disturbed Years,' 19

John the Terrible (John IV.), letters of, 18; position of, in Russian history, 18, 59

Judaic Christianity, life depressing influences of, 334

'Kalevála,' epic poem of the Finns, 10

Kalíki, songs of the, 6

Kantemír, son of a Moldavian prince, 23; satires of, 23; ambassador at London, 23 _n_

Kapníst, comedy writer, superficial satires of, 29, 212

Karamázoff, the brothers, 275

Karamzín, historian and novelist, educated at Moscow, 31; his _History of the Russian State_, 33; reactionary spirit of, 34; his history a work of art, 34; his sentimental romanticism, 35; references to, 65, 212, 291

Katénin, translator and imitator of Racine, 212

Katkóff, 144

Kavélin, philosopher and writer, 53, 292, 295

Kíeff, annals of, 13; disappearance of, from history for two centuries, 15; Græco-Latin Academy of, 20, 208

Kiréyevskiy, the two brothers, Slavophiles, 290, 292

Kishinyóff, 43

Knyazhnín, writer and translator of tragedies, 211; his comedies, 211

Kobýlin, Sukhovó, 220

Kókoreff, I. T., folk-novelist, 246-247

Kokóshkin, translator and imitator of Racine, 212

Koltsóff, poet, short note on, 201; references to, 261, 327

Korolénko, Vladímir, folk-novelist, 269 ; editor, 271, 272, 278 ; sketch of, 329-332

Kórsakoff, Rímskiy, music of, 13 ; his opera *John the Terrible*, 206

Kósheleff, political writer, 304

Kossítskaya, Madame Nikúlina, actress, 219

Kostomároff, *The Twelfth Century Rationalists*, 17 *n* ; mentioned, 291

Kotoshíkhin, historian, runs away from Moscow to Sweden, 22 ; writes a history of Russia, 22 ; advocates wide reforms, 22 ; his manuscript discovered at Upsala, 22

Kotzebue, success in Russia of translations from, 212

Kozlóff, poet, 65 ; his translations from the English and the Polish, 66

Krestóvskiy, Vsevolod, writer of detective stories, 197, 320

—— pseudonym, *see* Hvóschinskaya

Krüdener, Madame, a German mystic, 37

Krylóff, I. A., fable-writer, 63 ; his comedies, 64 ; his translations from Lafontaine, 64 ; his unique position in Russian literature, 65 ; references to, 29, 195, 212, 216

—— V. A. (Alexándroff), prolific play-writer, 238

Kryzhánitch, a South Slavonian writer, called to Moscow, 22 ; revises the Holy Books, 22 ; preaches reform, 22 ; exiled to Siberia, 22

Kúrbskiy, Prince, letters, 18

Kúrotchkin, translator, 205

LÁBZIN, a Christian mystic, 31

Lafontaine, translations from, 64

La Harpe, republican, 36

Lake Onéga, 5

Lamartine, 67

Lassalle, 97

Latin Church, prevented from extending its authority over Russia, 16

Latin families, 2

'Latinism,' Patriarch Níkon, accused of, 20

Lavróff, Peter (Mírtoff), Russian political writer, sketch of, his works, 300-301

Lay of Igor's Raid, The (*Slóvo o Polkú Igoreve*), a twelfth-century poem, 10-12 ; destruction of manuscript, in conflagration of Moscow, 1812, 10 ; compared with *Songs of the Nibelungs and Songs of Roland* for beauty and poetical form, 10 ; fragment showing general character and beauty of, 11 ; translation by Wiener, 12 *n* ; opera by Borodín, 12

Lazhétchnikoff, historical novelist, 68

Legends of saints widely read, 17

Lenan, 206

Leopardi, 206

Lérmontoff, Mikhail Yúrievitch, language of, 3 ; sketch of his life and works, 53-63 ; ancestry of, 53 ; writes verses and poems at the age of fourteen, 54 ; enters Moscow University, 54 ; enters military school in St. Petersburg, 54 ; writes a piece of poetry on the death of Púshkin, and is exiled to the Caucasus, 54 ; his descriptive poetry, 55-56 ; *The Demon* and *Mtsýri*, 57-58 ; his demonism and pessimism, 58 ; his prose-novel, *The Hero of Our Own Time*, 59, 62, 63 ; a humanitarian poet, 59 ; his deep love for Russia, 59 ; his dislike of war, 60 ; exiled a second time for fighting a duel, 60 ; death of, 61 ; references to, 65, 67, 68, 71, 92, 188, 189, 190, 194, 299, 322

Leroux, Pierre, mentioned, 242, 295

Levítoff, folk-novelist, sketch of his life and works, 260-263 ; exiled, 261 ; his extreme poverty, 261

Liberty, struggle for, 332

Literary criticism, in Russia, 310-326

Literature, a new vein in, 336 ; treasures of, in the thirteenth century, 15 ; a new era in, 27 ; social element introduced into, 89 ; of the Czechs, 2 ; of the Poles, 2 ; of the great Slavonian family, 2 ; of the Great Russians, 2 ; of the Little Russians, 4 ; of the White Russians, 4 ; freed from enslavement by Púshkin, 45

Lithuanian language, 2

Little Russian, language of, 4 ; old bards of, 5 ; struggle of, for independence, 39 ; the *hétman* Mazépa joins in the war against Peter I., 39

Lomonósoff, historian, studies in Moscow, 24; and at Kíeff, 24 ; sent to Germany and studies under Christian Wolff, 24-25 ; nominated a member of the St. Petersburg Academy of Sciences, 25 ; unfriendly reception of, 25 ; praised by Euler, 25 ; violent character of, 25 ; salary confiscated, 25 ; persecution of, 25 ; foundation of Russian grammar by, 25 ; 'Discourses' of, 26 ; his memoir on Arctic Exploration, 26 ; invents new words, 33

Longfellow, William Hadsworth, mentioned, 2, 206

Louis XI., position of, in French history, 18

Lubatóvitch, the trial of, 144

MACPHERSON, 67

Makovítskiy, Dr., 161

Málikoff, a 'populist,' 145

Mámin, novelist, 332

Márkovitch, Madame Marie (Márko Vovtchók), folk-novelist, 244-245, 246, 265, 273

Marriage, complicated ceremonial of, 6

Martýnoff, Russian officer, 60

Matchtétt, novelist, 332

Maude, Aylmer, *Life of Tolstóy* by, 145 ; mentioned, 147

Maugham, W. S., mentioned, 239

Maupassant, Guy de, mentioned, 272, 336

Maxímoff, ethnographer, 241, 243, 250

Máykoff, Apollon, poet, short note on, 203

—— Valerián, literary critic, 242, 316

Mazépa, ruler of Little Russia, joins Charles XII. against Peter I., 39 ; flight of, into Turkey, 39

Mazzini, Joseph, 97

Mediæval literature of Russia, 15-19

Mélnikoff (Petchérskiy), folk-novelist, 250

Mélshin, L., folk-novelist, 270

Merezhkóvskiy, Dmítriy, novelist and poet, translation from writings of, by Leo Wiener, 12 *n* ; sketch of, 333-334

Merimée, Prosper, 40

Méy, L., poet and translator, short note on, 206

Michelet, 325

Mickiéwicz, *The Crimean Sonnets*, 66

Midsummer Day, pagan songs of, 6

Mihailóvskiy, a gifted Russian critic, 139 ; his criticism of Tolstóy, 139-141 ; sketch of, 320-321 ; mentioned, 197, 311, 337

Mikhaíl (the first Románoff) introduces serfdom, 19

Mikháiloff, Mikhail, poet and translator, 206 ; condemned to Siberia where he died, 206 ; mentioned, 119

—— A., pseudonym of Scheller, 332

Mikháilovskoye, Púshkin's estate in the Province of Pskov, 43

Mill, John Stuart, 305

Mináyeff, D., poet and translator, 191, 206

Molière, mentioned, 209, 213, 216, 218

Monasteries, learning concentrated in, 17

Mongol invasion of Russia, the, 15

Mongol Khans help to build up the power of Moscow, 15

Mongols, their tales, 6, 7

Montesquieu, 26

Moore, Thomas, poems of, in Russian, 35, 206

Mordóvtseff, D. L.., novelist and ethnographer, 199, 250, 332

Morris, William, poet, 127

Moscow (Moskvá), conflagration of, in 1812, 10 ; first capital of Russia, 13 n ; monarchy consolidated, 15 ; centralised state at, 15 ; aid of Mongol Khans in building up its power, 15 ; State ideals substituted for those of local autonomy and federation, 15 ; combination of Church and State throw off Mongol yoke, 15 ; introduction of serfdom in, 16 ; 'a third Rome,' 16 ; Poles capture it, 18 ; general revolt of peasants in, 18 ; printing-office established at, 19

—— Censorship Board, 68

—— Church, criticism of dignitaries of, 17 ; formidable power of, 20 ; mixed origin of, 290

'Moscow Fifty,' trial of the, 144

—— Gazette, 139

—— Institute of Friends, 31

—— Mályi Teátr, 219

—— Stage, the, 218-220

—— Theological Academy, 24

Motcháloff, actor, 219

Müller, historian, 34 n

Murillo, Bartolomé, painter, 94

Musórgskiy, music of, 13

Mýshkin, 114

Myths, gradual evolution and migration of, 8

NADÉZHDIN, art critic, 312, 313, 322

Nádson, poet, 332

Nala and Damayanti, Hindu poem of, 35

Napoleon III., coup d'état of, 100

Naryézhnyi, historical novelist, 68

Nature, forces of, personified in heroes, 8 ; knowledge of, considered unholy, 17 ; knowledge of, condemned by Russian Church, 17

Naúmoff, folk-novelist, short note on, 269

Nefédoff, ethnographer and folk-novelist, 271

Nekrásoff, Nicholas, poet, sketch of his life and works, 187 ; his poverty, 187-188 ; co-editor of The Contemporary, 188 ; death of, 188 ; his pessimism, 191 ; his love of the peasant masses, 191 ; his struggle against serfdom, 192 ; his best poem Red-nosed Frost, 192 ; his poem about the Russian women in Siberia, 193 ; references to, 117, 177, 178, 196, 242, 255, 308

Nestor's Annals, 14

Netcháyeff groups, trial of, 144, 145

Newton, Sir Isaac, 26

Nicholas I., thirty years' reign of, 38 ; hangs five and exiles others of the 'Decembrists,' 38 ; references to, 48, 67, 178

Nicholas the Villager, 7

Nietzsche, egotism of, 278, 334

Nihilism in Russia, 107

Nikítin, poet, short note on, 201 ; mentioned, 327

Níkon, Patriarch, ambitions of, 20

Nineteenth century, first years of, in Russia, 33-36

Nonconformists, cruel persecution and migrations of, 19

Northern Russia, spoken language of, 3; special bards of, 6

Nóvgorod, annals of, 13 ; victories of, 14 ; early Protestant rationalism in republic of, 17

Nóvikoff, the first philosopher, 28 ; an apostle of renovation, 30 ; an organiser and business man, 30 ; starts a successful printing-office in Moscow, 30 ; his influence upon educated society, 30 ; organises relief for starving peasants, 30 ; accused of political conspiracy, 30 ; condemned to death, 31 ; imprisoned in fortress of Schlüsselburg, 31 ; released by Paul I., 31 ; falls into mysticism, 31 ; founded Institute of Friends in Moscow, 31

Novodvórskiy, folk-novelist, 332

OBLÓMOFF, OBLÓMOVISM, 167-176

Odóevskiy, Prince Alexander, Russian poet, 66 ; friend of the 'Decembrists,' 67 ; sent to Siberia, 67 ; becomes a friend of Lérmontoff, 67; his historical poem Vasilkó, 67

Odyssey, The, in Russian, 35

Oertel, novelist, sketch of, 327-329 ; his descriptive power, 328-329 ; references to, 250, 269

Ogaryóff, poet, 214, 294, 295 ; short note on, 299

Old Testament, books of, wide circulation in Russia of, 17

Olónets, province of, bards of, 7

Opera, early appearance of, in Russia, 13

Orlóff, a 'populist,' 145

Osmanlis, rule of, over Serbia and Bulgaria, 15

Ossian, 212

Ostróvskiy, sketch of his life and works, 221-234 ; placed under police supervision, 221 ; description of Poverty—no Vice, 222-224 ; extracts from The Thunderstorm, 224-230; his later dramas, 231-234 ; references to, 65, 213, 216, 220, 242, 243, 248

Ovid, pleasant talk of, 25

Ozeroff, writer and translator of tragedies, 211, 212

PAGANISM, return to, 16

Palm, A. I., dramatist, 237

Panáeff, Iván, co-editor of The Contemporary, 196; his novels, 196 ; his exquisite types of Russian women, 197

Paris, occupation of, by the Russian armies, 37 ; ideas of liberty in, 37

Pássek, explorer of folk-lore, 294

Peasants, widespread revolt of, 19

Persian language, 2

Pestalozzi, educational reformer 127

Péstel, a 'Decembrist,' 37

Peter I., violent reforms of, 22 ; historical significance of his reform, 22; realises importance of literature, 22 ; introduces

European learning, 22; establishes a new alphabet, 22; little interest in literature of, 23; his struggle against Charles XII. of Sweden, 39; reforms of, 208; opens a theatre in Moscow, 209

Peter III., *coup d'état* of Catherine II. against, 27

Petrashévskiy, a 'Fourierist,' 178; 'circles' of, 201, 307

Petrograd, Academy of Sciences, 24

Petropávlovskiy (Karónin), poet and folk-novelist, 270

Písareff, A. I., writer of vaudevilles, 213

Písareff, D. I., literary critic, sketch of, 318-320; confined in the fortress of St. Peter and St. Paul, 318; his death from drowning, 319; references to, 115, 124 *n*, 311, 325, 331, 333

Písemskiy, A. Th., novelist and dramatist, 236; short note on, 247-248; mentioned, 126

Plattner, lectures of, 31

Pleschéyeff, A., poet, short note on, 201-202; arrested with the 'Petrashévskiy circles,' 201; sent into the army, 202; pardoned by Alexander II., 202; mentioned, 191

Poetry, sin of, 17

Poland, first Russian Bible printed in, 19; constitution of, 36, 48

Polar Star, The, Hérzen's review, 296

Poles, old literature of, 2; invasion of Russia by, 18

Polevóy, P., historical novelist, founder of serious journalism in Russia, 312; references to, 313, 321, 325

Polezháyeff, Russian poet, student of Moscow University, 67; *Sáshka*, 67; dies from consumption, 67; mentioned, 294

Polish language, 2

Political literature, 284-306; abroad, 293-302

Polónskiy, poet, a friend of Turguéneff, 203; short note on, 203-204

Pólotskiy, Simeón, a high functionary of the Russian church and writer of mystery plays, 209

Pólovtsi, raid on, 10; Igor's band defeated by the, 11

Poltáva, Peter I. defeats Charles XII. of Sweden at, 39

Pomyalóvskiy, folk - novelist, 251; his notoriety, 252; his sketches from the life of clerical schools, 253; death of, 254; mentioned, 261

Pope, an Eastern, 20

'Popularism,' 333

'Populist' movement, 298, 332; influence of, upon Tolstóy, 144

Potápenko, novelist, sketch of, 335-336

Potyékhin, A. A., novelist and playwright, 236-237; folk-novels of, 247-248

Printing-office established in Moscow, 19

Procopóvitch, a priest and writer, 23; founds the Græco-Slavonian Academy, 23

Proudhon, mentioned, 127, 296, 322, 325

Prugávin, ethnographer and 'populist,' 145, 251

Pryzhóff, ethnographer, 251

Pskov, republic of, annals of, 13; struggles between poor and rich in, 14; province of, 43; early Protestant rationalism in, 17

Pugatchóff, a revolutionist, 32; leads peasant revolt against Catherine II., 49; history of, by Púshkin, 61

Púschin, a 'Decembrist,' 43.

Púshkin, Alexander, language of, 3; popularity of, 5; first great Russian poet, 12; beginning of his career, 12; melodious verse of, 33; sketch of his life and works, 40-53; his lyrics familiar in England, 40; neglected in Russia in the sixties, 40; appreciated in France and Germany, 40; his beauty of form, 41; his individuality and vital intensity, 41-42; his birth and ancestry, 42; his perfect mastership of the Russian language, 42; his knowledge of folk-lore, 42; educated at St. Petersburg at the Tsárskoye Seló Lyceum, 42; his reputation as a poet at school, 42; describes his shallow life in *Evghéniy Onyéghin*, 43; exiled to Kishinyóff, 43; joins the gipsies, 43; journeys to Crimea and Caucasus, 43; renders himself impossible at Odessa, 43; ordered to return to Central Russia, 43; his estate at Mikháilovskoye, 43; his 'Decembrist' friends, 43; returns to St. Petersburg and becomes chamberlain to Nicholas I., 43-44; his unfortunate marriage, 44; killed in a duel, 44; his early productions, 44-45; *Ruslán and Ludmíla*, 44; his simplicity in verse, 45; frees literature from enslavement, 45; his lyric poetry, 46-47; called the Russian Byron, 47; his epicureanism, 47; his stupendous powers of poetical creation, 48; his dramas, *Don Juan* and *The Miser-Knight*, 48; his comprehension of human affairs, 49; his most popular work, 49-53; extracts from, 52, 63, 351-353; his

prose-novels, 61; references to, 4, 28, 29, 41, 43, 47, 54, 56, 62, 65, 66, 68, 69, 71, 82, 89, 92, 117, 188, 189, 190, 194, 202, 212, 213, 216, 234, 287, 295, 312, 313, 317, 319, 336

Putívl, Yaroslávna awaits return of Igor in the town of, 11

Pyatigórsk, 60

Pyéshkoff, A. (Maxím Górkiy), 271-283; *see* Górkiy, Maxím

Pýpin, A. N., author of a *History of· Russian Literature*, 32 *n*; and a *History of Russian Ethnography*, 250

QUAKERS, their doctrine of non-resistance, 148

RACINE, JEAN BAPTISTE, mentioned, 65, 210, 212

Radíscheff, a political writer, 28, 31; receives his education in the Corps of Pages, 31; sent to Germany to finish his education, 31; his *Journey from St. Petersburg to Moscow*, 32; transported to Siberia, 32; commits suicide, 32; his book still forbidden in Russia, 32; London and Leipzig editions, 32 *n*

Ralston, translation of Russian *sagas* by, 10; mentioned, 63, 100

Rambaud, appreciation of Russian *sagas* by, 10

Raskólnikoff, 275

Rayévskys, the family of the, 43

Rázin, Stepán, terrific uprising of, 19

Rebellion, State and Church cruelly hunt down traces of, 19

Renaissance, great movement of, did not reach Russia, 18

'Rigorism,' 333

Rímskiy-Kórsakoff, music, 13

Rousseau, Jean Jacques, *Emile*,

127 ; mentioned, 125, 126, 137, 157

Rúrik, house of, 13

Russia, centres of development in, 13 ; main cities of South and Middle Russia laid waste by Mongol invasion, 15 ; invasion of, by Turks, 15 ; transformation of life in, 15 ; independent republics of, 15 ; years of great disturbance in, 18 ; invasion by Poles of, 18 ; period of serfdom in, 19 ; widespread revolt of peasants in, 19 ; semi-Byzantine and semi-Tartar State of, 22 ; takes a firm hold of the Black Sea, 28 ; begins to play serious part in European affairs, 28 ; servility of nobles in, 29 ; horrors of serfdom in, 29 ; federal principles in, 34 ; secret societies in, 37 ; abolition of absolute rule in, 37 ; republican federalism of old, 37 ; free thought stifled in, 38

—— Annals, richness of, 13 ; composition of, 14 ; historical facts and mythical traditions of, 14 ; high literary value of, 15

—— Church, proscribes the singing of epic songs, 12 ; revision of translations of the Holy Books, 19 ; split in, 19-21

—— drama, the, 208-238

—— epics, mythological features in heroes of, 8-9 ; Eastern origin of heroes, 8

Russian folk-lore, assimilation of Eastern traditions in, 9 ; origin of, 9 ; antiquity of, 9

—— Geographical Society, 7

—— 'intellectuals,' 250, 275, 332, 335, 341, 342

—— language, 1-39 ; richness of, 1 ; its pliability for translation, 1 ; musical character of, 2 ; adaptability of, 2 ; adopted many foreign words, 3 ; remarkable purity of, 3 ; most widely spoken, 3 ; unchanged roots of, 3 ; structural beauty of, 4 ; free from *patois*, 4 ; variety of pronunciation in, 4 ; unity of the spoken, 13 ; a dictionary compiled of, 27 ; value of the spoken for literary purposes, 33 ; syllabic form of, 33 ; melodiousness of the, 56 ; dictionary of, by Dal, 196

Russian literature, treasures of, in the thirteenth century, 15 ; a new era in, 27 ; social element introduced into, 89

—— novel, new element in the, 332

—— poetry, rhythmical versification of, 24

—— State, mixed origin of the, 290

—— society, looseness of habits of, 29 ; neglect of idealism in, 280 ; influence of Tchernyshévskiy's novel upon, 305 ; rapid succession of different moods of thought in, 334 ; hopeless sadness of intellectual portion of, 343

—— Theatre, Sumarókoff's development of the, 26-27 ; in the first years of the nineteenth century, 212-213 ; triumph of romanticism in, 212

—— verse, old, 23

—— versification, rhythmical form of, 12

—— women, struggle of, against society, 331

Rustem of Persia, legends of, 6

Ryépin paints Tolstóy behind the plough, 147

Ryeshétnikoff, folk-novelist, sketch of his life and works, 254-260 ; founder of the ultra-realistic school, 254 ; birth and ancestry of, 254 ; poetry of, 255 ; his unique position in Russian literature, 255 ; his sound truth, 255-260 ; references to, 246, 265, 273, 274

Ryléeff, a 'Decembrist' poet, 36 ; hanged by Nicholas I., 38 ; twice visited France, 38 ; magistrate at St. Petersburg, 38 ; circulation of his ballads in manuscript form, 38 ; references to, 38, 214, 215, 296

SÁDKO, personification of navigation, 8

Sadóvskiy, actor, 219, 221

Sagas, interpretation of, by early explorers, 8 ; Russia's precious national inheritance of, 10

St. Petersburg (now Petrograd), Academy of Sciences of, 24

Sakiamuni, despairing pessimism of, 143

Saltykóff (Schedrín), satirical writer, life and works of, 237, 306-310

Sáloff, folk-novelist, 270

Samárin, Yúriy, political writer, 304

Sand, George, 248

Satire, a favourite means of expressing political thought, 306; writers of, 306-310

Scandinavo-Saxon language, 2

Schedrín, see Saltykóff

Scheller (A. Mikháiloff), novelist, 332

Schépkin, 219

Scherbátoff, Prince, historian and collector of old annals and folk-lore, writes a history of Russia, 29, 34 n.

Scherbína, N., poet, 203

Schiller, the lyrics of, 41, 42 ; poems of, in Russian, 35 ; mentioned, 2, 54, 59, 299, 314

Schlosser, 207

Schlötzer, Academician and historian, 34 n, 213

Schlüsselburg, fortress of, 31

Schola, 7

Schopenhauer, philosopher, mentioned, 56, 142, 143

Scott, Sir Walter, mentioned, 65, 212

Sebastopol, Tolstóy besieged in, 117 ; the terrible Fourth Bastion of, 156

Serbian language, 2

Serfdom, introduced into the Tsardom of Moscow, 16 ; period of, in Russia, 19 ; definite introduction of, 19 ; horrors of, 29 ; brutalising effects upon society of, 30 ; spirited protest against, 35 ; abolition of, 249 ; growth of, 291

Serfs of the Church, heavy impositions on the, 20

Servia falls under the rule of the Osmanlis, 15

Shahovskóy, Prince, dramas of, 212 ; comedies of, 213

Shakespeare, William, mentioned, 2, 49, 54, 55, 96, 195, 206, 207, 212, 220, 234, 235, 313

Shakespearian fatalism, 258

Shelgunóff, Madame L. P., prose translator, 207

Shelley, P. B., mentioned, 2, 41, 54, 56, 189, 191, 205, 206

Shenshín, A. (A. Fet), a poet of art for art's sake, 204 ; a friend of Tolstóy and Turguéneff, 204, 144

Sheridan, 206

Shevtchénko, Little Russian poet, 68, 242, 294

Siberia, spoken language of, 4

Silistria, Tolstóy in the siege of, 117

Skabitchévskiy, Russian critic and historian of Russian literature, 189, 232, 239, 263, 286, 320, 321, 324 n

Slavonian family of languages, 2

'Slavophiles,' the, 288-293

Slyeptsóff, burlesque tales from popular life, 251

Smirnóff, Madame O. A. (*née* Rossett), a 'pietist,' 87
Smirnóva, Sophie, novelist, 332
Smith, Adam, 301
Smolénsk, Poles capture, 18
Society of Friends of Russian literature, assist the freemasons in spreading moral education among the people, 30, 323
Sokolóvskiy, A. A., translator of Shakespeare, 207 ; receives the Púshkin prize of the Academy of Sciences, 207
Solomon, despairing pessimism of, 143
Solovióff, N., playwright, 238
—— Vladímir, philosopher, 292
Song collectors, 250
Songs, incredible wealth of, 13
Song of Roland, beauty and poetical form of, 10
Song of the Nibelungs, beauty and poetical form of, 10
South-eastern Russia, prairies of, 10
South-eastern Steppes, encampments of Tartars in, 16
South Russia, annals of, 13
South Slavonian language, high perfection of, 3
South Slavonians, treasures of, folk-songs, 2
Spencer, Herbert, 286, 321
Spielhagen, 199, 207
Stankévitch, N. V., moral influence of, 288, 294, 314
Stanyukóvitch, novelist, 332
Stásoff, V. V., his theory of epic songs of Slavonic mythology, 8
Stepniák, political writer, 302
Sterne, Laurence, 32
Stowe, Harriet Beecher, 245
Stritter, historian, 34 *n*
Subbótin, the sisters, trial of, 144
Sue, Eugène, 185
Sukhovó - Kobýlin, playwright, 236
Sumarókoff, the 'Russian Racine,' 26 ; French education of, 26 ; dramas of, 26 ; contributed to the development of the Russian Theatre, 26-27 ; remarkable style of his letters, 26 ; plays important part in the development of Russian drama, 210 ; writes comedies, 211
Súzdal, land of, 13
Syutáeff, a Nonconformist peasant, 145, 148

TALES, astonishing wealth of Russian, 5 ; Aryan origin of, 6 ; Russian origin of, 6
Tartars, repeated raids of, into Russia, 16
Tasso, Torquato, 65
Tatíscheff, historian, superintendent of mines in the Urals, 24 ; wrote a history of Russia, 24 ; appreciates value of annals, 24 ; leaves no lasting trace in Russian literature, 24
Tchaadáeff, 'Decembrist,' 214
Tchaykóvskiy, Piotr Iliitch, composer, music of, 13 ; his opera, *Evghéniy Onyéghin*, 49
—— N. V., populist, mentioned, 145
Tchéhoff, Anton P., novelist and dramatic writer, sketch of his life and works, 336-347 ; originality of, 336 ; new vein in literature introduced by, 336 ; biography of, 337 ; death of, 337 ; the 'sorrow' of, 342 ; his dramas described, 344-346; influence of, 346 ; fabulous circulation of the works of, in Russia, 346 ; mentioned, 238, 269, 272, 278, 327
Tchernyshévskiy, political writer, sketch of his life and works, 303-306 ; birth and ancestry, 303 ; writes for *The Contemporary*, 303 ; his influence on Russian society, 305 ; exiled to Siberia, 305 ;

returns to Russia, 306; his translation of Weber's *Universal History*, 306; death of, 306; references to, 117, 119, 120, 135, 188, 289, 292, 311, 316, 319, 322, 323, 324, 343

Tchernyshóff, I. E., actor and playwright, 237

Tchertkóff, V., friend of Tolstóy, edition of Tolstóy's works by, prohibited in Russia, 137 *n*, 151, 302

Tennyson, Lord Alfred, mentioned, 191, 205, 206

Thackeray, William Makepeace, 196

Tolstáya, Countess A. A., 128

Tolstóy, Count Alexéi Konstantínovitch, historical novelist, dramatist and poet, 234-236; friend of Alexander II., 235; head of the Imperial Hunt, 235; mentioned, 190, 204, 205

—— Lyoff Nicoláievich, sketches of his life and works, 115-163; his first stories, *Childhood* and *Boyhood*, in *The Contemporary*, 115; his birth and ancestry, 116; orphaned at an early age, 116; his education, 116; enters the Kazáñ University, 116; enters the military service, 117; *The Cossacks*, 117, 125; his life during and after the Crimean War, 117-120; takes part in the siege of Silistria and in the battle of Balakláva, 117; besieged in Sebastopol, 117; his friendship with Turguéneff, 119; in search of an ideal, 120-124; his educational work, 126-128; his estate searched by gendarmes, 128; his intention to emigrate to London, 128; warns Alexander II., 128; his marriage, 128; family traditions, 128; sketch of *War and Peace*,

128-134; sketch of *Anna Karénina*, 134-136; profound change in his conceptions of life, 137; his love of the peasant masses, 142; his question 'What is Life?' 143; his dislike of revolutionists, 144; influence of the 'populist' movement upon, 145; his acquaintance with Alexéyeff, 145; his letter to, 145; reforms his life, 146; his plain food, 147; philosophical and religious reasons for his conduct, 147; undertakes a complete study of Christianity, 148; his interpretation of the Christian teaching, 148-157; his influence, 161; his disappearance, 161; his excommunication, 161; his death, 162; the great Rousseau of the nineteenth century, 163; references to, 3, 5, 37, 48, 62, 89, 92, 164, 165, 185, 186, 204, 220, 233, 236, 241, 242, 247, 248, 258, 264, 272, 302, 305, 322, 323, 324, 325, 326, 328, 336, 339, 346

Tolstóy, Nicholas, brother of L. N., death in France of, from consumption, 127

Tolstóyism, 149, 333

Traditions, astonishing wealth of Russian, 5

Transbaikalian folk-lore, 9

Tretiakóvskiy, son of a priest, 23; runs away to Moscow, 23; his melancholy career, 23; goes to Amsterdam and Paris, 23; studies at Paris University, 23; admirer of advanced ideas, 23; clumsy verse of, 23-24; returns to St. Petersburg, 23; poverty, neglect and persecution of, 23; great service to Russian poetry of, 23-24; ridiculous artifices of, 24; clumsy verses of, 33

Tsar's authority, divine origin of, 18

Tsárskoye Seló Lyceum, the, 42

Turanian language, 3

Turguéneff, Ivan Sergéyevich, last message of, to Russian writers, 1 ; language of, 3 ; popularity of, 5 ; melodious prose of, 33 ; sketch of his life and works, 92-115 ; greatest novel-writer of his century, 92 ; *Virgin Soil*, 95 *n* ; his lecture *Hamlet and Don Quixote*, 96 ; his early sketches, 98 ; his short novels, 98 ; extract from *Correspondence*, 99 ; pessimism of, 100 ; threatened with Siberia, 100 ; his novels, 100 ; his sketches, 101 ; sketch of his *Rúdin*, 101-102 ; extracts from, 103 ; his autobiographic tale *First Love*, 104 ; extracts from *Fathers and Sons* and *Hamlet and Don Quixote*, 107-111 ; wreck of his hopes in reform movement, 113 ; his death in Paris, 114 ; his prose poetry, 114 ; references to, 31, 40, 48, 53, 55, 62, 88, 89, 90, 115, 119, 145, 164, 165, 185, 186, 188, 193, 196, 197, 198, 199, 202, 203, 204, 220, 232, 236, 237, 241, 242, 243, 244, 245, 247, 248, 255, 259, 274, 275, 276, 288, 292, 295, 297, 299, 305, 317, 319, 322, 327, 330, 332, 336, 343, 344

Turguéneff, Nicholas, political writer, education of, at Moscow, 31 ; short note on, 301-302

Turks, tales from the, 6, 7

Tyúttcheff, poet, short note on, 202-203

Uhland, Ludwig, poems of, in Russian, 35

Upsala, Kotoshíkhin's manuscript discovered at, 22

Ural-Altayan language, 3

Uráls, Nonconformists' migration into depths of the, 19

Uspénskiy, Gleb, folk-novelist, sketch of his works, 263-267 ; references to, 241, 268

—— Nicholas, 251

Vasílieff, S., actor, 219

Venevítinoff, Russian poet, 66, 312, 313, 322, 324

Venguéroff, S., Russian critic and author of a biographical dictionary of Russian authors, 117, 189, 191, 321

Vereschágin, Vasíliy, Russian painter, 124

Verstóvskiy, *Askóld's Grave*, (opera), 13

Virgil, brilliant earnestness of, 25

Vladímir the Fair Sun, Kieff Prince, table of, 7

Voinaróvskiy, a friend of Mazépa transported to Siberia, 39 ; visited by Müller, 39

Volhynian Annals, 13-14

Volkhónskaya, Princess, Tolstóy's mother, 116

Voltaire, François, sarcasm of, 2, 210

Vorontsóva-Dáshkova, Princess, and Catherine II. in her *coup d'état*, 26 ; nominated president of the Academy of Sciences, 27 ; assisted in compiling a dictionary of the Russian language, 27 ; edits a review 27 ; her memoirs, *Mon Histoire*, written in French, 27

Vvedénskiy, prose translator, 207 ; translator of Dickens, 207

Wagner, operas and librettos of, 323

Weber, historian, 306

Weinberg, P., poet, translator, 206

Western Europe, languages of, 1 ; mediæval city-republics of,

15; struggle against influences of, 18

Western influences, struggle against intrusion of, 16

—— Slavonians, songs of, 35

'Westerners,' the, 288-293

White Russian language, 4

Whiting, 239

Wiener, Leo, his great knowledge of Russian literature, 12 *n*; author of *Anthology of Russian Literature from the Earliest Period to the Present Time*, 2 vols., 1902, 12

Witchcraft, important part of, in epic songs, 7

Wízin, Von (Fonvízin), writer of comedies, 28; creator of the Russian drama, 29; secretary to Count Pánin, 29; comedies of, 211

Wolff, Christian, 25

Wordsworth, simplicity of, 46, 205

Wycliff, popular Christian movement of, 148

YAKÚSHKIN, collector of folk-songs and ethnographic material, 250

Yaroshévitch, P. (L. Mélshin), folk-novelist, 270

Yaroslávna, Igor's wife, lamentations of, 11

Yazýkoff, Russian poet, friend of Púshkin, 66

Yúshkova, P. I., Tolstóy's aunt, 116

ZABYÉLIN, historian, 291

Zagóskin, historical novelist and comedy-writer, 68, 213

Zasódimskiy, folk-novelist, short note on, 251, 269-270

Zasúlitch, Véra, the trial of, 144

Zémstvo Statisticians, 250

Zheleznóff, *Urál Cossacks*, 250

Zhukóvskiy, poet, beauty of his translations, 35; distinctive features of his poetry, 36; his ultra-Romanticism, 36; appeals chiefly to women, 36; references to, 33, 43, 69, 71, 88, 205, 212

Zlatovrátskiy, folk-novelist, 267-269; his opposition to Uspénskiy, 268; his ethnographical novels, 268

Zola, Émile, mentioned, 90, 239, 240, 259, 343

Printed by T. and A. CONSTABLE, Printers to His Majesty
at the Edinburgh University Press

George Woodcock has been variously described as... 'Canada's Tolstoy,' 'a great human being, protean and in some understated way, magnificent,' and 'a kind of John Stuart Mill of dedication to intellectual excellence and the cause of human liberty.'
Toronto Star

WRITERS AND POLITICS
by George Woodcock

In *Writers and Politics*, George Woodcock examines how a group of writers including Pierre-Joseph Proudhon, Alexander Herzen, Peter Kropotkin, George Orwell, Graham Greene, Ignazio Silone, Franz Kafka, Rex Warner and Arthur Koestler use their powers of thought and writing in order to assist the establishment of social justice.

This book embraces a social approach to literature and thought. Woodcock discusses the difficult relationship writers have with the social structure within which they must work, and in particular, their relationship to movements that strive for a better world. For Woodcock, the individual and the social are intermingled in the work of the writer.

Paperback ISBN: 0-921689-82-9 $16.95
Hardcover ISBN: 0-921689-83-7 $35.95

George Woodcock has also written the following literary biographies:

OSCAR WILDE

The Double Image
...embodies the spirit in which Wilde is best read...
Quill and Quire
...leaves us most importantly with a sympathetic and balanced portrait of Wilde...
The Gateway

Paper ISBN: 0-921689-42-X $16.95
Cloth ISBN: 0-921689-43-8 $36.95

WILLIAM GODWIN

A Biographical Study
The book is brilliant...I hope Woodcock's book sells widely.
Ottawa Citizen

Paper ISBN: 0-921689-48-9 $16.95
Cloth ISBN: 0-921689-49-7 $36.95

PIERRE JOSEPH PROUDHON

A Biography
The first full-scale English-language biography of the prominent nineteenth-century social thinker. A solid and workmanlike effort.
Times Literary Supplement

Paper ISBN: 0-921689-08-X $16.95
Cloth ISBN: 0-921689-09-8 $35.95

APHRA BEHN

The English Sappho
...a valuable introduction to this remarkable woman who was a pioneer feminist, free spirit, liberated woman and professional writer during the Restoration
Ottawa Citizen

Paperback ISBN: 0-921689-40-3 $16.95
Hardcover ISBN: 0-921689-41-1 $36.95

THE COLLECTED WORKS OF PETER KROPOTKIN
Explorer, Agitator, Traveller, Writer, Sage, Prophet

Kropotkin was born a prince of the old nobility of Moscow, was trained as a page in the Emperor's court, and at twenty became an officer in the army. The discovery that he was engaged in revolutionary activities caused a sensation. He was arrested in St. Petersburg and held in prison for two years without trial. In disguise, he made his way to Sweden, then to England, where he took refuge. For the next forty-two years, he lived in exile doing scientific research and also wrote for various periodicals in many countries. He returned to Russia in 1917 after the Kerensky revolution, and was one of the early opponents of Lenin's government.

The Collected Works of Peter Kropotkin will be published by Black Rose Books over the next four years. Each volume is introduced by George Woodcock, one of Canada's most distinguished men of letters — journalist, poet, and author of more than forty books. The collection will contain some twelve volumes, including a biography written by George Woodcock and Ivan Avakumovic.

* * *

Already published in the series

MUTUAL AID
A Factor of Evolution
Kropotkin's powerful testimonial to humankind's historical inclination toward spontaneous co-operation...The viewpoint in this eloquent classic opposes doctrinaire Darwinsim.
Ottawa Citizen

Paperback ISBN: 0-921689-26-8	$19.95
Hardcover ISBN: 0-921689-27-6	$39.95

MEMOIRS OF A REVOLUTIONIST
This reissue of the anarchist prince's reminiscences capture Kropotkin's essence for readers new to him. His brilliant life-in-exile pre-Revolution political views and scientific theories give insights into doctrines of anarchism...
Ottawa Citizen

As well as providing a study of the early anarchist movement in Western Europe, *Memoirs* is an extraordinary portrait of the old Russia of Kropotkin's youth.

Paperback ISBN: 0-921689-18-7	$19.95
Hardcover ISBN: 0-921689-19-5	$39.95

THE GREAT FRENCH REVOLUTION

Rejecting his predecessors' narrow focus on politics and institutions and assimilating the research of contemporaries, Kropotkin anticipated debates on the...impact of the Revolution, that remain hotly contested and unresolved...The reader will find here a clear and lively exposition of themes and personalities that informs, and whets the appetite for more...a readable and insightful account.

Canadian Book Review Annual

Paperback ISBN: 0-921689-38-1   **$19.95**
Hardcover ISBN: 0-921689-39-X   **$38.95**

THE CONQUEST OF BREAD

In Kropotkin's own description, the book is "a study of humanity, and of the economic means to satisfy them."

[Kropotkin] envisioned a society in which men and women, joined by natural bonds of cooperative effort, would be rid of the artificiality of bureaucratic states and massive industrial complexes.

Connexions

Paperback ISBN: 0-921689-50-0   **$19.95**
Hardcover ISBN: 0-921689-51-9   **$38.95**

PETER KROPOTKIN

From Prince to Rebel

by George Woodcock and Ivan Avakomovic

In this special addition to the collection, Woodcock and Avakumovic present the most significant aspects of Kropotkin's life and thought: his formative years in Russia and the origins of his anarchist thinking; his years as an emigré in western Europe, and his last years in the Soviet Union.

Paperback ISBN: 0-921689-60-8   **$19.95**
Hardcover ISBN: 0-921689-61-6   **$38.95**

IN RUSSIAN AND FRENCH PRISONS

The one who is shut up in a prison is so far from being bettered by the change, that he comes out more resolutely the foe of society than he was when he went in.

Kropotkin's critique of the prison system shows from first hand knowledge the immense human suffering caused by prison life.

Paperback ISBN: 0-921689-98-5   **$19.95**
Hardcover ISBN: 0-921689-99-3   **$38.95**

To be published over the next four years

ETHICS	FIELDS, FACTORIES AND WORKSHOPS
A REBEL'S WORDS	FUGITIVE WRITINGS

BLACK ROSE BOOKS

has published the following books of related interests

Marie Fleming, THE GEOGRAPHY OF FREEDOM, The Odyssey of Elisée
   Reclus, Introduction by George Woodcock
Murray Bookchin, REMAKING SOCIETY
Murray Bookchin, TOWARD AN ECOLOGICAL SOCIETY
Murray Bookchin, POST-SCARCITY ANARCHISM
Murray Bookchin, THE LIMITS OF THE CITY
Murray Bookchin, THE MODERN CRISIS
Murray Bookchin, THE PHILOSOPHY OF SOCIAL ECOLOGY
Murray Bookchin, THE ECOLOGY OF FREEDOM
Noam Chomsky, LANGUAGE AND POLITICS
Noam Chomsky, RADICAL PRIORITIES
Noam Chomsky, PIRATES AND EMPERORS, International Terrorism in the Real
   World
William R. McKercher, FREEDOM AND AUTHORITY
Abel Paz, DURRUTI, The People Armed
Ida Mett, THE KRONSTADT UPRISING
John Clark, THE ANARCHIST MOMENT, Reflections on Culture, Nature and
   Power
Sam Dolgoff, THE ANARCHIST COLLECTIVES IN SPAIN, 1936-39
Sam Dolgoff, THE CUBAN REVOLUTION, A Critical Perspective
Sam Dolgoff, BAKUNIN ON ANARCHISM
Thom Holterman, LAW AND ANARCHISM
Dimitri Roussopoulos, THE ANARCHIST PAPERS
Dimitri Roussopoulos, THE ANARCHIST PAPERS 2
Dimitri Roussopoulos, THE ANARCHIST PAPERS 3

send for a complete catalogue of books
mailed out free
BLACK ROSE BOOKS
P.O. Box 1258, Succ. Place du Parc
Montreal, Quebec H2W 2R3 Canada

Printed by
the workers of
Editions Marquis, Montmagny, Québec
for
Black Rose Books Ltd.